DEPENDENT CONVERGENCE
The Struggle to Control Petrochemical Hazards in Brazil and the United States

C. Eduardo Siqueira
University of Massachusetts Lowell

Work, Health, and Environment Series
Series Editors: Charles Levenstein and John Wooding

CRC Press
Taylor & Francis Group
Boca Raton London New York

CRC Press is an imprint of the
Taylor & Francis Group, an **informa** business

CRC Press
Taylor & Francis Group
6000 Broken Sound Parkway NW, Suite 300
Boca Raton, FL 33487-2742

First issued in paperback 2018

© 2003 by Taylor & Francis Group, LLC
CRC Press is an imprint of Taylor & Francis Group, an Informa business

No claim to original U.S. Government works

ISBN-13: 978-0-89503-245-4 (hbk)
ISBN-13: 978-0-415-78433-7 (pbk)

Library of Congress Catalog Number: 2003044405

Library of Congress Cataloging-in-Publication Data

Siqueira, C. Eduardo (Carlos Eduardo), 1955–
  Dependent convergence : the struggle to control petrochemical hazards in Brazil and the United States / C. Eduardo Siqueira.
      p. cm. -- (Work, health and environment series)
Includes bibliographical references and index.
  ISBN 0-89503-245-7 (cloth)
  1. Petroleum chemicals industry--Brazil--Bahia (State) --Environmental aspects. 2. Petroleum chemicals industry--Texas--Environmental aspects. 3. Petroleum chemicals industry--Employees--Health and hygiene--Brazil--Bahia (State) 4. Petroleum chemicals industry--Employees--Health and hygiene--Texas. 5. Complexo Petroquímico de Camaçari--History. 6. Gulf Coast Waste Disposal Authority--History. 7. Hazardous substances--Government policy--Case studies. I. Title. II. Series.

  HD9579.C33B788 2003
  363. 738--dc21

                                                                            2003044405

Cover photo by Charley Richardson

Visit the Taylor & Francis Web site at
http://www.taylorandfrancis.com

and the CRC Press Web site at
http://www.crcpress.com

Table of Contents

INTRODUCTION 1

CHAPTER 1. Migration of Hazards: The Viewpoint of Actors in
a Newly Industrializing Country 7

CHAPTER 2. One Industry, Two Complexes, Two Companies 33

CHAPTER 3. Twenty Years of Petrochemical Production in Bahia 61

CHAPTER 4. Benzeno à Vista (Benzene Ho!): The Work
Environment Crises of COPEC 107

CHAPTER 5. Environmental Management Policies in Cetrel:
A Case Study of the Implementation of Pollution Control Policies
in the Periphery. 145

CHAPTER 6. Environmental Management Policies in the Gulf
Coast Authority: A Case Study of Pollution Control Policies
in the Center 181

CHAPTER 7. Dependent Convergence: Comparing Cetrel and
GCA Histories 215

APPENDIX 1. Research Design 239

APPENDIX 2. The Petrochemical Industry 247

APPENDIX 3. Timeline of the History of "Pólo Petroquímico
de Camaçari 249

APPENDIX 4. CETREL S.A. Environmental Policy 251

APPENDIX 5. Bayport Facility Industrial Users in 1997 253

Index 255

Introduction

No human being should have contact with this thing [chemical waste],
the place where it was disposed can not be cleaned up, nobody should harvest
anything there, nobody should drink water there either.

Manager of Rhodia in *Cubatão*, interviewed by
the German magazine *GEO*, July 1992 [1]

INTRODUCTION

In 1966, the French Progil Société Anonyme and the Brazilian Carbocloro S/A
jointly created Clorogil S/A, in Cubatão, state of São Paulo, to produce fungicides
(wood preservatives) such as sodium pentachlorophenolate—also known in Brazil
as "China dust"—in a plant known as "penta." The production of the fungicides
uses chlorine, phenol, and caustic soda and generates toxic persistent organic
pollutants, such as hexachlorobenzene (HCB), polichorinated byphenils (PCBs),
and dibenzodioxins, in the waste stream. In 1974, Rhodia, the Brazilian subsidiary of the French multinational Rhône-Poulenc, joined Clorogil to operate an
adjacent new plant, also known by the workers as the "pentatetraper" plant,
to produce carbon tetrachloride and tetrachloroethylene (also known as perc).
The "pentatetraper" plant also generated highly toxic hazardous wastes, such as
hexachlorobenzene, tetrachlorobenzene, and trichloroethylene.

For over a decade the workers in these plants handled these toxic and
lethal chemicals without any information on the hazards they posed. The death
of two workers from acute poisoning caused by pentachlorophenolate in 1975
precipitated enough pressure from workers and activists to close the "penta" plant
down in 1978, after inspections by the County Council to Protect the Environment
of Cubatão revealed extremely poor work-environment conditions. Many of the
other thirty "penta" employees had chloracne, the malodorous skin eruptions
caused by exposure to PCBs, and liver disorders. They were transferred to the
"pentatetraper" plant after the "penta" plant closed, despite the existing signs and
symptoms of occupational diseases. After many years of struggle to have their
health conditions recognized as work-related, Rhodia's sick and disabled workers
created in 1994 the "Associação dos Contaminados Profissionalmente por
Organoclorados" (ACPO, Association of Workers Occupationally Contaminated

by Organochlorines) to organize and strengthen their struggle against Rhodia and for just compensation for their diseases and disabilities.

Since the 1970s, both plants disposed of millions of tons of untreated chlorinated hazardous wastes either on-site or into rivers and soil around the "Baixada Santista," creating numerous hazardous waste sites. The people who lived near the plants and the waste sites were deliberately misinformed about the dangers these chemicals posed. The company at one point even donated the waste to poor neighboring communities as fertilizer! Uncontrolled population growth and increases in the volume of hazardous wastes as well as the area contaminated by them created arguably the worst environmental disaster in Brazil: Houses were built over highly contaminated soils, with contaminated sand, and located in an environment where the drinking water was also highly polluted with hazardous chemicals.

The combination of work environment and environmental pollution produced by the two plants set in motion a chain of occupational and environmental health incidents. In 1998 "the tetraper" plant was finally closed, but the remediation of the hazardous waste sites it generated is still ongoing. Almost all of the plant's former employees show signs and symptoms of diseases associated with exposure to polichlorinated chemicals [2]. The saga of these workers has become a tragic example of the human health impacts of polluting technologies exported to developing countries by multinationals.

Since the 1970s developed countries have often exported hazards, in the form of toxic substances, products, polluting technologies, factories, or hazardous wastes to developing nations. Numerous horror stories in the press and scientific studies of occupational health practices of multinational companies conducted by American and European researchers have created a strong body of evidence that indicates the widespread existence of double standards between developed and developing countries regarding workplace and environmental health and safety protections.

The international literature on the export or migration of hazards from developed to developing countries has for the most part focused on the perspectives of exporting countries. Serious concerns have been raised by observers in developed countries about the export of hazards, and remedies have been proposed that, on the one hand, emphasize home-country control of multinationals and, on the other, the development of international standards.

This book complements this body of literature and adds to the debate by focusing on the role of national actors in the importation of hazards, based on the experience of late-1970s developments in the petrochemical industry in Bahia, Brazil. Based on initial evidence that indicated long-term cooperation between the waste management company of the Camaçari Petrochemical Complex (Cetrel), located in the state of Bahia, Brazil, and the Gulf Coast Waste Disposal Authority (GCA), the waste management company for the Gulf Coast area of Texas, three case studies were conducted, describing and analyzing the process of importation.

The first is a case study of two benzene-related occupational and environmental health crises that affected the complex in the eighties; the second is a case study of the environmental policies adopted by the Brazilian company; and the third is a case study of the environmental policies carried out by the parallel waste management authority in Texas.

Two of these studies center around social struggles and the process of importation of technological hazards and controls in Bahia, resulting from cooperation among the Brazilian state, private Brazilian funds, and foreign capital. The cases address the historical and structural developments in the "Pólo Petroquímico de Camaçari," and Cetrel. The latter has a microlevel focus, while the former has a mesolevel focus. The third, the Gulf Coast Waste Disposal Authority (GCWDA or GCA) case study, is similar to what epidemiologists would call a "control" or referent to Cetrel's case.

The Brazilian company has been operating under pollution control standards and technologies for protecting the environment and workers that are quite similar to GCA's. This did not depend heavily on government-initiated regulation, but, in the case of worker health and safety protections, did rely on a young and militant trade union in the complex, which successfully pushed for government intervention and regulation by the end of the 1980s. Similarly, community concerns about environmental damage contributed substantially to the efforts by the Texan waste management authority to deal more effectively with pollution control. These similar pollution control trends are characterized in the book as "dependent convergence" between developing and developed countries. That is, the Brazilian authorities sought to copy control measures employed in the United States—indeed, they perceived that they had surpassed American conditions and looked to a petrochemical complex owned by BASF in Germany as a more advanced model.

The Brazilian cases indicate that social struggles and/or interaction among actors in developing and developed nations determine to what extent hazardous technologies are imported without environmental controls and to what extent their hazardous effects are controlled by these nations. "Dependent convergence" suggests that the future development of a more inclusive theory of export-import of hazardous technologies and products should take into account the dialectical relationships established between social actors, such as unions, businesses, and governments, that are present in the societies of exporting and importing countries. The development of this broader theory requires cooperation and solidarity between researchers and activists in both developed and developing countries, which is happening in the last few years, for example, in the struggle to ban asbestos from the world economy. The rapid formation and expansion of international networks—both "virtual" and "real"—to control the worldwide production and use of toxic substances and polluting technologies seem to suggest that the time for this theory has come and that it is very feasible to embark in such an endeavor.

Chapter 1 develops the theoretical approaches to analyze the case studies by discussing four major arguments: the export of hazards, the dependency perspectives, the theory of class formation, and the political economy of occupational diseases.

Chapter 2 offers background information on some of the main characteristics of the petrochemical industry, then situates the geographic, historic, and political-economic context of the Bayport and Camaçari complexes, as well as GCWDA and Cetrel.

Chapter 3 starts with an overview of the Brazilian national political context throughout the twenty-year history of the Camaçari complex, and then moves to a political-economic analysis of the history of the complex, emphasizing the evolution of the environmental management policies. It frames the twenty-year period in three different phases according to critical events that shaped the changes in environmental—and occupational—health policies. The unit of analysis for this chapter is the complex as a whole.

Chapter 4 is a case study of the two benzene crises that shook the complex—the major occupational health problem in its history—and how they affected national legislation for controlling benzene exposures.

Chapter 5 is a case study that examines the evolution of environmental—and, to a lesser extent, occupational—health policies in Cetrel, documenting how this company dealt with the air, solid, and liquid hazardous wastes generated in the complex throughout the twenty years.

Chapter 6 is a case study that reviews the critical steps in the evolution of GCA's environmental control policies, with particular attention to the evolution of the Bayport complex. It is a case study of the American counterpart to Cetrel, serving as a cross-national reference for comparisons. It does not cover, however, the evolution of GCA's policies in the same depth as the Brazilian case, because of limited time and resources [3].

Chapter 7 is a cross-national comparative discussion of the two case-studies. It offers a cross-country actor analysis, a comparative analysis of the policy outcomes described in the two cases, and a summary of the lessons learned through the comparison of the two case studies. It ends with the main conclusions of the book, under the umbrella of what I call "dependent convergence" between Cetrel and GCA. Appendix 1 describes the research design used for this study.

ENDNOTES

1. Sindicato dos Trabalhadores Químicos de São Paulo, ABC e Campinas, (São Paulo, ABC and Campinas Chemical Workers Union), "*Dossiê Caso Rhodia,*" Maio de 1995 *(The Rhodia Dossier, May 1995).*
2. *The Rhodia Dossier* provides solid evidence of the high levels of pollution found in the soils and water in different hazardous waste sites in the area. The state environmental agency, CETESB, the University of Campinas, the Pan American Health Organization

(PAHO), and environmental consulting companies have conducted numerous tests and clinical exams to measure chemical contamination and human health effects. For example, in 1991, CETESB found hexachlorobenzene levels 3,000 times over the levels accepted by the German Chemical Industry Federation. See [1], p. 26.

3. To compensate for these limitations, comparative perspectives with the United States were underlying factors throughout the whole research, giving it a comparative flavor from start to finish.

CHAPTER 1

Migration of Hazards:
The Viewpoint of Actors in a
Newly Industrializing Country

The international literature on the double standards and the migration or export of hazards to developing countries is not new [1, p. 61]. It gained momentum, however, in the early to mid-eighties, when scholars and activists interested in international occupational and environmental health focused their attention on the international impacts of recent developments in U.S. capitalism. These intellectuals were specially concerned with the impact of multinationals on consumers, workers, and societies in the Third World. The 1984 Bhopal disaster in India—when a Union Carbide plant released a large quantity of methyl isocyanate onto adjacent neighborhoods, killing and injuring thousands of people—added a lot of fuel to their apprehension and galvanized the attention of scholars in developing countries as well. Two publications published during this period embody the central issues [2, 3].

Most commentators in Ives' book argued that U.S. multinationals had been exporting banned products and technologies to developing countries without any government control, nor any safeguards for the health and safety of workers and consumers in these countries. The debate in this book revolved around the causes and the magnitude of the problem, and what policies and legislative tools were needed or could be developed to curb it [2].

Pearson's book had a broader approach to the debate. It contained pro-business as well as anti-business opinions and included contributions of authors from developing countries [3]. Some commentators warned that ". . . if multinational businesses do not set high standards of conduct for themselves, they could face increasingly rigid or inconsistent regulation and restraints" [3, Foreword, p. x]. Others claimed that Pearson analyzed the relocation of "dirty industry" through trade to and direct investment in so-called "pollution havens" and concluded that the problem has been exaggerated [3, Foreword, p. xv]. On the other hand, Scherr and Castleman argued otherwise. Scherr noted that "[t]he widespread use of pharmaceuticals, pesticides, and other dangerous products has spread across national borders much more quickly than the capability to assure their safe use" [3, p. 130]. Castleman argued that ". . .numerous examples suggest that worker protection in the multinationals' Third World plants has been markedly poor compared with that in U.S. operations" [3, p. 149].

From the late eighties on, the export of hazards and the double standards arguments were debated in academic journals and at public health conferences in the United States and elsewhere. While the debate gradually included the point of view of commentators from developing nations, it was still dominated by the perspectives of the exporters, i.e, the developed countries. Little attention was given to the perspectives of the importers of hazardous technologies.

This book tries to answer several questions related to the double standards argument: Did Brazil, a newly industrializing country, import hazards from the United States, a developed country, when it developed its petrochemical industry in Camaçari? Did it also import technology controls from these countries? If yes, how did the process of importation of hazards and controls take place? What was the model adopted to control these hazards? How did social actors in the state of Bahia, Brazil, influence the environmental and occupational health policies adopted to control these hazards? In addition, the text that follows seeks to discover how both societies approached and resolved the pollution problems created by petrochemical production; how different social actors in these societies interacted to create the paradigms and policies used to control—or prevent—petrochemical pollution; and what models were used to guide the policies adopted to control pollution problems.

This chapter discusses the theoretical framework that grounds the study of the development and evolution of the occupational and environmental health and safety policies in Cetrel and GCA. The theoretical framework to explain these policies is an interplay of four related currents of thought:

- the "export or migration of hazards" argument, as proposed by Castleman;
- the "dependency" perspectives—structuralist and historical-structural— which provide two different theoretical and methodological views of economic development in peripheral countries;
- the theory of class formation, which helps to inform my argument as a historical analysis of social struggles by new classes, which were formed and developed with the creation and expansion of the complex. These new classes formulated their ideology and politics vis-a-vis work-environment hazards as they responded to concrete social struggles around changes of occupational and environmental health policies; and
- the political economy of occupational disease argument, as outlined by Levenstein et al., which lays out a structural set of hypotheses on the social relations at the point of production that need to be analyzed in order to understand health and safety policies in developed countries.

THE EXPORT OR MIGRATION OF HAZARDS

In 1979, Castleman argued that ". . . as hazardous and polluting industries come under increasing regulation in industrial nations, some of the affected processes are exported, without improvement to make them less hazardous, to nonregulating countries where cheap labor is abundant" [4, p. 569]. He called these factories "runaway shops." Castleman also stated that ". . . U.S. pollution control laws and occupational health standards may soon lead to *wholesale exodus* in major industries, as manufacturers move overseas to avoid the large costs imposed here while continuing to sell their products in the USA" [5, p. 51]. (emphasis added).

Castleman's point was that industries would flee U.S. environmental and occupational health and safety regulations because compliance is too costly. Indeed, this "wholesale exodus" would encompass the following products or industries: asbestos textiles and friction products industries, arsenic and refined copper from primary smelters, mercury mining, primary refined zinc, pesticides, and benzidine dyes. The vinyl-chloride and steel industry were two potential candidates. In 1985, Levenstein and Eller criticized Castleman's argument as an overreaction and an exaggeration of the impacts of Occupational Safety and Health Administration (OSHA) regulations on businesses [5]. They argued that Castleman's warnings sounded very similar to the claims of the National Association of Manufacturers. Although motivated by different concerns, Castleman appeared to echo industry opposition to OSHA and the Environmental Protection Agency (EPA) regulations. His projections of capital flight were based on examples of only a few industries. Levenstein and Eller countered that available evidence did not support Castleman's assumptions that 1) OSHA regulation of U.S. industry has been effective; 2) U.S. industry in general must relocate in order to produce at acceptable costs (a technological assumption); and 3) companies comply with government regulations in both developed and developing countries [5]. Levenstein and Eller reviewed economic data and policy studies to demonstrate that there were no grounds to forecast a major capital flight from the United States as a result of regulation of business. They concluded that "OSHA is at best marginally effective; industry has provided some evidence that it can adjust to regulation if pushed to the wall (i.e., the vinyl-chloride case); and foreign investment statistics fail to show a regulation effect" [5, p. 57].

During the last fifteen years, Castleman and others have pursued the "double standards" or migration-of-hazards" argument. Their body of work has influenced the views of a significant number of public health professionals and intellectuals in the United States and elsewhere [see, e.g., 1, 6, 7]. In his most recent article on the subject Castleman defined double standards the following way: ". . . Companies have *on occasion* moved entire plants and exported banned products to developing countries, but *more often the export of hazards is less obvious unless one is able to make quantitative international comparisons*" [7, p. 87]. And, he continued:

"There have been many examples where multinational corporations have not been as thorough in controlling industrial hazards in developing countries as they were in their 'home' countries. The most numerous reports of this *double standard' have arisen in connection with asbestos and other ultra-hazardous materials, where substantial control of the hazards would represent a major share of overall costs of production and reduce sales in other ways*" (emphasis added) [7, p. 87].

This is a less diametric position and raises questions about the need for more direct research. Wheeler and Ashoka performed one such econometric analysis of international investment location decisions of U.S. firms and concluded that agglomeration economies or economies of scale are the dominant influence on investor calculations [8]. For developing countries, the most important factors for company location decisions are infrastructure development, stable international relations, rapid industrial growth, and a growing domestic market; for developed countries, the existence of specialized support services is the most important factor.

Castleman's argument in 1979 probably exaggerated the migration of hazards when he predicted the "wholesale exodus." His argument that multi-nationals "on occasion" export ultrahazardous chemicals to the Third World and maintain a system of double standards is correct. A wealth of evidence exists to demonstrate this [9, 10]. Bhopal is probably the most famous example, among many others. Nevertheless, it may be difficult or unreasonable to claim the existence of double standards in cases when multinational facilities in developing countries are the safest and most modern plants.

Evidence of this can be found in many countries in Latin America, lending some credibility to those who argue that the globalization or internationalization of the world economy may improve health and safety and decrease environmental pollution in Third World countries [11].

Birdsall and Wheeler came to such a conclusion in their study of the relationship between greater economic "openness" and increase in industrial pollution in Latin American countries. They suggested that "liberalization of trade regimes and increased foreign investment in Latin America have not been associated with pollution-intensive industrial development" [12, p. 137]. Relying on Chilean anecdotes and econometric evidence, they claimed that "protected economies are more likely to favor pollution intensive industries, while openness actually encourages cleaner industry through the importation of developed-country pollution standards" [12, p. 137].

That said, it is quite possible that two contradictory phenomena may have occurred simultaneously in Latin America. On the one hand, large, transnational companies exported new and cleaner technologies that allowed them to comply with developed countries' pollution control standards. Once established, they may push host governments to enforce tighter standards than the existing ones to gain competitive advantages over smaller companies of host countries. Export-driven industries in "open" host countries may also be forced to comply with social regulations of developed countries to gain access to their consumer markets. According to Birdsall and Wheeler, this seems to have happened in Chile, that is an extreme case of laissez-faire economics [12].

On the other hand, pollution-intensive industries may have been exported to less-developed countries in the 1980s as the Organization for Economic Cooperation and Development (OECD) countries made their regulations stricter in the 1970s [13]. The Birdsall and Wheeler analysis supports such a possibility. In turn, they claim that pollution-intensive industries (capital and material-intensive industries) have enjoyed protection in Latin America despite being heavy polluters. Thus, pollution havens would be found in protectionist instead of open economies.

Beyond the arguments related to different political positions, methodologies, and views of economic development, it is clear that data from different industries, countries, and periods could provide evidence in support of either view. In short, the migration-of-hazards argument is a good example of a hotly contested terrain between corporate and community, developed and developing nations' interests.

In an excellent and updated discussion of the migration of hazards, Karliner summarized what he called the three paths of migration of hazardous industries from the North (where most of the developed or industrialized countries are located) to the South (where the vast majority of the less-developed or industrializing countries are located) [14]:

- Pollution havens—In this path, the relocation of production and migration of hazards are due to strict environmental standards. Transnational corporations (TNCs) relocate their operations to the South, export their products or send off their hazardous waste primarily to avoid environmental regulations in the North [15-21].
- Package Deals—In this path TNCs move their operations to the South because of a package offered to them that includes the following comparative advantages of relocation: lax environmental regulations, as well as poor enforcement, low wages, and no unions. The best examples of this path are found in the maquiladora factories on the Mexican side of the Mexico-U.S. border. These assembly-line plants, owned by many U.S.-based corporations and now totaling more than 3,000, created what some American environmentalists and health and safety activists consider to be the worst cases of environmental pollution in the Americas [22-27].
- Marlboro Men—In this path economic globalization is the driving force for the migration of hazardous industries to the Third World. Corporations set up factories in these countries to export back to their home markets (export platforms), as well as to sell their products elsewhere. These products include cigarettes, polyvinyl chloride piping, cars, cornflakes, and several lines of consumer products. The tobacco industry migration coincided with a process

of saturation, stagnation, or decline of sales in developed countries, in part due to health concerns and regulations.

Thus, for most transnational or multinational industries, the export of jobs, capital, and hazards is related to capital expansion on a global scale. Stricter occupational health and safety or environmental control standards in developed countries play only a small role in this process, compared to cheaper labor, lack of or reduced tariffs, barriers to trade and investment, and tax incentives in developing countries.

On a more fundamental or structural level, the challenge is to analyze the process of economic globalization or expanded capital reproduction at the global level and its repercussions on local work and community environments. Today, these traditionally local issues are closely intertwined with economic decisions that follow a global logic. The global assembly line is the ultimate example of this process. Local environmental or occupational health problems derived from this production process are thus part of a global scenario. So are solutions to these problems.

THE STRUCTURALIST, GLOBALIST, OR ORTHODOX APPROACH TO DEPENDENCY

To understand the underlying tenets of Castleman and Navarro's assertion regarding the migration or export of hazards to developing countries, one must discuss the structuralist approach to dependency perspectives as posited by Andre Gunder Frank and Samir Amin, among others [28, 29]. There seems to be a clear correspondence between their approach and Castleman's and Navarro's viewpoints on the process of exporting hazardous chemicals, products, and technologies from developed to developing countries. In fact, I suggest that the latter applied the structuralist view of economic development in the periphery proposed by the former to explain how hazards migrate from developed to developing countries.

The world-system view, as elaborated by Frank, Amin, and Wallerstein, argues that the development of Third World capitalism is determined by the role of Third World countries in the process of capital accumulation on a world scale. Frank's approach represented a theoretical reaction against the propositions of the modernization theories, which held that "economic development occurs in a succession of capitalist stages" and that "today's underdeveloped countries are still in a stage, sometimes depicted as an original stage of history, through which the now-developed countries passed long ago" [30-42].

He argued against these notions on the grounds that

> . . . contemporary underdevelopment is in large part the historical product of past and continuing economic and other relations between the satellite underdeveloped and the now developed metropolitan countries. Furthermore,

these relations are an essential part of the structure and development of the capitalist system on a world scale as a whole [30, p. 3].

Frank's criticisms of the modernization theories countered the idea that the future of underdeveloped countries would be similar to the past of Western Europe and the United States in the sense that the development process would reproduce the various stages that characterized the social changes of the political, economic, and social systems of these countries [43, 44].

Another primary debate with the modernization theorists has to do with the argument that evident inequalities in income and cultural differences in underdeveloped countries were due to the existence of "dual" societies and economies in these countries. In a nutshell, the frame of the modernization argument characterized one part of dual societies as rich, modern, and relatively developed because it had continuous relations with the capitalist world; the other part was poor, backward, and underdeveloped or precapitalist due to its lack of capitalist relations with the developed world. Frank's refutation to the theorists theorized that

> ... [t]he expansion of the capitalist system over the past centuries effectively and entirely penetrated even the apparently most isolated sectors of the underdeveloped world. Therefore, the economic, political, social and cultural institutions and relations we now observe there are the products of the historical development of the capitalist system no less than are the seemingly more modern or capitalist features of the national metropolises of these underdeveloped countries [30, p. 4].

Thus, in the capitalist world system, some countries are *metropolises* or *centers* or *core* (synonyms include industrialized or developed countries) and others are *satellites, peripheries,* or *dependent* (synonyms include under-developed, less-developed, industrializing, or developing countries). The conception that the development of the core countries comes at the cost of the under-development of the periphery is central to this approach. According to Frank:

> ... Any serious inquiry, then, into the differences in origins of the historical experiences and subsequent development paths of the various regions of the New World must begin with an examination of the historical process of capital accumulation on a world scale, since that was the driving force of the various processes in the New World which were integral parts of the world process, and go on to consider how it was mediated through differing modes of production in the various parts of the World which correspond to the differing—though related—roles these regions placed in the worldwide process [cited in 45, p. 185].

The world capitalist system structurally determines the international division of labor, whereby "core" countries export technologies and capital, and periphery countries export raw materials and in some cases consumer and durable goods. By the same token, developing countries import technology and capital, and metropolises import primary products (food and raw materials) and cheap manufacturing products.

The imperialist metropolises develop this international division of labor and accumulate capital from it. As technology changes and the organization of capitalist expansion changes, developing countries are assigned different tasks in this division of labor. Following the logic of this approach, this book argues that transnational companies, as major organizers of capital expansion from the metropolises to the periphery, would export hazards from developed to developing countries whenever needed for the process of capital accumulation in the former countries. Less-developed countries would become "pollution havens" due to their subordinate role in the world economy.

The industrialization of developing countries and all changes in the process of periphery development/ underdevelopment were seen by Frank as a result of the development of productive forces in the metropolises. Amin disagreed with this conception. He argued that anti-imperialist forces such as national liberation movements imposed the industrialization of the periphery on the monopolies of the center. Moreover, the changes in the international division of labor are in part a result of the anti-imperialist struggles in the periphery [cited in 45, p. 187]. Amin also ascribed a more important role to the national liberation movements in imposing changes in the economic order than technological changes or contradictions in the development of the metropolises.

The structuralist approach to dependency proposed by Frank and Amin adopts one of the views of the nature of the state in less-developed countries (LDCs), the instrumentalist view, which depicts the state as an instrument for the administration of the dependent role of these economies in the capitalist world system. Therefore, the role and the form of the weak state in the periphery are determined by the exigencies of the process of capital accumulation and the international division of labor, leaving little room for national class conflicts to influence state policies. By emphasizing the weight of outside influence on the local state, world system dependency theorists "take the emphasis off local capitalist development, domestic class struggle, the autonomy of the state, and the shift of struggle to the State" [cited in 45, p. 190].

As Frank posited:

> Indeed, this dependent, and in this sense weak, character of the state in the Third World—dependent financially, technologically, institutionally, ideologically, militarily, in a word, politically, on the international bourgeoisie(s) and their metropolitan states—may be regarded as the fundamental characteristic of the Third World state [cited in 45, p. 189].

Furthermore, the transformation of the world capitalist economy in the post-Second World War period created world economic conditions that would prohibit developing countries from being able to accumulate capital "within the narrow confinements of the national (and even state) capitalist mode of production in the era of neo-imperialism" [cited in 45, p. 191]. According to this theoretical framework, any political aspirations of national bourgeoisies in the periphery are condemned as hopeless. We must understand the Castleman and Navarro discussion of export of hazards in the context of this world-systems theory.

While Castleman and Navarro's export-of-hazards, migration-of-hazards, or double standards arguments may help explain some of the structural trends that determine some practices of transnational companies in developing countries, it is not sufficient to explain other political-economic situations that occurred during the 1970s in some semiperipheral countries such as Brazil [46]. In other words, while their argument may correctly explain cases where multinational corporations export hazards to developing countries without adequately protecting workers and the environment, it falls short of explaining cases where the nation-state and national actors in developing countries are the major factors behind the creation or importation of the hazards. This is the case that is addressed later in this book when the origins and development of Cetrel and the Camaçari Petrochemical Complex are discussed in detail.

The 1970s was a period of rapid economic growth in Brazil, the so-called Brazilian miracle. A military dictatorship following an import-substitution, pro-growth development economic model and ideology decided to make major public investments in economic infrastructure, including the construction of two petrochemical complexes. One of these was the Camaçari Petrochemical Complex.

This petrochemical complex generated a variety of occupational and environmental hazards leading to work environment exposures that had to be controlled or mitigated in some fashion. Occupational and environmental policies and regulations were implemented throughout the eighties and nineties to address the pollution problems generated by the complex. To understand this development, one must examine the social struggle and the interaction between and among national actors, i.e., the Brazilian state, the Brazilian bourgeoisie, and the Brazilian subordinate classes.

THE HISTORICAL-STRUCTURAL, RELATIONAL, OR UNORTHODOX APPROACH TO DEPENDENCY

I believe that the historical-structural approach to dependency as proposed by Cardoso and Faletto, Petras, or Evans best contributes to understanding this development in Brazil. This approach leads to a view of dependency within the context of local social struggle. An economic system is dependent when "accumulation and expansion of capital cannot find its essential dynamic component inside the system" [47, p. xx].

Class struggle between popular movements and ruling classes at the national level plays the most important role in determining historical events in these countries. According to Cardoso and Faletto, their approach "is both structural and historical: emphasizes not just the structural conditioning of social life, but also the historical transformation of structures by conflict, social movements and class struggle. Thus our methodology is historical-structural" [47, p. x]. They wrote that while

> ... structural analysis of dependence aims to explain the interrelationships of classes and nation-states at the level of the international scene as well as at the level internal to each country, dialectical analysis of that complex process includes formulation of concepts linked to the effort to explain how internal and external political domination relate to each other [47, p. x].

The logic of world capitalist accumulation and imperialist penetration in developing countries is very important—as proposed by the structuralist approach—but it does not mechanically determine their economic and political development. On the contrary, the interests of foreign capital may be internalized by local groups and promote national development. Instead of emphasizing the self-perpetuating structural mechanisms of dependency, Cardoso and Faletto argued that different dependent countries have histories that are the result of the different historical instances "at which sectors of local classes allied or clashed with foreign interests, organized different forms of state, sustained distinct ideologies, or tried to implement various policies or defined alternative strategies to cope with imperialist challenges in diverse moments of history" [47, p. xvii]. They agreed with the notion that capitalist development in the periphery is conditioned by the world economy, but they concentrated on the particular countries rather than on the general world economy. Their focus was on the inter- and intra-class struggles that take place at the periphery, and they submitted that these struggles had significance for the local as well as the world capitalist development. Moreover, the dependent state is viewed as a ruling-class mechanism for appropriating local resources for capital export, and a mechanism for establishing and maintaining bourgeois hegemony. The economic development at the periphery is conditioned by crises and developments in the world system, but the dependent state is primarily responsible for organizing the internal market and the local accumulation of capital.

The history of the economic development and industrialization of Latin America proposed by Cardoso and Falleto shows how the characteristics of dependent states in Latin America are similar to the capitalist states in core countries. Carnoy observed that, as in Poulantzas and in opposition to the above-mentioned instrumentalist view of the nature of the state, their approach to dependent states sees the state as a primary arena for class conflict, since national popular movements or groups may force this state to democratize [48]. In short, Cardoso's and Faletto's approach is a political-economic view of dependency that gives more autonomy to politics, as opposed to the instrumentalist view of Frank's world-systems theory, which is overly deterministic.

Petras and Brill argued along the same lines for a relational approach to the problems of development:

> . . . The world economy cannot be understood as merely the aggregate of the parts that comprise it. But neither can nation-states, regions, nor classes be reduced to an expression of the whole. Nation-states, regions, or classes can only be understood in terms of their own specific logic. The existence of a world economy does not in any sense imply its homogeneity [49, p. 9].

These scholars believe that domination is a consequence of particular relations that evolve between states and classes within and between regions. Third World countries have the ability to change these relations as new class forces and alliances emerge. These new class relations are capable of redefining "the nation's role in the world market and its relations within the Third World" [49, p. 9]. They also criticized the overemphasis on structural economic determinism of the globalist approach to dependency and argued that globalist views propose a rather static view of the capitalist system, in which social relations are conceived as unequal, without much possibility for change [51]. I believe this is one of the most profound and solid criticisms to the structuralist approach to dependency. For further discussion on this issue, see [45, p. 187].

These characteristics of globalist theories were responsible for the creation of categories such as "core" and "periphery," "which serve both to describe and classify countries according to representative attributes and to analyze those attributes in terms of deduced 'relations' arising from particular models of social and economic action" [44, p. 4]. As theorized by the structuralist approach to dependency, human agency in both developed and developing countries is considered to have minimal if any role in explaining the relationship between core and periphery countries. Wooding criticized structuralist analyses of the state by arguing that "they do not give much import to the actions of classes as collective manifestations of individual rebellion" [52, p. 59]. By analogy, his critique seems to indicate that there is little room for "class struggle" or "class consciousness" at the national level in the globalist or world system's approach to dependency.

Evans' study of economic development in Brazil follows Cardoso's and Faletto's approach to dependency, examining the attempts of the Brazilian state to promote the expansion of the role of local capital in two instances: the capital goods and petrochemical industries during the period 1974-1979, two clear examples of dependent development in a "semiperipheral" or "newly industrializing country" [53, pp. S211-S212]. He maintained that the Brazilian case is a nontraditional case of industrialization whereby the state intervenes as an economic and political actor to create a "local bourgeoisie," which is a departure from the "conventional paradigm of capitalist industrialization" [53, p. S211]. Thus, the Brazilian state plays a central role in peripheral capitalist development by coordinating an alliance with transnational corporations and local capital.

The bureaucratic authoritarian state that developed after the Brazilian coup d'etat of 1964 becomes the centerpiece that pushes forward accumulation in strategic industries, such as the capital goods and petrochemical industries [54]. In an initial phase that lasted about ten years, the state builds an alliance with international capital to promote economic development and restore capital accumulation, after "eliminating the threat to the capitalist order" posed by the populist and nationalist unrest of the sixties. The weak local bourgeoisie is temporarily pushed to the side while the state rebuilds the political and economic conditions for bourgeois hegemony. In a second phase—the economic miracle is the end result of it—the state actively "tutors" and subsidizes the activities of the local bourgeoisie. The state actually "reinvents" the local bourgeoisie, creating a solid alliance with it to leverage its economic and political power. A triple alliance or tripod (tripé, in Portuguese) is formed: the state, the local bourgeoisie, and international capital become partners in developing a dependent economy.

Although some observers argue about the nature of the alliance and the relative power of these three actors in promoting national economic development, it is indisputable that the empirical evidence in the two cases mentioned above favor Evans' analysis [55, 56]. As Evans and Guimarães submitted, the Brazilian state clearly acted as a "tutor" with the technobureaucracy representing a class fraction—state bourgeoisie—and performing the hegemonic role in reinstating the temporarily weakened power of the private local bourgeoisie [57, 58].

Thus, the Brazilian regime of the 1970s defies classification as state capitalism. Abranches summarized the situation the following way: "With civil society devoid of autonomous political organizations, all political transactions are mediated by state structure. Thus, politics becomes an affair circumscribed to the bureaucracy of the state" [cited in 53, p. S217].

In the capital-goods sector, state attempts failed and generated political opposition to the military regime among local entrepreneurs. In the petrochemical industry, the existence of a powerful state enterprise within the sector (Petroquisa) was critical to the state's ability to restructure the industry. Evans claimed that what came out of this attempt was " . . . an interesting oligopolistic community in which state and private local capital are thoroughly integrated and similarly organized" [cited in 53, p. S210]. He proposed that concentrating the analysis on such oligopolistic communities "represents the most promising strategy for understanding the local side of dependent capitalist development" [cited in 53, p. S210]. Moreover, this understanding "should focus on the concrete forms of oligopolistic community that are created and particularly on the way in which state and private capital are synthesized in different sectors" [cited in 53, p. S243].

THE THEORY OF CLASS FORMATION

Guimarães and Castro performed an extensive review of the American and Brazilian literature on class formation. They contributed their own insights to it before applying this theory to explain class formation in Brazil and Bahia, in particular the formation of the petrochemical fraction of the Brazilian working class [59-61]. They grounded their analysis on concepts such as *class capacities, class interests, class identity, class consciousness, class hegemony,* and *factory regime.*

Class capacities operationally mean the concrete practices of a class, expressed through unions, political parties, community or neighborhood associations, student organizations, and the family. Different classes build and develop their class interests through the workings of these institutions, where they may find their ideological resources (a common language, tradition, theory, and worldview), their material resources (talents, skills, money) and their organizational resources (shaping of networking and resource mobilization for action).

Class interests are defined by Marx as "goals that are somehow imputed to the members [of a class], such as the goals they would have had if fully aware of the causes of, and possible remedies to, their situation" [cited in 57, p. 59]. The use of this criterion to define interests is opposed by liberals and pluralists who believe that to impute interest to classes and individuals is a nonempirical and nonverifiable procedure and propose instead the reliance on self-definitions of interests. Marxists disagree with liberals and have to explain "the mechanisms by which the working class becomes conscious of its class interests and the circumstances that inhibit or stimulate these mechanisms" [cited in 57, p. 62].

Traditional Marxist analysis of class consciousness, based on Marx's "Prologue to the Contribution of a Critique of Political Economy," tends to be economistic because it overdetermines the role of the development of productive forces as the motor of social change.

According to Castro and Guimarães, this overstress leads to the underestimation of the role of human agency in social change, that is, the role of objective forces is overemphasized, and the "concrete analysis of the concrete event" is downplayed. They argued that, on the one hand, classes are a result of objective structural positions in capitalist production; on the other, they are also constituted as an effect of social struggles that are not singly determined by the nature of production relations [57].

Classes are structured by the totality of economic, political, cultural, and ideological relations. Thus, class formation should be characterized as a continuous movement whereby classes are permanently organized, disorganized, and reorganized throughout capitalist development according to the struggles that give them concrete historical existence. In turn, *class consciousness* is not the same as class formation, since the former "simply means that a group of people occupying empty places have acquired common interests and a common social identity," while the latter "refers to the process by which these and not other interests were formed at a given moment" [57, pp. 18-19].

Classes should be understood as historical subjects within certain structural limitations that men and women face to live their own history, because there exist concrete structural limitations to political successes of different social classes. The limitations originate from structural conditions as well as from particular forms of subjectivity and collective solidarity, which take into account the intentionality of social actors. A fundamental concept to understand classes is the notion of *class identity,* which refers to "struggles between classes and about classes, i.e., struggles which define a class identity" [57, p. 18]. It is therefore "impossible to reduce class formation to a process in which certain segments within the class structure base their interests on the economic and material conditions of social production" [57, pp. 18-19].

Factory regime is defined by Burawoy in the following way:

> We shall distinguish the labour process, conceived as the coordinated set of activities and relations involved in the transformations of raw material into useful products, from the political apparatuses of production, understood as the institutions that regulate and shape struggles in the workplace—struggles which I call the "politics of production." Factory regime refers to the overall form of production, including both the political effects of the labour process and the political apparatuses of production [cited in 57, p. 4].

Burawoy identified three types of production politics in advanced capitalism: the despotic, the hegemonic, and the hegemonic despotic. He focused on national variations of hegemonic regimes by comparing two similar workshops in Chicago and Manchester, England, as well as comparing Japan with Sweden. Market despotism or despotic factory regime is the common early capitalistic regime where "the despotic regulation of the labor process is constituted by the economic whip of the market" [63, p. 588; 64, 65, 66].

Hegemonic factory regimes developed after World War Two in opposition to the despotic regime and are characterized by "bureaucratic regulation, in which rules are used to define and evaluate work tasks and govern the application of sanctions" [63, p. 589]. Moreover, in this period social-insurance legislation and state intervention to limit managerial domination reduced workers' dependence on wages. The "pure" coercive character of the despotic regime was replaced by consent in the hegemonic regimes, without eliminating coercion.

Hegemonic despotic regimes emerged as a consequence of the 1970s' crisis in profitability in advanced capitalist states. Mechanisms for the regulation of conflict and a minimal social wage enforced by the state laid the basis of this crisis; i.e., "[U.S.] hegemonic regimes established in the leading sectors of industry placed such constraints on accumulation that international competition became increasingly threatening" [63, p. 602; 67].

Advanced capitalism responded to the crisis of Fordism by creating areas of production—such as the U.S. sweatshops—where labor protections, minimum wages, and health and safety regulations are similar to the conditions prevailing in peripheral countries. This is what some commentators, such as Alejandro Portes, called the peripheralization of the core [cited in 63, p. 603].

The de-industrialization of the United States in industries such as the auto, steel, electrical, etc., coupled with the changing balance of class forces and the changing processes of capital accumulation at the international level paved the way for the rise of the new hegemonic despotism. In this new regime, labor and capital interests continue to be coordinated, but "whereas before labor was granted concessions on the basis of expansion of profits, now labor makes concessions..." [63, p. 602].

Burawoy summed up the hegemonic despotic factory regime when he wrote that "the new despotism is not simply the arbitrary tyranny of the overseer aimed at *individual* workers (although that happens too) but the "rational" tyranny of capital mobility aimed at the *collective* worker" (emphases in the original) [63, p. 588].

Guimarães asserted that "in the particular historical situation I have studied, workers' class identity was more delineated in the production sphere and in immediately related institutions, such as unions, than in any other setting" [57, pp. 99-100]. Consequently, the study of the factory regime or "work management" enables the theorization of the political process of hegemony and consent as it is manufactured at the plant level. Moreover, it adds the political sphere to the traditional study of labor processes.

While in the latter, "capital always dominates labor and relations are unconsciously and forcefully experienced," in the former, workers' organizations "bargain interests and forge consent or dissent" [57, p. 101]. Class formation then becomes a process of adaptation or resistance. Following this theoretical framework and adapting it to the Brazilian situation, the two Brazilian scholars explained the emergence of the new Brazilian labor movement of the late seventies to early eighties by a set of determinations originating in many levels or instances and institutions, the most relevant of which being the political system, the state, the factory regime, and the communities where workers live. Besides, they showed how conditions specific to the petrochemical industry of Bahia coupled with the political system and the state defined a factory regime that is a political space within the plants. This political space is what fed and launched the formation of the petrochemical working class in Bahia.

The historical analysis produced by Guimarães and Castro provides me with essential theoretical elements to discuss the origins and evolution of general and specific health and safety work-environment conflicts in the Camaçari complex until the mid-eighties. Their background work also enables me to try to explain in more than superficial ways why health and safety as well as environmental protection policies developed as they did afterward.

THE POLITICAL ECONOMY OF OCCUPATIONAL DISEASE

Levenstein, working with Tuminaro, Wooding, et al. suggested a set of structural hypotheses on relations among four key social actors in the work environment—labor, management, health professionals, and the government—which taken together may reveal the political economy of the work environment in the United States and other developed countries [68-70]. However, in Chapter 4 I apply their structural hypotheses to analyze the development of work environment crises in the Brazilian Camaçari petrochemical complex.

Levenstein et al. focused their theoretical questions on the political economy of occupational diseases under the assumption that they are the indicators or tracers for workplace exposures and hazards. According to them, the political economy of occupational disease requires attention to four major areas of concern:

1) the production of disease
2) the perception or recognition of disease
3) control measures
4) compensation for affected workers

The Production of Disease

Occupational diseases emanate from the production of goods and services, whereby workers are exposed to materials, machines, technologies, and work practices that may be hazardous to their health and well-being. The choice of technologies is an engineering and political-economic decision subject to social imperatives and constraints, which in turn determine the possibilities for labor-management cooperation or conflict regarding organization of work, the scale of production, inter- or intra-firm competition, and the impact of industry structure on workers' health. Labor-market issues such as "the relative scarcity of labor as a whole or of particular types of labor will influence choices in production, the resultant hazards associated with labor in particular industries, the options available to labor, and the pressure exerted on management to improve working conditions" [68, pp. 26-27].

The Recognition of Disease

The perception of workplace disease is determined by the social locus of the observer in the social relations of production. This idea was well-defined when the authors stated:

> While ill health may appear to be an "objective" matter, political-economic considerations are important in the perception of disease. Observers of worker health occupy different, and sometimes opposed locations in the system of production. Therefore, they bring to their understanding of occupational disease viewpoints directed or constrained by other, sometimes more important, determinants of their positions [68, pp. 26-27].

Workers perceive disease differently from management and "will mobilize around occupational health hazards and perceived disease if the hazard is believed to be drastic and the effects serious" [68, p. 27]. Health professionals hold different ethics and perceptions depending on their role in the system of production. For example, physicians who are labor allies in unions perceive occupational diseases very differently from state or company "docs."

It appears that there are three distinct orientations to the perception of industrial disease, or three ethical orientations: the scientific ethic, the public health ethic, and the engineering ethic.

The scientific ethic stresses a conservative approach to information about health effects, leaning toward the requirement of conclusive proof or incontrovertible proof of disease related to particular occupational exposures. It stresses the study of factors that determine causation, attempting always to separate them from the ones that only show association between exposures and disease. The public health ethic stresses prevention of workplace injuries and illnesses. The engineering ethic stresses efficiency in production.

To understand how the perception of occupational illness is mediated by the state and the legal system requires that one focuses on three concepts or characteristics of modern government in capitalist societies: hegemony, bureaucracy, and class conflict.

Hegemony suggests that the dominant class presents itself as guardian or guarantor of the interests and sentiments of the whole society, including subordinate classes. An instrumental theory would suggest that the state merely serves the interests of the dominant capitalist class and intervenes in social-economic matters to mediate and contain class antagonisms in a way that preserves the legitimacy and stability of the system. Accordingly, the state and the legal system function to mediate and reinforce existing class relations, and to legitimate and mystify dominant class power. However, the history of health and safety in the United States clearly shows that the state is also a central arena for class conflict and that the law and nature of the hegemonic state are not reserved for the exclusive use of the dominant class. Legal outcomes of class conflict and partial victories by subordinate classes can force the dominant classes to concede or can win limitations to the exercise of power by industry.

A middle-class stratum of bureaucrats usually administers the state for the capitalists. Sometimes these two social classes have conflicting views about workplace protections and regulations, creating a political space for labor to gain more or stricter state intervention on production. Therefore, the impact of bureaucrats with their public health or professional ethic may be significant enough to shape implementation of laws, regulations, and state intervention in class conflicts. Along the same lines, the impact of the quasi-scientific, bureaucratic-legal stance of judges and public health practitioners must not be underestimated.

Control Measures

Political-economic aspects also affect the control of occupational diseases because of economic and political decisions regarding the most cost-efficient allocation of a limited amount of financial resources. In turn, control measures are often heavily associated with notions derived from societal concepts such as private property ownership, the role of the state, and the best social means to limit the negative effects of technology. Two common and complementary models exist to control technological hazards: The industrial hygiene approaches tend to concentrate on the elimination and reduction of hazards through engineering control, administrative controls, or personal protective equipment; and the clinical approaches tend to concentrate on removing the worker from the exposure instead of eliminating or reducing the exposure.

Compensation for Occupational Diseases

The workers' compensation system is geared toward handling accidental injuries rather than occupational diseases. The system is presumed to encourage preventive measures for reducing or eliminating occupational diseases. However, financial considerations play a very important role in the definition of diseases, shifting the burden of proof to the employee. Usually, the emphasis that both labor and management place on compensating harm or monetizing the risk translates into less attention and effort toward preventing the occurrence of harm or the probability of the risk.

In controversial situations that often happen, medical uncertainty about the etiology of occupational diseases puts labor and management at cross-purposes regarding the influence of individual behaviors or attitudes in the causation of disease. A well-known example is the role of smoking behavior in controversies about long-term effects of chemical or asbestos exposures and lung cancer. In short, ". . . [a]ttempts by workers to gain protection from the economic effects of occupational disease affect the definition of disease and the subsequent research on occupational health hazards as well as research on the implementation of control technologies" [68, p. 33].

The set of structural hypotheses delineated by Levenstein and colleagues for developed countries such as the United States will be partially used to frame the historical evolution of work environment policies in the Camaçari complex as well as in Cetrel. These Brazilian policies will be contrasted with the ones that developed in the Bayport complex and in the GCWDA Bayport plant. These hypotheses identify the major players in the work environment and spell out the most important areas around which the players establish their identities, interests, and strategies regarding health and safety issues. To make an analogy using medical terms, these authors describe the anatomy of work environment actors. The next logical step would be to relate this anatomy to the physiology of the workplace, making these sets of hypotheses historical and concrete. By using a theater metaphor, one should conceive these actors as the key actors that "act out" the open-ended historical script of real work-environment conflicts.

CONCLUSION

In this chapter I reviewed the main four interrelated theoretical constructs that I will use to perform a historical-structural analysis of work environment policy development in one company of the Camaçari petrochemical complex, as suggested by Cardoso, to understand industrial development in the periphery. The focus on the viewpoint of Brazilian actors is based on the idea that the petrochemical complex was born as a major industrial development that produced a wide variety of occupational and environmental hazards, whose creation is a result of a triple alliance among national and international actors. The foreign component of this alliance played a small role in determining what would be produced, by whom, and how, as was the case with other heavy industries in newly industrializing countries. This scenario contrasts with Castleman's export of hazards argument. Hence, it is more correct to talk about the importation of hazards by national actors within a nation-state than to discuss the export of hazards by transnational corporations. It is even more correct to speak of the relationships between national and foreign actors, since foreign and national technology and expertise complemented each other in the process of transforming raw materials into petrochemical goods and treating the wastes generated by petrochemical production.

This new development in the history of the Brazilian petrochemical industry also created two new classes or fractions of classes—social actors—in Bahia, whose formation and development is part of the social history that would allow me to explain what these two classes did to deal with the unavoidable process of production, perception, control, and compensation of occupational diseases generated by petrochemical production. Thus, the introduction of complex technological hazards in developing countries creates development, hazards, disease, hazardous waste, pollution, and new social actors who build institutions, ideology, and political resources—in a word, class capacities—to deal with those. The scenario that arises seems quite complex and difficult to decipher. Only the use of theoretical arguments that facilitate the understanding of the complex relationships between and among economic and social structures and history; development and industrial production; export and import of hazards and controls; work and community environments; state, class, and society, would enable me to try to make some sense of it. That is why I decided to approach the set of problems reviewed here from the distinct angles suggested by these arguments. Other contributions will also be explored in the following chapters of this research, all with the conscious intention of rendering simpler the petrochemical complexities, the social struggle, and the control of technological hazards in the "Pólo Petroquímico de Camaçari."

ENDNOTES

1. Barry Castleman, "The Double Standards in Industrial Hazards," in [2, pp. 61-89].
2. Jane Ives, ed., *The Export of Hazards*, Routledge & Kegan Paul, Boston, 1985.
3. Charles Pearson, ed., *Multinational Corporations, Environment, and the Third World: Business Matters*, World Resources Institute, Duke University Press, Durham, N.C., 1987.
4. Barry Castleman, "The Export of Hazardous Factories to Developing Nations," *International Journal of Health Services*, 9(4), pp. 569-606, 1979.
5. Charles Levenstein and Stan Eller, "Exporting Hazardous Industries: 'For Example' Is Not Proof, " in [2, pp. 51-59]. Other observers contested Castleman's assertion from a different angle. Royston, for example, stated that the "technical standards of the plants operated by multinationals in different countries tend to be similar, just because it is managerially simpler to standardize. As a result, the pollution control features of plants operated by multinationals in developing countries are likely to be closer to those operating in the industrialized countries than to those of plants operated by local companies in the same host country" [3, p. 17]. For a survey of legal, economic, technological, and policy issues involved in the export-of-hazards debate, see the above-mentioned publications.
6. Barry Castleman and Vicente Navarro, "International Mobility of Hazardous Products, Industries and Wastes," *International Journal of Health Services*, 17(4), pp. 617-633, 1987.
7. Barry Castleman, "The Migration of Industrial Hazards," *International Journal of Occupational and Environmental Health*, 1(2), pp. 85-96, April-June 1995. Castleman is the main author in the field of international occupational and environmental health who deals with the export of hazards issue.
8. David Wheeler and Ashoka Mody, "International Investment Location Decisions: The Case of U.S. firms," *Journal of International Economics*, 33(1-2), pp. 57-76, 1992.
9. For an extensive, though a bit outdated, compilation of this literature, see [10]. For a more recent summary of double standard cases, see [7, p. 88].
10. Thomas Mac Sheoin, "The Export of Hazardous Products and Industries: A Bibliography," *International Journal of Health Services*, 17(2), pp. 343-363, 1987.
11. Cited by George Martine, "Urbanização e Desenvolvimento Sustentável: Oposição ou Sinergia?" in Tania Franco, ed., *"Trabalho, Riscos Industriais e Meio Ambiente: Rumo ao Desenvolvimento Sustentável?"* EDUFBA, CRH, FFCH, UFBA, (Salvador, Brazil: 1997, p. 55. This argument has been advocated by the defenders of the North American Free Trade Agreement, Free Trade Agreement—or Area—of the Americas (FTAA), the World Trade Organization (WTO), and other regional trade agreements.
12. Nancy Birdsall and David Wheeler, "Trade Policy and Industrial Pollution in Latin America: Where Are the Pollution Havens?" *Journal of Environment and Development*, 2(1), pp. 137-149, Winter 1993.
13. The OECD was created in 1960 by thirty mostly developed countries as a forum for these nations to promote democracy and market economies. More details at www.oecd.org, accessed in February 2002.
14. Joshua Karliner, *The Corporate Planet: Ecology and Politics in the Age of Globalization*, Sierra Club, San Francisco, 1997, pp. 148-159. Although the author focused for the most part on environmental regulations in his analysis, the same paths

occur for occupational health and safety regulations. The following discussion is based on his approach to the issues.

15. For information on the export of pesticides, see [16, 17]. In these publications the author also describes the "circle of poison." The "circle" begins at the site of production, where millions of pounds of toxic chemicals are discharged into our air and water every year during the manufacturing process. It then extends to the country of use, where pesticides threaten the health and safety of untrained and unprotected workers. Most pesticide poisonings occur in developing countries that lack the proper training and access to even the most rudimentary protective equipment. The circle is completed when harmful residues come home to American dinner tables on imported food. Marquardt also mentioned that about 25 percent of the U.S. export pesticide market consists of the export of banned or unregistered pesticides (about 100-150 million pounds per year).

16. Sandra Marquardt, "Never-Registered Pesticides: Rejected Toxics Join the 'Circle of Poison,'" *Greenpeace Report,* p. 24, July 1990.

17. Sandra Marquardt, "Stopping the Export of Banned Pesticides," *Biography & News/Speeches & Reports,* 33(6), pp. 798-803, December 1990.

18. For a good description of the export of asbestos to Latin America, see [19]. Brazilian authors also adopted Castleman approach to denounce the export of hazards to Brazil in the asbestos and chemical industries; see [20, 21].

19. Mario Epelman, "The Export of Hazards to the Third World: The Case of Asbestos in Latin America," *New Solutions,* 2(4), pp. 48-56, Summer 1992.

20. Fernanda Giannasi and Annie Thébaud-Mony, "Occupational Exposures to Asbestos in Brazil," *International Journal of Occupational and Environmental Health,* 3(2), pp. 150-157, April-June 1997.

21. Carlos M. de Freitas, Marcelo F. de S. Porto, and Carlos M. Gomez, "Acidentes Químicos Ampliados: Um Desafio para a Saúde Pública," in Tania Franco, ed., *Trabalho, Riscos Industriais e Meio Ambiente: Rumo ao Desenvolvimento Sustentável?* EDUFBA/CRH/FFCH/UFBA, Salvador, Brazil, 1997, p. 27.

22. AFL-CIO affiliated unions, the U.S. Congress, and nongovernmental organizations have sponsored comparative studies between Mexico and U.S. occupational and environmental standards prior to and after the enactment of the North American Free Trade Agreement. For a sample of this rapidly growing literature see [23, 24, 25]. For a good Mexican study, see [26]. For a good American study on environmental health conditions in a maquiladora area, see [27].

23. Coalition for Justice in the Maquiladoras, *The Issue Is Health: Toxic Samplings, Environmental Conditions and Health Concerns along the U.S./Mexico Border,* p. 80, San Antonio, Texas, 1993.

24. U.S. General Accounting Office, *U.S.-Mexico Trade: The Work Environment at Eight U.S.-Owned Maquiladora Auto Parts Plants,* Government Accounting Office-General Government Division, p. 45, Washington, D.C., 1993.

25. L. Kochan, *Las maquiladoras y las Substancias Tóxicas: Costos no Divulgados de la Producción al Sur de la Frontera,* AFL-CIO, Publication No. 186.2600-0490-5 , p. 15, Washington, D.C., 1990.

26. Roberto Sanchez, "Health and Environmental Risks of the Maquiladora in Mexicali," *Natural Resources Journal,* 30(1), pp. 163-186, Winter 1990.

27. Rafael Moure-Eraso et al., "Back to the Future: Sweatshop Conditions on the Mexico-U.S. Border. I. Community Health Impact of Maquiladora Industrial Activity," *American Journal of Industrial Medicine*, 25, pp. 311-324, 1994.

28. There has been a long-lasting debate among scholars in political science, sociology, and economics about what the proper status of the concept "dependency," dependencia or dependence should be. Is it a theory? A perspective? An approach? A school of thought? The answer to these questions involves a discussion about epistemological and philosophical ideas that are far from semantic. Since it is not my intention here to solve or reproduce this debate, I will adopt the criteria formulated by Packenham, who used the term "dependency perspectives" to include different approaches to dependency. For further discussion on this topic, see [29].

29. Robert Packenham, *The Dependency Movement: Scholarship and Politics in Development Studies,* chap. 1, Harvard University Press, Cambridge, Mass., 1992.

30. Andre Gunder Frank, "The Development of Underdevelopment," in J.D. Cockroft, A.G. Frank, and D.L. Johnson, eds., *Dependence and Underdevelopment: Latin America's Political Economy,* 1st ed., p. 3, Anchor Books, Garden City, N.Y., 1972.

31. Many authors agree that the dependency perspectives were a counterargument against modernization theories proposed in the U.S. and Latin America. For a sample of the political works on modernization cited and/or criticized by different authors of dependency perspectives see [32, 33].

32. Gabriel Almond, "The Development of Political Development," in Weiner Myron and Samuel Huntington, ed., *Understanding Political Development,* pp. 437-490, Boston: Little Brown, 1987.

33. Seymour M. Lipset, *Political Man: The Social Bases of Politics,* Doubleday, Garden City, N.Y., 1960.

34. Samuel Huntington, "The Change to Change: Modernization, Development and Politics," *Comparative Politics,* 24(3), pp. 283-322, April 1971.

35. Edward Shils, *Political Development in the New Society,* Mouton, London, U.K., 1965.

36. The most famous economic writings seem to be [37, 38].

37. Walter Rostow, *Politics and the Stages of Economic Growth,* Oxford University Press, New York, N.Y., 1971.

38. Alexander Gerschenkron, *Economic Backwardness in Historical Perspective,* Harvard University Press, Cambridge, Mass., 1962.

39. For Latin American examples, see [40, 41, 42].

40. R. Redfield, *The Folk Culture of Yucatan,* Chicago University Press, Chicago, 1940.

41. Jacques Lambert, *Le Brésil; structure sociale et institutions politiques,* Paris, 1993.

42. Albert O. Hirschman, *The Strategy of Economic Development,* Yale University Press, New Haven, Conn., 1958.

43. For an excellent criticism of modernization or neo-modernization theories, see [44]. In his devastating criticism of modernization theories, Petras wrote that ". . . the problem with modernization theorists was that they asked the wrong questions, looked at the wrong units and failed to understand their own past, present and future. In a word, the starting point for an analysis of the development problematic was with their own paymasters—the complex network of research centers, state and corporate interests that funded them—who were unwilling to fund critical studies of the long-term, large-scale power and profit structure invading the post-colonial societies . . . [44, p. 33].

44. James Petras, "Declining Empire, Passing Theory," in James Petras and Morris Morley, eds., *U.S. Hegemony under Siege: Class, Politics and Development in Latin America,* pp. 31-40, Verso, New York, 1990.

45. Cited in Martin Carnoy, *The State and Political Theory,* p. 185, Princeton University Press, Princeton, N.J., 1984.

46. The use of the term semiperipheral here is derived from the classification proposed by the postdependence world system approach that, in the words of Petras, "sought to describe the development of capitalism in terms of a stratified, functionally inter-related global market containing three levels (a core, semi periphery and periphery), and to trace historically the mobility of nations within what is dubbed a single capitalist world economy" [44, p. 40]. For further discussion on this approach, see [44].

47. Fernando Henrique Cardoso and Enzo Faletto, *Dependency and Development in Latin America,* p. xx, University of California Press, Los Angeles, Calif., 1979.

48. Carnoy discussed the different views on the dependent state in chapter 7 of his book. According to him, Frank's view of dependent states emphasizes the nature of the state in Third World countries as "far more *an instrument* of foreign than local capital" [45, p. 193]. Cardoso and Faletto, on the other hand, emphasized that national actors and national struggles have shaped the nature of dependent states, which are not instruments of foreign capital.

49. James Petras and Howard Brill, "The Tyranny of Globalism," in [50, pp. 3-20].

50. James Petras, *Latin America: Bankers, Generals, and the Struggle for Social Justice,* Rowman & Littlefield, Totowa, N.J., 1986.

51. Although the detailed account of this criticism is beyond the scope of the discussion entertained here, it is worthwhile to quote Petras when—after claiming that globalist and neoclassical views of the market are similar—he wrote that ". . . [a]ctors do not form purely economic relations under formally equal conditions. Relations are comprised of different levels of interaction; political, economic, ideological and social—combined, unequal and in contradiction. These relations are not static—as they are extended and reproduced and are also transformed. The transformative processes can be understood in terms of abstract logic, but the concrete patterns that manifest them are historically specific [50, p. 4].

52. John Wooding, "Dire States: Workplace Health and Safety Regulation in the Reagan/ Thatcher Era," Ph.D. dissertation, Brandeis University, 1990.

53. Peter Evans, "Reinventing the Bourgeoisie: State Entrepreneurship and Class Formation in Dependent Capitalist Development," *American Journal of Sociology,* Supplement, 88, pp. S210-247, 1982.

54. This is O'Donnell's characterization of the state that developed in the South Cone of South America after military intervention in the mid- and late sixties. In this state ". . . political power is turned over to "techno-bureaucrats" who must repress the popular sectors on the one hand and gain the confidence of international capital on the other" [emphasis in the original] [53, p. S216]. See [51] for more on this characterization.

55. For an example of this argument see [56].

56. Consuelo Ahumada, *El Modelo Neoliberal y su Impacto en la Sociedad Colombiana,* Editorial El Áncora, Bogotá, Colombia, pp. 77-79, 1996. Ahumada disagrees with the notion that the local bourgeoisie was a partner in the alliance. Instead, she believes it

was subordinate to the interests of international capital and played a minor role in the alliance.

57. Antonio Sérgio Guimarães, "Factory Regime and Class Formation: The Petrochemical Workers in Brazil," Ph.D. dissertation, University of Wisconsin Madison, 1988, pp. 86-92, 186-187.

58. Guimarães formulated a typology of capitalist states specially useful to Latin America along two axes: One axis is based on the presence or absence of bourgeois leadership; the other axis is based on the presence or absence of working-class acceptance. He suggested four types of state: the liberal state or bourgeois dictatorship, the hegemonic state or bourgeois hegemony, the authoritarian state or bureaucratic rule, and the dictatorial state or bureaucratic dictatorship. According to this typology, the Brazilian state of the 1970s falls under the last two categories in different periods, depending on the presence or absence of compromises with the working class [57]. While O'Donnell called it bureaucratic-authoritarian, most progressive intellectuals in Brazil preferred to call it a dictatorial state or military dictatorship.

59. Antonio S. Guimarães and Nadya Castro, "Movimento Sindical e Formação de Classe—Elementos para uma Discussão Teórico Metodológica," *Caderno CRH*, vol. 4, p. 39, 1987. For a sample of their collective work see [60].

60. Antonio S. Guimarães, Michel Agier, Nadya Castro, and Tania Franco, "Classes, Trabalho e Diferenciação Social: A Bahia nos Anos 80," *Caderno CRH*, vol. 12, pp. 1-109, Editora Fator, Salvador, Brazil,1990.

61. For a thorough discussion on the class formation in the Camaçari petrochemical complex see [53]. These authors [53, 59-60] produced a wealth of studies of class formation and development in Brazil, Bahia, and in the petrochemical complex. They used the theoretical contributions of many Brazilian and American intellectuals, such as the well-known American authors Erik Olin Wright, Michael Burawoy, and Adam Przeworski, to frame their approach to class formation.

62. Earlier in the same publication Guimarães rejected the identification of working-class interests with ". . . a priori economic motivations, losing track of the rich process of political and ideological struggles over the definition of class interests" [57, p. 17].

63. Michael Burawoy, "Between the Labor Process and the State: The Changing Face of Factory Regimes Under Advanced Capitalism," *American Sociological Review*, vol. 48(5), pp. 587-605, 1983.

64. Another way of interpreting this factory regime was proposed by Druck, who— following the French Regulation approach—wrote that it is characteristic of the Fordist pattern of development. Estabrook submitted that according to Lipietz and other regulationists, Fordism is an accumulation strategy within the monopoly stage of capitalism. Fordism is also ". . . noted specifically for its qualities of mass-production, centralized state-led regulation and intervention in the market, rapid growth of mass-consumerism, and a capital-labor accord which ensured industrial peace by providing workers high wages and substantial benefits" [65, p. 36]. To other regulationists, Fordism represents a ". . . way of organizing society as a whole, as far as *it enunciates a development framework—a linkage between an intensive accumulation regime and a 'monopolist' or 'managed' regulation mode—that demarcates a certain phase of capitalist development in the center: the years of unprecedented prosperity (the 'golden era')"* [emphasis in the original] [66, p. 27]. For Druck's discussion, see [66].

65. Thomas Estabrook, "Labor/Community /Environment: The Spatial Politics of Collective Identity in Louisiana," Ph.D. dissertation, Clark University, 1996.
66. Graça Druck and Angela Borges, "Crise global, terceirização e a exclusão no mundo do trabalho," *Caderno CRH*, No. 19, pp. 23-45, 1993.
67. French and American regulationists call this the crisis of Fordism. For example, Estabrook wrote that Harvey "asserts that Fordism foundered in the 1970's in the U.S. because of its rigidity: in production investments; in labor allocation and contracts; in the unstoppable growth of the Welfare State despite dwindling tax revenues; and in the close interrelationship between organized labor, big business, and the government" [65, p. 36]. For a rich discussion on the crisis of Fordism, see [65, pp. 35-50].
68. Charles Levenstein and Dominick Tuminaro, "The Political Economy of Occupational Disease," *New Solutions*, 2(1), pp. 25-34, Summer 1991.
69. Charles Levenstein, John Wooding, and Beth Rosenberg, "The Social Context of Occupational Health," in Barry Levy and David Wegman, eds. *Occupational Health: Recognizing and Preventing Work-Related Disease,* 3rd ed., Little Brown and Company, Boston, pp. 25-49, 1995.
70. Michael Lax, "Workers and Occupational Safety and Health Professionals: Developing the Relationship," *New Solutions*, 8(1), pp. 9-16, 1998.

CHAPTER 2

One Industry, Two Complexes, Two Companies

FUNDAMENTALS OF THE PETROCHEMICAL INDUSTRY [1, 2]

The petrochemical industry was born in the early twentieth century in Germany and the United States and became one of the largest industrial sectors of modern developed societies after the Second World War. The industry spread to Western Europe in the fifties and to Japan in the sixties. Economic data show that the industry reached market saturation in the United States, Western Europe, and Japan by the mid-seventies, when it expanded to many developing countries in Asia, the Middle East, and Latin America.

This historical development of the industry is closely related to its upstream economic linkage with the oil industry, which refines crude oil or natural gas (raw materials) to provide the feedstocks for petrochemical production. The petrochemical industry may be considered a branch of the chemical industry, dependent upon petroleum-based raw materials, exposing it to the cyclical booms and busts of the oil industry.

The spatial location of the petrochemical industry in proximity to oil and natural gas fields, as well as its organization in petrochemical complexes adjacent to or downstream from refineries, to take advantage of intra- or intercompany economies of scale, is due to historical, macro-economic, and micro-economic aspects.

The historical aspects that determined this industrial agglomeration are related to the process of inventing new refining technologies by oil companies—motivated by the demand-pull for fuels and strategic materials (such as rubber) during World War Two—that allowed the commercial use of previously wasted by-products. Therefore, American and European petrochemical complexes tended to branch out of refineries in order to transform the basic chemicals produced by oil cracking into value-added petrochemical goods.

The macro- and micro-economic aspects that caused the geographic concentration of the petrochemical industry derive from its internal static and dynamic economies of scale, which force firms to try to reduce unit costs associated with increases in the volume of production. The former refers to "savings based on engineering principles which tend to reduce unit costs as the size of plant increases" [2, p. 121]. The latter refers to the "benefits of accumulated experience, which are usually expressed in the form of learning curves or experience curves" [2, p. 121]. Some of the factors that affect the economies of scale of the petrochemical industry include the large construction and operation costs of plants, access to technology and raw materials, distance from consumers and size of markets, the hazardous nature of its processes, the continuous-flow mode of operation, the size of corporations, and the need for a skilled workforce and a well-developed industrial infrastructure. The combination of these and other important factors, such as product life cycles, and vertical and horizontal integration, determines the economic push for industrial agglomeration in selected areas. Chapman concisely summarized the essence of the rationale for geographic concentration of the petrochemical industry when he noted that

> ... the massive capital sums involved in the construction of bigger and bigger units tend to emphasize the commitment of individual companies to existing sites, not least because of the knock-on effects generated by functional linkages between interdependent processes [2, p. 142].

The most common feedstocks for petrochemical production are natural gases such as ethane, propane, and butane, and liquids such as naphtha, which are typically transformed into olefin gases such as ethylene, propylene, or butadiene by cracking in refineries. As long as oil is refined to produce gasoline and other fuels, naphtha and light gases will be generated. Aromatics such as benzene, toluene, and xylene cannot be derived from natural gas and are commonly extracted from gasoline or naphtha. While naphtha generates a wider variety of basic chemicals than natural gas, it is more expensive than natural gas.

Appendix 2 displays the chain of production involved in changing olefins and aromatics into plastics, resins, synthetic fibers, and rubbers. Plastics and resins followed by synthetic detergents and fibers are the three largest outputs of the industry.

Downstream from the petrochemical industry a variety of industries may consume its products: the auto industry, the construction industry, the packaging industry, the textile industry, and the toy industry, among many others. By displacing competing raw materials such as wood, tin, glass, and paper, the early petrochemical industry became a mature propulsive industry that created many forward linkages with these essential economic sectors. As a result, it grew continuously between the fifties and seventies—the golden age of the international petrochemical industry—through technological breakthroughs, and process and product innovations. Due to its broad downstream linkages, the petrochemical industry exemplifies well the notion of "growth pole" adopted by governments and regional development agencies, in developed as well as developing countries, to promote economic development in less-developed or peripheral regions [3].

From a technological perspective, the petrochemical industry has always required a great deal of research and development (R&D) in organic chemistry and chemical engineering to develop processes capable of breaking and combining chemical molecules and compounds. For the most part, the R&D activities occurred within large corporations based in developed countries, which patented the innovations and kept them as proprietary sources of international competitive advantage. Nevertheless, the competition among these corporations eroded the relative advantage of a technological monopoly within a short time frame because, depending on the profitability of the product or process considered, competitors would sooner or later find a way to break the monopoly. Therefore, "technological monopolies based on process innovation rarely last long in petrochemicals" [2, p. 99].

Faced with this reality, companies have to weigh the relative economic advantages of keeping the technology monopoly or licensing it; in other words, companies have to assess how long they will keep a given patent monopoly before licensing it. The emergence of the petrochemical industry in the developing countries is a clear result of the process of technology licensing, coupled with the industry's commercial need to expand its markets beyond the United States, Western Europe, and Japan. In some cases, such as Argentina or Australia, foreign direct investment in the 1960s by oil and chemical multinationals was responsible for the migration of petrochemical production to these countries. In others, such as Brazil, Mexico, South Korea, or Venezuela, the initiative of governments was essential in establishing or expanding the industry, within the framework of import substitution policies [2, chap. 7; 4].

These countries imported a high-tech petrochemical industry that is capital-, energy-, and raw materials-intensive. Moreover, the industry creates high levels of pollution and evolves within the cyclical up and down swings of oil markets. Last, but not least, it is dominated by large oil and chemical corporations, some of which are the richest and maybe the first global corporations in the world [5].

As the new and minor players in this global industry, "peripheral" countries have in a very short time gone through the same industrial life-cycle curve that occurred in developed countries. At the international level they are facing tougher competition than the developed countries did. "Peripheral" countries for the most part started petrochemical production when this industry was already mature in the core countries and this fact, in and of itself, created many opportunities and challenges that will be discussed in the next sections and later in the book.

Here it suffices to note that, on the positive side, "peripheral" countries adopted modern production and environmental control technologies that had already been consolidated in the core countries. On the negative side, the former countries imported environmental and technological problems for which solutions are very difficult to find, even in the wealthiest nations.

Besides, the continuous change in international consumer markets has created a "race" among giant developed countries' corporations for competitive advantages in innovations in production and environmental pollution-control technologies, which tends to keep companies in "peripheral" countries in a constant state of "catching up." For example, while in the 1990s some of the large multinationals slowly adopted pollution-prevention and/or clean technologies, developing countries are struggling to buy costly pollution-control technologies that had been adopted in the 1980s in developed countries.

In a word, the importation of an inherently "dirty" industry had its own "unplanned" complexities, not the least of which is chronic technological dependence.

THE BAYPORT INDUSTRIAL PARK: "CAPITALIST PLANNING IN A MARKET-CAPITALISM ECONOMY" [6]

Background

The Bayport Industrial Park, located on the edge of Upper Galveston Bay in Pasadena, Harris County, Texas, was developed in the late 1960s by a real-estate development subsidiary of Exxon called Friendswood (now Exxon) Land Development Company (see Figure 1). The park is surrounded by the urban communities of La Porte, Clear Lake, Shore Acres, and Pasadena, about twenty miles south of Houston (see Figure 2). Exxon started the development of the

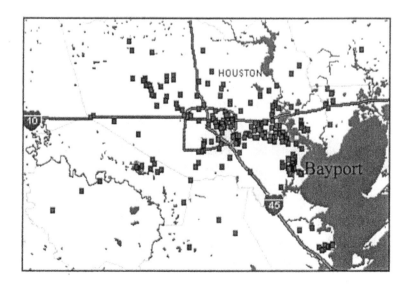

Figure 1. Geographic location of the Bayport Petrochemical Complex.

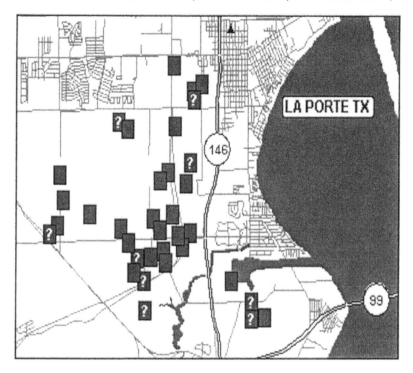

Figure 2. The Bayport Petrochemical Complex. Squares represent
plants in the Bayport Complex.

Bayport Industrial Park by selling the 9,000 acres of usable land it owned to oil, chemical, and petrochemical companies. To attract businesses to the Bayport Park, Exxon built a port, rail spurs, a system for freshwater distribution, and a small wastewater treatment plant prior to the time that Environmental Protection Agency (EPA) regulatory requirements took effect. Exxon developed the initial infrastructure for the implementation of a large industrial park whose industrial wastewater would be treated at the Bayport treatment facility. Thus, the waste-water plant preceded most of the facilities that came to Bayport. By 1974, the park had about ten operating companies.

The Bayport Park started as a planned chemical and chemical specialty integrated complex, where materials produced or plants were complementary. Later on it changed to compatibility among plants and producers instead of integration among producers. Thus, competition between two plants located in this industrial park may eventually occur. Most companies in the complex use natural gas as feedstock, although naphtha is also used. Each company buys its own feedstock from a supplier (refineries and chemical producers) located in the

50-mile Houston Ship Channel or in adjacent areas in the Gulf of Mexico, where the American oil and petrochemical industry is heavily concentrated [7].

Companies also have individual arrangements to obtain utilities such as steam and water. There are no centralized utilities and maintenance facilities in the complex. The only centralized facility that deals with the liquid industrial effluents is the GCWDA Bayport wastewater treatment facility. Many facilities in the complex are subsidiaries of large, global, American-based corporations— such as Rohm & Haas, ARCO, Goodyear, Oxychem, Hunstman, and Dupont— that produce chemicals, plastics, or synthetic fibers. Moreover, these corporations have followed the continuous petrochemical market trend over the years toward the production of fine and specialty chemicals [8, 9].

The political economy of the Bayport Industrial Complex may be characterized the following way:

First, it is a petrochemical complex composed of privately owned, small and medium-size plants with an average of seventy-five to 100 workers, which mostly produce second- and third-generation petrochemical products.

Second, the complex is but one complex in the largest oil and petrochemical production area in the world, the Gulf Coast region, in a state where in the 1990s about a quarter of the world's chemical production took place [10, p. 3]. The Gulf Coast region of Texas is the dominant center of petrochemical production in the United States. The state of Texas has built in the post-World War Two period a vast industrial infrastructure for oil and petrochemical production in the region, including a network of pipelines, ports, cargo terminals, rail system, and access to feedstock and customers of chemical and petrochemical production. For example, the Bayport complex has two privately owned liquid cargo terminals, and access to Southern Pacific Railroad Co. services and to Highway 146, which connects to the major interstate road system. Within a radius of 20 miles there are the Amoco, Lyondell-Citgo, and Exxon refineries. The Bayport complex may be described as one of the links in the Gulf Coast chain of petrochemical production [11].

Third, as a result of being the largest source of chemical raw materials and energy in the United States, Texas developed regulatory and tax environments friendly to petrochemical businesses. Not only have the oil, chemical, and petrochemical industries been a major part of the state economy for at least five decades, but also the corporate hegemony of the oil, chemical, and petrochemical industries is solidly established in political, social, and cultural matters. In addition, the regional expertise in environmental regulation, engineering, construction, and waste treatment and disposal makes Texas more attractive to international petrochemical businesses.

Fourth, the Bayport complex is an offshoot of the booming economy of Texas in the late sixties to early seventies, which set off another wave of industrial concentration of petrochemical companies in a resource-rich and wealthy region of the United States. As mentioned above, well-developed economies of scale favored agglutination of petrochemical production in the Gulf Coast. Given the overall pro-business environment in the state, the installation of the initial group of facilities in the Bayport complex should be seen as a result of market-driven corporate planning that tried to take advantage of optimistic supply and demand forecasts for specific petrochemicals, such as polypropylene, as well as competitive advantages resulting from location and economies of scale.

One of those competitive advantages is the centralized treatment of liquid industrial waste, as a former president of the Association of Bayport Companies (ABC) candidly noted: ". . . since GCA is a major drawing card for industrial facilities to Bayport" [12]. The state of Texas has traditionally subsidized the infrastructure needed for industrial development and offered tax incentives to attract companies to the area, paving the way for the investment in Bayport by large multiplant American and foreign-based multinational corporations (German, Japanese, Dutch, and British) that may lead the national or world market in their specific production capabilities [13].

A corollary of corporate power in the area is shown by the weak unionization in Bayport. The former Oil, Chemical, and Atomic Workers International Union (OCAW) represented workers at only two of the fifty companies listed in 1998, Calgon and Petrolite, while the International Union of Operating Engineers represents workers at Arco Chemical. The perspective offered by area former OCAW leaders is that Bayport companies were able to keep their workplaces free from labor unions by matching employees' wages, benefits, and health and safety programs in nonunionized plants with the ones in unionized workplaces. Therefore, it appears that the former OCAW might only indirectly influence important aspects of labor-management relations in the area—a situation that is also very different from Camaçari, as chapter 3 will show [14].

The GCWDA was created by the Texas state legislature in 1969 in response to an environmental crisis in the Galveston Bay area. The municipalities located in this region, such as Houston, Pasadena, and Texas City, were treating (i.e., disinfecting) the wastewater only against the biological hazards of municipal sewers, which was a common trend at the time. They were not removing the biochemical oxygen demand load (BOD), a tracer of chemical contamination, of the polluted industrial wastewater originating in the many petrochemical plants alongside the Houston Ship Channel. In the late 1960s, industries were discharging approximately 425,000 pounds per day of BOD into the channel, giving a black color to the water and killing marine life.

This untreated wastewater was discharged into the bay, killing aquatic life and threatening the shrimping, fishing, and tourist industries of the second most-productive seafood estuary in the United States. The lack of attention to industrial wastewater treatment was responsible for the high levels of pollution found by the Texas Water Quality Board Galveston Bay study, which was also supported by the Federal Water Pollution Control Administration [15].

The Gulf Coast Waste Disposal Authority
(GCA OR GCWDA) [16]

The sixty-first Texas State Legislature created the Gulf Coast Waste Disposal Authority as a political solution to the immediate and potential environmental crises identified in this study, since it was determined that the existing governmental structures (over 150 different units) and powers were not adequate to implement regional programs such as the one required to control the pollution of the Houston Ship Channel and the Galveston Bay watersheds.

The rationale underlying the new regional public agency was to coordinate these governmental units, to counter the proliferation of ineffective small treatment plants, and to control the discharge of heavy quantities of industrial waste into a major estuarine system that crossed county boundaries. State senator Croce sponsored senate bill 225, which created GCWDA, modeled after the German Ruhr Valley Authorities—the Ruhrverband and the Emschergenossenschaft—which had been in charge of dealing with the management and treatment of industrial pollution in the Ruhr river watershed [17, 18].

The authority was established as a conservation and reclamation district, a unit of local government, and body politic and corporate of the state of Texas, with broad statutory powers. Despite the claim of some authority officials that it is a pioneer and a unique form of government in the United States, it is institutionally similar to other regional authorities that manage ports, transit, and other regional public services. Perhaps its innovative character lies in the fact that GCA focused on regional water pollution and solid waste control before this institutional model of dealing with environmental pollution had spread to other areas of the United States [19].

The GCA was given the power to acquire, own, and operate regional wastewater treatment facilities, and to help industry and municipalities secure bond issues for financing waste treatment and disposal facilities. If so approved by voters, it could levy a tax up to 10 cents per $100 property valuation. The voters defeated this tax measure in November 1970, which caused the board to determine that GCWDA policies should correspond to the ones of an implementing agency, instead of an enforcement agency. In other words, the agency was steered into the role of a facilitator of wastewater pollution control in the Houston-Galveston area.

The GCA was also directed to adopt and enforce rules such as establishing minimum standards of operation for all aspects of solid waste handling, including storage, collection, incineration, and sanitary landfills. Although GCA was also empowered to develop and enforce water pollution control and waste disposal standards, and to adopt rules and regulations pertaining to all subjects within its control, it is not a regulatory body. The authority has to hold public hearings, consult with the state Texas Natural Resources Conservation Commission (TNRCC is a merger between former independent state agencies such as the Texas Water Quality Board and the Air Control Board), and the state and federal

Environmental Protection Agency to ensure that its standards do not violate environmental regulations set by these agencies. Davis expressed well the claimed uniqueness of GCWDA when he wrote that:

> We [GCWDA] had a silk glove on the one hand and a sword in the other. We have been hailed by some as the last hope for pollution free waters and by others as a hiding place for polluters. Actually, we are neither of these, but we have become competent operators of waste treatment plants with a highly skilled technical staff [18, p. 2; 20].

The authority's territory consists of the area inside the boundaries of Chambers, Galveston, and Harris counties, including the Houston metropolitan area and reaching Galveston in its Southern tip. It is governed by a nine-member board appointed by the governor (3), the commissioners' court of the three counties (3), and a council of mayors of each of the three counties (3). The board directors serve two-year staggered terms. The authority employs and pays the salary of a general manager, who implements board policies and directs staff efforts.

The authority received only limited funding from the state in the first years of operation, without any assistance from the local or federal governments. To survive, it had to be self-funding. Once the voters rejected its right to collect taxes in the early seventies, authority officials set service rates that guaranteed the financial sustainability of its operations as well as devised other ways of supporting its activities. One such way is to provide technical assistance to cities, counties, and industries in the area in return for payment. GCWDA's management model for operating its industrial wastewater facilities is characterized by a fee-for-service and the voluntary participation of industries and local governments that contract with the agency for the provision of regionalized treatment services [21].

It wasn't until 1973 that the first three contracts for industrial wastewater treatment facilities were signed: The first contract with Union Carbide Corporation in Texas City paved the way for regional waste control in the Texas City industrial area; the second had Monsanto pipe wastewater to the same facility, the 40-acre facility. By 1974 both companies were on stream. The third contract with Amoco Oil and Amoco Chemical in Texas City generated the American Plant by 1975.

The first industrial contract for the joint treatment of industrial wastewater of five participating industries was also signed in 1973, leading to the issuance of bonds to acquire, expand, and construct the Washburn Tunnel Facility, located in the banks of the Ship Channel [22]. In 1974, GCA signed a contract with Friendswood to operate the Bayport wastewater treatment facility. In 1976, GCA acquired the facility from Exxon. The joint treatment system implemented in Bayport combines the treatment of industrial and domestic wastewater in a single facility. Customers of the Bayport treatment plant are charged according to their hydraulic, organic, nitrogen, and total suspended solids loading. According to an early GCA publication, "The advantages of a joint waste treatment facility are the economies of scale as a result of less operational overhead, usually combined with better operational efficiency of the waste treatment plant" [23, p. 10].

The collection and treatment process adopted in Bayport may be roughly summarized the following way: The industrial and domestic wastewater are collected through a system of sewer lines, lateral lines, trunk lines, and interceptor lines that transport the liquid wastes to two open, concrete-lined channels; one for process and municipal wastewater streams (Bio-San) containing biological wastes and incinerable wastes, and another for "clean" streams composed of cooling water blow down and other wastewater with low levels of contaminants [24].

These channels transport the waste streams to the treatment works or facility, where they are submitted to a conventional three-stage treatment process: the primary, secondary, or general activated sludge process, and tertiary stages of wastewater treatment [24].

THE CAMAÇARI PETROCHEMICAL COMPLEX: "SOCIALIST PLANNING WITH CAPITALIST IMPLEMENTATION" [25]

The title of this section summarizes the major contrast between the Brazilian and American petrochemical complexes: the fact that the former was a planned state intervention in a capitalist economy, which was characterized erroneously by a former Brazilian executive cabinet member as "socialist" planning. The Bayport complex was also planned, but with much less state participation in the process. Instead, in Texas the bulk of the planning followed corporate investment priorities and oil and petrochemical market economics.

Background

The Camaçari Petrochemical Complex (COPEC in Portuguese) is located 40 kilometers (about 25 miles) north of Salvador, capital of the state of Bahia—the richest state in the poorest region of Brazil, the Northeast—between the watersheds of the Joanes and Paraguaçu rivers, and over the largest groundwater reserve of the state, the São Sebastião aquifer (see Figure 3). The Camaçari area is where the main sources of water supply for the metropolitan region of Salvador intersect, making it an environmentally strategic area [28, p. 68]. The construction of this complex started in 1971 in an area covering 235 square kilometers (about 58,000 acres) in the counties of Camaçari and Dias D' Avila, both within the metropolitan area of Salvador. The urban centers of these two counties are located four and three miles from the complex, respectively. The complex started operating in June 1978 with about twenty-seven companies, seventeen of which

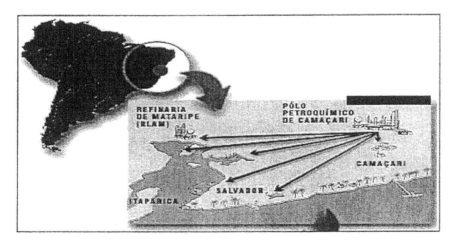

Figure 3. Geographic location of the Camaçari Petrochemical Complex.

were added by new petrochemical companies to an existing group of companies located in Camaçari.

By 1985 the complex had thirty-two companies: one public company, seven joint ventures of state and local capitals, nine tripod joint ventures of public-private and foreign capital companies—each with a third of the shares—two joint ventures of private and foreign capitals, six private companies, and seven foreign-owned companies [26, pp. 223, 509]. The ownership of seventeen of these companies was divided among seven Brazilian groups—three of them from Bahia: the Mariani group with five companies, the Banco Economico group with three, and the Odebrecht group with one. The other four groups were based in São Paulo. Some of the foreign groups that participate in the complex are the Japanese Nissho-Iwai, Sumitomo, and Mitsubishi, which are partners in three companies; the German BASF; the American Dow Chemical; and the French Rhone-Poulenc [29, 30]. The companies that constitute the complex are organized in a trade association called COFIC (Comitê de Fomento Industrial de Camaçari or Committee for the Industrial Foment of Camaçari), which formally represents them in external interactions with the local, state, and federal governments, as well as with different segments of the Brazilian society.

The "Pólo Petroquímico de Camaçari" is actually an industrial park composed of chemical, petrochemical, and other industries such as copper, cellulose, textile, and breweries, spread over four geographic locations: the basic complex area—where the majority of chemical and petrochemical companies are located; the north industrial area—where Cetrel is located; the east industrial area—where the copper refining industry and the breweries are located; and the west industrial area—where the industries that do not depend on the flow of raw materials produced in the complex are located. Moreover, there is a special-use area where the COFIC, the Centro de Recursos Ambientais (CRA, the state of Bahia environmental Agency) branch office, and other private institutions are located.

The COPEC is the most important industrial complex in Brazil, producing a range of intermediates for plastics, synthetic fibers, detergents, fertilizers, pharmaceutical goods, and petroleum and natural gas derivatives. In total, it produces more than 150 chemical products, divided into first-generation (olefines and aromatics), second-generation (e.g., styrene and toluene-diisocyanate), and third-generation (polymers such as polypropylene and polyvinyl-chloride) petrochemical products [31]. According to Guerra, since most companies in the complex produce a single product and have a low level of integration among them, intrasectoral synergism is almost impossible [32, p. 63]. Chronologically, it is the second Brazilian petrochemical complex (the first and oldest is located in Capuava, state of S. Paulo), the largest petrochemical complex in the southern hemisphere, and one of the largest in the world. The infrastructure of this integrated complex includes:

- Copene, the Companhia Petroquímica do Nordeste, is the basic petrochemicals and utilities center or "central" [33]. It is the main company of the complex, producing the first-generation chemical inputs out of naphtha (the main raw material) and gasoil, and the utilities—electric power, steam, compressed air, and clarified and demineralized water.
- Ceman, the "Central de Manutencão," is the industrial maintenance and repair company.
- Cetrel, the hazardous waste-management company, provides solid and liquid hazardous waste treatment.
- An integrated transportation network is composed of internal roads connected with highways, rail spurs, and ports; and pipelines, such as the ethylene pipeline that connects Copene with the Alagoas Chlorochemical Complex, located in Alagoas, a state in the north of Bahia.

The oil feedstock is mostly provided by the state-owned monopoly company Petrobrás, which refines local or imported oil in its Landulpho Alves refinery (RLAM), located about 20 miles from the complex. It is worth noting here that the oil reserves available in Bahia were never considered sufficient to support long-term petrochemical production in the region, which reinforces the importance of the industrial decentralization criterion as the main reason for locating the complex in Bahia.

The Political Economy of the "Pólo Petroquímico de Camaçari"

Evans' discussion of the petrochemical industry in Brazil maintains that the Camaçari Petrochemical Complex was an outcome of General Ernesto Geisel's II

National Development Plan (PND) [34-36]. As an offshoot of the Brazilian economic "miracle" of the late sixties to early seventies, the PND drew up a long-term economic development plan to develop Brazil's infrastructure in order to turn the country into a "developed" country in a short period. The "basic inputs" industries, such as the petrochemical and capital goods industries, were targeted as high priorities for investment. The "Pólo" was located in Bahia as a result of an economic-development strategy that favored regional development and industrial decentralization, promoted the import substitution of essential products, and the expansion of nationally owned industries.

This developmentalist strategy assumed that the creation of a large industrial structure in the Northeast would not only polarize (the Portuguese word "Pólo" means pole) the economic growth of the Brazilian Northeast upstream and downstream from the complex, but would also provide the country with much-needed petrochemical goods. As a result, Brazil would reduce its economic dependency on foreign countries to get these valuable goods. However, to achieve this result, the Brazilian state needed to create "strong entrepreneurial structures" supported and leveraged by the state apparatus. Evans argued that a state-sponsored local bourgeoisie was created through the initiative of state bureaucrats who directed the investment of around 2.5 billion dollars to guarantee local private capital participation in the planned petrochemical development. The state oil monopoly company, Petrobrás, through its subsidiary Petroquisa, coordinated a triple alliance—the tripartite model—among foreign, local private capital, and state capital to establish joint ventures in the production of second-generation chemicals. Petroquisa also organized Copene, selected the sources of technology, and chose its own partners in the undertaking.

A variety of federal agencies, in particular the old National Bank for Economic Development (BNDE), backed the local private investment with low-interest loans, tax subsidies, fiscal and economic incentives, market and pricing protections for the products, and feedstock supply at lower-than-international-market prices. This quite-decentralized state apparatus successfully bankrolled the local bourgeoisie, transforming local capitalist structures without using typical "free market" competition among capitalists. The Brazilian state forcefully pursued a strategy of cooperation with selected local and national private capital along the lines of "managerial capitalism." Thus, private and state capital became tightly integrated in a "tripé" (tripod in English) with foreign capital [37].

Foreign capital was invited to participate in the tripé as a way of allowing Brazil to gain access to capital and technologies not available domestically. The French Oil Institute (IFP in French) advised the Brazilian government in 1971 on the adequate scale of production for Copene and downstream companies [38]. French companies licensed their technology but were not interested in participating in the tripartite model. Japanese economic groups, on the other hand, not only advised the Brazilian government about the best mix of raw materials and scale of production for the complex, but also became the second largest investors after Petroquisa. Guimarães summed up the political-economic process brought about by this major capitalist development: "... the oligarchy in power [in Bahia] effectively obtained, through federal resources and economic alliances with the state bureaucracy, and international and national capitals, the displacement of the economic axis of Bahia from agriculture to petrochemicals ..." [26, p. 216].

Thus, the Bahian bourgeois leadership exercised its hegemony by organizing and conducting the compromised transition from a previous liberal project of oil-petrochemical industrial development, in which local financial capital would be associated with foreign capital, to a state bureaucracy-led industrialization. The immature Bahian bourgeoisie temporarily lost the direct leadership of its own hegemonic project by making concessions to the newborn regional techno-bureaucracy, as well as to the federal and state apparatuses created by the military after the coup d'etat of 1964. In short, a planned regional economic development led by middle-class nationalists paved the way for the "re-invention" of the Bahian bourgeoisie that later re-instituted its power and command as the new petro-chemical fraction of the industrial bourgeoisie [39]. ·

Petrobrás, a symbol of the victory of the nationalists, has invested large sums of money in the Recôncavo Baiano region of Bahia since the mid-fifties, stimulating the development of the construction, metallurgy, minerals, and other industries in the metropolitan area of Salvador [40]. In the sixties, Bahia received 41.3 percent of the state subsidies for the industrialization of the Northeast, contributing to the growth of the relative share of the industrial sector in the state's Gross Internal Product (GIP). In 1950, agricultural production was almost half of the GIP; in 1980, it was only 12 percent of the GIP. The industrial sector's share grew from 20 percent in the 1970s to more than 30 percent in the mid-eighties. In 1980, Bahia received 42 percent of all investments made in intermediary goods and 36 percent of all investments in the capital-goods sector in the Northeast. In the 1990s, Bahia became the fastest-growing state in the Northeast, the poorest region of Brazil, and the sixth richest state in Brazil. The industrial sector was responsible for 38.4 percent of the state GIP by 1998 [41, chap. 1].

Over three decades, what initially appeared to be a state-driven oil enclave in Bahia changed dramatically. An example of this change is the reversal of the chronic internal trade deficit between the Northeast and the Southeast: In the fifties Bahia exported cocoa, sugar cane, and precious metals to developed countries at a low exchange rate and imported manufactured goods; the federal government would collect the foreign exchange generated and finance the industrial development of the Brazilian Southeast. Bahia, in turn, imported the more expensive and value-added manufactured goods from the Southeast, creating a chronic internal trade deficit that amounted to $400 million dollars/year [42]. The continuous inflow of public investments in the state created a situation where, in the eighties, Bahia would export value-added petrochemical goods to the Southeast, generating an internal trade surplus. Furthermore, the local accumulation in the state economy increased the importance of the local bourgeoisie and attracted out-of-state private capital to Bahia.

This unequal trade triangle among Bahia, foreign countries, and the Southeast in the fifties played an important role in the arguments Bahia intellectuals put forth in defending the need to reduce national disparities between the Southeast and the Northeast of Brazil by industrializing the Northeast. An influential group of well-known Brazilian scholars, politicians, businessmen, and military leaders has converged around this position since then.

The Social Structure

It goes without saying that this rapid industrialization also radically transformed the social structure of the state. Whereas in the fifties one could see the social map as typical of a "traditional agricultural society" led by the financial elite, in the eighties there was further segmentation in the dominant as well as in the subordinate classes [43]. The old financial, commercial, and export bourgeoisie lost ground to the new petrochemical bourgeoisie, a monopoly-based industrial bourgeoisie. Some members of the traditional sectors actually became the "reinvented" leaders of the new entrepreneurial class. Clemente Mariani is a good example. Once the president of the "Banco da Bahia," he later became the owner of several petrochemical companies in the complex.

A modern working class and a new layer of a relatively well-paid middle class in the state, service, and industrial sectors appeared on the social scene. Chemical and industrial engineers, skilled workers, small businesses, business managers, and a host of other professionals found work and employment in the area. While experts from the more developed Southeastern region of Brazil migrated to Bahia, the state of Bahia invested in human resource development by sending recent graduates to the Southeast and overseas to learn new skills that would be useful to the new Bahian petrochemical industry [44].

These two subordinate classes were born integrated into one of the most dynamic sectors of the national economy, i.e., they are classes that have national impact in economic, political, and social terms, as chapters 3 and 4 will convey. Moreover, the factory regimes "lived" in the modern Bahian factories depended on new forms of management of work "which were simultaneously more authoritarian and more rational" [26, p. 218]. As Guimarães wrote:

> [T]he prevailing factory regimes in petrochemical factories have been unable to obtain workers' consent as they did in the past [the class compromise of the populist period], thus generating a vigorous process of working class formation based upon on an ensemble of subjective and objective conditions [26, p. 218; 45].

As mentioned in chapter 1, the creation of the Camaçari complex gave birth to a new working class in Bahia.

An Introduction to Sindiquímica

In April 1963 the ASPETRO (Association of Petrochemical Industry Workers) was founded under the auspices of the strong SINDIPETRO (Refinery Workers Union), representing about 340 workers. Oil drilling workers belonged to a different union called STIEP (Union of Oil Drilling Workers), which had turf battles with SINDIPETRO related to organizing workers within the oil industry. Brazilian labor law did not allow ASPETRO to bargain for economic and other important labor relations matters on behalf of refinery workers. Since the association was legally classified as a pre-union entity, it relied on the support of SINDIPETRO and Petrobrás to survive.

Over a short period of time all members of the newly formed association joined SINDIPETRO, which provided the association with all the infrastructure (an office, union hall for meetings, etc.) needed to have regular operations. This association was created in a political conjuncture when the Brazilian government—the Goulart administration—supported an alliance with labor unions in general and specifically with the strategically important oil workers union [46]. It was a period of intense state activism during which the Goulart administration, continuing the policies of the Vargas national-populist regime, supported strong state intervention in the economy to promote independent economic development through import substitution.

The political agenda of both the federal government and the Brazilian labor movement in the turbulent years of 1963-64 favored fundamental structural economic and political reforms in Brazil, the so-called "reformas de base"("basic reforms"). Labor leaders in Bahia were strongly influenced by the ideas of the Brazilian Communist Party (PCB), which defended the political strategy of a national front against imperialism; the front would lead Brazil toward a national, democratic, and popular revolution. Moreover, Copeb was seen as a strategic future economic development for the state of Bahia with the introduction of the petrochemical industry in the state economy [47].

Unfortunately, the ASPETRO did not get its official trade-union recognition from the Ministry of Labor before the coup d'etat. It took fourteen years for the association to be granted official union status. Meanwhile, it barely survived the political repression and de-mobilization that occurred after 1964. In 1978, the same year the Camaçari Petrochemical Complex started its operations, Sindiquímica was chartered as the petrochemical workers' union. Chapter 3 will discuss the evolving role of this "sindicato" in shaping the environmental and occupational health policies in the complex. Chapter 4 will focus on the major health and safety struggles led by Sindiquímica.

Brief History of the Creation of the Complex

The factual history of the creation of the "Pólo" can be summarized in the following critical events.

In 1967 the governor of Bahia invited the InterAmerican Development Bank (IDB) to send a mission to Bahia to study and guide the development of the petrochemical industry in Bahia. The mission's report recommended as a high priority that a study on the integrated development of the "Recôncavo Baiano" region of Bahia be performed. This project was carried out by a consulting group headed by one of the most important intellectuals of the nationalist development ideas in Bahia, Rômulo Almeida. He argued in a 1969 report, based on an economic analysis of the potential Brazilian market for petrochemical goods, that Bahia would be an excellent location for the creation of a second petrochemical complex in Brazil [48]. The report argued that its comparative advantages, such as access to feedstocks and the existence of a small industrial park in the area, were ideal. The report also suggested an initial list of petrochemical commodities that could be produced in Bahia [48, 49].

At the national level, the São Paulo petrochemical companies lobby argued that Bahia was not a proper location for the expansion of the Brazilian petro-chemical industry due to its distance from the consumer markets of the richer Southeastern region. Instead, they proposed the expansion of the first Brazilian petrochemical complex located in S. Paulo. As a result, a political struggle between the regional interests of the two states took shape within the Brazilian government. Despite the political strength of the S. Paulo lobby, the Bahian lobby was able to persuade high-level authorities to invest in Bahia.

In January 1970, the Board of Administration of Petrobrás made the landmark decision of supporting the development of the petrochemical industry in Bahia. It committed to supplying natural gas, naphtha, propilene, and ammonia for the industrial projects approved by the National Oil Council (CNP) and the Executive Group of the Chemical Industry (Geiquim). In May 1970, the Brazilian president, Gen. Médici, announced his decision to create a petrochemical complex in Bahia, the Petrochemical Complex of the Northeast [50]. In an effort to facilitate the presidential decision, the governor of Bahia declared an area of 233 square kilometers located in Camaçari as a public area.

In July 1971, the Industrial Development Council of the Ministry of Industry and Commerce (CDI-MIC) issued Resolution 2/70, which established that a) Petrobrás should lead, through Petroquisa, the implementation of projects in the "Pólo do Nordeste" (Petrochemical Complex of the Northeast); and b) an Inter-Ministerial Working Group should be created to determine the essential measures needed for the creation of the complex, the scale of production, the pricing policies, and the financial, technological, and entrepreneurial structures for the units.

Since the working group could not achieve internal consensus around which industrial projects to support, it hired the "third-party" French IFP to study the economic viability of the Camaçari complex. The IFP supported the investment in Bahia. Based on this feedback, the federal government decided to end the continuous political pressure of lobbyists representing S. Paulo interests by formalizing a political compromise where both Bahia and S. Paulo would win.

This was the essence of the "Exposição de Motivos" (decision rationale) 213/71, signed by the Ministries of the Interior, Industry and Commerce, Mines and Energy, Planning, and Treasury, which established that the consolidation of the "Pólo Petroquímico de São Paulo" and the implementation of the "Pólo do Nordeste" were complementary. This resolution also gave Petroquisa the assignment of

> . . . promoting the formation of a pilot company, which details the technical and economic activities for the companies comprising the petrochemical complex, including the second generation industries which will use the basic petrochemicals produced by the basic petrochemicals producing unit [Copene] [51].

In addition to the criteria defined by the "Exposição de Motivos," the main industrial policy criteria used were the definition of a scale of production close to the prevailing optimum international level; the choice of the best available technologies; and the constitution of a cooperative modus operandi in the areas of utilities, ancillary services, and infrastructure [2].

Once the political roadblocks were eliminated (or neutralized), the federal government took the necessary steps to make the complex a reality. Copene was created in 1971 to design the basic plan for the complex, covering the production schemes, physical schedule, investment program, shareholder participation, etc. In 1972, the state governor, Antonio Carlos Magalhães, created the "Coordination for the Implementation of the Infrastructure of the Complexo Petroquímico de Camaçari-Copec," which formulated the "Plano Diretor de Camaçari" or the blueprint of the complex, covering the industrial zoning, the preservation of the environment, the road systems, the adaptation of the Port of Aratu, the electric energy system, and the treatment of industrial waste.

One of the most publicized early environmental protection initiatives of Copec was the creation of a buffer zone or greenbelt area around the complex, to avoid land occupation close to the production facilities as well as to dilute the air pollution originating in the complex[52]. It appears that the state of Bahia followed the advice of Masaji Kawasaki, a consultant of the Japanese Consultant Institute, who visited Bahia in 1972, and adopted a variety of environmental pollution control technologies that had already been tested in Japanese petro-chemical complexes [53].

The location of the petrochemical complex in Camaçari is attributed to favorable conditions such as availability of feedstocks nearby (refinery), fiscal incentives, the preexistence of "pioneer" industrial projects in the area as well as integration with other economic initiatives in neighboring states, easy access to port, and the availability of a large supply of water and energy [54].

The Central de Tratamento de Efluentes Líquidos (Cetrel)— Empresa de Proteção Ambiental (Centralized Treatment of Liquid Effluents—Environmental Protection Company)

Cetrel was created in 1975 by the state of Bahia Law 3,369 [55]. Law 3,369 mandated that the company should have a group of executives and an advisory board composed of three to five members each, whose terms would be three years, with reelection allowed. In practice, Cetrel had three executive officers: the "director-superintendent," representing the state Secretariat of Industry, Commerce, and Tourism; the administrative director, representing the participant industries, and the technical director, representing the state Secretariat's of Science and Technology Center for Research and Development (CEPED). The administrative director used to be a Copene headquarters' employee from Rio de Janeiro, instead of an employee from the Camaçari facility [56].

By 1982, the total workforce in Cetrel totaled 220: three directors, nineteen college-level professionals (ten engineers), eighty-seven high-school level technical employees, and 111 skilled, semiskilled, and nonskilled blue-collar employees [57].

Law 3,369 also prescribed that the state had to own at least 51 percent of the voting shares, while individuals and private companies could own the remaining shares. Shareholders were guaranteed annual dividends of at least 6 percent of the shares' nominal value. Although it was incorporated as a tax-free, for-profit joint venture between state and private capital, it has always operated as a not-for-profit public utility, charging customers at cost. For the first twelve years of operation, the state of Bahia owned 70 percent of the shares, divided between the Center for Research and Development (40 percent) and the state of Bahia [58]. Private industry's division of the remaining 30 percent of Cetrel's shares was proportional to the contractual service provided to each company.

Cetrel started its centralized wastewater treatment operations in 1978, had a one-year temporary shutdown due to construction problems, and restarted its operations in February 1979. It was built in a modular fashion to allow for the future growth of its treatment systems as the complex expanded.

As the company name indicates, the *first environmental system* operated by Cetrel is the liquid organic effluent system, which consists of the collection, treatment, and discharge of the organic effluents discharged by Copec industries. This system includes an underground pipeline network 30 kilometers long (about 19 miles), three lift stations, and the wastewater treatment plant; in the very beginning, it had nine industries connected to it—seven petrochemical companies and two breweries—creating a volume of 14,000 m^3/day of sanitary and industrial wastewater. By 1982, the wastewater treatment facility treated 31,100 m^3/day, a volume of wastewater equivalent to what is produced by a city of 550,000 inhabitants.

The contract fees charged to the customers to treat the organic effluents were calculated according to the biochemical oxygen demand (BOD), the total amount of solid particles suspended (TSS), and the flow in each industry effluent. Due to the ability of the wastewater treatment plant to treat both sanitary and industrial wastewater, all companies that had facilities in the petrochemical complex had to participate in the Cetrel system, whether or not they generated any industrial wastewater.

Cetrel's decision to adopt the centralized industrial wastewater treatment model—innovative in Brazil—was based on a worldwide trend in favor of this model during the 1970s. As mentioned before, Germany pioneered this wastewater management model in its Regional River Authorities, which was later adopted in Japan and the United States [59]. Copec planners and the first Cetrel managers had actually visited the German and GCWDA facilities in the Houston-Galveston area before deciding to implement the centralized secondary treatment of the industrial liquid effluents through the use of biologically activated sludge [60].

As a matter of fact, the decision to adopt this treatment process and other elements of GCWDA's waste management "model" involved a close interaction with GCWDA. For example, in 1978, two Cetrel managers visited the GCWDA industrial wastewater treatment facilities and were impressed with the Bayport facility. They spent a total of five weeks in GCWDA to learn how the authority and the Bayport plant operated. In 1979, two other managers visited GCWDA for a week [61]. GCWDA documented the visit of the Brazilians in its February-March 1978 issue of its newsletter *Comments*, which reads: "Brazilian Wastewater Technicians Study Industrial Facility Questions." In the March 1979 issue, under the headline, "Visitors from Home and Abroad," the report summarized the visit:

> During a seven day visit to industrial and municipal plants, two Brazilian engineers *scrutinized* Gulf Coast Authority operations prior to start-up of a regional waste treatment plant in Bahia, Brazil. The South American plant, Central de Tratamento de Efluentes Líquidos , S.A. (Cetrel), processes wastewater from several industries in a set-up *similar to* the Authority's Bayport operation (emphases added) [62, p. 2].

The *second environmental system*, introduced in 1980 at Cetrel, is the inorganic effluent system (SEPAR). It consists of four dams, three lift stations, pipelines, and nine-mile long, cement-built, open channels, which drain an area of 60 square kilometers. Together these components collect the clean (organic-free) streams of storm, process, and industrial refrigeration waters, carrying this untreated effluent to the sea by way of the Capivara Pequeno river, which flows into the estuary of the Jacuípe River. Customers pay a fee-for-service tariff based on their flow during dry and rainy seasons.

The *third environmental system* operated by Cetrel is the solid hazardous waste treatment and disposal system, which consists of specially designed hazardous-waste landfills and oil landfarming. The biodegradable oil sludge is disposed of on the surface of the landfarm plots to mineralize. The nondegradable solid hazardous waste is pretreated whenever necessary and confined in the landfills [63].

According to the public relations manager of CETREL and many company documents and publications, the Camaçari Petrochemical Complex is the first "ecological experience in Brazil" [64]. It is beyond doubt that the Camaçari complex is the first modern industrial complex in Brazil that took some form of environmental pollution control into consideration since its initial planning stages. Nevertheless, the public relations and media messages arguably claimed that Camaçari is a modern, centralized industrial complex, where *almost all forms* of environmental damage were avoided due to its strict adherence to environmental controls [65]. The main reason for this claim is the existence of Cetrel to manage and treat the hazardous wastes generated in the complex.

ENDNOTES

1. The discussion of the petrochemical industry developed here is aimed at introducing the reader to basic notions, definitions, and concepts that will be used throughout this book. It is based on several chapters of *The International Petrochemical Industry* [2].
2. Keith Chapman, *The International Petrochemical Industry: Evolution and Location,* Basic Blackwell, London, 1991.
3. The premise of the "pôle de croissance" (growth pole) model is that an industrial development has the economic ability of acting as a "pole" that generates national and regional economic development through its multiplier effects upstream and downstream. According to Chapman, this notion was developed by the French economist Perroux [2, pp. 11, 261].
4. Import substitution policies were aimed at producing nationally petrochemical goods that had been previously imported, especially basic petrochemicals such as polyethylene [2, chap. 7].
5. Some of the major players in the industry include Exxon, Mobil, Amoco, Shell, British Petroleum, Rhone-Poulenc, BASF, Hoechst-Celanese, Mitsubishi, Zeneca, Dow Chemical, Dupont, Enimont, and Union Carbide. All the leading companies are Fortune 500 companies.
6. The account that follows is based on interviews with Gulf Coast Waste Disposal Authority (GCWDA) staff, especially the Bayport plant manager, and internal documents from GCWDA. In contrast to the Brazilian complex, there seems to be a paucity of accessible information on the historical development of the Bayport Industrial Complex. Therefore, I also relied on indirect information about Bayport obtained from corporate publications, books, and documents. I use the terms Bayport Industrial Park or complex to refer to the Texas petrochemical complex. The subhead of the chapter calls attention to the contrast between the underlying Brazilian and U.S. political-economic frameworks that help explain the creation of the complexes.
7. Chapman wrote that ". . . the Houston Ship Channel is, for example, flanked by an almost uninterrupted procession of oil refineries and petrochemical plants over a distance of approximately 25 km . . ." [2, p. 264].

8. Fine and specialty chemicals are generally defined as "high-value/low-volume materials that are synthesized or refined to exact specifications while specialties are sold on the basis of performance" [9, p. 3]. Fine and specialty chemicals include pharmaceuticals and agricultural products. Allegedly stricter environmental regulations and pressures as well as the "constant need to supply value-added chemical products" drove innovation in the 1990s' $200 billion/year fine-chemicals market [9, p. 3].

9. Rick Mullin, "Fine & Specialty Chemicals: An Era of Innovation on the Molecular," *Chemical Week*, World Wide Web edition, www.chemweek.com, 150(14), 38, p. 3, April 8, 1992.

10. Gregory Morris, "Texas Looks to Build Downstream: Petrochemical Strengths Underpin," *Chemical Week*, www.chemweek.com, 150(21), 32, p. 3, May 27, 1992.

11. Nevertheless, the Bayport complex is one of the largest petrochemical complexes in the world. The 1995 aerial photo of the complex produced by Landiscor Aerial Information and sponsored by Exxon Land Development has a subtitle that reads "Bayport: Petrochemical Capital of the World."

12. Marcel Olbrecht, *Bayshore Sun* (Texas), p. 4, May 1988. The Bayport complex companies are represented collectively by an association called Association of Bayport Companies (ABC), which has been active mostly in regulatory air and water pollution issues affecting the neighboring communities of Clear Lake, Pasadena, Shore Acres, and La Porte.

13. It is worth mentioning here that Louisiana competes with Texas for this investment, sometimes creating a situation where the two states wage a true "war" of incentive packages to attract new businesses. From the perspectives of the corporations, this interstate competition for investment allows them better bargaining conditions vis-a-vis the states.

14. Jim Lefton, former Oil Chemical and Atomic Workers International Union Staff Representative for District 4, and Gulf Coast former OCAW local union leaders. Interview by author, tape recording, Pasadena and Texas City, Texas, March 1998.

15. The Galveston Bay study was one of the studies of estuaries authorized by the Clean Water Restoration Act of 1966, under the National Estuarine Report. This information is part of the unpublished presentation on the Gulf Coast Waste Disposal Authority, prepared by Corwin Johnson for presentation at the organizational meeting of the board of directors of GCWDA in Webster, Texas, 1970. Several local press reports and company documents of this period described the serious water pollution of Galveston Bay. For examples, see League City (Texas) *News Citizen*, Friday, May 1, 1970; *Houston Chronicle*, Friday, May 8, 1970; or Professor Richard Leuba, assistant professor of engineering of Antioch College, Ohio, June, 4, 1970, to GCA (letter in the historical files of the Gulf Coast Waste Disposal Authority, Pasadena, Texas).

16. This account is based on GCWDA internal publications and documents, newspaper reports, and on a personal interview with Charles Ganze, a long-time GCWDA employee who was the current industrial operations manager; tape recording, Pasadena, Texas, May 1997.

17. The purpose of the bill reads: ". . . To establish an instrumentality for developing and effectuating for Chambers, Galveston and Harris counties, a regional water quality management program including provision of waste disposal systems and regulation of disposal of waste," quoted in Gulf Coast Waste Disposal Authority, Legislative

Analysis and History, unpublished anonymous manuscript from GCWDA's historical files, available at the library of the Authority in Pasadena, Texas. The first general manager of GCWDA, L. Jack Davis, wrote that the imitation of the German model was actually motivated by a visit of senator Edward Muskie, Representative Jones, and other federal officials, to these authorities. They were impressed and excited by the model and stimulated its adoption in the U.S. [18].

18. L. Jack Davis, "A Basin Authority for Treatment of Industrial Wastes," unpublished and undated paper obtained at GCWDA's files, p. 1.

19. Susan Caudill, a *Houston Post* reporter, wrote: ". . . There is nothing like the authority in Texas, Cole [Criss Cole, the senator who wrote GCA's bill] said. The closest thing to it [GCA] in the country is the Los Angeles Sanitary District in California, which builds facilities and assesses cities and individuals for effluent treatment," *Houston Post,* Sunday, February 8, 1970.

20. In the same paper Davis referred to GCA as an "unbiased referee," an "unbiased intermediary," or a regional agency with a mantle of government [18]. After interviewing some GCA staff and reading a great deal about this agency, it is my impression that GCA has consolidated its image as a quasi-governmental institution, in-between government and industry.

21 To keep in line with the main arguments entertained in this book, I will concentrate on the industrial operations of GCA, with special emphasis in the Bayport plant, because Cetrel managers who visited GCA used this plant as a model.

22. The five initial customers were Champion International, a paper mill, Crown Central Petroleum, Petro-Tex Chemical, Air Products and Chemicals, and Atlantic Richfield (ARCO).

23. Gulf Coast Waste Disposal Authority, *Five Year Status Report,* 1970-75, (Pasadena, Texas, 1975). Operational overhead includes labor costs, purchased materials, and laboratory analyses of waste streams. Operational efficiency includes cost reductions that originate in "the effect of economy of process which very frequently comes into force when joint facilities are employed" in Joe Teller, "Economic Considerations of Joint Waste Treatment," unpublished paper available at GCA's historical files, p. 3, 1973. It seems that the most common of potential process economics is the adjustment of pH that may occur when combining acidic with basic waste streams discharged by two different industries, i.e., the acidic waste would be neutralized by the basic waste without the need of adding salt to neutralize the acidic waste. Therefore, costs are reduced by jointly treating compatible waste streams.

24. This is a compilation of several descriptions of the same process available in GCWDA publications. Most of it was taken from the Gulf Coast Waste Disposal Authority, *1975-76 Status Report,* Pasadena, Texas, 1976. Over the years these treatment stages became somewhat more sophisticated as new waste streams were added. Whenever relevant to the arguments of this study, the changes in the process will be discussed in chapter 6.

25. The discussion that follows is based on a variety of official company documents, newspaper reports, and the dissertations of Antonio Sérgio Guimarães [26, p. 546] and Luciana Darwich [27, p. 162]. The quote in the headline for this section is attributed to a former Brazilian minister, Fabio Yassuda, according to the report "A História do Pólo II: Ajudamos os Argentinos e Apelamos aos Japoneses," by David Oliveira, *A Tarde,* Salvador, Bahia, June 29, 1988.

26. Antonio Sérgio Guimarães, "Factory Regime and Class Formation: The Petrochemical Workers in Brazil," Ph.D. dissertation, University of Wisconsin-Madison, 1988.

27. Luciana Darwich, "Gerenciamento Ambiental no Pólo Petroquímico de Camaçari," [Environmental Management of the Pólo Petroquímico de Camaçari], master's thesis, Núcleo de Pós-Graduação em Administração [Graduate Studies in Management], Universidade Federal da Bahia, May 1996.

28. Angela Borges and Angela Franco offerred this characterization of the area in "Mudanças de Gestão: Para Além do Muro da Fábrica" [Management Changes: Beyond the Factory Walls], Salvador, Brazil: Caderno CRH, EDUFBA, 1997.

29. Karliner noted that these three Japanese groups are among the six largest sogo sosha, or trading companies of Japan. For more discussion on the economic and environmental activities of Japanese corporations in other Asian countries, see [30, pp. 5, 115-132].

30. Joshua Karliner, *The Corporate Planet: Ecology and Politics in the Age of Globalization*, Sierra Club, San Francisco, 1997.

31. This classification is common in the Brazilian petrochemical industry. Synonyms for these terms are primary or basic chemicals for first generation, petrochemical intermediates for second generation, and petrochemical products for third generation.

32. Osvaldo Guerra, "Desafios Competitivos para a Petroquímica Brasileira," [Competitive Challenges of the Brazilian Petrochemical Industry], Salvador, Bahia, Cadernos CRH, no. 21, 1994, pp. 48-67. Guerra also argued that the companies in the Camaçari complex are incapable of achieving adequate scales of production, revenues, and the "critical mass" needed to develop technological innovations.

33. The word used in Portuguese to denote the centralized raw materials, utilities, and maintenance units is "central."

34. Peter Evans, "Collectivized Capitalism: Integrated Petrochemical Complexes and Capital Accumulation in Brazil," in Thomas Bruneau and Philippe Faucher, eds., *Authoritarian Capitalism: Brazil's Contemporary Economic and Political Development*, pp. 85-125, Westview Press, Boulder, Colo., 1981.

35. The discussion that follows is also based on chapter 3 of Guimarães [26] and the report [36].

36. *Anais: Seminário Internacional da Indústria Petroquímica:* Pólo, 10 Anos, Salvador, Bahia, 1988. This consists of the proceedings of the seminar sponsored by a Brazilian business newspaper similar to the *Wall Street Journal*, *Gazeta Mercantil*, São Paulo, Brazil, and by industry associations and unions to celebrate the tenth anniversary of the "Pólo Petroquímico de Camaçari." Most leaders of the industry as well as the state intellectuals or bureaucrats who contributed to the planning and implementation of the complex participated in the event, synthesizing the history of the first ten years of the complex. This document for the most part confirmed the previous political-economic analyses put forth by Guimarães [26] and Evans [34], notwithstanding the expected differences in approach. Though I did not find any explicit mention of the role of the first oil crisis in the creation of the complex, it is fair to postulate that this crisis contributed significantly to it, since Brazil was (and still is) an oil-importing country. Therefore, the complex fit nicely within Brazil's strategy of reducing the importation of expensive oil and petrochemical goods to offset trade-balance deficits.

37. Guimarães, citing Suarez, seemed to agree with Evans when he noted that "the emergence of Copec came at a time when there was a confluence of interests between the goals of the dominant class, the nationalist interests of the state bourgeoisie under

president Geisel, and the interests of a number of international chemical giants, mainly German and Japanese, who were looking for new investments in the Third World" [26, p. 186].

38. Chapman mentioned Sercovich to point out the importance of the technology transfer process between France and Brazil. According to Chapman, the choice of Technip, a French state-owned engineering firm, as a "principal agent supervising the design and construction of the country's [Brazil] third petrochemical complex in Rio Grande do Sul," was due to its willingness "to offer most in terms of communication of expertise to native Brazilians" [2, p. 149].

39. Guimarães stated that the Bahian leaders or cadres of this petrochemical fraction "were extremely forceful in leading the triple alliance" [26, p. 217]. The economic evolution of the Brazilian Northeast and Bahia appears to support the points made by Guimarães.

40. Recôncavo Baiano is a thirty-mile radius region around the All Saints Bay and Salvador, where the oil platform of Bahia is located. In the fifties, the Landulfo Alves refinery was built in Mataripe county. For almost three decades—mid-1950s through early 1980s—Bahia was one of the largest oil-producer states in Brazil. For more details about the economic development of Bahia, see [26, chap. 3].

41. Vladson Menezes, "Tendencias da Economia Baiana," Governo da Bahia, Salvador, 2000. Available at http://www. seplantec.ba.gov.br. Accessed in March 2002.

42. The nonadjusted dollar figure was mentioned by Paulo Cunha [36, p. 55].

43. The literature reviewed by Guimarães seems to unanimously describe this social structure as a top layer of agro-export interests composed of bankers, big exporters, and importers, ". . . followed by the sugar cane barons, other landowners, big wholesale businessmen and industrial entrepreneurs in tobacco, cocoa and construction" [26, p. 169]. The small state bureaucracy included some members of the ruling elite, a stratum of high officials such as lawyers, civil engineers, physicians, and professional politicians. The dominant class depended in large part on the rental of land and property as well as on official posts. Below the top layer there was a small segment of petty landowners, petty businessmen, professionals in the liberal arts, and a large segment of civil servants. In addition, there was a large layer of middle peasants, artisans, and self-employed skilled workers. At the bottom of the social pyramid were the unskilled, the unemployed, and the journeymen.

44. According to Francisco Fontes Lima, a sanitary engineer who played a major role in the technical aspects of the operations of Cetrel from the very beginning and who was its technical director for two terms. (Interview by author, tape recording, Salvador, Bahia, July 1997). Lima mentioned that the state Center for Research and Development (CEPED) sent about 100 technicians to foreign countries and other more developed areas of Brazil to learn how to manage scientific and technologic development in the areas of nutrition, mineral resources, and petrochemicals.

45. Later in this chapter and in chapters 3 and 4 I will discuss further the class formation and factory regimes in the Camaçari complex.

46. The João Goulart administration was overthrown by the military on March 31, 1964. The military regime lasted until 1985. João Goulart, the last civilian president before the coup d'Etat, defended the national populist ideology established by the late Getúlio Vargas, the founder of the "New State." Goulart believed that unions were an indispensable tool for the harmonious progress of labor and capital (national bourgeoisie) against foreign capital.

47. Copeb was the abbreviation for the original Complexo Petroquímico da Bahia—Petrochemical Complex of Bahia, that later became the Copec, Complexo Petroquímico de Camaçari—Camaçari Petrochemical Complex.
48. "Development of the Petrochemical Industry in Bahia," 1969.
49. By the mid-fifties, Rômulo Almeida was one of the state intellectuals who led the state-sponsored Economic Planning Commission (the state Department of Regional Planning), which formulated the First Plan for the Development of Bahia (PLANDEB in Portuguese). The plan suggested the creation of the Aratu Industrial Park (Complexo Industrial de Aratu or CIA), located near Camaçari. The park was composed of a few companies that processed propene and other by-products of oil refining in the Landulfo Alves Refinery.
50. The largest newspaper of Bahia, A Tarde, dedicated a special edition to celebrate the tenth anniversary of the "Pólo." In this edition, it reported that Gen. Geisel, the president of Petrobrás, stated in January 1970 that "Petrobrás will not any longer be interested in building roads for the Government of Bahia: Petrobrás is now interested in building Petrochemistry in Bahia." ["A História do Pólo–I: Uma Batalha disputada palmo a palmo com SP," A Tarde, p. 6, Salvador, June 29, 1988].
51. "Getting to Know Copene," at the company Web site at www.copene.com.br/hist-i.html.
52. This account is based on two articles of the newspaper A Tarde, June 16, 1976, and June 29, 1988, p. 42, as well as in my interview with a former director of Cetrel. The greenbelt is a man-made green area composed of pine, eucalyptus, and other native trees, which is supposed to reduce air pollution levels by acting as an environmental filter. Although this concept is considered outdated and unsupported scientifically today, it was regarded very differently in the seventies, when environmental protection technologies to reduce air emissions were still incipient in Brazil.
53. A Tarde, June 29, 1988, p. 42. According to a former Cetrel manager I interviewed, the Japanese had copied American ideas in establishing integrated petrochemical complexes in Japan.
54. Transcript of the videocassette, "10 Anos de Petroquímica no Nordeste" ["10 Years of Petrochemicals in the Northeast"], in Anais, p. 10. The location of the complex above the São Sebastião aquifer, the source of the water supply for the metropolitan region of Salvador, has been an important source of conflicts, discussed later in this book.
55. Diário Oficial do Estado da Bahia, 21/1/1975. (The "Diário Oficial" is similar to the U.S. Federal Register.) The law established that Cetrel, among other responsibilities, had to coordinate the operation of the entire liquid effluent system, sanitary and industrial, in the area of the "Pólo Petroquímico de Camaçari," including the pipelines, the lift stations, the wastewater treatment plant, and all the elements necessary to the operational integrity of the system; study, design, and promote the execution of all developments necessary to treat the future effluent loads that may be generated in the area; advise the industries, whenever required, on how to do primary treatment of their industrial wastewater; and establish acceptable discharge limits for industries to follow.
56. Personal interview with Fontes Lima, former Cetrel director, Salvador, Bahia, July 1997. He suggested that this appointment of a "stranger" to represent the companies in Cetrel was an indication of the limited involvement of Cetrel's industrial clients in its internal affairs. This situation changed in the late eighties.

57. Cetrel brochure, undated, "Estação Central de Tratamento de Efluentes" (the literal translation would be Effluent Treatment Central Plant).
58. Cetrel was initially part of the State Secretariat of Mines and Energy. In May 1979, state Law 3,696 moved it to the Secretariat of Industry, Commerce, and Tourism.
59. The BASF petrochemical complex in Ludwigshafen also had such types of wastewater treatment plants. Moreover, according to Fontes Lima (personal interview, July 97), the Japanese mission that visited Brazil in the early seventies transferred to Brazilians the knowledge the Japanese had about this wastewater treatment model.
60. A process already briefly described above. Chapter 5 will detail the treatment system adopted in Cetrel to the extent necessary for comprehension of environmental or occupational health policy issues.
61. The current GCWDA industrial operations manager, Charles Ganze, also visited Camaçari a few times since the early eighties. An informal relationship between managers of Cetrel and GCWDA has developed within the last twenty years, facilitating the exchange of experiences between both companies.
62. The report goes on to state that ". . . General Manager Edgard Teles Sobrinho and Francisco Fontes Lima, planning consultant, amassed information concerning all phases of operations in an effort to open Cetrel with as few snags as possible. They spent two days at the Bayport plant . . ." [*Gulf Coast Comments,* vol. 7, February-March 1979, p. 2. Actually, by 1979, the Cetrel wastewater plant would be restarted because it had had initial construction problems in 1978.
63. Here I briefly describe the first three environmental protection systems because these were implemented within the first three years of the operation of the complex. Later I will expound on the environmental protection systems in more detail, as well as their historical evolution.
64. For a sample of these documents, see: *Cetrel: A Natureza em Boas Mãos* (the environment in good hands), undated brochures published by the Secretaria da Indústria, Comércio e Turismo (state Secretariat of Industry, Commerce, and Tourism), Antonio Carlos Magalhães and João Durval administrations. These governors belonged to the party that supported the military dictatorship (Arena, whose name changed to PDS by the late seventies) and were in office from the early through the mid-eighties. See also *Copec: An Integrated Industrial Complex,* undated bilingual brochure published by Copec and the same state secretariat; *Cetrel: the Environment in Good Hands,* undated internal publication. I also reviewed several other publications that convey the same message.
65. For a good example of the claim mentioned, see *A Tarde,* Saturday, March 11, 1978, and Francisco Fontes Lima and Francisco Alves Pereira, "Avanços no Tratamento de Resíduos Industriais," (Advancements in the Treatment of Industrial Wastes) *Bahia, Análise & Dados,* CEI, I(4), pp. 66-74, March 1992. Conversely, the first Brazilian petrochemical complex, located in Cubatão, state of São Paulo, is a "horror story" that has taught many lessons on what happens when minimal environmental precautions and controls are not implemented. During the seventies and eighties, the Cubatão area had the worst air pollution in the country, as well as a host of environmental and health problems.

CHAPTER 3

Twenty Years of Petrochemical Production in Bahia

This chapter focuses on the evolution of work environment and environmental policies in the "Pólo Petroquímico de Camaçari," state of Bahia, Brazil. It elaborates further the process of importation of technological hazards and controls by summarizing the 20-year history of the "Pólo." The chapter presents the critical events, theory-driven structural as well as historical aspects, that help explain the evolution of work environment and environmental health policies. It is an effort to undertake the "concrete analysis of the concrete case," emphasizing the interaction among national social actors, and bringing international actors into the discussion whenever relevant. As referred to in chapter 1, Petras, Cardoso, and Guimarães proposed this as the best approach to explain historical developments in peripheral countries. In addition, Levenstein et al. offered a set of structural hypotheses to interpret historical developments at the workplace level in developed countries.

Here, I apply their theoretical arguments to the Camaçari case to suggest that the environmental and occupational health policies adopted in the "Pólo" (and also in Cetrel) are a result of the interplay of social, economic, political, and ideological factors. These factors combined in different moments to facilitate or hinder the control of environmental and occupational health impacts of petrochemical production in the complex, reflecting the balance of power among actors.

To account for both the historical and structural aspects of the argument, I divided the history of this complex into two overlapping periods [1]. The first phase ranges between the start-up of the complex in 1978 and the late 1980s, when the industry experienced its consolidation.

I borrowed a human-development metaphor to title this phase "From Infancy to Maturity," to account for its essential driving forces, i.e., a period of rapid growth that propelled the Bahian petrochemical industry into the national scene. By the end of this phase there is the transition period of the EIA/RIMA (Estudo de Impacto Ambiental/Relatório de Impacto Ambiental in Portuguese) or Environmental Impact Study/Report (EIS/EIR in English) studies of the late eighties [2].

I treat this period as a distinct period because that is when the most important changes in environmental policies in the complex started to take place, a result of the combination of a new state administration and industry plans to expand the complex.

The second phase is the period during and after the expansion of the complex in the nineties, when companies implemented their economic restructuring and adopted the Chemical Manufacturers Association Responsible Care program and the International Standardization Organization 9,000 and 14,000 series standards.

NATIONAL POLITICAL- ECONOMIC ASPECTS: FROM THE "LOST DECADE" TO THE NEOLIBERAL DECADE [3]

The period between 1978 and 1985 is the period during which the majority of the Brazilian people mounted its political offensive against the military regime. The only legal opposition party, the Movimento Democrático Brasileiro (MDB, changed to Partido do Movimento Democrático Brasileiro [PMDB] in the late 70s) gained strength in all state and national elections held between the mid to late 1970s and the early 1980s, electing state governors in 1982 in some of the most important states in the country. A significant majority of the Brazilian society turned massively against the military regime as a result of the impacts of recessionary monetary policies driven by the foreign-debt crisis of the 1980s, when the International Monetary Fund (IMF) imposed the structural adjustment program (SAP) on the Brazilian government [4-8].

According to Bello, the aim of the SAP was

> . . . to weaken domestic entrepreneurial groups by eliminating protectionist barriers to imports from the North and by lifting restrictions on foreign investment; to overwhelm the weak legal barriers protecting labor from capital; and to integrate the local economy more tightly into the North-dominated world economy [9, p. 5; 10].

Used by the Reagan and Thatcher administrations, among others, to open Third World economies, the SAP forced Brazil to agree to major economic reforms in order to get loans that would relieve the country from balance-of-payments deficits or from the burden of servicing the debt owed to private foreign banks. The conditions attached to the approval of IMF loans compelled the government to reduce public spending, cut subsidies to agriculture, liberalize imports, remove restrictions on foreign investments in industry and financial services, devalue the currency, increase prices of basic foods such as wheat and sugar, and last but not least, privatize state enterprises. Therefore, by the early 1980s, unemployment, high inflation, and lowering wages and standards of living combined with the lack of democratic freedoms to energize a broad-based democratic movement. Student unions, labor unions, neighborhood associations, and professional associations representing lawyers, physicians, and journalists, formed a broad coalition that took to the streets to protest these policies and demand an end to the military regime [11].

The revitalized labor movement organized national independent confederations that mobilized workers from almost every trade. A wave of strikes against significant wage losses and the economic recession spread all over the country. The 1984-85 unsuccessful campaign for the direct election of a civilian president unified the grassroots mobilization for economic and political changes, and created a powerful civil disobedience movement.

The growth of the democratic forces coupled with the poor performance of the economy accelerated the internal political divisions within pro-regime forces, allowing a somewhat peaceful democratic transition to a limited liberal democracy. Limited democracy because, as in other countries in South America, the military in Brazil were able to keep tight control over the civilian government during the first post-dictatorship administration, the Sarney "New Republic" [12].

The Sarney administration, also called the Brazilian "democratic transition" regime, represented a political coalition of former moderate allies of the military regime, liberal democrats, and some left-of-center forces. This administration gradually reinstituted the basic freedoms of assembly and speech. As a result, a variety of new political parties, labor confederations, environmental groups, and nongovernmental organizations appeared on the national scene.

A new modern constitution, incorporating in the Brazilian supreme law—a fairly progressive body of legal concepts and social concerns—was approved in 1988, after two years of intense public debate. In essence, a civil society flourished during this transition regime to an extent never before seen in Brazil. With some success, this strong grassroots movement of social and political resistance forced the transition regime to challenge orthodox IMF policies, but the structural causes of the economic crises that unfolded during the early 1980s' foreign-debt crisis remained throughout the eighties [13, 14].

Although, after the mid-eighties, the social mobilization mentioned above went through a period of peaks and valleys, it strongly affected the first direct presidential elections in 1989. In the second round of these elections, Lula, the left-of-center metalworker and Workers Party candidate, faced the right-wing candidate Fernando Collor. The latter, who represented a mix of the neoliberal agenda—disguised under modernization slogans—with populist anticorruption goals, won by a small margin. With this victory, the Brazilian right started to regain political momentum.

The Collor administration deeply embraced the principles of the *"Washington Consensus,"* and implemented them right away. Collor followed to the letter the IMF and World Bank-recommended privatization program, which included the large state-owned steel mills, public state banks, and several other public enterprises [15, 16]. Collor, however, could not stay in power long enough to finish this privatization program. The Brazilian press played a major role in disclosing an underground corruption ring that was directly linked to and controlled by the president and his close allies. In 1992, as a result of strong public pressure, the Brazilian Congress impeached Collor.

While the neoliberal agenda suffered another temporary setback, it has been fulfilled even more forcefully by the current Fernando Henrique Cardoso administration, which expresses the local victory of the ideology of globalization of the world economy. Therefore, after many years of internal resistance against the global neoliberal agenda, Brazil finally—and officially—became a full member of the free market economies by the mid-nineties [17]. The offensive of this neoliberal ideology goes hand in hand with the dominance of the speculative "casino" economy of the nineties and authoritarian trends in the executive branch of government—all almost uncontested by the lack of alternatives to globalization among progressive forces [18-24].

This neoliberal ideological perspective is summed up in Bello:

> In this school of thought [the neoliberal], the history of Latin America in the post-war period is the history of a collective error in the terms of the economic course chosen, and of the design of the accompanying institutions. To correct that error, the long period during which the public sector has the center of economic stage has to be brought to an end, and a radical remedy applied: *the withdrawal of the producer State and assisted capitalism, the limiting of State's responsibilities to its constitutional commitments, a return to the market for the supply of goods and services, and the removal of obstacles to the emergence of an independent entrepreneurial class* (emphases added) [9, p. 31; 25; 26].

FIRST PHASE: FROM INFANCY TO MATURITY [27]

Industry: Ten Years of Unconditional State Support

In the first few years of the complex's operation, the internal market demand for petrochemical products was sufficient to have all plants operate at full capacity, encouraging the planning of short-term expansion in production. By 1981, however, Brazil faced a deep economic recession that significantly affected the consumption of plastics and durable goods. According to Gradin and Guerra, the petrochemical industry in Camaçari had to export its overproduction to survive this first decline in demand [28, p. 19; 29; 30]. Gradin even praised the planners of the complex for their anticipation of potential reductions or increases in internal demand, which enabled companies to export their excess production in bad economic times [28]. Although by some accounts the international markets were already saturated, exports grew from $74 million in 1980 to more than $200 million in 1981, a 169.5 percent increase [30, p. 5; 31]. In addition, from a trade deficit in petrochemicals of $380 million in 1980, the industry evolved to a $609 million surplus in 1985 [32, p. 27]. On average, the Bahian petrochemical industry exported around 34 percent of its production [29, p. 61]. Therefore, from very early on, foreign markets played the role of a safety valve for cyclical reductions in internal consumption.

Firms in the complex learned early in their development that, although the bulk of their production was targeted at the Brazilian market, they had to consider foreign markets in their strategic business plans. Suarez suggested that government subsidies also helped to keep the industry afloat through reductions in the prices of naphtha and gas, transferring an estimated $3,57 million per day to the industry [33, p. 425].

This reduced internal demand remained until the end of 1984, when the Brazilian economy picked up steam again and created a bottleneck for basic petrochemical production. Demand far outgrew supply in 1986, causing firms to import petrochemical goods. A trade deficit of about $1 billion accumulated. By then it was clear to industry leaders that an expansion in capacity was urgently needed to remove the bottleneck for the production of polyethylene. As a result, accelerated industry growth scenarios dominated the national scene in the following years.

By 1987, the Brazilian government approved the "National Petrochemical Plan," which included an increase in capacity in Copene from 460,000 tons per year to 910,000 tons per year. The total investment amounted to about $850 million. Continuously favorable world market conditions in 1987 and 1988 yielded good profit margins that underscored a climate of overt optimism toward future growth. This optimism was quite visible in the 1988 celebration of the ten years of the petrochemical complex, when some of the most important business leaders and intellectuals assembled in Bahia to discuss the prospects of the Bahian and Brazilian petrochemical industry.

The analyses offered at this meeting by leading industry experts, state bureaucrats, and executives resulted in a true "State of the Industry" report. The main themes debated on that occasion ranged from the origins and development of the industry in the Northeast, to the diagnosis of its current situation, to the role of the state and the private sector in the future expansion of the industry [34]. Not even a single line in the annals of the meeting mentioned any environmental or occupational health and safety problems in the complex [35].

Industry's Diagnosis

The Brazilian petrochemical industry, in particular the Camaçari branch, was universally recognized as a successful example of government planning to promote industrial deconcentration, decentralization, and regional economic development. By 1988, the regional industry was a strong and internationally competitive industry, able to leverage the development of agriculture, food, textiles, domestic appliances, and packaging industries; in addition, it created around 50,000 jobs. The industry was also claimed to be responsible for the generation of taxes, wages, and benefits amounting to $.5 billion per year. As a result, a national entrepreneurial sector developed without harming the dynamic participation of international groups [36, p. 10].

During the initial ten years, the industry achieved a level of efficiency, productivity, and scale of production that paved the way for its short-term expansion. The growth of the petrochemical sector in Brazil "drove an accelerated process of industrial maturation" [32, p. 29]. Business managers, professional staff, and skilled workers accumulated a wealth of experience in managing industrial projects and operating petrochemical plants that was uncommon in peripheral countries.

The "Achilles' heel"of the industry was said to be insufficient know-how about the production of fine and specialty chemicals, and lack of downstream processing industries in Bahia. Nevertheless, the Brazilian state and society were ready to introduce or strengthen these strategic developments in the Bahian petrochemical industry [37, p. 116; 38, p. 32].

Role of the State

The relative maturity of the industry, the end of a cycle of government investment, and the beginning of a new cycle with the "National Petrochemical Plan," posed new challenges to the expansion of the petrochemical industry in Bahia. While the Brazilian government was central to the creation and initial expansion of the industry—especially through regulation, promotion, and financing of private investment—it could no longer continue to invest in industrial growth to the same extent as in the late 1970s to early 1980s. By the late eighties, a new "transition" phase had started. The now-mature private capital (i.e., business class) was expected to take the lead in the new investment cycle and reduce the state participation in the petrochemical sector. A financially bankrupt and heavily indebted government was expected to allow the private sector to direct the future of the industry in a free market economy. In a word, some industrial leaders clearly advocated a change in the tripartite model toward a bipartite model—an association of private Brazilian capital and foreign capital, led by the former.

Most commentators argued that the central question the meeting had to address was the new role of the Brazilian government regarding industrial development in the nineties.

The predominant view proposed that the state should focus on a new industrial technology policy that promoted research and development in universities, research centers, and technology institutes. The industry should be deregulated and privatized, but the state should support technological development so as to facilitate technological innovation. These commentators seemed to agree that while on the one hand the industry was still relatively modern by international standards, on the other, it ran the risk of soon becoming outdated due to the low levels of investment in research and development [39].

Reflecting the existing climate in the country in the late 1980s, some representatives of private industries claimed they were ready to coordinate and organize capitalist growth in the petrochemical industry. According to them, the government should take bigger steps to encourage free markets and free enterprise, as well as focus on the traditional functions of government in liberal democratic societies, such as education and technology research. They said the government should also promote foreign trade by opening the country's internal market to foreign imports, which in turn would stimulate the modernization of the economy through international competition.

In addition, industry leaders argued that the Brazilian economy faced the great challenges of foreign competition and had to increase its productivity in an open-market society. Last, internal market forecasts suggested the urgent need for expansion in the production of first- and second-generation petrochemicals.

In short, the themes outlined here demonstrate that, by 1988, subsectors of the Bahian petrochemical bourgeoisie not only had the intention of controlling their own economic and political destiny, but had also formulated (or agreed with) a larger ideological agenda to conduct the economic development of the country—the neoliberal agenda.

Labor: Ten Years of Militancy

Chapter 2 laid out the historical events that led Guimarães to argue that the class formation of petrochemical workers in Bahia was marked from the very beginning by the fusion of political, trade-union, and state activism: Political activism because of the strong influence of left-of-center political leaders in shaping the union agenda; union activism due to the history of labor strikes and struggles against private employers, the federal, and state governments; and state activism because in the years before the 1964 coup d'etat, the Goulart administration—following the Vargas model—supported strong state intervention in the economy to promote independent economic development [40, p. 26].

Further, Guimarães suggested that the history of the petrochemical workers' unions in Bahia (Sindiquímica and Proquímicos) clearly illuminates 1) the importance of the political party—up to the late seventies, two communist parties (the PCB and the PC do B), after the late seventies the Workers Party (PT)—as the agency that guides union practices, and 2) the centrality of the political system as the main guide to explain the limits of these practices. Therefore, he claimed that Sindiquímica has to be understood as a progressive labor union that has always had a strong leftist political agenda, an anti-imperialist ideology, and that shared with other progressive Brazilian unions the political preference for general political issues, instead of shop-floor politics.

Organizing Under Adverse Conditions

Sindiquímica had to struggle permanently to defend its membership base against the well-known "divide and conquer" strategy used by petrochemical employers to divide the workers into separate and somewhat-rival "sindicatos."

These employer actions were always countered throughout the eighties by strikes, rallies, and slowdowns in production, with the strong support of the affected workers [41]. In 1980, maintenance workers who worked for Ceman were reclassified as metalworkers by the Brazilian Labor Ministry. Hunger strikes developed at Ceman against this change, because maintenance workers felt that they would lose fringe benefits if they were forced to join the less-active Metalworkers Union.

In 1983, chemical workers were reclassified after an unfavorable labor court decision on an employer-driven lawsuit. Consequently, Sindiquímica lost legal jurisdiction over them, forcing chemical workers to join the new "court-mandated" Chemical Workers Association. In 1985, the leadership of Sindiquímica responded with the formation of an independent association of chemical workers called Proquímicos, reorganizing chemical workers who used to be members of Sindiquímica. During a period of about four years (1985-1989), three organizations coexisted: an ephemeral and weak employer-controlled chemical workers association, the Astquímica; a worker-controlled association that later became a union, the "sindicato" Proquímicos; and Sindiquímica. In 1989, the latter two officially merged into a unified Sindiquímica.

This brief account of union organizing conflicts indicates that on the one hand, employers always showed animosity toward union organizing; on the other, that Sindiquímica was vulnerable to attacks at the shop-floor level, despite its political militancy and ideological commitment to build an independent labor movement in Bahia.

This weakness notwithstanding, the concentration of a young, relatively high-skilled, and politicized workforce in a few factories facilitated the emergence of a radical grassroots movement. The latter resulted from these young workers' ability to share their prior experience in the student movement's massive rallies of the late 1970s against the military regime. A young cadre of radical union activists gradually mobilized the petrochemical workers against the factory regime of the complex [33, p. 433; 42]. While the first direct negotiation between labor and management took place in 1978, the first confrontation happened during the bargaining campaign of 1979, when about 2,000 workers gathered in the union hall. Following the 1979 contract, the petrochemical workers in Bahia were the first group in Brazil to win the right to factory committees and automatic wage corrections [43].

The Factory Regime in Camaçari

According to Guimarães and Castro, the particular conditions that characterized the factory regime of the petrochemical industry in Bahia during the first ten years were [40, p. 27; 44; 45]:

1. Companies had monopolistic control over markets for feedstock, final products, and labor. Studies on the management of work in the industry in Bahia showed that business managers tried to stabilize the high-skilled

workforce through the creation of a human resource management style that is characteristic of the hegemonic factory regimes described by Burawoy (see chapter 1). These managers defined an internal (to the petrochemical industry) labor market that included a clear career ladder to promote upward mobility, teamwork coupled with shiftwork, and good fringe benefits. Human resource management was designed to maximize the use of skilled labor and minimize the use of unskilled or semiskilled labor. The literature on the effect of this "politics of production" in Bahia argued that the performance of teamwork combined with shift-work created solidarity bonds and camaraderie among supervisors, team leaders, and operators. In addition, it argued that process operators developed an industry-specific identity, based on their technical qualifications and understanding of the risks involved in petrochemical work.

2. Privatization of management through the privatization of capital owner-ship occurred in some initially state-owned companies. This "privatiza-tion of the state bourgeoisie" happened when the federal government launched a program in 1978 to invest capital in the private sector. The government financed stock purchases at a low interest rate, facilitating the privatization of Copene. It also created a stockholder holding company called Norquisa, allowing second-generation petrochemical companies to determine Copene's policies. Therefore, investments in the petrochemical industry became private capitalist investment. In turn, petrochemical workers refused any regionalist or nationalist justification for accepting "capitalist exploitation."

3. The high income of process operators made them a privileged group within the local labor force, because they also had the possibility of accessing or trying to access alternative sources of subsistence. However, these operators did not see their high wages as a privilege, but as insuffi-cient payment for bad working conditions in the plants.

4. Authoritarian and informal relations of subordination collided with a very bureaucratic and highly hierarchical management structure. Over the years some charismatic managers developed an "enlightened-despot" management style that was a widespread source of conflicts with shop-floor workers.

5. The reasonably well-developed control of work tasks and skills was delegated to operators, who were reasonably well-educated by Brazilian standards.

Based on a detailed study of the factory regime in one plant in the complex, Guimarães maintained that the factory regime created resentment and unrest among operators, who, due to their class capacities, have always been the avant-garde of petrochemical workers [33, 46]. According to Guimarães, workforce stability and the rigidity in the technical division of labor ended up stifling career mobility by creating career structures that limited upward progression. In this "funnel-shaped" career ladder, promotions became limited.

Shiftwork has always been a source of conflict due to its negative health and social effects, causing poor physical and mental well-being, as well as disrupting family and social life. Wage losses to high inflation, work environment exposures to chemicals, physical hazards—such as heat and noise—and psychosocial hazards (". . . the physical and emotional exhaustion of factory work, as well as its low potential for creativity") were also a permanent source of dissatisfaction [33, p. 360; 47, p. 374].

Every year Sindiquímica and Sinper (the employers' "sindicato") would bargain over these and other conditions [48, 49]. High-level managers would sit down with union leaders to negotiate the economic clauses of contracts, in a fairly civil fashion. On the one hand, this cooperative labor-management relationship guaranteed that the contract would be respected by management. On the other, the union would not challenge management's right to manage the plants as they wished. All in all, there seemed to coexist a confrontational as well as a cooperative relationship between management and labor.

By 1985, however, the rules of this bargaining game were undermined by decreasing real wages, increasing grassroots militancy, and politicization of workplace issues—such as hierarchical rigidity, management's arbitrary promotions, and unhealthy working conditions. The development of these contradictions at the grassroots level promoted the emergence of a more radical leadership within the union. This grassroots-based leadership wanted to change the rules of the game by denouncing the previous cooperation with management at the bargaining table and by advocating for the creation of a "new syndicalism" affiliated with the rapidly growing Central Única dos Trabalhadores (CUT). The traditional communist leadership lost ground to the new generation of workers' party activists, whose syndicalist agenda dominated the general strike of 1985.

The General Strike of 1985 [49, 50]

Because the strike of 1985 was a landmark event in the political struggle between workers and managers in the complex and had a major impact in the overall labor-management relations, I will summarize its causes and consequences in order to substantiate the arguments I make later in this chapter.

In the 1984 collective bargaining campaign, workers of four plants went on strike. Copene, the heart of the complex, almost went on strike as well. Employees of Copene were very dissatisfied with management during the year after this bargaining campaign. Moreover, conditions within Copene prior to the strike turned into very embittered disputes between operators and management. In this workplace, conflicts became more virulent, union solidarity more difficult to develop, and repression stronger. Managers challenged workers' courage and ability to shut the processing units down by overtly saying that they did not believe that the workers "had the guts" to do it. Authoritarian labor-management relations had been slowly but surely deteriorating, creating all the necessary ingredients for worker rebellion.

Sindiquímica's leadership knew that in order to have a successful strike they needed to shut Copene down, interrupting the supply of basic petrochemicals to downstream companies. Negotiations between the employers' "sindicato" and the workers' "sindicato" came to a standstill after ten rounds of talks. The strategy adopted by the employers was one of parsimonious concessions on economic and benefits issues, and no concessions at all on items that involved the organization of work and industrial relations. For example, employers would not agree to recognize shop-floor union committees or six-hour shifts.

The meeting of all workers in August 24, 1985, decided for the strike after grassroots activists and union leaders who worked in plants with poor labor-management relations agitated for a general strike [51]. Most of the union leadership was in favor of a settlement, but agreed to democratically respect the will of the majority. The strike started August 27 at 12:00 A.M.

The union was able to control many companies using the approach of "swelling" the facilities, i.e., the night-shift operators stayed in the plants instead of leaving when the morning-shift operators arrived early in the morning [52]. By the end of the first strike day, most plants were either occupied by union activists (around thirteen facilities) or operating very slowly. Shortly after, the union was successful in shutting the whole complex down. To accomplish that, however, workers had to forcefully occupy some facilities and take their operation over from management. In some facilities, civil disobedience became widespread.

Conflicts with the police occurred in the complex area. A fierce battle for the hearts and minds of the public developed between the employer and the workers' "sindicato." Court decisions favored Sindiquímica by considering the strike legal, but favored employers by demanding that Copene be evacuated. After reestablishing production in this strategic facility, employers fired about 120 workers, half of them from Copene. All strike activists and leaders in this company, including two union officers, were immediately fired.

In the end, petrochemical workers ended up losing the battle in terms of economic or political gains, but temporarily strengthened their collective organization and solidarity. The chemical workers, who at this point were not yet represented by Sindiquímica, were able to settle with the chemical companies one by one. This strike was arguably a collective struggle for civil rights within the gates of the plants, and against authoritarian factory regimes. It brought to the fore the need for new industrial relations in the petrochemical sector in Bahia [53]. Workers wanted a new managerial style, in which management would be democratic and responsive to workers' demands, and which replaced the one implemented by state technobureaucracies during the military regime.

As a result of the strike, Copene downsized the workforce and implemented a more participatory management style that included quality control circles. It also invested in public relations campaigns and cultural initiatives, such as music festivals, restoration of historic sites, and adoption of public schools, to clean its bad public image. In the years after the strike, management regrouped and successfully combined repression with persuasion tactics to neutralize the union.

By the late eighties, the beginning of the economic restructuring of the industry combined with national political realities to add another layer of obstacles to members' allegiance to the radical and aggressive Sindiquímica discourse. The "sindicato" started to lose hundreds of members, aggravating its political decline. One union leader explained this loss of power and support with the following words: "[M]anagement got sick of losing battles and successfully organized its counter-attack" [54]. A more profound analysis that corroborates this opinion was provided by Oliveira, who discussed the evolution of the union press in the nineties. According to her, businesses understood then "the need to speak to society, de-legitimize the movement, and legitimize its interests in partnership with society," while Sindiquímica's ideological discourse lost receptivity in a period when, after the redemocratization struggles mentioned above, society was partially demobilized and not interested in a very militant and radical line of political discourse [55, pp. 25, 43].

Guimarães added that the Brazilian labor movement lost hegemony after 1986-1987, since it was not able to communicate universal perspectives to society. Instead, this movement continued to convey a particularistic, self-centered approach to workers' interests that alienated the rest of society [56].

Occupational Health Policies: The "Silent Wall" Breaks Down [57]

By almost all accounts, occupational health policies during the first phase of the "Pólo" took a typical and common "back seat" to production. Work environment exposures to highly hazardous chemicals and occupational injuries did not constitute a serious concern to policy makers, employers, or employees [58]. Occupational health injuries and illnesses, however, have always been part of the day-to-day life of petrochemical workers. For example, in 1979, a disgruntled Sindiquímica officer broke the silence around occupational accidents by disclosing the occurrence of thirteen workplace deaths caused by inhalation of poisonous gases, falls, electric shocks, and explosions [59].

Given the large number and amount of hazardous chemicals produced and handled by companies in the complex, information on storage and handling of hazardous chemicals was at best unevenly distributed. Using benzene as an example of the general level of awareness and concern for chemical exposures in the complex, a high-ranking manager stated:

> . . . There was general awareness and knowledge regarding basic engineering aspects of working with benzene, i.e., the choices of materials for equipment—such as flanges, pumps and pump seals—that were involved in

benzene production. Nonetheless, day to day workplace monitoring only occurred in companies that had foreign partners with prior experience with benzene [production] (Dupont, for example) [60].

Thus, awareness of and concern about benzene exposures depended on the managerial composition of a given company. If a foreign partner had prior knowledge of benzene hazards, that was incorporated into company policies and procedures. Beyond basic engineering aspects, the overall awareness of benzene hazards and exposures was quite limited. Companies did not routinely monitor chemical exposures. Large companies had in-house occupational physicians and/or nurses to attend injuries and perform periodic exams. Some limited training on personal protective equipment, safety procedures, and fire prevention took place, at least annually, during the "Internal Week to Prevent Occupational Accidents." In sum, safety-related activities combined with clinical medicine to shape company programs in the occupational health area.

Adding insult to injury, the political situation of the country until the mid-eighties did not help the development of health and safety activism in the complex either. It took the emergence of a serious health and safety crisis in Cetrel and several other companies for health and safety policies to change, as chapter 4 will demonstrate. By the end of this phase, the "silent wall" showed cracks and fissures.

National and State Environmental Health Policies: "The Solution to Pollution Is Dilution"

The reconstruction of the environmental health policies implemented in the first phase of the complex seems to indicate that Brazilian officials—implicitly or explicitly—followed the pollution control paradigm common at the time. "The solution to pollution is dilution" logic seems to underlie and give meaning to the implementation of the greenbelt (described in chapter 2) as both a physical barrier to land squatters and an air pollution filter between communities and the industrial area. Following the same model, the adequate (i.e., according to technical specifications) installation of high smokestacks and the proper siting of the utility plant would combine with prevailing winds to disperse air pollutants toward the sea and avoid population exposure to air pollutants [61]. Surface water pollution would be controlled through the treatment of liquid effluents at Cetrel, which received the largest investment in pollution control. Groundwater pollution would be controlled by developing a permit system that would limit the number of business users. Solid-wastes collection, classification, treatment, and disposal would be taken care of by state-regulated landfills.

This menu of policies would control all the environmental pollution generated in the complex. The "Plano Diretor do Copec" (Master Plan of the Complex) guided the design and implementation of the environmental management policies adopted during this first phase. Cetrel would be the main institution in charge of overseeing environmental quality around the integrated petrochemical complex [62].

In a comment that reveals the strong faith—commonly held among technocrats—in the effectiveness of pollution control technology, the State of Bahia Secretary for Mines and Energy declared:

> This [industrial wastewater treatment] system will be able to minimize the typical pollution generated by the "Pólo Petroquímico" to very acceptable levels, allowing the discharge [of the effluent] into the sea and demonstrating that, in Camaçari, the government is effectively taking responsibility for avoiding pollution at any cost [63-65].

It is not surprising that the engineers in charge of designing and implementing pollution control in the mid-seventies used foreign technologies to control the pollution created by other imported technologies. Monosowsky wrote that the development of environmental policies in Brazil—among them industrial pollution control policies—were inspired by the 1972 United Nations Conference on Human Environment held in Stockholm [66-68]. After having its official "pollution equals progress" position defeated in the conference, the Brazilian government created the Secretaria Especial do Meio Ambiente (SEMA)— Special Secretariat of the Environment—which slowly inaugurated a new phase in Brazilian environmental policies [69]. Industrial pollution control, however, was treated by government officials as a mere "technical matter."

In addition, the classification of the petrochemical industry as a "national security" activity, under the exclusive purview of the federal government, caused decisions affecting this strategic industry to be heavily influenced by the executive branch. Air control parameters followed U.S. Environmental Protection Agency (EPA) maximum allowable concentrations for particulate matter, sulfur dioxide, carbon monoxide, and photochemical oxidants [70].

According to Monosowsky, the regulations enacted privileged ". . . a problem, industrial pollution, an agent, the industry, and a responsibility for pollution control (the State). The strategy adopted consisted of reduction of emission of pollutants by installing control equipment, in order to achieve the air quality standards . . . established in the regulation" [66, p. 19]. Since Brazil did not manufacture this air pollution control equipment, Brazilian companies had to import it from developed countries. This is exactly what engineers in Bahia did; they tried to control the air pollution emitted by the smokestacks [71-73].

In 1983, the federal government enacted the "Política Nacional de Meio Ambiente"—National Environmental Policy—which regulates the application of the Brazilian Environment Act of 1981 [74]. The environmental policy aimed at

> The preservation, improvement and recuperation of the environmental quality that supports life, in order to guarantee, in the country, [adequate] conditions for socio-economic development, for national security interests and the protection of the dignity of human life [68, p. 201; 75].

The Environment Act created two new institutions: 1) The "Conselho Nacional de Meio Ambiente" (Conama)—National Council of the Environment—directly linked to and charged with assisting the president in designing environmental policies. The CONAMA should also coordinate the creation of "State Councils of the Environment"; and 2) The "Sistema Nacional de Meio Ambiente" (SISNAMA)—National Environment System—whose higher decision-making body was CONAMA. The SISNAMA included all governmental institutions that deal with environmental issues at the federal, state, and local levels.

Among many conceptual innovations, this new national policy incorporated the "polluter pays" principle, environmental zoning, the need for environmental impact assessment of development projects, licensing and reviewing of actual or potential polluting activities, financial incentives for the production and installation of pollution control equipment, and the creation or absorption of environmental technology to improve environmental quality [76].

The CONAMA resolution 001 of 1986 regulated the "Avaliação de Impacto Ambiental" (Environmental Impact Assessment or EIA in the U.S.), including the participation of society in formal public hearings to discuss the environmental impacts of economic projects [77].

Monosowsky observed that, in spite of the Brazilian environmental regulations being modern and advanced, there was a large gap between rhetoric and reality. The Brazilian environmental legislation was harmonious with international standards by the late eighties, but the concrete conditions and the means used for its application were very limited.

On the one hand, there was a wide gap between environmental policy and national economic development strategies. On the other, social control of decisions that affected the environment was handicapped by civil society's lack of power to include noneconomic criteria in economic development decisions [66, p. 23; 78; 79].

At the state level, the picture is quite similar. The first institutional step toward environmental planning was the creation of the "Conselho Estadual de Proteção Ambiental" (CEPRAM)—State Council of the Environment—through state Law 3163 of October 4, 1973 [80]. The institutional origin of the state environmental agency lies in the 1970s' Programa de Meio Ambiente (Promam) of the Centro de Pesquisa e Desenvolvimento (CEPED)—Environment Program of the Center for Research and Development—mentioned in chapter 2. It became the Coordenação de Ciencia e Tecnologia (Coordination of Science and Technology) in 1980 [81].

Law 3858 of November 3, 1980, created the "Sistema Estadual de Administração dos Recursos Ambientais (SEARA)—State Environmental Resources Management System—expressing a broader approach that emphasized the rational use of natural resources. The SEARA actually articulated a pioneer understanding of environmental management in the country, one that went beyond the narrow view of industrial pollution control that had up to then limited the action of CEPRAM. This new vision aimed at incorporating environmental concerns into sectoral and intersectoral economic planning, including environmental variables as priorities in any public or private economic initiative [82]. After the promulgation of the constitution of the state of Bahia, SEARA gained the status of a constitutional "system to manage environmental quality, protection, control, and adequate use of natural resources" [81]. CEPRAM became the highest decision-making body in the system, expanding the participation of civil society by giving representatives of the public equal representation in the tripartite council—the other members were the state and environmental organizations [83].

By 1983, the CCT became the Centro de Recursos Ambientais (CRA)—Environmental Resources Center—the state of Bahia environmental agency [84]. In its initial activist phase (1983-1984), the CRA implemented environmental permitting and enforcement mechanisms, trained a critical mass of professionals, tried to decentralize its functions throughout the state, and formulated the first "Action Plan" for environmental protection. Yet, very early in its development, it was obstructed by a state administration that represented the political interests of the local oligarchy. Business interests in the complex and in other areas of the state were able to successfully neutralize the agency, alleging that CRA enforcement could prevent their economic growth [85].

After this short-lived activist period, CRA concentrated on the development of its internal bureaucratic and administrative structure. Enforcement activities slowed down substantially. Well-qualified human resources left the agency to the private sector in search of better wages and working conditions. Others were laid off. Industry started to capture the CRA.

In summary, despite the institutional, legal, and political progress made during the early eighties, the environmental pollution generated by the "Pólo" during its first phase was not clearly identified and recognized. Neither the state apparatus nor businesses developed policies, practices, or procedures that could tackle the large magnitude of the environmental impact of the complex in the air, water, and soil. Nonetheless, the overall mobilization of the Brazilian civil society in the mid-eighties did not take long to reach Bahia. The local democratic forces defeated the regional conservative oligarchy in the historical gubernatorial elections of 1985, electing Valdir Pires the state governor. A new window of opportunity for changes in environmental policies opened up with the expansion of the complex while the state administration was in the hands of this democratic coalition.

THE TRANSITION PERIOD: THE EIA/RIMA "SOLUTION TO POLLUTION IS POLLUTION CONTROL"

The positive internal market conditions of the mid-eighties had encouraged the prosperous petrochemical industry in Bahia to propose the expansion of sixteen companies and the construction of two new plants in the Camaçari complex [86, p. 12]. Guerra placed this expansion strategy within the scenario of future growth in the Brazilian market combined with forward integration of the Brazilian industry, i.e., the integration of basic commodities with fine chemicals and downstream processing industries [29, p. 31; 87].

Anticipating new legal requirements for an Environmental Impact Assessment prior to future construction or buildup of petrochemical industries, the state of Bahia performed the "Review and Update of the Master Plan of Copec" in 1987, to assess the environmental impact of the complex in the area affected by it. This unfinished study concluded that companies in the "Pólo" did not have effective control over the hazardous wastes generated nor over the impact of these wastes on the environment [88; 89, p. 96].

A full assessment of the environmental impact of the complex did not surface until 1989, when companies in the complex formally requested environmental permits (Licença de Ampliação in Portuguese) to start their construction projects.

An industry leader suggested that by 1987-88 the state of Bahia had "started to adopt a more intelligent idea of partnership with industry, involving it in decisions and sensitizing companies to manage their wastes responsibly and more intelligently" [90]. He also claimed that state agencies had revised their previous "command and control" philosophy and offered companies a new way of doing business [90]. Simultaneously, the state administration reviewed what needed to be done and the environmental problems that needed to be corrected in the complex.

Franco reviewed the main findings of the EIA/RIMA (EIS/EIR in English) and offered a sharp criticism of the environmental damage that had accumulated in the affected area during the eighties [91, 92]. Her main argument was that these documents not only showed that the environmental management of the complex had been inadequate, but also provided evidence of the lack of concern of businesses and the state about the environment.

Though it is beyond the scope of this research to discuss these findings in detail, it is important to summarize the main conclusions of the environmental diagnosis advanced in these documents [89, pp. 92-93; 93]:

1. The complex negatively affected the quality of the groundwater and surface waters in the county of Camaçari. The São Sebastião aquifer, the Capivara Pequeno river, the Santa Helena dam, and tributary rivers, were found to be polluted [94]. This aquifer might be irreversibly polluted in the medium term if immediate actions were not taken.

2. Soil degradation, contamination, and erosion were detected, causing the soils around the complex to have high permeability and low resistance; furthermore, the illegal dumping of toxic hazardous wastes and their improper storage in drums kept in open yards could affect the groundwater.

3. Significant deforestation, as a result of indiscriminate land use, and reductions in the fauna and flora were found to be a serious problem.
4. Air quality was poor, due to pollution by hydrocarbons (specially volatile organic compounds such as benzene), sulfur dioxide, and nitrous oxide.
5. The health conditions of the neighboring urban populations were not properly assessed due to the lack of reliable health and epidemiological data. Workers' health data showed the presence of respiratory and neurological disorders, hearing loss, leucopenia, and mercury poisoning.

The EIA/RIMA concluded that, even before the expansion of the complex, the petrochemical industry had created environmental impacts of high magnitude. These impacts had already reached alarming proportions in some cases and demanded urgent measures for their mitigation and control. Darwich wrote that the 1989 EIA/RIMA were a landmark in the evolution of environmental policies in the complex because: a) they assembled, for the first time in the life of the "Pólo," a wealth of good environmental information and data; b) they pointed out the potential threat to the environment of the planned expansion of the complex; c) they demonstrated the lack of effective and complete control over the environmental impacts of petrochemical production in the area affected [95].

The ability of the EIA/RIMA to expose the past—and forecast the future—environmental pollution generated by the complex was in great measure a consequence of the new political situation in Bahia in the late 1980s. The presence of progressive professionals in the state agencies who were in charge of implementing the new environmental laws enabled the consultants who had been hired to perform and evaluate the study to have the necessary independence and freedom. Furthermore, Sindiquímica, environmental groups such as the Grupo Ambientalista da Bahia (GAMBA), and representatives of professional associations that organized lawyers and journalists, formed an unprecedented ad hoc coalition to debate the reports in the public hearing held at Camaçari. The press was forced to cover in detail a variety of the aspects analysed in the documents, reflecting a new era of environmental awareness and activism in Bahia [96].

Responding to this—now public—environmental crisis, the CEPRAM approved and the CRA implemented Resolution 218/89, granting industry a *conditional permit* to move forward with the expansion of the complex. The complex could expand, provided that industry complied with a series of mandatory recommendations and measures to increase control of environmental and occupational hazards, under the coordination of the Gerencia de Meio Ambiente (GMA)—Environmental Management Division—of COFIC. In addition, companies had to take measures to clean up past environmental damage.

The Environmental Management Plan of COFIC

The GMA was created "to search for a harmonious relationship between technology and the environment, using all types of resources available in the companies and/or in public or private institutions, collecting and channeling diffuse knowledge, and forming a collective consciousness on commitments and responsibilities" [97, p. 12]. The GMA elaborated on the two-volume Master Plan to guide the design and implementation of the mitigation measures suggested in the EIA/RIMA. The main foundations of the plan [98] are: co-participation and co-responsibility of the companies affiliated with COFIC in addressing environmental issues, using the CRA and CEPRAM as references, since the community and the firms are represented in the latter; partnership between government and industry, based on the triad cooperation-consultation-commitment; balance between development and environment, by managing the risks inherent in production and handling of hazardous substances in such a way as to allow the community to safely enjoy the benefits derived from these products; responsibility of each company in formulating its own environmental management and policies; and self-control of the whole environmental management system through mechanisms based on the law.

The GMA would continuously guide, coordinate, and follow up on the implementation of the mitigation measures, in particular those concerning monitoring systems for air, groundwater, and surface water monitoring [99]. The GMA would also provide technical assistance and guidance on environmental matters; propose and implement business policies to manage the environment in the complex; gather data necessary to support an adequate management of the environment; allocate financial resources to allow the CRA to supervise the activities developed; elaborate on and/or propose standards to control the pollution of the air, water, and soil; improve the governmental structure in charge of regulating the environment; and promote human resources development through courses, seminars, and conferences.

Business response to the environmental crisis diagnosed and synthesized in the EIA/RIMA seems to indicate that the "environmental awareness or maturity" of the industry had reached a new level by the late eighties. Instead of reacting to day-to-day incidents, hiding the environmental damage resulting from the operation of the plants, and "hiding their heads in the sand," business leaders formulated a new strategy to manage environmental issues. This new plan indicates that they could no longer treat environmental issues as unfortunate externalities of petrochemical production. As occurred in the United States and other developed countries, corporate environmentalism arrived in Bahia through a conscious act of the ruling class, when its behavior was challenged by organized communities, labor, and environmental groups—the organized fractions of Brazilian subordinate classes [100].

To face this particular aspect of a growing political threat coming from below, a project to gain control of environmental management took shape in the late eighties, although not isolated from the drastic transformation striking the industry at the national and international levels [101]. The overall political and economic reorganization brought about by restructuring the petrochemical industry in Bahia was the heart of the new hegemonic project of the petrochemical bourgeoisie for the nineties. In a word, the post-Fordist program and the neoliberal agenda "came to town."

SECOND PHASE: THE MAKING OF A GLOBAL, RESTRUCTURED, AND NEOLIBERAL COMPLEX

Industry: An "Oligopólo" Develops [102]

The economic recession that started in 1989—and continued through the mid-nineties—combined with the new economic policy of the Collor administration and the temporarily unfavorable national and international market conditions, to delay the expansionist plans of the petrochemical sector in Bahia [103]. Marking a discontinuity between the old import-substitution and the new neoliberal models, the Brazilian government opened the petrochemical market to external competition by reducing import tariffs and cutting price subsidies to naphtha; it also announced the program to privatize and deregulate state-owned enterprises, including the ones in the petrochemical sector. In addition, Lopes observed that this down cycle of the Brazilian petrochemical industry was magnified by the international oversupply of petrochemical products, resulting from expansions in capacity in the Asian Tigers since 1987 [104].

Guerra, on the other hand, asserted that the local industry had several negative structural externalities that hindered its ability to compete successfully on the internation scene: It did not have an "endogenous technology innovation nucleus," making it vulnerable to better foreign technologies; it needed to implement a new organizational paradigm based on the quality of human resources and automation; it had low industrial integration, hindering its ability to achieve competitive scales of production and intra-sectoral synergisms; and it had difficulty in responding to the cyclical fluctuations of markets by shutting units down, as multinational corporations can do [29, p. 63].

Thus, the sudden bleak economic panorama that developed in the early nineties explains to a large extent why business leaders decided to restructure the industry at that time. In a matter of a few years, the optimistic industry prognosis had turned into a competitive nightmare. From the vantage point of the industry, the formerly protectionist policies were broken during a strong recessionary and inflationary period, exposing all of the local petrochemical industry's weaknesses and forcing it to go through surgical restructuring to survive. While in the first phase managers had viewed foreign markets as "safety valves" to alleviate problems in a protected internal market, now they had to worry about importation of cheaper petrochemical goods. Foreign production started to compete with national production.

Druck argued that, from the perspective of businesses—and in addition to internal economic and political factors—the process of globalization of markets demanded new managerial practices and technologies. These, in turn, required the introduction of the concept of quality as the main business principle. She also submitted that these work-management changes expressed a local crisis of "peripheral Fordism," in spite of its socially excluding character in Brazil [105].

According to Borges and Druck, Brazilian Fordism was born with the import substitution industrialization model, which followed the American industrialization model in developing mass production of durable goods and mass consumption. However, the social exclusion and income concentration of the Brazilian version of Fordism makes it an incomplete or peripheral Fordism. In contrast to developed countries' Fordism, businesses and the state did not bargain with unions on the Fordist organization of work.

Workers' consent was achieved mostly through coercion via authoritarian labor-capital relations. In addition, mass consumption was limited, and no welfare state existed. Conversely, some Brazilian intellectuals argued that there was privatization of welfare in some large and medium-size companies using public subsidies. The latter claimed that the Brazilian government supported corporate welfare instead of social welfare.

It appears that in the early nineties the Camaçari complex started the process of importing ideas and concepts that had been the leitmotifs of productive restructuring in the "center." An "epidemic" of *competitiveness, productivity and quality* discourses spread in business-consulting circles and the press, reproducing locally the process that had taken place in the mid-eighties in the United States and Europe.

The "Japanese model," already in use in a few forward-thinking companies in Brazil, turned into the new modern management style. Total Quality Management (TQM) and contracting-out practices joined the already known concepts of Just-In-Time (JIT), Statistical Process Control, and Quality Control Circles, fashioning the updated menu of managerial techniques [106-108].

Copene became the first South American petrochemical company to get ISO 9002 certification, which represented the utmost symbol of the new management paradigm. It also introduced the Total Productivity Management (TPM) model in the area, which is based on ". . . the participation of all Copene's employees to achieve a sole objective: maximum efficiency of the productive process" [109].

Contracting out was the central element of the "Japanese model" adopted in the petrochemical complex in the nineties, first and foremost to reduce costs. Combined with massive downsizing, contracting out epitomized the fundamental qualitative change in management policies and culture [107, pp. 132, 138; 110]. Several layers of mid-management were also cut in the process of reducing the workforce, contributing to widespread job insecurity throughout the complex. No job was secure any longer.

To achieve labor flexibility, firms extended the contracting out of support— such as cleaning, food, transportation, security, heat, ventilation and air conditioning (HVAC)—as well as productive services such as maintenance. Furthermore, it became common practice to have one contractor subcontract the management of its contract to another contractor, generating a "contracting-out chain" [111].

As a result of widespread contracting out, the petrochemical workforce became fragmented and divided into a minority of permanent (or formal) and a majority of temporary (or informal) workers. In general, contractor workers are low-skilled, poorly trained, work longer hours in the most dangerous jobs and under bad safety conditions, have lower wages, no formal relationship with their employers, and no benefits [112].

Conversely, the high-skilled permanent workers are well-trained, but had to acquire new skills (polivalencia in Portuguese or multiskilling in English), work in multiple jobs, and perform a variety of tasks. These new rules of the production game also demanded a "realignment" of employees to their employers' view of the world and to company values. Employees were persuaded, through TQM programs, to change the way they think "about the world around them, especially the world of work" [113].

A new organization of work developed, characterized by the flexibility of workers, integration of tasks rather than specialization, and the interchangeability of tasks and workers through team-based work [114, p. 62]. While permanent workers might still have had their union contracts, some fringe benefits, and better treatment than part-time contractor workers, the rapid increase in part-timers drove working conditions down for both. The fragmentation of the workforce and high unemployment derived from contracting out and downsizing hampered solidarity ties among workers, allowing management to reinforce its already authoritarian management style without organized collective resistance [115].

Another essential element of this productive restructuring has been the centralization and concentration of capital and the automation of operations, in order for the chemical and petrochemical sectors to achieve higher productivity and competitive economies of scale.

The Brazilian Odebrecht corporation took advantage of the national privatization program, and financial difficulties in some of the original family-based shareholder groups, to increase its shares in many companies in the complex within the past five years [116-118]. According to Lopes, Brazil has followed international market trends toward the formation of oligopolies and vertical integration of firms through mergers and associations between companies and their controlling groups. As a result, the Brazilian petrochemical sector may have become more competitive at the international level and increased its profit margins [119, 120].

While the productive restructuring of the petrochemical industry was an ongoing process throughout the 1990s, the cyclic nature of the national and international markets determined its rhythm and depth. By 1994-1995, with the recovery of these markets, the industry's commercial and financial panorama switched back to overt optimism. The delayed expansions were finally completed and new projects emerged [121, 122].

By the end of the decade, the bipartite association between larger Brazilian groups and foreign capital was the dominant trend. State participation was substantially reduced. It is reasonable to assume, however, that sooner or later the participation of foreign capital in the complex may increase due to the strategic integration of national markets, suggested by the formation of the Mercosur in the South Cone of South America. This regional market fully integrates the markets of Argentina, Uruguay, Brazil, and Paraguay—with Chile and Bolivia partially integrated—into a substantially larger market, which may attract the interest of the larger multinational corporations [123].

After going through all the structural changes described above, the Bahian petrochemical industry of the end of the nineties had become, without a doubt, a globally integrated and economically restructured industry—a "lean and mean" complex—whose leaders follow most if not all of the prescriptions of the neoliberal ideology. In this sense, it is currently a neoliberal complex.

Labor: Going "Down the Hill"

After two initial years of relative mobilization of the rank-and-file during contract negotiations in the nineties, it appears that Sindiquímica's power declined. In September 1989, the union negotiated a relatively good contract for its members. However, after the Collor administration took office in March 1990, employers toughened their relationship with the "sindicato." They violated the contract, especially the wage-increase and job-stability clauses, to counter the reduction in profitability caused by the economic recession cited above. The labor-management relationship turned sour. Sindiquímica tried to resist by mobilizing the members against this violation of the salary-increase clause of the contract. A media campaign was designed to rally the members behind the idea that the employers had cheated the union.

During the 1991 collective bargaining campaign, some plants went on strike to enforce that clause of the contract (clause four). The union appealed to the courts. The Supreme State Labor Court ruled in favor of the union, forcing the employers to pay the wage increases. However, the Sinper appealed to the Supreme Federal Labor Court, which overruled the state court decision after intense lobbying from petrochemical businesses.

After 1992, the already difficult situation worsened a great deal. The impacts of massive layoffs appeared in full force. Economic data reveals that petrochemical workers lost their middle-class status as wages failed to keep up with very high inflation rates. The average real wage decreased from around $1,000 per month to $500 per month between 1982 and 1992 (some observers assess the losses as high as 258 percent in ten years). Consequently, workers had to move to cheaper neighborhoods, cut their annual vacations, put their children in public schools, and keep their cars longer.

Oliveira suggested that the "sindicato" press showed some positive changes in the early nineties that indicated that a learning process had occurred within the leadership, probably related to their participation in electoral campaigns at the national, state, and local levels. The newsletter became more professional as journalists were hired to advise the union and write articles. Billboards and multimedia programs were added to the communication tools used to publicize union issues. A radio program started broadcasting in July 1992. The overly ideological language was tuned down, with more emphasis given to an efficient and professional writing style. Polls performed to assess the influence of the revamped newsletter on the membership demonstrated that the union still bore a good reputation and had broad support and credibility [124].

Nevertheless, in spite of all the changes in shape and form, and the continued support from the membership, the CUT's syndicalist style of unionism lacked a more elaborate message to sensitize the grass roots. The leadership gradually alienated the grass roots by its confrontational political and ideological discourse. Oliveira concluded that this gap between leadership and the rank and file occurred because of 1) the economism of the leadership prevented it from prioritizing health and safety issues, which had become very important to the members after the benzene crisis of 1990; 2) workplace and societal changes stimulated individualism within the rank and file, and 3) Sindiquímica's avant-garde replaced the previous ideological discourse with a propaganda discourse that did not perceive and take into account the modified consciousness of the members [125]. In summary, she argued that the union leadership did not understand the broad consequences of the new measures taken by the Collor administration, which pushed the industry to quickly adopt new work-management practices that had profound negative implications for the working class [55, pp. 70-73; 126].

According to the classification proposed by Burawoy and adapted by Guimarães to Bahia, the factory regime during the first phase of the complex was an authoritarian version of hegemonic factory regimes. Following the same framework, the second phase should be seen as the introduction and consolidation of the hegemonic-despotic factory regime in Bahia [127].

I think that this change in factory regimes summarizes well the fundamental change in the rules of the labor-management relationship. Management authoritarianism increased even further with the consolidation of the post-Fordist economic restructuring. Sindiquímica lost several thousand members—the so-called power in the numbers—to automation, downsizing, and contracting out, and it was not able to build a counter-hegemonic program to guide its remaining membership. While businesses gained power, the union weakened.

The reasons for this are still under debate in Brazil. Druck offered an interesting explanation for the decline of labor through a complex and multifaceted argument that theorizes on the relationships among the globalization process, the productive restructuring, and the labor movement in Brazil [20; 128].

First, she asserted the main sociopolitical dimensions of globalization. Globalization is defined as a political, cultural, and economic reality as well as a result of political decisions taken by global oligopolies and banks, and a few national governments. Therefore, it is not a mechanistic consequence of technological progress or competitive evolution of markets. Neither is it an inexorable result of the objective development and modernization of technology.

Social actors made globalization happen. Intercapitalist competition does not explain everything. She countered that the economism of several analyses of globalization actually hides the human agency of social and political actors to convey its irreversibility and unavoidability. The message implicit in these positivist arguments is that "there is no alternative" to globalization. These arguments invite social conformism and end up naturalizing social events.

Instead, she saw globalization as a structural movement of capitalism, where there is concentration and centralization of capital combined with the growth of micro-, small, and medium-sized businesses; the latter are a direct offspring of outsourcing and contracting-out networks.

Citing Hobsbawn, she diagnosed globalization as a capitalist response to the social, moral, and political crises of modern times, explicitly recognized only after the fall of "real socialism." Through globalization, the rationality of modern society reaches its maximum limits. Humankind's subordination to the logic of markets, goods, costs, and benefits naturalizes social events and the relationships established with nature and within society itself. The world becomes more and more alike, although inequality between the rich and the poor increases to levels never before seen. In a word, the subordination of peripheral countries to industrialized countries intensified during the eighties and nineties.

Second, she argued that productive restructuring is another structural movement that occurs at the point of production. It is part of the redefinition of U.S. economic hegemony vis-a-vis Japan and Germany. Cost reduction, flexibility of labor markets and work, and neutralization of conflicts between labor and capital gain prominence in the corporate agenda. The struggle for hegemony at the workplace places the indoctrination and co-optation of workers at the center of management's discourse. TQM and new training policies are implemented to achieve these goals [129]. However, this search for hegemony is coupled with despotic work-management policies, contracting out, and downsizing.

Third, she defined neoliberalism as ". . . a conjunctural political-economic project that supports the ideal ideological framework to consolidate economic restructuring within the context of globalization" [20, p. 29]. While the latter two are long-term structural movements, the former is a short-term program. Neoliberalism became hegemonic in the nineties in Brazil and impregnated the society with the "cult of the market," modifying all prior cooperation and solidarity patterns. Individualism was reinforced in opposition to collective action;

competition was stimulated in contrast to social solidarity; the market and "stuff" were elevated to the condition of "subjects"; a privatizing view of society was disseminated, while everything that is public was demoralized. The ideology of the "end of history" was defended as the only possible social, political, historical, and economic order [130]. While globalization and productive restructuring establish "the material and objective conditions in the current phase of capitalist development, neoliberalism offers the subjective conditions necessary to realize the connection and the interlacing between them to the fullest extent" [20, p. 32].

Last but not least, Druck pointed out that, as a consequence of the Fordist crisis, labor crises arose at the point of production. The fragmentation and dismantling of factory work organization undercut the workers' sense of collective identity and weakened the strength of the "sindicatos." Growing unemployment forced workers to formulate individual survival strategies. These changes combined with the deregulation of labor markets and contracting out to promote the growth of individualism, and to undermine class identity and solidarity. Instead, workers developed a different kind of self-identification; now they are either first-class permanent workers or second-class part-time workers.

This destruction of the traditional factory culture led to a union crisis, which was bolstered by the ideological and political crisis stemming from the lack of hope and alternatives to capitalism after the fall of the Berlin wall. Thus, otherwise radical and militant labor leaders adopted a defensive position, searching for negotiated solutions that did not disrupt the new capitalist order. "Sindicatos" gradually lost the ability to mobilize and unify the rank and file and were forced to follow the new rules. Simultaneously, union members lost interest in politics. In this context, neocorporatist trends within the Brazilian working class were reinforced. Permanent workers wanted to keep their status at the expense of a broader unity with the underemployed.

As downsizing progressed in Camaçari, permanent workers turned into contractor employees, and Sindiquímica lost members to weaker service unions that organize food, cleaning, security, and maintenance services [131]. Therefore, the dynamics of contracting out in the complex had two opposite effects: Some smaller service-sector unions grew, and the industrial unions shrank. The impact of this process over labor union unity has been very negative; instead of joining forces to fight the common enemy, industrial unions and service unions have been fighting over representational jurisdiction and raiding each other [132].

While in the eighties the Brazilian labor movement had a broad political perspective and was able to mobilize workers beyond specific trade and group demands, in the nineties this perspective seemed to disappear. Tactics were confused with strategies, and business unionism was counterposed to syndicalist unionism as a better solution to the new problems posed by restructuring. Lula's defeat in the 1989 and 1994 presidential elections added to the progressive labor unions' declining political momentum. Furthermore, progressive Brazilian union leaders tended to use the European experience as their reference for good unionism. With the crisis of European unions, they had less and less inspiration to their praxis.

The Central Única dos Trabalhadores (and Workers Party) affiliated labor unions also showed confusion in their political-ideological discourses; on the one hand, they fiercely opposed neoliberalism; on the other, they did not seem to have clear understanding of the changes happening at the workplace. In sum, this confusion expressed difficulties in associating globalization, economic restructuring, and neoliberalism.

By 1997, Sindiquímica merged with Stiep/Sindipetro—the refinery and oil drilling workers' union—to form the Sindiquímica-Sindipetro labor union. The merge of "sindicatos" seems to be a global common trend in situations where labor is being successfully attacked by corporations, losing power to larger and larger oligopolies. In the new "Oligopólo Petroquímico de Camaçari" of the nineties, this is the last bastion of resistance for the working class.

Occupational Health Policies: "The Turtles Want to Preserve the Petrochemical Workers" [133]

After the benzene crisis of the early nineties, described in detail later in the book, health and safety issues achieved high visibility for the rank and file, as well as for Sindiquímica's officers. During 1991, the union newsletter *Grave* systematically denounced occupational accidents, spills, explosions, and deaths in companies in the complex. In addition, the shift of hazards from permanent to contractor employees became evident in many headlines and reports [134]. Therefore, in contrast to the first phase, health and safety moved temporarily to the front seat of the union car. By the early nineties, Sindiquímica had a medical department that regularly collected and analyzed data on occupational injuries, illnesses, and deaths in the complex.

Special issues of the newsletter publicized basic descriptive, occupational epidemiology data on work-related morbidity, classified by disease, occupation, employer, etc. The worsening of work conditions and increasing unemployment, however, forced union leaders to concentrate their efforts on responding to the overwhelming employment crisis of the early nineties. The union's agenda increasingly focused on unemployment and jobs. Health and safety struggles were given a lower priority, though never as low as in the first phase [135].

Reacting to the increase in union activity, employers upgraded health and safety conditions in some plants and implemented health and safety policies, training, and procedures. As the title of this section illustrates, Sindiquímica believes that companies did (and still do) less than necessary to prevent and control the serious chemical and physical hazards of chemical and petrochemical workplaces. However, most social actors agree that the overall level of chemical hazard awareness and control in workplaces in the complex undoubtedly improved in the nineties [136]. With the more recent drive to get certification by the International Standardization Organization (ISO) 14,000 standards series, a few companies are starting to integrate health and safety with environmental issues.

Another important trend of of this new phase was exposed by Franco and Afonso, who collected data that suggests a process of transfer of risks within companies; in a sample of fifteen industrial sites in the Salvador Metropolitan Region, contractor workers had more accidents than permanent employees. For example, in 1988 more than 50 percent of occupational accidents affected permanent workers. In 1992, 65 percent of the accidents affected contract workers [137, 138].

If one combines this dangerous trend with the obsolescence of machinery and equipment, it is easy to postulate that dangerous conditions are in gestation in the complex. Young, less-skilled, and poorly trained contractor workers are told to repair and maintain fifteen- or twenty-year old tanks, machines, and pipelines that need to be replaced. Moreover, employers are cutting costs by reducing the size of the maintenance workforce and stretching equipment usage to dangerous limits. Corrective maintenance is replacing preventive maintenance [139].

The picture that appears to emerge indicates that while on the one hand the overall health and safety conditions inside the plants may have gotten better, on the other, new causes for concern are developing. While permanent employees may be working under safer and healthier conditions, contractor employees may bear the brunt of short-sighted human-resource policies that are shifting chemical risks to them as well as exposing them to potentially very harmful conditions.

If the experience of the U.S. petrochemical industry in the eighties is any indication of what the future may hold for Camaçari, plant blowups and catastrophic releases of hazardous materials should be expected as a result of poor standard operating procedures for the maintenance of chemical plants.

National and State Environmental Health Policies: "The Solution to Pollution Is Voluntary Pollution Control"

CEPRAM resolution 620/1992 authorized the operation of the expanded facilities, provided that companies complied with and implemented a series of requirements. These requirements included monitoring of groundwater, surface, and navigational waters; air-quality monitoring of the area affected by the complex; source control of pollutants; risk mapping; implementation of self-monitoring procedures, and development of an emergency response plan [140]. While the state of Bahia, through CEPRAM and CRA, set the guidelines of *what* companies needed to do to manage the environment in the area affected by the complex, it did not determine *how* these guidelines should be complied with. To answer the question of *how* companies managed environmental—and occupational—matters, it is necessary to understand this particular managerial aspect with respect to the overall reorganization process that took place within the firms.

All state-owned companies were totally or partially privatized during the nineties, including Cetrel, which became the "green seal" of the complex with the implementation of the environmental plan of COFIC. Together with the GMA of COFIC, Cetrel took over the environmental management of the complex, extending to all media the well-established, centralized, wastewater management strategy—which sees the complex as one single point source composed of an aggregate of facilities, or a condominium of individual companies [141]. In this new scheme, each company was supposed to take care of its own releases into the environment, while Cetrel managed the solid, air, and liquid hazardous wastes, monitors all environmental media, and helps companies improve their pollution-control performance [142]. Therefore, the operation of almost all aspects of environmental management in the complex came under the control of a private company controlled by the polluters.

By the mid-nineties, the process of replacing the command-and-control regulatory strategy of state intervention by voluntary and cooperative compliance ended, culminating in a strategic shift in the state-private sector relationship that made it friendlier to the private sector. A landmark of this change to market-based and management-oriented instruments for environmental management was the Brazilian Chemical Industry Association's (ABIQUIM) introduction of the CMA Responsible Care Program in Bahia in 1994.

In contrast to the eighties, the picture suggested by business managers, labor, community groups, state officials, and the press in the nineties, emphasized the lack of or the limited union and societal influence on environmental management policies. The rise of corporate dominance at the country and state levels skewed the already tilted playing field even more toward the interests of the business community. State agencies, in particular the CRA, have gradually abdicated their enforcement power and replaced it by partnerships with corporations, transferring environmental pollution-control functions to the private sphere, where company managers have the last say about company procedures and policies.

It appears that the 1990s' trend of integrating the Brazilian petrochemical industry with the global petrochemical industry—the globalization of the "Pólo"—has had clear environmental-management implications. On the one hand, the industry imported the ideology and politics of what Mann and Karliner called "corporate environmentalism" [143, 144].

Corporate intellectuals quickly adapted this corporate model to national and local Brazilian realities, framing it as a modernization of business environmental practices, which were widely disseminated during and after the Earth Summit, held in Rio de Janeiro in 1992.

On the other hand, nongovernmental organizations, labor, and progressives feel overwhelmed by the business hegemony in the field and have not been able to counter this environmental "there is no alternative" agenda. Therefore, a most likely scenario is the continuation of the voluntary ISO and Responsible Care programs in the near future, led by Cetrel.

In turn, Cetrel managers claim that this internationally unified set of environmental management systems and policies (and public relations messages), reflecting the corporate control of environmental pollution, is applied in Camaçari to a degree that surpasses its application in Texas [145]. The verdict on the extent to which the adoption of these global policies and management systems will turn the Camaçari complex into a green complex is an ongoing discussion in local business and academic circles. Business intellectuals argue that global and national free markets have driven and will keep driving businesses to do the right thing in the long run, while progressives partially or totally reject this thesis, claiming that past environmental damage caused by petrochemical production suggests otherwise [146].

CONCLUSION

With the understanding that this debate is not a choice between black and white, I tend to agree with the latter. By reviewing the three phases of the twenty-year history of the complex, I laid out the marked differences in the environmental and occupational health policies implemented.

During the first two phases of the complex, labor, the state, and communities had at times decisive influence on the design and outcomes of environmental and occupational health policies. The militant reaction of these social actors against the environmental and occupational health crises forced businesses to increase control and mitigate the impact of petrochemical production. Conversely, in the third phase, these actors have had much less influence on business practices. Hence, whatever materialized next has been, for the most part, a result of profit-driven, market-oriented decisions over the use and abuse of local natural resources to produce petrochemical-derived commodities. In a word, business hegemony has controlled the playing field.

Unfortunately, the hegemonic logic of capitalist decisions regarding environmental protection in the United States and other industrialized countries has shown that, while it is urgent to move to cleaner technologies that prevent environmental pollution, businesses tend to focus on short-term, "band-aid" measures. Left to free market forces, the end result of mainstream practices of petrochemical and chemical business has been the worsening of long-term environmental pollution.

Commoner summarized this anti-environmental logic in the United States when he stated that "[f]or the first time in the 3.5 billion-year history of life on this planet, living things are burdened with a host of man-made poisonous substances, the vast majority of which are now even more prevalent in animal tissue and the elements than they were twenty years ago when Earth Day first imposed itself on popular consciousness" [cited in 144, p. 60].

Since complex managers have a track record of following the mainstream corporate America way of thinking about environmental problems, which translates into newer and more sophisticated end-of-pipe, pollution-control technologies, I have no reason to be optimistic. While environmental pollution may be under voluntary, "state of the art," end-of-pipe control, much more needs to be done. Probably, it will take at least another decade before pollution prevention and cleaner production-policy strategies emerge as an alternative way of preventing instead of curing environmental pollution. In the meantime, new crises may arise that will require state, community, and labor intervention to resolve.

ENDNOTES

1. I believe that the overall classification proposed here apprehends the critical events in the different conjunctures that contributed to the changes in environmental and occupational health policies observed in the complex. However, it does not include all the factors that may have contributed to policy changes. Like a movie director, I edited these twenty years of history by cutting the whole "twenty-year historical footage" into a narrative that focuses on the most important events or trends in each period. In addition, I zoomed the camera in on the social actors proposed by the authors mentioned above.
2. Since the major work environment crises in the complex, the benzene crises, occurred during the first and second phases, I address them separately in chapter 4 due to their relevance to the arguments developed in this book.
3. The low or negative macroeconomic growth, high foreign and internal debts, and high inflation rates in many countries in Latin America resulted in deteriorating social indicators, such as infant mortality and education levels. Hence, the 1980s were nicknamed "The Lost Decade." The political-economic aspects examined in this section should be viewed as the main causes of the social struggles that led to the re-democratization of Brazil, the "New Republic" transition regime, and the consolidation of the neoliberal agenda in the nineties.
4. The large Brazilian foreign debt accrued during the seventies and multiplied very quickly with the steep rise in international interest rates. Nilson Souza noted that the Brazilian foreign debt increased by $35 billion between the late 1970s and the early 1980s as a result of the "increase in interest rates imposed internationally by the U.S. Government" [5, p. 228]. When Mexico defaulted on the payment of its foreign debt service in 1982, a financial crisis shockwave spread throughout the Americas. To bail out the banking sector of developed countries, the International Monetary Fund demanded that debtor countries implement the so-called structural adjustment programs (SAPs). These are in turn a new name for the structural adjustment loans formulated in the last years of Robert McNamara at the World Bank. There is a massive literature that addresses the causes and effects of the Latin America debt crisis. For good examples of this literature, see [6-8].
5. Nilson Souza, *'Plano' FHC: Economia em Marcha À Ré,* Rio de Janeiro: Instituto do Trabalho Dante Pelacani, p. 228, 1994.

6. Michael Tanzer, "Globalizing the Economy: The Influence of the International Monetary Fund and the World Bank," *Monthly Review*, 47, 4, pp. 1-15, September 1995.

7. Consuelo Ahumada, "El Modelo Neoliberal y su Impacto en la Sociedad Colombiana," [The Neoliberal Model and its Impact on Colombian Society], El Áncora Editores, Bogotá, pp. 51-54, 1996.

8. Kevin Danagher, ed., "IMF/World Bank Wreak Havoc on Third World," in *50 Years Is Enough: The Case Against the World Bank and the International Monetary Fund*, South End Press for Global Exchange, Boston, pp. 20-22, 1994..

9. Walden Bello, Shea Cunningham, and Bill Rau, *Dark Victory: the United States, Structural Adjustment and Global Poverty*, Pluto Press, London, 1994.

10. For a sharp criticism of SAPs, see "Structural Adjustment Programs," *In Focus*, vol. 3, no. 3, April 1998. *In Focus* is a joint project of the Interhemispheric Resource Center (IRC) and the Institute for Policy Studies (IPS), Washington, D.C.

11. The slogan used to express popular discontent with the IMF policies was "Fora daqui o FMI." It means that the Brazilian people wanted the IMF "out of" Brazil. This slogan also called attention to the fact that the Brazilian government was subservient to IMF's social and economic policies.

12. José Sarney, a long-term conservative ally of the military regime, was the vice-presidential candidate on the Tancredo Neves ticket. Tancredo Neves was an experienced moderate politician who assembled a broad coalition against the military regime. He died before taking office, and Sarney became president of the "New Republic" regime. Guimarães argued that these societal conditions not only favored the radicalization of the working class in Bahia (discussed later in this chapter), but also fractured the hegemony of the regional petrochemical bloc, which relied heavily on the military regime to keep its power base.

13. Nilson Souza condensed the first four years of the eighties in [14, p. 151]. He asserted that the main structural economic contradiction in Brazil is the one between *dependent* capitalist production relations and the progress of productive forces, i.e., a contradiction between economic dependency and national development. Therefore, he claimed that during the eighties the political economy of Brazil went through different junctures that reflected the evolution of the conflict between imperialist forces (and interests) on one side, and democratic-nationalist forces on the other. The IMF and the military dictatorship regime expressed the interests of the former, while the democratic-nationalist alliance expressed the interests of the latter. Although his analysis is limited to only four years and has a militant tone that reveals commitment to a particular radical interpretation of the social struggles in the country, it outlines with precision some of their fundamental reasons.

14. Nilson Souza, *Sim! Reconstrução Nacional!* [*Yes!, National Reconstruction*], Global Editora, S. Paulo, 1984.

15. Latin American progressive commentators tend to agree that the document "Washington Consensus" guided and synthesized the Latin American economic policies adopted in the 1990s. The "Washington Consensus" is an expression created by the economist John Williamson of the Institute of International Economics (IIE) to name the structural reforms proposed by international finance community representatives, conservative "think-tank" ideologues and the U.S. government. According to Ahumada, in November 1989, the IIE organized the conference, "Latin

American Adjustment: How Much Has Happened," during which economists of eight Latin American countries (Peru, Bolivia, Mexico, Brazil, Colombia, Venezuela, Chile, and Argentina) identified ten points that constituted the base for an ample consensus regarding economic reform in Latin America. These points were: fiscal discipline, cuts in public spending, financial and trade liberalization, privatization of state-owned enterprises, overvaluation of currencies, deregulation and protection of property rights, and openness to foreign investment [7, p. 54]. Druck also wrote that the "Washington Consensus" had three main economic goals: 1) the stabilization of Latin American economies, 2) structural reforms to reduce the size of the state, deregulate markets, and liberalize trade and finance, and 3) open national economies to international investment [16, p. 18].

16. Graça Druck and Tania Franco, "A Degradação do Trabalho e os Riscos Industriais no Contexto da Globalização, Reestruturação Produtiva e das Políticas Neoliberais," in Tania Franco, ed., *Trabalho, Riscos Industriais e Meio Ambiente: Rumo ao Desenvolvimento Sustentável?* Salvador: EDUFBA, pp. 15-27, 1997.

17. Ahumada wrote that Brazil was considered by the international finance community to be the "black sheep" of Latin American countries, because of its reluctance to apply this community's package of neoliberal policies in a consistent fashion [7, pp. 56-57]. After Brazil started to implement this agenda, especially after the privatization of state-owned enterprises, it was praised in several conservative magazines, such as *The Economist* and *Business Week*.

18. The ideological dominance of the neoliberal ideology is also a global phenomenon that has concerned progressive intellectuals all over the world since the fall of the Berlin Wall. Paul Sweezy called it the "there is no alternative" or TINA ideology. For examples of the massive literature on the debate regarding this issue, see [6; 7, pp. 51-65; 9; 19; 20; 21; 22; 23; 24].

19. Kari Levitt, "Toward Alternatives: Re-Reading the Great Transformation," *Monthly Review,* 47, 2, pp. 1-16, June 1995.

20. Graça Druck, "Globalização, Reestruturação Produtiva e Movimento Sindical," [Globalization, Productive Restructuring and Trade-Union Movement], *Cadernos CRH,* no. 24-25, pp. 21-40; 1996.

21. *The Nation,* 263, no. 3, 1996, has many articles on globalization. Particularly relevant are: Jerry Mander, "The Dark Side of Globalization," pp. 9-13; Martin Khor, "Colonialism Redux," pp. 18-19; Helena Norberg-Hodge, "Break Up the Monoculture," p. 20.

22. Richard Barnet, "The End of Jobs," *Harper's Magazine,* pp. 47-52, September 1993.

23. Bruce Campbell, "The Global Economy at the Close of the Twentieth Century," *New Solutions,* 5, 4, pp. 16-23, Summer 1995.

24. Ute Pieper and Lance Taylor, "The Revival of the Liberal Creed: The IMF, the World Bank, and Inequality in a Globalized Economy," unpublished paper presented at the Economic Policy Institute conference, "Globalization and Progressive Economic Policy," Washington, D.C., June 21-23, 1996.

25. Another definition of neoliberalism is cited by Joshua Karliner: "As opposed to political liberalism—a term commonly used in the United States to define the philosophy of those who favor government intervention for the social good—the term *neoliberalism,* which is regularly employed in much of the world, should be understood to refer to a set of economic policies rooted in the old free-market economic

liberalism epitomized by Adam Smith's Wealth of Nations. Today's neoliberalism can be defined as including the following components: the primacy of the market, the reduction in public expenditures for social services, the reduction of government regulation, and privatization of state-owned enterprises" (emphasis mine) [26, p. 2].

26. Joshua Karliner, *The Corporate Planet: Ecology and Politics in the Age of Globalization*, Sierra Club, San Francisco, 1997.

27. Appendix 3 graphically displays the timeline for the twenty-year history of the "Pólo."

28. Victor Gradin, president of the Empresas Petroquímicas do Brasil, in *Anais: Seminário Internacional da Indústria Petroquímica: Pólo, 10 Anos*, Salvador, Bahia, 1988. Gradin stated that the plants were designed with a built-in 20 percent production overcapacity relative to projected internal market demand to prevent future supply shortages. According to him, if supply shortages occurred, companies would have to import basic petrochemicals. See also [29]. For more information on this period, see [30].

29. Oswaldo Guerra, "Desafios Competitivos para a Petroquímica Brasileira," (Competitive Challenges for the Brazilian Petrochemical Industry), *Cadernos CRH*, no. 21, pp. 48-67, 1994.

30. *A Tarde*, Salvador, Bahia, Caderno Economico, p. 5, December 26, 1981.

31. In *Jornal do Brasil* (Rio de Janeiro), June 26, 1989, special report on the eleven years of the complex, Francisco Teixeira commented that the industry was able to export with marginal costs and profits to an international market that had, at the time, compressed prices. The industry was allegedly successful in this "great export effort" because of the internally "managed" prices of naphtha as well as the cooperation among the producers of basic and intermediate chemicals, and of final products.

32. Claudio Frischtak, *Anais: Seminário Internacional da Indústria Petroquímica: Pólo, 10 Anos*, Salvador, Bahia, 1988.

33. Cited in Antonio Sérgio Guimarães, "Factory Regime and Class Formation: The Petrochemical Workers in Brazil." Ph.D. dissertation, University of Wisconsin Madison, 1988. Guimarães considered this government subsidy a tax on the Brazilian people since Petrobrás increased the price of gasoline, oil, and gasohol to compensate for it. Therefore, it supported "the steady performance of the industry during the recession," p. 425.

34. Since the origins and implementation of the industry were discussed in chapter 2, I will focus here on the remaining issues.

35. My interviews in Bahia in July 1996 and 1997 with key labor and management informants suggest that industry leaders did not consider health and safety a serious problem up to the benzene crises described in chapter 4. Another possibility to account for the lack of recognition of these issues may be that business leaders kept them under the carpet for as long as they could.

36. Transcription of videocassette, "10 Years of the Petrochemical Industry in the Northeast," *Anais: Seminário Internacional da Indústria Petroquímica: Pólo, 10 Anos*, Salvador, Bahia, 1988, p. 10.

37. Ernesto Geisel, former president of Brazil and major supporter of the industry, *Anais: Seminário Internacional da Indústria Petroquímica: Pólo, 10 Anos*, Salvador, Bahia, 1988. The development of fine chemistry and downstream industries in the complex has been on the agenda of the petrochemical bourgeoisie for a long time. An example

of this is the headline of the newspaper, *O Globo* (Rio de Janeiro): "Química Fina: A Bahia Crê, Promove, Estimula. E as Empresas Canalizam Investimentos" (Fine Chemistry: Bahia Believes, Promotes, Stimulates. And the Companies Channel Investments). The basic points of a national operational strategy to promote investments in this sector of the industry are laid out in this story [*O Globo*, p. 23, October 29, 1982]. See also "Bahia reabre discussões e mostra um Pólo Petroquímico viabilizado,"(Bahia reopens discussions and shows a viable Petrochemical Complex), *A Tarde*, Nov, 21, 1980. In the early 1980s, the governor of Bahia and the federal government jointly launched a program to stimulate investments in the production of fine chemicals such as pesticides and drugs. Guerra noted that the association among an Italian company (Liquipar), Petroquisa, and Norquisa made viable the creation of Nitroclor, that is a kind of "feedstock center" for the production of fine chemicals. See [38, p. 32].

38. Oswaldo Guerra, "O Futuro Industrial de Camaçari," *Bahia An &Dados,* CEI, 2, 3, pp. 26-36, 1992.

39. Among those industrial leaders were José Mascarenhas, president of the Industrial Federation of the State Bahia (FIEBA), one of the "founding fathers" of the complex; Cláudio Lobo Sonder, president of Hoechst in Brazil; Félix Bulhões, president of White Martins, a manufacturer of industrial gases; Edson Musa, president of Rhodia (former Rhone-Poulenc) of Brazil; and Álvaro Cunha, director of the Odebrecht group.

40. Antonio S. Guimarães and Nadya Castro, "Movimento Sindical e Formação de Classe-Elementos para Uma Discussão Teórico-Metodológica," *Caderno CRH*, no. 4, pp. 1-39, 1987.

41. Jorge Nóvoa et al., *Cronologia, Ação e Organização dos Petroquímicos Baianos 1963 -1987* (Chronology: Action and Organizing in the Petrochemical Workers of Bahia 1963-1987), Projeto "O Movimento Operário e Sindical Petroquímico da Bahia," Centro de Recursos Humanos, Universidade Federal da Bahia, Salvador, July 1989, unpublished manuscript. The "sindicato" also fought the employers in court through lawsuits, appeals, and other legal tools.

42. Guimarães noted that these young workers would meet in preparatory courses for the complex, ". . . some in college, others having just finished high school. Their aspirations were to gain autonomy from their families, earn high salaries in a technical profession, and enjoy the benefits of a privileged company" [33, p. 433].

43. One union leader I interviewed considered this to be the best Sindiquímica contract ever. This is a reasonable assessment, since management made concessions to the union under the fear of the disastrous consequences that a strike would cause in the very first year of its life. In addition, the "sindicato" was much better organized during the campaign than management, as claimed by Guimarães, who quoted the following statement from an activist: "[W]e [the union] got in 1979 more than we could handle" [33, p. 446].

44. Antonio S. Guimarães and Nadya Castro, "Classes, Regimes Fabris e Mudança Social," *Caderno CRH*, vol. 12, pp. 23-31, 1990.

45. As referred to in chapter 1, I will dwell on the contributions of Guimarães and Castro to review the history of the petrochemical working-class formation in Bahia, taking advantage of the fact that many of their studies occurred before 1988. However, these

and other authors in Bahia developed a substantial literature on class formation that is beyond the scope of this research.

46. In chapters 4, 5, and 6, Guimarães discussed in detail the factory regime of a state-owned plant in the complex. In chapter 7, he examined operators' dissatisfaction with work and resistance in the same factory. He asserted that the combination of education, skills, and political radicalism enabled this subgroup to be the avant-garde of the whole class [33].

47. In the words of Guimarães, "The shift worker has absolutely no doubt that his life will be shorter than that of other workers. This realization is especially widespread among operators and analysts" [33, p. 374].

48. The account that follows is partly based on [49]. This paper discussed the reasons for and the consequences of the complex-wide strike of 1985.

49. Antonio S. Guimarães, "Desobediência e Cidadania Operária: O Conflito Industrial em Camaçari no Ano de 1985," Diversidade e Dinâmica Regional do Sindicalismo, relatório de pesquisa, Cedec/CRH, Salvador, Bahia, unpublished manuscript, 1989.

50. Guimarães wrote that he observed the events described here personally. Jorge Nóvoa et al. also documented in detail the local press and union press coverage of the 1985 strike [41].

51. Copene employees played a major role in having the 1985 strike approved, because they encouraged rank-and-file members to vote against the opinion of the union officers and activists who wanted to settle the contract.

52. By doing this, the union was able to have enough personnel in the plants to safely shut down the different processing units.

53. In the same period that the working class took on the managerial class of the complex, Cetrel workers started to flex their muscles against management, a situation that is discussed in chapter 4.

54. Paulo César, health and safety officer of Sindiquímica, personal communication with author, June 1997.

55. Solange Oliveira, "O Dizer e o Silenciar: O Discurso do Sindiquímica nos Anos 90," unpublished monograph presented to the Graduate Course in Communication, School of Communication, Federal University of Bahia, 1995. Oliveira used the analysis-of-discourse method to understand the contents of the union newsletter *Grave* and other press materials.

56. Antonio S. Guimarães, "Repensando uma Década—A Construção da Cut na Bahia nos Anos Oitenta,"(Rethinking a Decade—The Making of Cut in Bahia in the Eighties), UFBA, CED, Bahia, 1995 [cited in 55, p. 43].

57. I owe this characterization of the first phase to Moema Gramacho, who meant that health and safety issues were hidden from workers during most of this phase. See chapter 4 for more details.

58. This conclusion was offered to me in almost every interview I conducted, with the exception of a couple of managers. Overall media coverage, newspaper articles, and company materials confirm the notion that environmental pollution has always been more visible than occupational health issues.

59. This was reported by the newspaper *Tribuna da Bahia* (Salvador, Bahia) with the following headline: "Falta de Segurança no "Pólo" Aumenta Acidentes"(Lack of Safety in the "Pólo" Increases Accidents). This newspaper was the only in Bahia (at the time) that reported on subjects considered "dangerous" or politically sensitive,

since the military regime used to censor press reports [*Tribuna da Bahia*, p. 13, February 15, 1979].

60. Fernando Paes de Andrade, former superintendent of Copene, interview by author, tape recording, Salvador, Bahia, July 1997.

61. The inferences made here are based on my interview with Paes de Andrade, July 1997, who recounted the pollution-control initiatives undertaken in this phase of the complex.

62. The company slogan during this initial phase read, "Cetrel, the environment in good hands," i.e., Cetrel should be trusted as the environmental steward of the complex.

63. Although I may be losing a bit of the meaning of the statement by translating it almost literally into English, I believe that the thrust of the secretary's view is clear. See *A Tarde* (Salvador), June, 13, 1975. This statement illustrates the state's adherence to the assimilative capacity paradigm, which assumes that "humans and ecosystems can absorb [assimilate] a certain amount of contamination without being harmed," [64, p. 3]. For a more in-depth discussion of assimilative capacity see [65, chaps. 2, 3]. Assimilative capacity is defined as "the ability of ecosystems to assimilate a substance without degrading or damaging its ecological integrity" [65, p. 31].

64. Joel Tickner, *The Networker*, The Newsletter of the Environmental Science and Health Network, vol. 3., no. 1, pp. 1-28, March 1998.

65. Tim Jackson, ed., *Clean Production Strategies: Developing Preventive Environmental Management in the Industrial Economy*, Lewis Publishers, Boca Raton, Forida, 1993.

66. Elisabeth Monosowsky, "Políticas Ambientais e Desenvolvimento no Brasil," (Environmental Policies and Development in Brazil), *Cadernos Fundap*, 9, 16, pp. 15-24, 1989 (translated from Portuguese by the author).

67. At the Stockholm conference, the Brazilian delegation opposed proposals for adopting international standards for environmental protection, because "Brazil rejected any concerted effort by countries to curb the industrial growth of developing countries," cited in [68, pp. 199-200]. As one Cetrel manager mentioned in a newspaper story in 1990, "twenty years ago, smoke coming out of smokestacks symbolized progress."

68. João Carlos Pimenta, "Multinational Corporations and Industrial Pollution Control in São Paulo, Brazil," Charles Pearson, ed., *Multinational Corporations, Environment and the Third World: Business Matters*, Duke University Press, Durham, N.C., 1987, pp. 198-220.

69. SEMA was responsible for environmental conservation and the rational use of natural resources, within the Ministry of Internal Affairs.

70. The state of S. Paulo pioneered the importation of U.S. EPA emission standards for suspended particulate matter and sulfur dioxide, which later became national standards. Pimenta noted that "virtually all standards adopted in S. Paulo are based on the U.S. Environmental Protection Agency" [68, p. 213]. Furthermore, he wrote that S. Paulo state's Environment Act was enacted in 1976, focusing almost exclusively on pollution control. As a result of the act, CETESB (Environmental Sanitation Technology Company) was created and became the most effective environmental protection agency in the country [68, p. 205].

71. Karliner pointed out that the regulation of environmental pollution "has resulted in a significant decrease of some pollution over the last thirty years in the triad of the

European Union, the United States and Japan. By forcing polluters to invest large sums of money in pollution control technology, it has also given rise to a multibillion dollar 'environmental industry' dominated by some of the world's largest corporations" (emphasis in the original) [26, p. 34].

According to Commoner, ". . . the U.S. environmental regulations were guided by a common strategy: they took effect only after pollutants were detected in the environment. Then and only then did the laws call for action. Pollution levels were determined: their ecological and health effects were evaluated; on that basis, levels of 'acceptability' were determined; emission standards designed to achieve these levels were established; and finally polluters were told to install emission controls that were supposed to meet these standards" (emphasis in the original) [72, p. v].

72. Barry Commoner, Foreword to Richard Grossman and R. Kazis, eds., *Fear at Work: Job Blackmail, Labor and the Environment*: New Society, Philadelphia, 1991.

73. Therefore, judging by the similarities, I am led to believe that Brazil imported this U.S. regulatory model and the paradigm upon which it is based.

74. Law 6,938 is the Brazilian Act. Executive Decree 88,351 regulates the application of the act through the National Environment Policy.

75. I slightly changed the translation of the Brazilian law proposed in Pimenta's text.

76. After the enactment of the new policy, environmental planning had to be done through Environmental Impact Assessments (EIAs in English, AIAs in Portuguese) and environmental zoning. In 1985 the Ministry of Urban Development and Environment was created.

77. This resolution opened a democratic channel for social participation during the decision-making process that occurs prior to state licensing or permitting of economic development projects.

78. This situation also occurs in the U.S. and other developed countries, as publicly denounced by American and European environmental justice advocates. For references on the massive literature of public participation in decision-making regarding development projects, see chapter 3 of [79].

79. Brian Clark, Ronald Bisset, and Paul Wathern, "Environmental Impact Assessment: A Bibliography with Abstracts," Mansell Publishing, London, 1980.

80. The start-up of large industrial units in the metropolitan area of Salvador (Aratu) and the federal government decision to locate the second Brazilian petrochemical complex in Camaçari were two important determinants of this state law.

81. This account of the facts is based on an interview with a former director of CRA, who has been involved with environmental management in Bahia for over twenty years, and on some of the unpublished manuscripts produced by the project "Analysis of Aspects of the Environmental Management Model of the Camaçari Petrochemical Complex." This project was funded by FINEP (a federal government agency) and carried out between 1995 and 1998 by the "Núcleo Interdisciplinar de Meio Ambiente" (NIMA)—Interdisciplinary Center for the Environment—of the Federal University of Bahia.

82. The law determined the integration of environmental values (dealing with urbanization, industrialization, and human settlements issues) into the budgeting processes of local governments; the law also laid out the conceptual guidelines for environmentally sound technology development. I based this characterization of the law on

the unpublished manuscript, "O Pólo Petroquimico e a Questão Ambiental," which was part of the project cited in [81].

83. Law 3858 also adopted, as the national decree did, a systemic approach to environmental management in the state. It included a variety of stakeholders in the implementation of environmental policies, instead of concentrating all state interventions in a single environmental agency.

84. The CRA is an autarchy under the Secretariat of Planning, Science, and Technology that implements environmental policies and coordinates, according to the directives of CEPRAM, the actions of all state secretariats. It also functions as the executive secretariat for the state council (CEPRAM), providing it with technical and administrative support.

85. It is also important to emphasize that, at the time, the Bahian civil society was not yet active in environmental issues. The argument that regulations and enforcement prevent economic freedom is also commonly used by conservative business lobbyists and ideologues in the United States. In this sense, the debate that took place in Bahia is part of the international debate on the role of government in controlling environmental pollution. For more discussion on this issue, see [26, chapter 2].

86. Hidroconsult, "Relatório de Impacto Ambiental Para a Ampliação do Complexo Petroquímico de Camaçari," June 1989, unpublished manuscript.

87. He also noted that this strategy was not risk-free due to the saturation of international markets for petrochemical commodities (such as polyethylene), and the high investments needed to create a national high-tech fine and specialty chemicals industry controlled by big multinational corporations.

88. Darwich remarked that this study neither indicated effective solutions to the environmental problems of the "Pólo," nor demonstrated the existence of enough knowledge within the state apparatus to launch the implementation of environmental protection programs in the firms [89, p. 96].

89. Luciana Darwich, "Gerenciamento Ambiental no Pólo Petroquímico de Camaçari," master's thesis, Núcleo de Pós-Graduação em Administração, Federal University of Bahia, May 1996.

90. Personal interview with Paes de Andrade, July 1997. This business leader's account of the process before the EIA/RIMA was marked by his view of the state as a bureaucracy that did not cooperate with business. Therefore, he favored changes in the state toward more cooperation with business interests.

91. Tania Franco, "Trabalho Industrial e Meio Ambiente: A Experiencia do Complexo Industrial de Camaçari/Bahia," (Industrial Work and the Environment: The experience of the Camaçari industrial complex), in George Martine, ed., *População, Meio Ambiente e Desenvolvimento: Verdades e Contradições*, Campinas: Unicamp, 1993, pp. 69-100.

92. Franco expressed a popular view of the Left in Bahia regarding the lack of state enforcement of environmental regulations, which is attributed to business power to prevent the action of CRA and other state agencies [91].

93. This summary is based on Darwich [89, pp. 92-93]. Though one should not overestimate the power of documents to effect social change, I would argue that the EIA/RIMA catalyzed the struggle that took place among industry, the state, labor, middle class professionals, and community groups to modify the environmental

management of the complex. In a word, representatives of a variety of interest groups in Bahia participated in one form or another in the debate.

94. Franco divided the discharges of industrial pollutants into the waters in three phases: In the first phase, between 1971 and 1979, the initial industries in the area discharged their untreated effluent into the Bandeira river, an affluent of the Joanes river. In the second phase, after Cetrel was built in 1979, the treated industrial effluent was discharged into the Capivara Pequeno river (affluent of the Jacuípe river), reaching the sea indirectly. A third phase started in 1992 with the implementation of the submarine outfall, when the sea became the final receptor for the treated industrial effluent. Franco charged that the outfall shifted pollution from the rivers to the sea [91, p. 82].

95. Darwich cited Asher First as the source for her conclusions [89, p. 94].

96. Examples of press coverage are seen in the headlines for the stories, "Pouco foi feito para a defesa do Jacuípe,"(Little was done to preserve the Jacuípe), "Pólo vai hoje a julgamento," ("Pólo" goes to trial today), and "População de Camaçari inquieta"(Population of Camaçari unsettled). See *A Tarde*, March 4, 1989, and August 15, 1989 (p. 2) for the first two, and *Jornal do Brasil* (Rio de Janeiro), August 13, 1989 (p. 14) for the latter. The press reports in the period enabled faculty of the Federal University of Bahia (such as Eduardo Machado and Asher First) to publicly manifest their disagreement with some of the mitigation measures proposed in the RIMA. The most controversial of those was the construction of the submarine outfall, aimed at discharging the organic and inorganic industrial effluents directly into the sea. The reports also mentioned that participants in the public hearing requested unsuccessfully that CRA postpone approval of the RIMA to allow for more public input into the decision to license the expansion of the complex.

97. "O Pólo Petroquímico de Camaçari e a Questão Ambiental"(The Camaçari Petrochemical Complex and the Environmental Question), unpublished manuscript produced by the NIMA project cited in [81].

98. Here I only comment on the parts of the plan that describe its most important points.

99. The programs stimulated by the GMA at the plant level were: Program of Environmental Management, Program of Environmental Audits, and Waste Minimization Program. The plans and projects included Air Quality Monitoring Plan, Liquid Effluents Monitoring Plan, Groundwater Monitoring Plan, Hazardous Wastes Plan, and the Technical Standardization Plan. I will go over the implementation of these plans by Cetrel in chapter 4. Volume two of the Environmental Management Plan discusses the theoretical bases of these plans, expounding on the U.S. experience with environmental pollution control for each media. In this volume it is mentioned several times that Brazil follows the U.S. EPA regulations for air, water, and hazardous wastes.

100. Corporate environmentalism was defined by Karliner as ". . . the melding of ecological and economic globalization into a coherent ideology that has paved the way for the transnationals to reconcile, in theory and rhetoric, their ubiquitous hunger for profits and growth with the stark realities of poverty and environmental destruction" [26, p. 31]. Karliner noted that the 1992 Earth Summit held in Rio de Janeiro, Brazil, marked the coming of age of corporate environmentalism [26, p. 31].

101. I am referring here to the growth of the Workers' Party at the national level, the benzene crises described in chapter 4, the popular mobilization around the Constitution of 1988, etc.

102. I created the neologism "oligopólo" to connote the concentration of capital that has occurred in Camaçari in the nineties, since the nouns that denote this process in Portuguese and English have the same Greek root, oligopólio in Portuguese and oligopoly in English. Hence, oligo-pólo, to play with the word "pólo," which is how the complex is known in Bahia.

103. According to the Brazilian Association of the Chemical Industry, the reduction in the petrochemical and chemical goods markets amounted to $1 billion by 1991 [29, p. 62]. By 1992, the complex had close to 8,000 workers in about sixty industries and produced 2 percent to 3 percent of the world's benzene production. Despite the reduction of 4 percent in the GNP and widespread bankruptcies in the country, most companies in the complex survived the crisis.

104. Vitor Lopes, "Indústria Química Brasileira: Panoramas e Perspectivas" (Brazilian Petrochemical Industry: Panorama and Perspectives), unpublished manuscript, DIEESE, Subseção Sindiquímica, Salvador, April 1996. Lopes is an economist who advises Sindiquímica on economic matters.

105. For a rich discussion on the subject, see Angela Borges and Graça Druck, "Crise Global, Terceirização e a Exclusão no Mundo do Trabalho,"(Global Crisis, Contracting Out and the Exclusion in the World of Work), *Caderno CRH,* no. 19, pp. 23-45, 1993.

106. Simultaneously, in 1990 the Brazilian government launched the "Programa Brasileiro da Qualidade e Produtividade" (Brazilian Quality and Productivity Program), which aimed at promoting quality in the economy. The program was not a government program, but a ". . . program to mobilize actors representing society (government, business, workers, and consumers), based on new role for the State—less intervening and executive and more coordinator—and on a new citizenship environment (. . .) [107, p. 119].

107. Graça Druck, "Flexibilização, Terceirização e Precarização: A Experiência dos Sindicatos," in [108, pp. 117-158].

108. Tania Franco, ed., *Caderno CRH,* "Trabalho, Riscos Industriais e Meio Ambiente: Rumo ao Desenvolvimento Sustentável?" EDUFBA, Salvador, BA, 1997.

109. "Quality and Environment" section of former Copene Web site http://www.copene. com.br/qualidade-i.html accessed August 1998 (new site: http://www.braskem.com.br).

110. Druck also noted that reduction in costs became an obsession for an entrepreneurial class that was used to protectionist policies and could not consider investment in new technologies as a choice. Besides, they had always bought technology packages from foreign countries. According to Sinper data, the employers' "sindicato," there were 14,982 permanent employees in 1989 and 6,627 by 1995. This number seems to agree with a guesstimate based on research data from Sindiquímica which suggests that about 8,260 workers were laid off between September 1990 and August 1993. Even though there may remain some doubts regarding the exact numbers, these figures show the drastic reduction in the size of workforce in the first years of the 1990s [107, pp. 132, 138].

111. In Brazil the word used for contracting out is "terceirização," a word associated with the idea that a third party (terceiro in Portuguese) would be involved in delivering services to a given employer. Therefore, the hiring party transfers responsibilities or activities to a third party. If the contractor uses a subcontractor to manage part of the contracted-out services, a fourth element is introduced, creating what Druck calls a "cascata de subcontratações (chain or cascade of subcontractors) or quarteirização (inclusion of a fourth party). Franco described the work trajectories of contractor employees as marked by a downward spiral of first losing a permanent job, then becoming a contractor worker with fewer benefits and wages [108, p. 230]. Then, after becoming a contractor worker, the worker would rotate among different contractors, being hired and fired in a vicious cycle that depended on the maintenance schedules and demands of host companies. When these workers got sick, this work history was replicated in a long journey among health clinics, because they had to go to several of them to get their perceived morbidity diagnosed and treated. To make matters worse, seldom do these clinics establish the relationship between work and disease.

112. The deterioration in working conditions described here is called "precarização" in Portuguese, a word that connotes the worse job and work conditions of contractor employees.

113. I owe this remark to Charley Richardson, an American, pro-labor, staunch TQM critic.

114. Joan Greenbaum, "The Forest and the Trees," *Monthly Review*, 46, 6, p. 62, 1994.

115. Recently, petrochemical employers sponsored a national campaign to get rid of the fifth shift, a victory of the labor movement that forces employers to expand the size of the workforce to account for shiftwork. In 1988 it became part of the new Brazilian constitution. The Odebrecht group is one of the main supporters of the elimination of this protection.

116. By the end of 1997, the Odebrecht group was responsible for over 50 percent of the net income of the Brazilian chemical industry. According to the National Confederation of Chemical Workers (CNQ), it entered the chemical sector ten years earlier by buying minority shares in private companies. Later, the corporation bought, as part of the Privatization Program, the federal government's shares in most of the companies where it had participation. Today, through the Empresas Petroquímicas do Brasil— EPB—the Odebrecht group is an oligopoly that controls all the steps in the production of thermoplastic resins, the main input for the production of pvc-based plastic products. See [117, 118].

117. Informe CNQ (Conselho Nacional dos Químicos), "Carta de Porto Alegre," no. 2, June 1997.

118. Vitor Lopes, *Grupo Odebrecht: Caracterização e Desempenho* (Odebrecht Corporation, Characterization and Performance), DIEESE, Subseção Sindiquímica Salvador, Bahia, July 16, 1996.

119. Vitor Lopes, "A Indústria Química: Retrospectiva 1995 e Perspectivas," DIEESE, Subseção Sindiquímica, Salvador, Bahia, unpublished manuscript, 1996.

120. As an economic advisor to Sindiquímica, Lopes reviewed the main trade newsletters and magazines regularly before outlining the trends and perspectives of the Brazilian petrochemical industry. Therefore, his conclusions [119] are supported

by the material provided in these publications, as I could attest after reading some of the same sources.

121. A good example of this business optimism is the prognosis offered by a director of Petroquisa, Eduardo Fonseca e Silva, who claimed that every two years a new ethylene plant needs to be built in Brazil to feed the growth of the internal market [122, p. 24].

122. Marcelo Fairbanks, *Química e Derivados*, xxxi, 334, p. 24, 1996.

123. This South American-oriented growth of the Brazilian petrochemical industry of the mid- to late nineties has shifted the geographic concentration of new investments to the South and Southeast of Brazil and away from Bahia, located in the Northeast. In turn, this modification in investment patterns is a significant shift from the decade between 1985 and 1995, when Copene absorbed most of the new venture capital [104, p. 3]. It appears that Dow Chemical, which already has a large plant in the outskirts of the complex, has also bought shares in companies in the complex recently. Rumors have it that it will broaden its participation in the complex in the future.

124. Poll results showed that Sindiquímica still exercised a strong leadership over the rank and file. As many as 82.8 percent of the workers polled read the newsletter as soon as it was distributed to them at the plant gates or in the buses. Of these, 63.6 percent rated the newsletter as good, while 88.7 percent indicated that the information in the bulletins and newsletters was reliable [55, p. 16].

125. See chapter 4.

126. While Oliveira may be right in identifying some of the causes for Sindiquímica's political mistakes, it is important to highlight here that the deck was stacked against the working class as a whole in Brazil in the early nineties, despite the particular orientations and/or experience of each "sindicato." Union communication strategies do matter, but only to a limited extent, in a period when deep structural political, economic, and ideological changes take place. In addition, the problems that petro-chemical workers faced during the restructuring of the petrochemical industry in Bahia also occurred in other developing countries and the United States. Though Sindiquímica may plausibly be accused of "childhood's malady of leftism" or political extremism, the rise of neoliberalism was a nationwide phenomenon that goes well beyond local realities. It was, in a way, a right-wing counteroffensive against progressive forces' victories in the eighties.

127. According to American union leaders I interviewed, corporate hegemony in the petrochemical industry also defeated the resistance of the Oil, Chemical, and Atomic Workers International Union (OCAW). These leaders suggested that, in the early and middle eighties, U.S. petrochemical businesses changed the traditional hegemonic factory regime into a hegemonic despotic regime as part of worldwide economic restructuring. In March 1998, I interviewed Jim Lefton, the international staff repre-sentative for OCAW in District 4, which includes Texas, and Glen Erwin, an OCAW Occupational Safety and Health Educational Coordinator (OSHEC), who has over twenty-five years of experience in the industry. According to the latter, after the national 1980 OCAW strike, the oil industry was restructured, and the workforce was dramatically downsized. As a result, OCAW local unions lost much of their political and financial power.

128. According to Druck, Sindiquímica had about 6,100 members by 1995, out of a total of 12,000 chemical and petrochemical workers in the state of Bahia (a 51 percent

unionization rate). By 1982, when the complex was in a booming period, there were around 30,000 petrochemical workers in the state [data: 107, p. 144]. See also [110] for more data on downsizing.

129. For a solid critique of these training programs, see Charley Richardson, "TQM: Tricks and Traps," unpublished manuscript, Department of Work Environment, University of Massachusetts at Lowell, 1996.

130. Observers in developed countries may notice that big similarities between these ideas and the ones that were espoused in the United States and Europe, especially the United Kingdom, during the Reagan and Thatcher period.

131. While there were around 30,000 petrochemical and chemical workers in Bahia in the booming period of the complex, in the nineties there were not more than 12,000, of whom about 6,000 were union members—a union density of about 50 percent [107, p. 144].

132. This has occurred despite the fact that they may belong to CUT and support the Workers Party, i.e., although they may have similar political perspectives. This is an overwhelming example of how neocorporatist beliefs are dividing the Brazilian labor movement.

133. This was the headline of a pamphlet the union issued during the 1992 bargaining campaign, aimed at criticizing and ridiculing employers' environmental propaganda. The pamphlet claimed that employers were more concerned with the positive image they would get by supporting ecological causes than by protecting workers on the job. To counter the complex green marketing, Sindiquímica issued a special Eco-92 (the Eco Summit of 92) newsletter headlined, "In defense of life: Against the green make-up," where the "sindicato" denounced the green propaganda of Cetrel and the complex, criticized the petrochemical companies for the environmental impact of production, and listed other serious environmental impacts caused by oil drilling and refining in the state of Bahia [in *Grave*, special edition, June 27, 1992].

134. Examples of these headlines are: "Leucopenia afasta 36 na Copene," (Leucopenia removes 36 from work at Copene), April 3, 1991; Contaminação: Vamos Dar um Basta! (Pollution: Let's Say Enough!), April 8, 1991; Saúde na Estireno: 87 atingidos (Health in Styrene [company name]: 87 affected), July, 22, 1991; Insegurança no Pólo: 4 acidentes graves em 7 dias (Lack of safety in the "Pólo": 4 serious accidents in 7 days), May 1992; Incêndio na Prochom (Fire at Prochom [company name]), June 1, 1996. These are just a sampling of the many stories covered by the union newsletter, showing that health, safety, and environmental issues have risen within the sindicato's priorities. Oliveira argued that whereas health and safety issues became a priority to union members, they were not properly addressed by the leadership in the 1991 and 1992 collective bargaining campaigns. It appears that only Moema Gramacho, the health and safety director, was *really* committed to the issue [55, p. 47].

135. Moema Gramacho has been a popular leader of petrochemical workers since the early nineties. In 1997 she took office as a state representative for the Workers Party.

136. Darwich interviewed Sindiquímica representatives in 1995 and presented this feedback in her dissertation. I interviewed Sindiquímica representatives in 1997

and got similar answers about how they perceived occupational health management in the complex in the nineties.

137. For more details on the discussion on the transfer of risks, see Tania Franco and Roseli Afonso, "Acidentes de Trabalho e Mobilidade dos Riscos Industriais na Bahia" (Occupational Accidents and Mobility of Risks in Bahia), in [108, p. 211]. This process of risk transfer appears to have occurred in the United States as well, according to the conclusions of a study conducted by the John Gray Institute of Lamar University [138]. As a result of the 1989 Phillips 66 plant explosion and fire in Texas, OSHA commissioned a study to examine the use of contract labor in the U.S. petrochemical industry. For more details on this issue, see [138].

138. John Gray Institute, "Managing Workplace Safety and Health: The Case of Contract Labor in the US Petrochemical Industry, Beaumont, Texas, Lamar University System, 1991.

139. This pessimistic scenario is based on the observations of an experienced maintenance worker with whom I talked during my bus trips to Cetrel. It is also supported by other interviews with maintenance workers conducted by Federal University of Bahia professors Tania Franco and Eduardo Machado. For an account of workers' views on work- environment hazards in the complex, see Tania Franco, and Mina Kato, "Os Riscos Ambientais e os Indivíduos," (Environmental Risks and the Individuals), in [108, pp. 215-241].

140. See [89, p. 103] for a complete list of requirements.

141. Interview with Carlos Eugenio Menezes, director-superintendent of Cetrel, *Litoral Norte* (Bahia), June 1994. Mr. Menezes was asked, "What does Cetrel mean to the petrochemical complex?" He answered with the following words: "Today, Cetrel's investment reached 200 million dollars [total investment up to 1994]. This in and of itself shows its importance. Cetrel is the firm in the complex that monitors, controls, and treats all the liquid and solid wastes generated by the Camaçari Petrochemical Complex, which is one of the largest in the world, with an investment of 6 billion dollars." Chapter 5 will further elaborate on Cetrel's ISO 14,001 certification process.

142. For example, according to information provided in Copene's former Web site [http://www. copene.com.br] (accessed August 1998), it invested in liquid industrial effluent monitoring, air emissions reductions and control, solid waste elimination, safer transportation of hazardous materials, modern firefighting equipment, and accident-prevention campaigns (new site: http://www.braskem.com.br).

143. For Karliner's definition, see [100]. Mann summarized the institutional matrix of corporate environmentalism in the following way: ". . . Corporate polluters derail environmental regulations in Congress; corporate pollution managers make lucrative deals that neither restrict polluters nor effectively clean up the toxins, government agencies set up ostensibly to protect the environment become captive to the polluters and pollution managers; and corporate boards of directors co-opt the most malleable and greedy environmentalists to clean up their image—but not their products" [144, p. 6].

144. Eric Mann, "Environmentalism in the Corporate Climate," *Tikkun*, 5, 2, pp. 60-65, 1990.

145. Asked whether Cetrel quality was comparable to American or European firms, Menezes declared that "[t]here's no doubt about that. Our job regarding safety

and environmental treatment places us on a level equivalent to any industry of American or European origin" [141].

146. These opinions were briefly presented throughout this chapter and will be further elaborated upon in chapters 5, 6, and 7. Chapter 5 will examine this controversy in the context of Cetrel's policies, which have become the avant-garde of the complex. For an excellent review of these opposite views, see [26, chapters 1, 2]. For a good summary of business views, see the interview with José de Freitas Mascarenhas, one of the "founding fathers" of the complex, in Cetrel's *BEM-TE-VI, Jornal da Cetrel*, no. 10, November 1992. For a harsh criticism of business practices in Bahia, see [91, 108].

CHAPTER 4

Benzeno à Vista (Benzene Ho!):
The Work Environment
Crises of COPEC

The international occupational safety and health community has known for some time now that benzene and organic solvents are hazardous substances that can cause serious health effects. Yet, as happened with many other chemicals, such as lead and mercury, workers and professionals in Bahia had to fight for a long time to demonstrate the relationship between negative health effects such as leucopenia and workplace exposure to benzene. This chapter will provide a historical account of the social and political struggles that ensued around benzene exposures in two important moments during the "life" of the Camaçari complex.

The first, a small crisis, occurred in Cetrel in the mid-eighties. The second crisis took place in Nitrocarbono in the early nineties, spreading to all benzene processing facilities in the complex. The adoption of the integrated petrochemical complex model with naphtha as the main feedstock for the production of base petrochemicals in the industrial area of the complex had enormous consequences for workers' exposures to benzene and other organic solvents.

Five companies in the complex process benzene to produce second-generation chemicals, while Copene, the raw material "central," produces large amounts of benzene. Ceman, the maintenance "central," does not produce or process benzene. It is responsible for the maintenance of the facilities in the complex, exposing maintenance workers during turnarounds and shutdowns. Cetrel, the industrial wastewater- treatment facility, exposed its employees to benzene, which was an industrial effluent of these companies.

The integration of benzene production and processing in the same industrial complex made sound economic sense in the seventies, justifying the importation of this notion from Japan [1-3]. However, as the two benzene stories will show, the occupational and environmental costs also increased. Thus, in Camaçari, workers may become exposed to benzene in every step of the petrochemical production process or, paraphrasing the U.S. Resource Conservation and Recycling Act (RCRA), from "cradle to grave."

Benzene is listed in most sources of information on the properties or toxic effects of hazardous materials [4]. It became one of the best studied chemicals in the world, a "star" hazard in the family of organic solvents, many of which—such as toluene and xylene—are also produced in Camaçari.

The two work environment crises described in this chapter do not tell the whole story about the occupational hazards that petrochemical workers in the "Pólo" faced in their work environments. Nevertheless, the crises clearly illustrate how benzene exposures became a "sentinel" to a much broader spectrum of chemical, physical, and safety hazards related to petrochemical production [5-7]. These benzene crises exemplify locally the historical development of the overall political economy of occupational disease in Brazil in the last 20 years. They not only show how unions perceived the adverse health effects of a toxic substance and mobilized against the working conditions that caused these exposures to occur, but also suggest the role of labor in causing legislative changes to protect workers against these conditions.

The chapter ends with the discussion of the benzene agreement, a negotiated compromise that represented a new standard-setting process in Brazil, whereby the three major players in the Brazilian corporatist tripartite regulatory environment—the state, labor, and business—built a cooperative venture to update the old benzene standard.

THE BENZENE CRISIS AT CETREL

Antecedents

Cetrel was created to treat the industrial effluents generated by the chemical companies in the complex. Before Cetrel started its treatment operations, existing companies such as Fisiba, Antarctica, and Ciquine dumped untreated wastes in the rivers around the complex. Right after the start-up of Cetrel's operations in 1978, excessive wastewater pressure burst the cement walls of the inorganic waste stream collection channels. Cetrel had to stop operating for about a year [8]. It restarted its operations in February 1979, after the civil engineering problems with the channels had been corrected. During this one-year period, raw industrial wastewater was discharged untreated into the Capivara Pequeno river.

During the first few years of operation, neither managers nor workers knew much about the hazards of operating the industrial wastewater treatment plant. In the initial employee training courses, about fifty employees—mostly operators—received training on the equipment, processes, and units they would operate. Some of them demonstrated curiosity and concern with potential exposures to carcinogens and other toxic chemicals that would be treated in the plant. But the training curriculum did not address chemical hazards in detail. Trainees would sporadically talk about or ask a question about potential job exposures to chemicals and work-related illnesses during the training, but they would not get clear answers. Neither did they get any written information about chemical hazards related to their jobs.

Roughly between 1978 and 1984, Cetrel operators and staff faced the uphill moments of the "learning curve" of plant operations. This rather young (most workers were in their twenties) and new workforce wanted the company to succeed in its operations, and made their best efforts, sometimes involving strong physical exertion, toward this goal.

The labor-management relationship tended to follow local cultural traditions and ideology, which pretended that all employees belonged to the "Cetrel family" [9, 10]. Company employees—formally called collaborators—played soccer and had picnics and leisure activities on weekends in a friendly atmosphere. During this initial period, employees could take home vegetables and fruits cultivated on the company grounds as an indirect, in-kind employee benefit. In this non-unionized company with few employees, camaraderie developed along the lines of cooperation and collaboration between labor and management. Employees and managers felt that the correct and optimal operation of the company was their common challenge. Employees also found it difficult to interact with other groups outside of Cetrel due to the company's shift schedules and modus operandi—workers were bused daily between their residences and Cetrel in an almost two-hour-long drive each way—without much time left for social activities [11, 12].

In spite of this common goal, not everything was peaceful and quiet. The first internal independent organizing actions taken by employees revolved around the issue of making job descriptions and classifications similar to those of other petrochemical companies in the complex. Cetrel had a different system that tended to reduce wages; for example, the operators found out that their salaries were almost ten times lower than the salaries received by other operators in the "Pólo." The Internal Committee for the Prevention of Accidents (CIPA) once tried to do something about the bad wastewater odors, but its chair was fired by the company, even though she represented management on the committee.

The Production of Disease

One of the important ways in which workers were exposed to chemicals occurred during their lunch and rest breaks. In addition to being exposed to organic chemicals when routinely collecting raw wastewater samples for laboratory analyses, and doing maintenance on machines and pumps, employees used to smell the odor of these chemicals in the air throughout the plant. Some of them suspected—out of pure common sense—that they might get sick in the future if that "cheiro" (odor) continued.

Many employees also were exposed to chemical vapors by walking around the aeration and settling tanks during lunch and breaks, or strolling around the tree-covered and pleasant company grounds. Administrative offices were located close to the tanks, allowing vapors to be smelled inside the offices. Employees would also smell organic chemical odors when prevailing winds changed direction throughout the shift.

A former Cetrel operator was exposed to benzene when he sampled and inspected emergency releases in benzene-processing companies. He recalls that once, after an accidental release, he had to wait for about a half-hour outside the gates of a plant and had to argue with the plant manager to be allowed into the plant to inspect its effluent.

Cetrel operators would normally inspect facilities in the complex in emergency situations, on weekends, and after 5:00 P.M., while Cetrel personnel from the effluent-control department would routinely check the effluents of these companies. Occasionally employees working in lift stations would be exposed to such high levels of toxic chemical vapors that they had to leave their work area, because they could not endure the acute symptoms caused by these vapors.

Personal protective equipment use was minimal and not supervised. Emergency response training was very poor. Confined space entries were highly unsafe. There were no standard operating procedures addressing the repair of pumps in confined underwater spaces—the confined spaces located inside wastewater tanks. Health and safety awareness was limited to conversations with peers about safety, electrical hazards, and accidents. Cetrel management did not seem to care much about the health and safety of its employees either. Moreover, in those times, the overall societal and employee health and safety knowledge and awareness were poor.

Nevertheless, during the first six to seven years (1979-1986) of Cetrel's almost 20 years of operation, the company became an example of good environmental management in Brazil. The politically controlled and censored press would portray the Camaçari petrochemical complex as a "clean petrochemical complex" that produced chemicals without harming the environment [13]. During the eighties Cetrel became a showcase for proactive pollution-control technology. Based on this reputation, a group of federal representatives from Rio Grande do Sul, where the next Brazilian petrochemical complex was built, visited Cetrel to learn about the good technology and management practices adopted.

This clean image held true until 1984, when some employees started noticing adverse health effects. Female employees started to suddenly faint without clear reasons or explanations. An informal company organizing committee composed of twelve employees tried to address its concerns with management. Management came up a with a sexist explanation to the committee's concerns. It claimed that the fainting was not a problem, because "women usually faint anyway" [14]. Using this rather sexist argument, Cetrel management dismissed the problem. Since the committee was unofficial, inexperienced, politically weak, and lacked alternatives, it had to swallow management's insensitivity without further action.

Shortly after, otherwise healthy and physically fit male employees also started to faint. The committee revisited the problem with management. The committee finally persuaded management, which authorized it to find competent professionals to investigate the source of the sickness. Interestingly enough, some committee members had already made—behind the scenes—their own informal contacts with professionals from the regional office of Fundacentro [15]. When management agreed with the committee about the need to investigate the origins of the employees' signs and symptoms, the stage had already been set.

The Fundacentro Health Hazard Evaluation: The Role of the Middle Class Expert in the Cetrel Work Environment Conflict

The scientific validation of workers' perception of the relationship between exposures to chemical hazards and adverse health effects came with the 1985 Fundacentro report. Fundacentro staff was called to perform a health-hazard evaluation (HHE) of Cetrel's work environment. At the time their experience in doing workplace inspections was minimal [16]. The team was new to the technical field of work-environment assessment and to the institution. Initially, these professionals did not want to carry out the HHE, because they felt that they did not have enough experience to conduct such a detailed study.

After consulting with more experienced staff from São Paulo, they came to the conclusion that it would actually be very difficult to assess workplace risks in Cetrel. On the one hand, little knowledge existed in Brazil about risks related to work in an industrial wastewater treatment facility. On the other, Cetrel received poorly identified and monitored liquid organic chemical wastes from the petrochemical complex, making the selection of chemicals to be sampled quite nonspecific. Despite their concerns, Fundacentro management assigned the work to them.

According to Fundacentro staff, Cetrel did not have any exposure-monitoring system, nor any written health and safety and industrial hygiene programs or policies. Employees told them that workers had fallen into settling tanks when trying to do maintenance work. Biological hazards were not controlled. Confirming the account of the employees, they also found Cetrel administrative offices to be located too close to the wastewater aeration and settling tanks. Cetrel was so poorly organized and managed that it became self-evident even to these young professionals that the company did not control any of the potentially hazardous exposures in the work environment. One of them classified Cetrel as a "chaos" regarding health and safety matters [17]. In short, they found Cetrel to be a real "mess" as far as health and safety issues were concerned.

The year-long HHE collected mainly qualitative data during walkarounds and field observations. The Fundacentro team did area sampling and monitoring for noise, lighting, and organic vapors, using somewhat inadequate monitoring equipment, such as Dräger tubes to measure organic vapors. They reviewed company medical records, searching for clinical evidence of exposures to organic chemicals, such as leucopenia and other clinical disorders. The HHE final report is divided into four sections. Section I is the introduction; section II addresses safety; section III addresses industrial hygiene; and section IV addresses occupational medicine. The most important findings of the HHE report are discussed in the Industrial Hygiene section [18]:

a) Noise levels were above Brazilian legal limits (similar to the U.S. ACGIH TLV levels of 85 dB/8 hour work shift) in the maintenance shop, in welding operations, and in control room # 4. The operator(s) used to sit inside the control room close to four noisy motors. The report considered this situation the most critical in Cetrel and recommended a variety of engineering controls and/or changes in work practices to reduce exposures and abate excessive noise levels.

b) Lighting of some workstations at the mechanical shop, at welding stations, and at the warehouse was found not to be in compliance with Brazilian regulations. The report also gave some recommendations to management on how to fix the inappropriate lighting.

c) Toluene and benzene concentrations were above Brazilian legal limits in some sampling stations for organic wastewater streams originating in petrochemical companies, such as Ciquine, Nitrocarbono, Estireno, etc. Some lift stations also had levels of these gases above Brazilian limits. A few sampling stations had very poor hygiene conditions, with strong foul odors and accumulation of sludge and garbage on the ground.

Investigators found high hydrogen sulfide levels in the pilot plant during the process of mercury and silver recovery from residues of the chemical oxygen demand test. In the chemical landfills employees were exposed to chemical vapors and aerosols without proper respiratory protection. Moreover, employees would use hammers and mattocks to unload solid hazardous waste from the drums, creating the potential for exposure to hazardous dust.

The report stated that the air sampling findings could not be conclusive regarding organic chemicals' concentration levels because maintenance turnaround, plant shutdowns, and equipment failures could potentially expose workers to high levels of hazardous chemicals. The report also provided management with information regarding alternative engineering controls and suggested changes in work practices to control exposures.

About 62 workers were found to have low white blood cell counts (below 5,000/mm^3 for total leukocytes or below 2,500/mm^3 for neutrophiles). Initially, a total of 22 workers were removed from work due to "benzenism." Additional clinical and epidemiological investigation concluded that twelve more workers could have developed leucopenia as a result of overexposure to benzene. The investigation of the suspected cases of work-related leucopenia turned into a political issue when Cetrel management decided to halt the continuation of the HHE, because it was revealing uncomfortable facts and exposing the company to obvious political and financial burdens [19].

After the industrial hygiene and the safety parts of the HHE had already ended, Fundacentro staff were told by their director that the study must not proceed. The medical staff of Fundacentro finished their incomplete medical evaluation report by recommending that Cetrel follow the case-management protocol for occupational leucopenia developed in São Paulo to tackle the problem of leucopenia in steel workers.

Disagreeing with management's authoritarian decision to stop the investigation, some Fundacentro staff refused to sign the final report. An internal political gridlock developed. The staff wanted political transparency regarding their findings, i.e., that their findings be communicated without political interference, but their views were not respected. Fundacentro ended up never officially issuing the report, which was kept in the director's office. The released version of the report was never signed by the authors. As indicated by Cetrel management's reaction to the partial report conclusions, Fundacentro's final report was kept hidden from Cetrel employees. The company doctor got a copy of the HHE report and hid it in his office (he was ironically nicknamed "Dr. Aspirin" by the workers in recognition of his expertise and "care" for the well-being of the employees, because he would prescribe aspirin for any kind of health complaints).

By now the members of the Internal Committee for the Prevention of Accidents strongly suspected that there was a toxic chemical exposure problem in Cetrel. They saw the Fundacentro staff do their work, but did not hear anything about the results of the health hazard evaluation for almost a year. An activist member of the CIPA received, in 1986, a confidential phone call from a technical member of the staff of Fundacentro, who told him that the HHE had found health problems in some workers. He was also told that the director of Fundacentro had not allowed the report to be written the way the technical staff wanted, and that there had been political censorship of the report conclusions. A day after hearing about it, the activist mobilized the organizing committee to ask management for the HHE report. Management denied the existence of any important health findings in it. During 1986, the committee spread the word within Cetrel, without identifying the source of the information, that the HHE study had clearly found high exposures to toxic chemicals in Cetrel's work environment.

Meanwhile, the state water and sewage utility workers, who worked for Embasa, were trying to change their employee association into a water and sewage workers union, Sindae [20]. Cetrel workers had been contacted and asked to join them. Cetrel employees had been unhappy about wages, working conditions, and health and safety issues. By now they were actively trying to organize their own "sindicato." They also included the release of the Fundacentro report as one of the main items of their organizing agenda.

After deciding to join Sindae, they elected one officer and one substitute in the first union slate. No sooner had Sindae been legally formed than Cetrel employees went on a strike that lasted for twenty-two days. They mainly wanted the same job classifications and salaries as other employees of the complex had. About 95 percent of the workers supported the strike.

The strike was victorious and ended with the signing of the first contract with the company, which called for the company to communicate the results of the report to all the employees. Yet, the workers decided to go on strike again in 1987 to enforce the contract in two areas: 1) the job classification and wages plan, and 2) the release of the Fundacentro report to the union.

The communication of the report findings to the employees became a difficult issue in the negotiations with management. The report was delivered to Cetrel's union representatives only after the local media had access to the results of the HHE study, and the intervention of the DRT (the regional office of the Labor Ministry) and CRA (the state environmental agency).

Cetrel management ended up recognizing the existence of health problems within the company. Cetrel employees also reacted with outrage when they discovered that the company physician had known the report results long before they did. Later in 1987 Fundacentro staff were invited to Cetrel to explain the meaning of the HHE results to the employees, who could not easily understand the technical-scientific language of the report. Sindae also searched for expert advice from other health professionals who worked with Sindiquímica.

From 1978 to 1987 the work environment conditions in Cetrel remained essentially the same. Fundacentro's report was the first and foremost piece of evidence to unravel the relationship between chemical exposures and health symptoms. This evidence allowed the employees to push for changes in safety and health conditions in the following years. As a consequence of this crisis, Sindae hired a part-time occupational health physician to implement a health-and-safety program for the whole union, started to agitate for an independent health-and-safety committee at Cetrel (in opposition to CIPA), and negotiated with Cetrel some job security and extra compensation for disabled workers. During 1988 and 1989, taking advantage of improved access to Cetrel workers, Sindae administered an employee survey to get feedback regarding health-and-safety conditions. Sindae used the data to denounce the poor work-environment conditions in Cetrel. Through these and other actions, the union gained political strength and increased employee control of workplace conditions, as expressed in the democratic election of all members of the group now called the "health committee" [21, p. 2].

Cetrel slowly responded to Sindae's pressure with partial wastewater treatment process changes, implementation of engineering controls, and environmental monitoring and training programs. On the other hand, Cetrel also countered the increasing union power by firing union activists and disabled workers.

Sindae gained political ground from the beginning of the benzene crisis in 1985 until 1991, when the situation started to change dramatically after the privatization of Cetrel. Job stability ended. Contracting out of workers expanded. Union access to the workplace became more and more difficult. In the words of a key union activist, the political conjuncture that developed during and after the privatization period allowed Cetrel to replace "old blood with new blood," regain power, and reestablish its control over the employees. Sindae lost not only political support in the company but also its ability to organize the rank and file to demand health-and-safety improvements. A relatively favorable situation for union activity quickly turned into a very adverse one.

The benzene crisis in Cetrel ignited locally an underlying problem that had permeated work environment struggles in Brazil for a long time—the workers' compensation issue. Given the fact that the Brazilian workers' compensation law classifies work-related leucopenia as a reason for temporary disability, Cetrel employees with leucopenia had to bear the brunt of the social stigma associated with disability. The stigma of benzene-related disability became such a controversial and tension-laden issue in Bahia that a local media outlet once called leucopenia the "AIDS of industry" after interviewing one disabled worker [22].

To address these social tensions, Cetrel's leucopenic workers formed an association. Their families also formed a social support group that received psychological care and therapy from social workers of the National Institute of Social Welfare (INPS). Some of these disabled workers were transferred temporarily to Embasa, as part of a two-year agreement between Cetrel, Embasa, and INPS. After the second year of the agreement (1989), Cetrel employees returned to Cetrel and were laid off, sometimes collecting a relatively good severance lump sum to restart their lives.

THE "OPERAÇÃO CAÇA BENZENO: LET'S TAKE THIS GHOST OFF THE AIR"

Historical Context

The history of Sindiquímica is a history of struggles and confrontation of workers with employers. Employers tried to divide the petrochemical workers' union by creating a parallel association to represent exclusively chemical workers, as referred to in chapter 3. The chemical workers resisted and organized their own association—Associação Proquímicos, which later became a union—Sindicato Proquímicos. This union finally merged with Sindiquímica to form a unified petrochemical and chemical workers' union in 1989, bringing to the unified Sindiquímica the person who would lead the health and safety issues for the union throughout the next ten years. Her name is Moema Gramacho.

Moema started dealing with health and safety in 1987, when she was elected a union officer of the "Sindicato Proquímicos." Her "transition" term lasted only a year, because all union officers resigned before the merger with Sindiquímica. Besides being a biologist by training, she fit well into the traditional union practice of assigning health and safety responsibilities to "rookies." She was the natural candidate to deal with health and safety problems. Over the years her comrades ironically nicknamed her "Saúde" (health, in Portuguese), due to her long-term persistence in trying to convince them that health and safety matters should become a very important subject for the union.

According to Moema, the history of health and safety in the Camaçari Petrochemical Complex had several phases. The period between 1978 and 1986 may be described as "the silent walls period" [23]. Her description is very similar to the description offered above for Cetrel. Petrochemical workers did not know much about chemical hazards, management did not inform workers about the hazards, nor did the union have access to information on chemical hazards. The complex propaganda alleged that it provided the best job conditions in the area; it was the largest industrial complex in South America; it meant needed progress and modernization to Bahia and Brazil, and that working there was good for everybody (see [13]).

While much stronger as a trade union than Sindae, Sindiquímica also had a weak internal structure to deal with health and safety issues during this initial period. In 1986, some union officers participated in the Eighth Brazilian National Health Conference, where they met many of the leaders of the Brazilian Public Health movement [24]. This national movement was discussing a new national health agenda for the Brazilian transition to a civilian democratic government after twenty-one years of military dictatorship.

The trade union leadership from Bahia learned about health and safety topics in the conference by interacting with local and national occupational health professionals, in particular some progressive occupational physicians from Bahia. One of them later became a health and safety advisor to Sindiquímica. After participating in the conference, Moema better understood the potential adverse health effects of petrochemical production and searched more aggressively for cases of occupational illnesses and workplace hazards in the plants.

She also realized the extent of underdiagnosis of occupational diseases in the state—an average of only ten cases had been officially diagnosed before 1986. These Bahian doctors told her that they worked under severe pressure in public clinics and hospitals not to diagnose occupational diseases, especially · when they affected a worker from the complex.

The first issue of the joint Sindiquímica/Proquímicos newsletter to focus on health issues dates from August 1986 and has the following headline: "Doenças do Pólo" (Diseases of the complex). This newsletter issue included a general discussion about the hazards of chemical and petrochemical work, the common occupational illnesses associated with it, the poverty of the Camaçari community, and an interview with the secretary of the environment for the city of Salvador [25, pp. 1-6].

Sindiquímica did not get much media coverage, unless occupational fatalities, accidents, or major incidents happened. When those injuries and fatalities occurred, union officers critiqued the companies' role in creating them and disputed employers' accounts of the facts, but only sporadically would they succeed in getting the media's attention. The "sindicato" would also complain to management about health and safety problems after the incidents, but it had little success in solving the problems brought to its attention by the members. In general, management would not only ignore these concerns but also "hide them under the carpet" [23].

The hegemonic safety ideology and culture promoted safety campaigns and programs as tools to achieve the safety goal of zero workplace accidents; all of these tools aimed at motivating employees to compete for accident reduction. Different sections in a given plant would compete for rewards based on their annual safety records. Sections with lower injury and accident numbers would be recognized and get rewards, the so-called "safety bingo" culture. The workers who had accident-free work histories would have better chances of promotions and receive some prize, as well as public recognition as exemplary workers during the Semana Interna de Prevenção de Acidentes do Trabalho (SIPAT)—Internal Week to Prevent Occupational Accidents [26].

The effect of these campaigns was that employees would not report injuries or incidents to avoid compromising the section's or company's accident record. This employer-friendly ideology would also claim that the accidents had happened as a consequence of particular cases of negligence or incompetence of individuals who had to be punished, the so-called "blame the victim" ideology [27, 28].

The main economic issues on the union bargaining agenda for the yearly contract negotiations were the recovery of wage losses to inflation and job stability. Union officers offered much political resistance toward including health and safety issues as main topics on the bargaining agenda. The health and safety items on the agenda were the reduction in hours of work, hazardous-duty pay, the creation of a Joint Toxicology Committee, the construction of an emergency care hospital to prevent and treat chemical poisoning; and the prevention and control of workplace accidents, chemical leaks, and spills, especially during plant construction and start-up [29].

This situation started to change after the formation, in January 1987, of the health and safety committee of the Central Única dos Trabalhadores (CUT, see chapter 3) in Bahia. This committee was created to unify the struggles of labor-friendly professionals and CUT-affiliated labor leaders—similar to the U.S. Committees/Coalitions for Occupational Safety and Health (COSH) of the AFL-CIO. It was composed of health professionals, such as occupational physicians who worked for the DRT or the INSS, nurses, nutritionists who worked in the complex, and other politically active professionals. A few union activists from Sindae and Sindiquímica also participated.

The committee sponsored the first Workers' Health Conference in Bahia to promote scientific and political discussions among union activists, professionals, and rank-and-file workers [30]. The CUT committee members realized that trade unions in the state needed to join efforts to increase their political power. They decided to concentrate their struggle on the occupational health problems that existed in the Camaçari petrochemical complex because it was the largest industrial concentration in the state.

The committee was instrumental in the creation of the Programa de Saúde do Trabalhador—Workers'Health Program (PROSAT)—which originated the CESAT in 1988, under the state of Bahia Health Department [31]. CESAT was a landmark in the effort to correctly diagnose and treat occupational health illnesses. In its first year of operation this clinic diagnosed about 250 cases of occupational disease, which grew to more than 800 per year in subsequent years.

The media also started to pay attention to the actions of the committee, which now had scientific backing for its claims and was perceived as more independent of labor-management conflicts. Before that, many journalists had seen it as a "sindicato" arm against employers in the complex. The CUT health and safety committee gained credibility and respectability. The committee advocated for the democratization of the CIPAs through their transformation into health committees elected by the rank and file without management interference; it advised many unions in the creation of health and safety departments, and it formulated a statewide health and safety agenda for the labor movement in Bahia. In sum, the CUT committee organically united and directed the actions of labor and occupational health professionals in Bahia [32, 33].

From the beginning Sindiquímica had a progressive view of occupational medicine practice. Physicians hired by the union as staff or advisors never focused exclusively on clinically oriented occupational medicine practice. The pro-worker, public health-oriented medical staff always looked for the relationship between workers' illnesses and injuries and work-environment conditions [34]. In the first three years of the "sindicato's" occupational health services (1987-1989), a total of about 500 people sought medical assistance from the service, 90 percent of them laid-off workers. By talking to the workers who came to the union office, the medical staff was able to make an indirect "diagnosis" of the workplaces in the complex [35].

Although, legally, employers have to inform workers about the results of preemployment or periodic medical exams performed in the companies [36], the trade union had only limited access to this information and could not actively search for information about cases or workplace exposures. Up to that point union leaders and staff worried mostly about serious sequelae of workplace injuries.

As detailed in chapter 3, in the late eighties the complex started laying off a large number of workers [37]. Some of the politically aware laid-off members would come to the union office bringing with them results of blood exams that showed low white blood-cell counts. About twenty-five to thirty laid-off workers from Nitroclor had low counts of white blood cells, constituting the first company represented by Sindiquímica where leucopenia had emerged as a big health problem. The prior discovery of cases of leucopenia in Cetrel had also alerted

Moema to this problem, since both situations had happened within a short time frame.

Sindiquímica tried unsuccessfully to push the DRT to investigate these cases. In spite of the lack of cooperation from state agencies, the union would commonly get information about work conditions in the plants through workers who would talk about their workplace conditions to the union staff. This mechanism was the only source of reliable information the union had. Shortly before the death of the Nitrocarbono physician [mentioned below], the "sindicato" had also criticized company physicians for not reporting workplace accidents and illnesses data (the CATs), as required by the Brazilian law [38]. Neither the union nor individual workers had access to this important source information.

In short, during the first phase of the development of health and safety in the union (in the 1980s), neither the union members nor the leadership were fully aware of the health problems in gestation within the plants. As Levenstein and Tuminaro suggested, the first decade of operation of the complex may be characterized as the years of production of disease [39]. Neither labor nor management had clearly recognized the hazards of petrochemical production. An overt social struggle around health and safety issues arose only when these two main actors recognized their own class interests and acted to defend them. That's exactly what the benzene crisis discussed below brought about.

The Nitrocarbono Crisis and the "Operação Caça Benzeno" Campaign

The pivot for the second benzene crisis was the death of two employees of Nitrocarbono in a three-month period. Nitrocarbono is a benzene-processing company that uses benzene for the production of caprolactam [40]. The Nitrocarbono occupational physician, Dr. Armando Sobrinho, died on July 6, 1990, and an operator, Antonio Lázaro de Freitas, died October 22, 1990. After the physician died, it appears that the attention given to benzene exposures increased dramatically.

According to the death certificates, the physician died of aplastic anemia, and the operator, of chronic myeloid leukemia. In the period between these deaths Sindiquímica wrote a letter to the DRT, in which it announced the possibility of other fatalities in Nitrocarbono due to high exposures to benzene [23]. When the second death occurred, the union gained so much credibility with the public that it became a legitimate and decisive actor in the crisis that broke out. Previous labor union claims became legitimized by the second death. Sindiquímica could no longer be accused of creating agitation or political propaganda, since it had been able to practically forecast the second death. Labor access to the media became easy. The deaths drew national headlines [41].

The "sindicato" took advantage of this favorable conjuncture to suggest that the raw materials producer (Copene), all benzene-processing plants in the complex

(Nitrocarbono, Nitroclor, Estireno, Ciquine), and the complex maintenance center (Ceman) could also have cases of leucopenia. The "sindicato" petitioned the DRT to investigate the fatalities and mobilized Nitrocarbono employees [42]. The DRT inspected Nitrocarbono and found more workers with low white blood-cell counts, which was the hematological thermometer for the crisis [43]. Yet, the employees did not know who was affected. The union demanded that the DRT remove affected workers from the job and inspect all companies in the complex that processed benzene to identify all the cases suspected of leucopenia. The union also contacted the Ministries of Labor and Health and requested their intervention in the crisis.

From the outset the Nitrocarbono management refused to admit that the two deaths were work-related and that employees might be affected by leucopenia. Nitrocarbono initially denied any exposures to benzene [44]. Union and governmental political pressure was aimed at shutting down Nitrocarbono, which changed its position during the process to admit that there might have been exposures to benzene there. Nitrocarbono employees had to go on strike for one day on October 30 to force the removal from work of all suspected cases. To persuade the technical staff of the Ministries of Labor and Health in Brasília to intervene, the union sent them some pictures showing visible corrosion of storage tanks at the Nitrocarbono plant, suggesting that leaks and spills could potentially occur [45].

The DRT inspected the facility in November 1990 and reported that among the white blood-cell tests assessed, there were two cases of leucopenia that required immediate removal from work (less than 4,000 white blood cells/ml of blood), and nineteen cases that should be considered "warning" cases (between 4,000 and 5,000 white blood cells/ml of blood) [46]. The report concluded that the health of Nitrocarbono workers was seriously threatened by an outbreak of leucopenia in the company.

Politically favorable conditions at the state level allowed state institutions such as CESAT to intervene in the crisis [47]. CESAT and Fundacentro worked together to investigate the situation in Nitrocarbono. CESAT conducted the medical and Fundacentro the industrial hygiene part of the investigation. Shortly after, Nitrocarbono reached a compromise with the union and agreed that a committee to assess the work environment be formed. The committee would be composed of four elected members who would have job stability for one year—the period agreed upon by both parties as necessary to perform the assessment [48].

Reacting to the crisis, the Brazilian president sent the ministers of Health, Labor, and Science and Technology in November 1990 to visit Bahia and come up with solutions. The ministers visited the area and publicly promised about $1 million in public funds to finance a massive program of occupational health surveillance in the complex, starting with the "hematological mapping" of all workers in the complex. They also declared that Nitrocarbono was not the only company where there were cases of leucopenia [49]. This cabinet-level response turned the benzene crisis into an officially recognized public crisis, whose impact went well beyond the initial target, Nitrocarbono.

A major source of contention between labor and management revolved around what to do with Nitrocarbono. The major debate question was: "Should Nitrocarbono be shut down immediately or not?" Sindiquímica and some government agencies, such as the DRT, advocated this course of action to prevent further cases. The federal government seriously considered this option [50]. Nitrocarbono management resisted. To solve the gridlock, a negotiated anticipation of the regular maintenance turnaround of Nitrocarbono took place instead of a mandatory shutdown.

The money promised by the federal government never appeared. The union put more pressure on the DRT to inspect all five facilities in the complex that handled benzene. The DRT inspectors who were labor friendly were finally "allowed" to inspect these facilities. Sindiquímica's prior experience with Nitroclor became public. Access to Copene, a company that used to be very secretive, was granted. As Table 1 shows, a true epidemic of leucopenia was unveiled.

During the same period, the national CUT leadership contacts with the progressive General Confederation of Italian Workers (CGIL in Italian) resulted in the launching of the CUT-affiliated Instituto Nacional de Saúde no Trabalho, the INST (National Institute for Workers Health) [51]. The first national campaign sponsored by the INST was the "Caça Benzeno" campaign, which entailed a large public campaign to educate workers who were potentially exposed to benzene all over Brazil.

Table 1. Suspected Cases of Leucopenia According to the Criteria of INPS Decree 01/86[a]

Company	Examined workers	Cases of leucopenia	Percent
Copene	1600	133	8.31
Ceman (Copene)	600	122	20.33
Ciquine	816	85	10.42
Nitroclor	444	80	18.02
Estireno	617	29	4.70
Nitrocarbono	442	23	5.2
Total	4519	472	10.45

[a]According to blood tests performed by the Division of Workplace Health and Safety of DRT in four companies and the tests performed by Copene and Nitrocarbono.
Source: Grave, Ano IX, No. 295, January 28, 1991, p. 1.

The campaign was inaugurated in Salvador, Bahia, in July 1991, the epicenter of the benzene crisis. However, before the crisis erupted in Bahia, over 1,000 workers of COSIPA (a large state-owned steel mill located in the state of São Paulo) had already been diagnosed with leucopenia and removed from their jobs [50, p. 3]. An association of disabled workers had already been organized there to represent the interests of disabled workers.

Sindiquímica, Sindae, Sindipetro, and the Metalworkers Union organized the "Operação Caça Benzeno" in Bahia. The campaign activities included a media campaign composed of radio, television, and newspaper interviews and ads; billboards around the state capital and the petrochemical complex; rallies at the gates of the main plants in the complex; pamphlets, fact sheets, stickers, and posters about the campaign (distributed in several states of Brazil); a professional video titled, "A Maldição do Benzeno" (The Benzene Evil), shown in union halls, neighborhood associations, and at the gates of the plants; and lectures given by the unions' occupational physicians.

The campaign logo and theme were adapted from the movie, *Ghostbusters*, very popular at the time. The campaign portrayed benzene as a bad ghost that had to be chased from the complex by rank-and-file action. Sindiquímica and CUT launched the campaign nationally in Salvador on July 3, 1991. This health and safety campaign was professionally designed and had a wide repercussion in the country. It soon turned into the largest labor-driven health and safety campaign ever in Brazil.

Moema believes that the change in behavior noticed in the employers, as well as the inclusion of many health and safety demands in Sindiquímica's bargaining agenda, was due to the success of this campaign. Oliveira wrote that the union press was effective in publicizing the crisis [52]. COFIC also polled the public after the campaign to assess how to deal with the employers' tainted image [53, 54]. Sindiquímica's systematic efforts of denouncing benzene exposures in the work environments of the complex appear to have worked to create this negative image in the eyes of the public.

Before this labor campaign, employers had been united against the union. Only a small group of company physicians would discuss health and safety problems with the union. When the media headlines successfully exposed the poor work-environment conditions in the complex, employers could not continue to claim that petrochemical production did not pollute the environment and was harmless to employees. They changed their strategy. They started to compete with labor for public support. A battle for the hearts and minds of the public developed during the campaign. As mentioned above, the unions used the *Ghostbusters* motif to popularize the idea that employees should hunt the "benzene ghost" off the air to eliminate exposures in the facilities of the complex. To counter labor's message, the largest employer of the complex hired advertising agencies to design billboards that portrayed its employees hunting benzene in the facility because of a company initiative.

The union coalition held employers responsible for the benzene exposures and demanded that they take action to control them. Employers countered that it was everybody's responsibility to control the problem, including the workers themselves. Only after overwhelming evidence made it clear that petrochemical workplaces caused disease and even death to petrochemical workers, did the employers propose that a study be performed by a neutral party to scientifically determine the causal link between exposures to benzene and adverse health effects. Sindiquímica rejected the proposal on the grounds that it was well-known within the international scientific community that benzene is a carcinogen that adversely affects the bone marrow. No more studies were necessary, they argued, to prove the causal link between benzene exposure and leucopenia, leukemia, or other cancers.

In 1991 the employers' "sindicato," Sinper, commissioned the Fundação José Silveira (FJS) to conduct epidemiology, toxicology, and industrial hygiene studies to investigate the relationship between benzene exposures and hemato-logic disorders in the complex. The overall objective of the studies was: "[t]o assess the occupational benzene exposures problem and their hemotoxic effects in workers of the Camaçari petrochemical complex—Bahia" [55, p. 1.11]. The FJS carried out three epidemiology studies: the first and most important was a nonconcurrent (or retrospective) cohort study; the second was a survival analysis study of the hematological parameters of the same cohort; and the third was a transversal study to compare the "hematological profiles" of exposed with nonexposed workers.

The industrial hygiene part of the investigation was weak, because it did not collect field environmental monitoring data. Investigators reported that during the walkaround in the facilities they noticed improper use of respirators and incorrect monitoring activities. Their report omitted existing data regarding benzene emissions that the companies themselves had collected for safety reasons. Besides, Fundacentro had also had access to some company data that showed benzene emissions of hundreds of parts per million. The report did not even mention it [56, 57]. In spite of its weaknesses, the industrial hygiene report concluded that there had been benzene leaks, spills, and overexposure in the past, as evidenced in some company operational records.

The Fundação José Silveira Benzene Studies

The most debated study was the nonconcurrent, or retrospective, cohort study, which evaluated the risk of severe hematologic diseases in workers exposed to benzene in the petrochemical complex between 1980 and 1991 [58]. The researchers collected data from medical records of the companies and through specially designed standard data collection forms. They also collected pertinent data on hemograms, bone-marrow biopsies, diagnoses of blood disorders, and other chronic pathologies associated with the use of medications that may influence the hematopoietic system. Death certificates were checked for cancer deaths in Salvador.

The study population comprised 17,453 workers; 13,100 of these worked or had worked in companies that produced or processed benzene, while 4,353 had not. Workers who worked in benzene processing companies were classified as exposed and compared to workers of two companies that did not handle benzene, who were classified as nonexposed. The study identified nine cases of diseases: three cases of leukemia, three cases of lymphomas, two cases of multiple myelomas, and one case of aplastic anaemia. Seven of this total worked in benzene-processing plants (exposed cases), while two did not (nonexposed cases). Although the study results are not statistically significant, they point to a greater risk of occurrences of blood disorders among the exposed workers [59]. In this cohort, the maximum benzene exposure time was eleven years and the mean exposure time was 4.38 years, which are less than the length of exposure needed for risk levels to reach the maximum [60, 61].

The study took about a year to finish and was allegedly done within acceptable scientific standards, according to local experts in the field and some of the investigators, who had academic appointments in federal Brazilian universities [62]. However, it appears that neither Sindiquímica nor progressive occupational professionals accepted the study results as legitimate, claiming that it was commissioned by employers to dismiss the existence of benzene-related problems in the complex [63]. Thus, the report was ignored by these two important stakeholders.

Many reasons could explain labor's reaction to the study. First, the struggle against the employers concentrated on leucopenia, which was not a major issue or finding in the retrospective study. Second, the employers created much suspicion around the research findings by using delaying tactics to release the final report of the study, which occurred only after intense political pressure [57, 64]. Third, the employers' official interpretation of the study findings was that it does not prove that there is an association between benzene and serious health effects in the workers of the complex [65]. Last but not least, labor has always had difficulties in supporting leucopenia as a good indicator for benzene overexposures, because leucopenia is a nonspecific symptom that can be caused by a variety of factors such as infections or parasitosis. Besides, Vasconcelos wrote that the Brazilian norm that established the hematological cutpoint for leucopenia has been under fire from employers for many years [66, p. 114].

The period of the two benzene crises was a period of intense fighting for the definition of the benzene problem in the Camaçari petrochemical complex. The argument between employers and labor organizations could be recapitulated as an argument revolving around three major questions: 1) the existence and size of the problem; 2) the causality of the problem; and 3) the solution to the problem [67, 68].

Existence and Size of the Problem

The main argument here centered around the existence and number of work-related cases of leucopenia in the complex. It is a complicated argument involving political, economic, social, and scientific aspects. In order to understand these aspects, it is necessary to briefly contextualize the discussion that took place in Brazil during the period when the benzene crises occurred [69].

The discovery of benzene-related leucopenia in Brazil came to the fore in S. Paulo in 1984, after state health agencies investigated benzene exposures in the Companhia Siderúrgica Paulista (COSIPA), a large steel mill where about 2,000 workers were found to have leucopenia between 1983 and 1992. COSIPA also commissioned an epidemiology study in 1985, which concluded for the work-relatedness of the hematologic alterations, in particular for white blood cells.

The Ministry of Social Welfare acknowledged the results of the study and established the criteria for the lower limits of normality for total blood leucocytes count as 5,000/mm^3 and 2,000/mm^3 for neutrophiles. The appearance of leucopenia cases in Bahia switched the technical discussion from steel mill to petrochemical exposures to benzene, but the criteria remained the same until an expanded new protocol was developed in Bahia in 1991 [70, p. 49; 71].

To make matters worse, the Brazilian scientific community did not agree upon accepted normal levels for blood-cell parameters. Physicians had been arguing about normal parameters for hemograms for a long time. One of them, Celso Guerra, became famous by claiming that blacks and mulatos would have lower white blood-cell count than whites. According to him, statistical data available in Brazil showed that about 5 percent of Brazilian workers would be found with leucopenia if the criteria were applied [66, p. 70]. In other words, leucopenia is not a synonym to benzene exposure. The argument lost some of its strength after the FJS transversal study in Camaçari, which did not support significant interracial differences in blood parameters.

Workers with white blood-cell counts lower than the legal criteria would be systematically removed from work as temporarily disabled, a measure aimed at preventing further damage to exposed workers. These workers could not return to work (as mentioned in the Cetrel case) until their workplaces had controlled exposures to a level below the Brazilian benzene tolerance value of 8 ppm—later reduced to 1 ppm for the petrochemical industry and 2.5 ppm for the steel industry [72]. Since the control of exposures often involves large expenditures with new equipment, engineering controls, and personal protective equipment, it has taken many years for employers to reduce benzene exposures. In the meantime hundreds of workers were removed from their jobs (especially in S. Paulo), creating serious political and economic problems for employers and the workers themselves [73].

Even though the hematological criteria had strong organized labor support and contributed to the protection of workers from further harm, it ended up causing unintended social consequences to the victims, who over time were fired by their employers instead of being reinstated to cleaner and safer workplaces. In short, the argument about the existence and number of cases of leucopenia in the complex had profound implications, over which organized labor and management waged a prolonged battle. In the end, business acknowledged the existence of the problem but accused labor of overstating the seriousness of the situation. Paes de Andrade, the former CEO of Copene, has the view that ". . . foi mais barulho que problemas reais" (. . . there was more "noise" about them than real problems in the complex) [74].

Causality of the Problem

The argument of the causal link between benzene and adverse health effects is closely intertwined with the recognition of the existence of leucopenia in the complex. The initial clinical and hematological evidence pointed in the direction of a positive association, but not necessarily causation. Employers reacted to this empirical evidence by claiming that well-designed epidemiological studies were needed to establish causation definitively. They paid for a large study, which concluded that there were somewhat strong indications, though not conclusive, that benzene exposure could increase the risk of certain forms of cancer, such as aplastic anemia and leukemia, in exposed workers. Organized labor claims were but reinforced by the study, although Sindiquímica did not agree with it.

The evolution of the political struggle between labor and management regarding this study may be summarized in the following chronological order:

First, employers delayed the release of the study results. Labor pressured for its immediate release. Secondly, business agreed to release it. Third, business used the results of the study as scientific proof to dismiss labor arguments on the causal link between benzene and leucopenia. Fourth, labor refused to validate the conclusions of the FJS study on the grounds that it only served to justify business inaction regarding control of benzene exposures.

In terms of substance, the arguments about the recognition and causation of leucopenia in the complex revolved around three main questions [66, p. 71]: the relationship between blood disorders and benzene exposures in the work environment, the establishment of normal values for blood parameters that should trigger removal from the workplace of workers with low white blood cell count, and the relationship between early detection of blood disorders and cancer.

Solution to the Problem

The argument here centers around the solutions to benzene exposure [23]. After releasing the study results, business blamed the union for a) the panic that the "Caça ao Benzeno" campaign generated among petrochemical workers, b) discrimination against the workers who might have nonoccupational leucopenia, and c) harming the working class as a result of the campaign. The logic of these accusations is based on the notion that trade union claims prevented new workers from getting jobs in the complex (because of fearmongering) and that the removal of affected workers from their jobs created unnecessary hardship to these workers, who could not find another job.

Following intense conflict about these three issues, employers invested a large sum of money in public relations to demonstrate their behavior change and to inform the public that benzene emissions were under control. They even reckoned that they had not been transparent and forthcoming in the past, but once society raised their awareness to their misconduct they permanently converted to a transparent relationship with the public.

This overt crisis made business modify its strategy. Business started arguing that it proactively espoused warranted programs, such as the Chemical Manufacturers Association's "Responsible Care" [75, 76]. Besides, they not only appropriated the risk-mapping idea from Sindiquímica, but did not allow the union to participate in its implementation in the workplace, either.

The intense and prolonged conflict triggered by the benzene crises in the Camaçari petrochemical complex was not fruitless. It contributed to the political momentum for a substantial change in the way standards and regulations are set in Brazil.

THE BENZENE AGREEMENT [77-79]

At the beginning of the 1970s, the Brazilian Ministry of Labor enacted Law 6.514 to create the Special Services for Safety Engineering and Occupational Medicine (SESMT), which was amended to its present version in 1978. The same law introduced the concept of Threshold Limit Values (TLV) for chemical substances in Brazil, setting the benzene's TLV at 8 ppm for a 48-hour workweek and the ceiling at 16 ppm.

Under Law 3.237 of July 1972, companies had to establish the SESMT to provide site-based clinical occupational health services to employees. This rule expanded the delivery of medical care based on the prevailing model of occupational medicine in Brazil, whose goal was to assure the maintenance of a healthy and productive workforce for capital. In the previous two decades, most industries had organized the provision of occupational medicine services focusing on clinical care, without much attention given to environmental issues and prevention of occupational diseases.

According to Freitas and Arcury, the large benzene producers organized these services with the following structural characteristics [80, p. 85; 81]: a) they were guided by positivist, unicausal theories of causation; b) they had the purpose of keeping the workforce "healthy" to work; c) they did not include the participation of workers; d) they had work environment controls built around quantitative evaluations and threshold values; and e) they were dominated by experts on work-environment issues, an inheritance of the previous influence of Taylorism and occupational hygiene.

Neither the Ministry of Labor nor the Ministry of Health was equipped to enforce quantitative tolerance levels. In general, these agencies would use qualitative criteria to determine compliance with regulations.

In the second half of the 1970s, a well-developed critical view about the consequences of late urbanization and industrialization in Brazil was presented. Some Brazilian social medicine intellectuals criticized the excessively biological and positivist approach of traditional occupational medicine professionals. As an alternative, they proposed the Marxist concept that work is a social process embedded in the social relations of production that occur between labor and capital. Laurell called this model the socio-medical model, which conceives the relationship between work and health as a complex relationship between social and biopsychological processes [81, p. 55]. The other approach, the traditional one, ". . . conceives work as an environmental condition that affects health because it exposes workers to hazards" [81, p. 56].

Thus, the socio-medical model posits that exposures to chemicals, occupational injuries, and illnesses result from the way work is divided, valued, and organized in society. This view refuted the idea that there was a natural history of occupational diseases and injuries; instead, workplaces become the loci for specific analysis of the social determination of the relationship between health and disease. Categories such as work, alienation, overload, subjectivity, satisfaction, and "desgaste" explain the social causation of occupational illnesses and injuries [82, p. 21; 83].

In a review of the historical development of collective bargaining around health and safety in Brazil, Costa stated that:

> . . . While the Italian labor movement assessed its ten years of struggle for better health conditions in 1978, a similar movement was starting to take shape in Brazil. This movement proposed an alliance between workers and professionals to create alternatives to effect changes in the work environment based on workers' participation and aiming at deep changes in the cultural, democratic and economic areas [83, p. 39, quoting D. Costa].

In 1978, the auto workers' strike in the ABCD region marked the emergence of an independent Brazilian labor movement on the political scene. The social movements in favor of workers' health developed within the context of a massive grassroots upheaval that took place in the late seventies to early eighties in the Brazilian auto industry [84, 85]. In 1979, the Inter-Union Committee for Workers Health (CISAT in portuguese) was created and promoted the first and second Workers' Health Weeks during the same year. Many initiatives developed to mobilize the rank and file for health and safety issues and to change the traditional, clinically oriented medical care services offered by the unions.

Labor unions built health departments within the unions with a view to fighting the old way of doing things and moving in the direction of a Brazilian version of the organizing model of unionism [86]. The criticism of the state-led, official model to deal with health and safety issues focused on the victim-blaming ideology, which attributed most workplace accidents and illnesses to "unsafe acts" of workers. To deal with these acts, the provision of personal protective equipment would be prioritized over engineering controls.

By the same token, workers would not participate in the formulation of policies and preventive measures to reduce workplace injuries, since these fell under the responsibility of occupational physicians and safety engineers. Technical staff working in company-controlled and state-mandated occupational health and safety services would take charge of allegedly technical decisions about the prevention of workplace injuries and illnesses.

In the early eighties, progressive union leaders and health professionals started to apply the newly formulated social medicine concepts to workplaces and to challenge the official version of occupational health. They joined efforts in São Paulo to create the Inter-union Department for the Study of Health and the Work Environment (DIESAT).

New counterhegemonic movements armed with a project to effect change in workplace health and safety developed through this interaction. One of them successfully put pressure on the Ministry of Labor to hire more health and safety personnel. Another connected movement linked the workers' movement to a broader public health movement, an international trend reinforced by the Alma Ata Primary Care Conference. By 1985, public occupational health clinics and workers' health programs flourished at the state and local level in São Paulo, all of which committed to include union representatives in the decision-making process. In some cases, union representatives participated as executive directors of the newly founded clinics [78].

Strikes and state intervention in companies to resolve health and safety problems grew increasingly common. However, a trend toward substituting top-down state intervention of professionals for workers' action still prevailed, a situation analyzed by Sass in the context of North America [87]. This paradox generated a new praxis that searched for a new role for the state, one where it would constitute only a "piece" of a pie that included the unions, employers, and technical institutions in the field.

The VIII National Health Conference and the First National Workers' Health Conference took place in 1986, generalizing the S. Paulo experience throughout Brazil. The broad political discussion of the "Sanitary Reform" movement to reform the Brazilian health system integrated work-environment issues into the public health agenda. The international connections with the Italian union leaders who took part in the creation of the Italian Workers Model greatly benefited Brazilian union leaders and health professionals, who tried to implement it there [88; 89, pp. 12-14]. The workers' health principles that characterize this alternative view included strong participation of workers in designing and evaluating the health services delivered in the clinics; the right of workers to be informed about chemical hazards (right to know); and the right to access medical records and medical surveillance in the workplace.

The 1980s were marked by struggles against chemical exposures in factories, against death and injuries at work, high noise and heat in the workplace, as well as a number of other physical and psychosocial hazards. Furthermore, this movement fought for changes in the relationship between the state agencies and labor, and in labor's view of health and safety matters. Collective bargaining agreements increasingly included health and safety language to prevent occupational injuries and illnesses, and to democratize the CIPAs (Internal Committees for the Prevention of Accidents).

The Development of the New Benzene Regulations

In 1982, the ministries of Labor and Health promulgated an ordinance forbidding the manufacturing of products containing benzene in their composition but allowing the presence of benzene as a contaminant agent in concentrations up to 1 percent in volume. In June of 1983, a new regulation mandated the limit of 50 mg phenol/l of urine as the biological tolerance level (LTB) for phenol— a benzene metabolite—in urine and 30 mg/l as its normal value.

In 1983, the Metal Workers Union of Santos, S. Paulo, started mobilizing union members against benzene exposures in the Companhia Siderúrgica Paulista (COSIPA). In 1985, a worker died in a pesticide (benzene hexachloride-BHC) manufacturing plant called Matarazzo, which was later shut down by the S. Paulo state labor department. Also in 1985, dozens of cases of leucopenia were discovered in another steel mill, the Companhia Siderúrgica Nacional (CSN).

Many technical conferences and seminars were held to discuss benzene-related issues in the same period. Employer representatives and labor representatives fought ideological, political, and technical battles about benzene, especially as to the existence of benzene-related leucopenia.

One of the results of these battles was the discovery of high benzene exposures all over the country. In turn, different government agencies moved toward regulating different aspects of benzene production. In 1986, an interagency committee formed to deal with the problems of COSIPA in S. Paulo came up with a proposal to characterize the diagnosis of chronic intoxication to benzene. Workers exposed to benzene with less than 4,000 total leukocites/mm^3 of blood or less than 2,000 neutrophiles/mm^3 were supposed to be diagnosed with leucopenia. In 1986-1987, the Ministry of Social Security used this proposal to elaborate institutional criteria for diagnosis and procedures for rehabilitation of affected workers. These regulations determined how medical surveillance should be conducted by the existing company-based SESMT.

In 1991, the state of Bahia created a protocol to control benzenism and other occupational hematological diseases in the Camaçari Petrochemical Complex. In 1992, the Center for Sanitary Surveillance of the S. Paulo Health Department created a tripartite group that elaborated a standard to control benzene in S. Paulo. This group was composed of regional offices of federal government agencies, state government agencies, universities, and labor unions. It was the first experience in Brazil where a tripartite group elaborated an occupational health standard.

This standard was enacted as a state regulation covering only the state of São Paulo. It classified benzene as a carcinogen; changed the strictly numerical criteria previously established to interpret blood test results; redefined criteria for considering individual leucopenia cases as cured, i.e., a return to normal white blood-cell count would not be enough to determine cure; did not adopt the notion of a biological tolerance level for benzene exposures; pointed out other effects related to benzene exposures; and required that companies develop a Program to Prevent Benzene Exposures (PPEB) involving several areas of management— production, operation, maintenance, and other sectors within the companies. By 1992, the Brazilian senate approved the International Labor Office (ILO) Convention 136 and ILO Recommendation 144, which had language on carcinogenic substances, on how to protect workers against benzene poisoning, on substitution of carcinogens wherever possible, on medical surveillance, and other relevant topics.

In 1993, the Division of Workers Compensation of the Ministry of Social Welfare (MPAS) constituted another group to review the 1991 National Institute of Social Insurance's benzene regulations, which followed the above-mentioned S. Paulo criteria of 1986-87. The group, composed of representatives of the ministries of Labor, Health and Welfare, produced a new federal standard on benzene poisoning. Again, the 1992 S. Paulo regulation served as the model for it, as well as the resolutions of the National Seminar on Exposures to Benzene and Other Mielotoxics, held in 1993.

Despite the regulatory initiatives regarding benzene exposures that developed between the mid-eighties and the mid-nineties, the main regulation on benzene, the Ministry of Labor Norma Regulamentadora (regulatory norm) NR-15, had not yet been modified. This changed during the administration of Walter Barelli, an old friend of labor who became the minister of labor after President Collor was impeached on corruption grounds in 1991. He replaced a rightist union leader who was caught accepting bribes from business. In spite of the presence of a generally conservative executive administration, the momentum was favorable for labor law reform. The new minister wanted to promote a liberal system whereby there would be industry-wide labor-management contract negotiations—Contrato Coletivo de Trabalho— without the presence of the state (à la the Italian model), in opposition to the traditional Brazilian corporatist system.

Dr. Raquel Rigotto, who was placed in charge of the Safety and Health Division of the Ministry of Labor, constituted in September of 1993 a technical advisory group to review the NR-15. The appointed group included professionals from several states who had had previous experience with benzene issues. The objective of the group was to ". . . situate the question of benzene exposures within the state of the art knowledge available nationally or internationally, in order to technically subsidize the revision of standards and the definition of a national policy" [80, p. 93]. Representatives from the steel and chemical industries challenged many of the new concepts introduced into the debate on letters sent to the Ministry of Labor. They also complained about not having been invited to participate in the advisory group. The group issued its final report, "Technical Subsidies to the Safety and Health Division of the Ministry of Labor" (SSST/MTb) in 1993. The Ministry of Labor administration that had planned this revision resigned by March 1994, precipitating the enactment of Ordinance 3 of the Safety and Health Division. This ordinance provoked a strong reaction from businesses.

The National Tripartite Agreement: A New Way to Formulate Work Environment Regulations in Brazil [90]

Ordinance 3 included benzene as an addition to four other substances that had already been classified as carcinogens in another ordinance since 1978. In the most controversial section, it read that: "no exposure or contact, by any route, with these substances, must be allowed." Further, it also read that ". . . no exposure means to enclose processes or operations, using the best available engineering methods. Workers must be adequately protected so as not to have any contact with the carcinogens. . . ." The use of phenol levels in urine as biological tolerance levels was also removed from Annex 2 of the NR-7. Article 5 gave employers ninety days to comply with the regulation.

The reaction from business was immediate. The National Confederation of Industry (CNI) contacted the new Labor Ministry, Marcelo Pimentel—an old friend of business who had replaced Barelli—requesting an immediate stay of the ordinance and suggesting the creation of a tripartite technical commission to regulate the controlled use of benzene within 270 days.

Businesses argued that ". . . benzene production would be made unfeasible by this ordinance because it determined the adoption of enclosed processes that would not allow any worker contact with the product, i.e, the existing TLV of 8 ppm would have to fall to 0 ppm in risky areas" [80, p. 94]. Besides, the deadline was allegedly too short. This reaction to the new benzene ordinance was an unusual one. For the first time in the Brazilian history of employer participation in standard setting, businesses called for a tripartite commission to negotiate and solve the "impasse."

This unusual behavior may be explained by a convergence of factors that created favorable conditions for a compromise between labor, the government, and businesses:

• Labor and government were already on board.
• A governmental decision on the matter had already been made.

- The quick development of new benzene regulations at the state and local level, especially in S. Paulo, Rio de Janeiro, Minas Gerais, and Bahia.
- A favorable political conjuncture that supported the implementation of collective bargaining negotiations between labor and businesses without much political confrontation. This agenda had been promoted by Barelli before his resignation.

In March 1994, the new head of the Safety and Health Division postponed the deadline for compliance for ninety days. In August, this same division officially invited labor and employer unions to constitute a "Technical Working Group," which had to present a proposal to regulate work environment monitoring and control of benzene, and medical surveillance criteria for benzene exposures. The Technical Group had broad, albeit unequal, participation of professionals representing labor confederations, national and local business organizations, academia, and government agencies. Businesses tried to get the upper hand in the very first meeting of the group by presenting an elaborate proposal that tried to recover power and control over the work environment.

Labor countered by mobilizing disabled workers' grass-roots organizations and labor-friendly professionals who worked at the state and local level and who had been shut out from participating. September 2 was a National Mobilization Day Against Benzene Contamination, which helped labor counter business power inside the group. Internal struggles developed between August and September for control over the rules of the game within the Working Group. Finally, after much bickering, the Tripartite Working Commission was formed, including equal representation of the three parties. It was composed of representatives of the ministries of Health, Labor, Social Welfare, FUNDACENTRO, Confederations of Industrial Workers, Metalworkers, CUT, Força Sindical, the National Confederation of Industries, ABIQUIM, and the Brazilian Steel Industry Institute [91].

The commission met for a year divided into several subgroups and became a forum for intense negotiations among the parties, which looked for competent technical advice before coming to political compromises. Discussions developed around three axes: the need to restrict and control benzene use, environmental health matters, and the creation of permanent mechanisms for negotiations among the stakeholders.

The commission reached gridlock on several issues, such as the establishment of technological reference values, which were based on the technical feasibility of controlling exposures. Labor representatives proposed to set the values at .3 ppm, with a deadline of 18 months for compliance. Employers proposed 5 ppm and 5 years. Internal disagreements between business representatives also occurred, especially between petrochemical industry representatives from Bahia and S. Paulo. The CUT took advantage of this lack of consensus and negotiated a separate agreement with employers from Bahia, which set the value at 1 ppm in petrochemical workplaces, with a compliance deadline of December 1997.

Labor also had its small disagreements. For example, CUT and Força Sindical disagreed on the power and autonomy that should be given to health and safety committees in the workplace. CUT had a more radical approach by proposing the creation of new, independent, and democratically elected workplace committees. F. Sindical proposed giving more power and autonomy to the existing CIPAs. They settled by giving more autonomy to the CIPAs.

In September 1995, the commission concluded its work and came up with a comprehensive benzene standard that covered all companies that produce, transport, store, use, or manipulate benzene or liquid mixtures that contain 1 percent or more of benzene in volume. The commission produced one agreement, one ordinance, and two normative technical instructions. The normative technical instructions provide uniform methodologies to conduct benzene monitoring and medical surveillance.

The major aspects of the agreement were [92]:

- The creation of the Permanent Benzene Commission (CNP) as a stable vehicle for negotiations among stakeholders. It constitutes a tripartite, interinstitutional forum for discussions, negotiations, and follow-up of the agreement.
- Employers have to write a Program to Prevent Occupational Benzene Exposures (PPOEB) within six months after the date of the agreement. The program should detail all health surveillance and environmental monitoring developed in the facilities covered.
- The establishment of a certification process to recognize compliance with the standard.
- A mandatory national registry of benzene producers, consumers, and transporters to be developed within thirty days of the agreement.
- The setting of Time Weighted Technological Reference Values (VRT-MPT) of 1 ppm for the petrochemical industry to be achieved by December 1997, and 2.5 ppm for the steel industry, to be achieved by December 1998. In rare instances, this compliance schedule may be extended to December of 1999. The VRT-MPT is a negotiated value that refers to the concentration of benzene in the air considered feasible from a technological perspective. It reflects the recognition by all parties that there are no safe levels for exposure to a carcinogen, indicating a quite dramatic change in the traditional view that adopted U.S. TLVs to regulate chemicals.
- The creation of benzene working groups (GTB) to follow up the elaboration, development, and implementation of the PPOEB. Employers have to give access to all company records regarding benzene solicited by the GTB, provide administrative support to the GTB, remunerate the work of GTB members as regular work, and train GTB members on benzene. The contents

of the training course, which should have a minimum of twenty hours, are spelled out in detail in the agreement.

- Companies that do not comply with the agreement will pay the highest fines allowed in the Brazilian regulation NR-28. The fines collected will be targeted to fund research, seminars, and other events aimed at preventing occupational benzene exposures.

In December 1995, the Ministry of Labor promulgated Ordinance 14, which removed benzene from the list of five cancer substances and created Annex 13-A to the NR-15, after the Ministry of Labor had given businesses successive extensions to comply with Ordinance 3.

According to Ferreira, the tripartite agreement was a positive step. He believes that since the government is unable to enforce the law, consensus may work better [57]. Besides, a critical mass of skilled occupational health professionals was created in the process of discussing and writing the agreement and the ordinances.

The national registry of benzene producers, consumers, and transporters went into effect immediately. The CNP was inaugurated in March 1996. Many GTBs have been created. The follow-up process for the agreement is slowly moving forward. A major roadblock for the implementation of the benzene agreement is the compensation of disabled workers. This difficult question involves compensating workers, recognizing diseases, and allowing workers to go back to work environments that may not have controlled benzene exposures.

The federal government agency that pays disability insurance, the INSS, wants to shed the financial burden of paying for the disability [93]. It wants to release or discharge disabled workers as soon as possible. Not all government agencies that participate in the CNP agree with this policy. Consequently, internal disagreement within the government has contributed to paralyzing the action of the CNP. This contradiction derives from the fact that workers have been on disability for many years, because the law does not allow workers to go back to their previous jobs without the employer either controlling work environment exposures or accommodating workers in jobs that are free from exposures to benzene.

The INSS wants to consider disabled workers cured of leucopenia and shift the compensation burden to the companies. The companies do not want to reinstate these long-gone workers. Workers are clinically able to go back to work, but must not go back to workplaces that may expose them to benzene levels higher than the new VRT. This situation is worse at COSIPA.

The state of S. Paulo DRT recently investigated COSIPA and found that the company still has an inadequate medical surveillance system in place. The industrial hygiene activities that should be part of the Plan to Prevent Environmental Risks (PPRA) are poor as well. Despite the progress embodied in the agreement, it appears that organized labor has had difficulties in making sure that businesses comply with it [94]. Recent increases in unemployment levels as well as downsizing of major manufacturing industries have put an enormous burden on workers, who are forced to put aside health and safety concerns, such as chemical exposures, and direct their efforts toward the preservation of jobs.

As Asher wrote for the U.S. context: "To preserve their jobs workers sometimes chose to avoid confrontations about accidents or exposure to occupational diseases" [95].

CONCLUSION

Following Levenstein's approach, the analysis of the two benzene crises and the benzene agreement reveal the political economy of occupational disease in petrochemical production, and the social context of occupational health in Brazil. Benzene was a catalyst around which labor, the state, and business articulated their political, ideological, and organizational resources to recognize, regulate, control, and compensate work environment hazards. At the same time, the struggle that developed around the benzene exposures concentrate many of the elements that are usually present in work environment crises in developing and developed countries. In this respect, these historical events are but a particular example of more general phenomena that tend to occur in capitalist societies, in the center or in the periphery, where profits and accumulation of wealth constitute the principles that determine how production is organized.

The first crisis in Cetrel started to uncover the reality that petrochemical workers do get ill if exposed to the chemical substances used in petrochemical production, even when these workers are involved in the tail end of the production process—the treatment of industrial wastes. As a result of the conservative nature of the political forces that dominated the Brazilian state at the time, it had a quite limited intervention in this crisis, contributing mostly to investigate the situation through the HHE.

Business representatives inside the state apparatus tried to cover up the results of the HHE. Middle-class labor allies inside the state leaked the information, which allowed Sindae to organize the rank-and-file against the bad working conditions in Cetrel and to shake the particular aspects of the factory regime that produced diseases at Cetrel. Acting as an indirect boost to Sindae's fight, Sindiquímica shook the foundations of the existing authoritarian factory regime in the complex when it shut the whole complex down in 1985. This young and still-inexperienced fraction of the working class in Bahia started to exercise its collective power at the same time that the Brazilian transition to a democratic regime gained steam.

The three main actors in the political economy of occupational disease started to openly and aggressively flex their muscles, in the process learning how to deal with new health and safety matters that had broad political, economic, and social implications. The first crisis was a small conflict, a kind of rehearsal for the bigger crisis that happened in the early nineties, because management control over the production processes prevented workers from getting information about benzene and other chemical exposures. Yet, it already displayed miniature versions of the explosive ingredients that the Nitrocarbono situation uncovered.

It took about ten years for the conflict regarding health and safety in the work environment to fully arise. By the time the second crisis happened, the three main work-environment actors (state, business, and labor) already had prior experience, enabling them to exercise their class capacity at the local and national levels. The Nitrocarbono battle manifested the tactics and strategies of an all-encompassing and dynamic "war of positions." Reacting to the wide repercussion of the death of the physician, business, labor, and the state brought their local and national organizations to bear on the solutions to the crisis, probably driven by strategic calculations about the impact of the crisis on their future power.

Organized labor led a successful local and national campaign to change business behavior and promote change in the work-environment policies in the Camaçari complex and elsewhere. Arguably, Bahia became the epicenter of a larger national work-environment crisis, whose origin was born in São Paulo. The left-of-center state administration intervened at the local level, through the action of progressive state bureaucrats and organized labor allies within the state apparatus, to force business to control work-environment hazards. At the federal level, three cabinet members of a conservative administration landed in Bahia to soften the bad publicity generated by the death of the company doctor, a middle-class ally of the ruling class [96].

Business initially staged defensive actions of denial and refusal to accept the unfavorable circumstances. As the crisis developed, the previously comfortable business hegemony regarding health and safety conditions in the complex showed clear signs of fracture, at least judging by media coverage and poll results. Businesses reacted strongly to this fissure with a large public relations campaign and a series of actions to neutralize labor with "objective," "scientific" answers to the crisis: They commissioned the FJS study to achieve this goal; they invested large amounts of money to persuade society that they knew how to control the hazards; and they implemented engineering controls and monitoring programs to evaluate work-environment hazards.

Society at large was invited to take sides by endorsing one of the opposite versions of the facts presented in the press and media. It appears that, at least for a while, the public took the side of labor and demanded corrective actions from business. Although it is difficult to document this argument, business and labor's interpretations of the public reaction lend support to it. Paes de Andrade, one of the most important business leaders of the Bahian petrochemical industry, confirmed this interpretation when he submitted that the only time that Sindiquímica affected environmental management decisions was during the benzene crisis [1, 97].

From the beginning, it became clear to the actors involved that the solution to the crisis demanded significant changes in Brazilian regulations of benzene.

A wide range of issues such as benzene tolerance levels, medical surveillance, and workplace monitoring needed to be addressed in order to stabilize the solutions to the crisis. This is what the national benzene agreement seems to have accomplished, as implied by Ferreira when he stated that "everybody learned" during the process [57].

ENDNOTES

1. Fernando Paes de Andrade, interview by the author, tape recording, July 1997, Salvador, Bahia. Paes de Andrade is a former CEO of Copene and a former superintendent of COFIC. In this capacity he chaired the board of Cetrel. He currently works for Trichem, a firm that is part of the Odebrecht group. Evans wrote that this strategy of integrating petrochemical companies lost its economic viability in the eighties [2]. For further discussion of this question, see [2].
2. Peter Evans, "Collectivized Capitalism: Integrated Petrochemical Complexes and Capital Accumulation in Brazil," in [3, pp. 85-125].
3. Thomas Bruneau and Philippe Faucher, eds., *Authoritarian Capitalism: Brazil's Contemporary Economic and Political Development*, Westview Press, Boulder, Colorado, 1981.
4. For example, see the lists produced by OSHA, EPA, National Toxicology Program (NTP), International Agency for Research on Cancer (IARC), etc. These lists account for extremely hazardous chemicals, hazardous chemicals, carcinogen substances, or priority lists for research and control of chemical exposures. The lists are generally found as appendices to environmental or occupational standards such as the OSHA Hazard Communication Standard, the EPA Clean Air or Clean Water acts. For the IARC and the NTP cases, the lists may also reflect research priorities for the agencies.
5. For a good discussion of the epidemiology of occupational injuries and illnesses of chemical and petrochemical workers in Bahia, see [6, p. 178]. Rego and Pereira's review, based on the health-care service provided by Sindiquímica, shows that hearing loss, leucopenia, respiratory diseases, mental health disorders, sequelae of work accidents, and back problems are—in this order—the most important causes of ambulatory care visits [6].
6. Marco Antonio Rego and Rosana Pereira, "Acidentes e Doenças do Trabalho no Complexo Petroquímico da Bahia," in [7, pp. 159-187].
7. Tania Franco, ed., *Trabalho, Riscos Industriais e Meio Ambiente: Rumo ao Desenvolvimento Sustentável?* EDUFBA-CRH/FFCH/UFBA, Salvador, Bahia, 1997.
8. This account of the facts is based on personal interviews with present and former employees of Cetrel who asked to remain anonymous. The interviews were conducted during the months of June and July 1997, Salvador, Bahia.
9. Cetrel's management style could be qualified as "paternalistic management": a style where "there is a personalization of industrial relations," or where there is "a superposition of industrial relations, family structures, and kinship relationships in the workplace" [10, pp. 55, 69]. For further discussion of this characterization of the dominant management style in the state-owned petrochemical companies in Bahia, see [10].

10. Antonio S. Guimarães, "A Gestão do Trabalho na Indústria Petroquímica: A Forma Geral e a Variante Paternalista," *Caderno CRH*, vol. 12, pp. 55-69, 1990.
11. Antonio S. Guimarães, "Factory Regime and Class Formation: The Petrochemical Workers in Brazil," Ph.D. dissertation, University of Wisconsin, Madison, 1988.
12. Guimarães described a very similar picture in his study of another petrochemical plant in the complex. He also provided data on the average age of the work force in that plant, where almost 80 percent of the workforce was under forty years old [11].
13. Some newspaper headlines and stories that illustrate this statement are: "Pólo Petroquímico: Maior estação do País vai evitar a poluição" (Petrochemical Complex: Largest wastewater plant in the country will avoid pollution), *A Tarde* (Salvador), June 16, 1976; and "Sistema de coleta, transporte e tratamento de efluentes líquidos vai ser inaugurado" (System to collect, transport and treat the liquid effluent will be inaugurated), p. 8, March 11, 1978. In the latter story, it is said that all industrial activity generates pollution. However, the government concern with environmental protection in the complex was such that it implemented state-of-the-art pollution-control systems to abate the chemical pollution created by the production of petrochemical products.
14. Interview with Cetrel employees, June and July 1997, Salvador, Bahia.
15. Fundacentro is a public Brazilian foundation affiliated with the Ministry of Labor whose functions and objectives are analogous to the U.S. National Institute for Occupational Safety and Health (NIOSH).
16. Personal interview with two anonymous members of the team that performed the health-hazard evaluation, tape recording, July 1997, Salvador, Bahia. I kept their names confidential since both still worked in this institution at the time of the interview.
17. Personal interview with Fundacentro staff, July 1997, Salvador, Bahia.
18. "Levantamento das Condições de Segurança, Higiene e Medicina do Trabalho, Cetrel—Central de Tratamento de Efluentes Líquidos SA," unpublished manuscript available at the regional office of Fundacentro, 1985, Salvador, Bahia.
19. To understand all aspects involved in Cetrel's reaction, an explanation of the Brazilian Workers Compensation Law is needed. This point will be further elaborated in this chapter. See also [73].
20. The union is called Sindicato dos Trabalhadores de Água e Esgotos do Estado da Bahia, or Sindae for short.
21. *Bem te vi, Jornal da Cetrel*, year 1, no. 5, April 1992.
22. Interview with Cetrel employees, June/July 1997, Salvador, Bahia.
23. I owe this characterization to Moema Gramacho, former health and safety officer of Sindiquímica. Interview by the author, tape recording, June 1997, Salvador, Bahia.
24. More details about this period are provided later in this chapter.
25. *Grave*, Especial de Saúde (Salvador), no. 1, Agosto 1986.
26. The SIPAT is a traditional policy adopted by Brazilian manufacturing employers to dedicate one week in a given year to raising workers' awareness of occupational accidents. One of the activities of the week would be a ceremony where a variety of prizes and certificates were given to the safest sectors and workers in the companies.
27. This underreporting of injuries and illnesses as a consequence of "safety bingos" and the victim-blaming ideology are well-known to American health and safety activists. For more details on this subject, see [28].

28. Jordan Barab, "Ways and Means of Safety: Labor's View," speech delivered at the 1998 Annual Conference of the New England Water Environment Association, Boston, Massachusetts, January 27, 1998.

29. Personal interview with Fundacentro staff, July 1997, Salvador, Bahia.

30. "Histórico da Comissão de Saúde da CUT-BA," draft unpublished paper by Moema Gramacho.

31. CESAT is the state occupational health clinic, which played a major role in the Nitrocarbono benzene crisis described later in this chapter.

32. John Wooding described how this alliance developed in the United States [33].

33. John Wooding, "Dire States: Workplace Health and Safety Regulation in the Reagan/ Thatcher Era," Ph.D. dissertation, Brandeis University, 1990.

34. The Department of Preventive Medicine of the Federal University of Bahia had a residency in occupational medicine that formed a generation of progressive occupational physicians, who became labor union staff. After completing the first year of their residency, the students received the Public Health Specialist degree. By the end of the second year, the students were licensed as occupational physicians. The department adopted the concepts of social medicine formulated by Asa Cristina Laurell, Ana Maria Tambellini, Sérgio Arouca, and others in Brazil. Most of these Bahian professionals had connections to the CUT.

35. *Grave,* Especial de Saúde, January 24, 1995.

36. Brazilian Law 614, section V, article 168.

37. *Grave*, Ano VIII, no. 23, November 14, 1990, reported about 180 layoffs in five companies in the complex. The headline of this report read: "As recordistas em demissões (outubro 90)." (Companies that have record lay-offs [October 1990]), p. 2.

38. The CAT (Comunicacão de Acidentes do Trabalho) is the form that licensed physicians have to complete to report occupational accidents with loss of work days. Company physicians must report them to the Ministry of Labor (DRT) or State Health Secretariats.

39. C. Levenstein and Dominick Tuminaro, "The Political Economy of Occupational Disease," *New Solutions*, 2, 1, pp. 25-34, Summer 1991.

40. Caprolactam is white, crystalline solid or flakes, with an unpleasant odor. It is used in the production of textile and industrial fibers, and engineering plastics.

41. The media coverage for these deaths became hot news in Bahia for a significant period during 1990-1991. Some of the most important media outlets in Brazil also reported on the issue, such as the newspapers *O Globo* (Rio de Janeiro) and *Gazeta Mercantil* (São Paulo). Some of the key actors in the process attributed this increased media coverage to a "class bias" by the media, whose coverage of the events expanded significantly after the doctor died. It may also be argued that his was the first death that bore a credible potential relationship to benzene exposures.

42. The account that follows is based on the "Dossiê Benzeno," which is a compilation of several sources put together by Sindiquímica to summarize many press and official reports about the benzene crisis. These sources included local newspaper clips from *A Tarde* (the largest newspaper in Bahia) and *Tribuna da Bahia* (Salvador, Bahia), *Grave* (the union newsletter), copies of letters sent to government agencies, and documents produced as a result of the intervention of these agencies. The period covered by the dossier ranges from 1985 to 1991. November 1990 was the climax of the crisis.

43. In 1986, the Ministry of Social Welfare defined specific criteria for benzene intoxication (benzenismo) that included removal from work and workers' compensation for affected workers. The criteria set the lower limit for normal total white blood cells at 5,000/mm^3 and 2,000/mm^3 for neutrophiles.

44. C. Ferreira, fictitious name of a Fundacentro staff member. Interview by author, tape recording, July 1997, Salvador, Bahia.

45. Brasília is the capital of Brazil, where the headquarters of all ministries are located.

46. Delegacia Regional do Trabalho (DRT) Bahia—Ministério do Trabalho e Previdencia Social, Divisão de Segurança e Medicina do Trabalho, November 1990.

47. At the time, the governor of Bahia, Valdir Pires, represented a broad political front that included most left-of-center political forces. His secretary of health, Luis Humberto Teixeira, was a progressive politician who fully supported the work of CESAT during the crisis.

48. Termo de Compromisso entre Nitrocarbono S/A e Sindicato dos Trabalhadores nas Indústrias e Empresas Petroquímicas, Plásticas e Afins do Estado da Bahia, November 1990.

49. *O Globo*, November 2, 1990.

50. *A Tarde*, November 8, 1990, p. 3. The headline on this page reads: "Government studies the interdiction of Nitrocarbono."

51. The contacts between the progressive Brazilian and Italian labor movements were not a coincidence. They were an offspring of a long-term relationship between Brazilian and Italian public health intellectuals who were members of Communist parties in both countries. A good example of the Italian influence in Brazil is the adoption in the latter of the Italian workers' model as a guideline for action and organizing around health and safety issues. More discussion on this topic is provided later in this chapter.

52. Solange Oliveira, "O Dizer e o Silenciar. O Discurso do Sindiquímica nos Anos 90," unpublished monograph presented to the Graduate Course in Communication, School of Communication, Federal University of Bahia, 1995.

53. *Grave*, ANO X, no. 332, March 23, 1992, reported that COFIC announced the results of this poll, which showed that 52 percent of the population polled did not trust the companies in the complex, 33 percent trusted, and 15 percent did not know. Fifty-eight percent did not believe that the complex was safe; 88 percent believed that the complex caused respiratory diseases in neighbor communities; and 79 percent agreed that if you work in the complex you were likely to become ill. According to the report, the superintendent of COFIC, Paes de Andrade, reacted to these numbers stating that companies should invest more in communications and public relations. Paulo Jackson, president of Sindae between 1986 and 1992, stated that after the deaths in the complex, the industry's image changed drastically. The public realized that the complex was not what the media sold. ". . . If the 'Pólo' creates jobs, if the complex generates tax revenues, and if the 'Pólo' generates wealth, it is also true that it generates disease, cancer, and that it can kill" [54].

54. *Bem te vi, Jornal da Cetrel*, year 1, no. 9, October 1992 (emphasis mine).

55. *Estudo da Exposição Ocupacional ao Benzeno e Seus Efeitos Hematotóxicos em Trabalhadores de Indústrias Processadoras de Benzeno no Pólo Petroquímico de Camaçari—BA*, Relatório Técnico, Salvador, Março de 1992.

56. According to C. Ferreira, the industrial hygiene part of the FJS study never got much credibility due to its gross lack of data, which made it look conceptual and vague [57].

57. C. Ferreira, personal interview with author, July 1997, Salvador, Bahia.

58. The severe hematologic diseases investigated included: leukemia, aplastic anaemia (also known as pancytopenia), paroxysmal nocturnal hemoglobinuria, lymphomas, myelofibrosis, myeloid metaplasia, trombocythemia, and multiple myeloma.

59. The incidence density was 12.45 for the exposed and 9.87 for the nonexposed, while the incidence density ratio (IDR) was 1.26 (C.I.= 0.26 - 6.07, p = .05). The standardized incidence ratio for the exposed workers was 198 for leukemia, 909 for aplastic anaemia, 45 for lymphoma (C. I.= 24-722, 23-5065, and 9-128, respectively, p = .05). The standardized mortality ratio for the exposed workers was 206 for leukemia, 588 for aplastic anaemia, and 88 for lymphomas (C.I.= 25-744, 15-3277, and 18-256 respectively, p = .05). All these morbidity and mortality ratios are commonly used in epidemiology research to assess the relative risks of disease between populations exposed or nonexposed to risk factors (benzene in this case).

60. In a nonconcurrent cohort study undertaken by Yin and collaborators in China, 28,460 workers exposed to benzene, from 233 companies, were compared with 28,257 non-exposed workers. The study found an excess of deaths for leukemia equal to 5,74. The risk of contracting leukemia increased with length of exposure, reaching its peak at fifteen years, after which it began to decline [61].

61. João Barberino et al., "Incidence and Mortality of Hematologlc Disorders Among Petrochemical Workers in the Northeast of Brazil," unpublished manuscript (available from the author), 1997.

62. Personal interview with João Barberino, one of the members of the team that conducted the study, Salvador, Bahia, July 1997. Barberino had a master's degree in community health at the time the study was done. He is presently pursuing his doctoral degree in epidemiology at the Instituto de Saúde Coletiva (ISC) of the Universidade Federal da Bahia (UFBA).

63. My personal interviews with labor activists and occupational health physicians who work for Sindae and Sindiquímica in Salvador confirm this opinion.

64. *Grave*, Boletim Especial de Saúde, 03-27-92. The headlines of this special health issue of the newsletter read: "Effects of Benzene. Sinper omits results of research," p. 1.

65. José Saraiva, superintendent of COFIC, to Ronaldo Martins da Silva, technical advisor to the Centro de Recursos Ambientais (CRA), Camaçari, Bahia, June 17, 1993, available from author. Annexed to the letter is a document written by Dr. Helton Rosa, occupational health advisor to COFIC, who clearly stated in one of its concluding comments that ". . . the study results do not indicate that the observed effects had been determined by exposure to benzene."

66. Fernando Vasconcelos, "Causa e Norma na Medicina do Trabalho—O Caso do Benzenismo,"(Cause and Norm in Occupational Medicine—The case of benzenism), Master's thesis, UFBA, Salvador, 1994.

67. Ozonoff summarized the successive arguments put forward by the asbestos industry the following way:
"Asbestos doesn't hurt your health.
OK, it does hurt your health, but it doesn't cause cancer.
OK, asbestos can cause cancer, but not our kind of asbestos.
OK, our kind of asbestos can cause cancer, but not the kind this person got.

OK, our kind of asbestos can cause cancer, but not at the doses to which this person was exposed.

OK, our kind of asbestos does cause cancer, and at this dosage, but this person got this disease from something else—like smoking.

OK, he was exposed to our asbestos and it did cause his cancer, but we did not know about the danger when we exposed him, but the . . ." [68, pp. 68-69].

68. Dan Fagin and Marianne Lavelle, *Toxic Deception: How the Chemical Industry Manipulates Science, Bends the Law, and Endangers Your Health*, Carol Publishing Group, Seacaucus, New Jersey, 1996.

69. For a detailed account of this issue see [66, pp. 68-79].

70. "Protocolo de Intenções para Controle do Benzenismo e outras Doenças Hematológicas Ocupacionais no Pólo Petroquímico de Camaçari," Salvador, BA, 1991 [71, p. 49]. This protocol expanded the federal criteria by creating additional criteria for the diagnosis of the hematological alterations addressed in the former. It established that workers who had white blood-cell counts below 4,000/mm^3 should be followed up through at least three consecutive hemograms done fifteen days apart. The protocol was a product of the work of an interinstitutional commission composed of state government agencies, universities, the regional medical council (CRM), and the Hematological Society of Bahia.

71. "Benzeno: Subsídios Técnicos à Secretaria de Segurança e Saúde do Trabalho," São Paulo: FUNDACENTRO, FUNDUNESP, 1995.

72. In the next section, these issues are discussed in detail.

73. After the first fifteen days of disability, the amended Brazilian law puts the burden of workers' compensation on the government, with the employer complementing the wages. In spite of having job stability for a year, disabled workers suffer a drastic reduction in income and quickly become marginalized due to their legal inability to work, even when they feel they are able to work.

74. Paes de Andrade, personal interview with author, tape recording, July 1997, Salvador, Bahia.

75. This business behavior is very much in sync with corporate arguments conceived by the Business Council for Sustainable Development (BCSD) [76, pp. 47-48].

76. Joshua Karliner, *The Corporate Planet. Ecology and Politics in the Age of Globalization*, Sierra Club, San Francisco, 1997.

77. The account that follows is based on [78].

78. Danilo Costa, "Negociações Coletivas e a Saúde do Trabalhador" [79, pp. 39-45].

79. Mario Bonciani, coord., *Saúde, Ambiente e Contrato Coletivo de Trabalho: Experiencias em Negociação Coletiva*, LTr Editora, São Paulo, 1996.

80. Nilton Freitas and Arline Arcury, "Negociação Coletiva Nacional Sobre o Benzeno" [79, pp. 71-117].

81. Asa Cristina Laurell, "Research on Work and Health in Latin America: The Perspective of Social Medicine," *New Solutions*, 5,4, pp. 53-63, Summer 1995.

82. The process of desgaste was defined by Laurell as "the loss of workers' biological or psychological capacities, effective or potential, including all bio-psychological processes" [83, p. 21].

83. Asa Cristina Laurell, coord., *Para la Investigación en Salud Ocupacional*, serie Paltex, Salud y Sociedad 2000 no. 3, capítulo 1, pp. 13-35, Organización Panamericana de la Salud, Washington D.C.: 1993.

84. This movement originally concentrated in four counties of São Paulo state: Santo André, São Bernardo do Campo, São Caetano do Sul and Diadema, respectively. Hence the abbreviation ABCD. For further details on the Brazilian auto workers strike and movements, see [85].

85. John Humphrey, *Capitalist Control and the Workers' Struggle in the Brazilian Auto Industry*, Princeton University Press, Princeton, N.J., 1982.

86. Organizing model is defined as "a model of unionism that involves and empowers the membership in actions and decisions that affect them—whether bargaining for a contract, recruiting new members, settling a grievance, or lobbying on a bill in the legislature," *Labor Research Review*, no. 17, p. vi, Spring 1991.

87. Robert Sass, "A Strategic Response to the Occupational Health Establishment," *International Journal of Health Services*, 26,2, pp. 355-370, 1996. Sass' North-American critique appears idealistic, given the political context; in Brazil, with an increasingly militant movement in place in the period described, his comments seem to be warranted.

88. The Italian Workers Model, or the Union Model, is a research methodology originally elaborated by a group composed of workers and union activists at a Fiat factory, professionals (psychologists, physicians, and sociologists) and students. The model was applied by workers at thousands of workplaces in Italy in the late sixties and early seventies, challenging prior research paradigms that depended on professional dominance of research. The Italian labor movement had a wave of strong mobilization in this period and was able to apply the model throughout Italy. As a result of the thousands of studies conducted and the action that developed around them, the Italian society legitimated and incorporated working conditions and related issues into the new public health policy known as the Sanitary Reform. Brazilian intellectuals were strongly influenced by this experience. For more details about this movement, see [89, pp. 12-14].

89. Asa Laurell, Renee Loewenson, and Christer Hogstedt, "Participatory Approaches in Occupational Health Research," International Development Research Center, Ottawa, Canada, unpublished manuscript, December 1993.

90. The account that follows is based on [80, pp. 93-98].

91. Força Sindical is a centrist unofficial labor confederation with some presence in the metal workers and petrochemical workers unions.

92. *Acordo e Legislação Sobre Benzeno*, Fundação Jorge Duprat Figueiredo de Segurança e Medicina do Trabalho [FUNDACENTRO], São Paulo, 1996.

93. The Instituto Nacional de Seguro Social (INSS) is part of the Ministry of Social Welfare (MPAS). It is responsible for workers' compensation in Brazil.

94. Personal interview with Rita Fernandes, occupational physician of Sindiquímica, tape recording, July 1997, Salvador, Bahia.

95. Robert Asher, "Organized Labor and the Origins of the Occupational Safety and Health Act," *Labor's Heritage*, January 1991, 66.

96. President Fernando Collor was later impeached by the Brazilian congress on the grounds of corruption.

97. This interpretation of the role of Sindiquímica in shaping business response agrees with Moema Gramacho's.

CHAPTER 5

Environmental Management Policies in Cetrel: A Case Study of the Implementation of Pollution Control Policies in the Periphery

INTRODUCTION

This chapter is a case study of the historical evolution of environmental management policies and practices in the Central de Tratamento de Efluentes Líquidos–Empresa de Proteção Ambiental, the hazardous waste management and treatment company of the "Pólo." I divide the history of Cetrel into two distinct phases that take into account the major changes in its practices, responsibilities, ownership, and policies.

The first phase is the period of Cetrel as a state-controlled or quasi-state company; the second phase is the privatized Cetrel that had to implement CEPRAM resolutions suggested in the EIA/RIMA (discussed in chapter 3). In each of the two phases I will address, chronologically, the environmental pollution control systems adopted. After Cetrel' s privatization, it expanded its legal pollution control responsibilities, strengthened connections to the firms in the complex, and radically modified its modus operandi. In short, it restructured the delivery of waste management and treatment services, because of the new ownership and environmental control requirements [1].

FIRST PHASE: CETREL AS A PUBLIC COMPANY— "THE ENVIRONMENT IN GOOD HANDS"

The first three environmental protection systems implemented by Cetrel were the organic effluent, the inorganic effluent, and the solid hazardous wastes treatment system.

Industrial Wastewater Treatment

The industrial effluents are collected, transported, and treated at the centralized industrial wastewater treatment plant (ETE, in Portuguese). The wastewater treatment process in the early eighties can be summarized in the following steps [2].

First, metal bar screens in lift stations removed bulky items such as paper or wood. Then the water was piped to equalization basins, where the industrial effluent was homogenized and aerated. *Second*, the equalized mixture (liquor) passed to the primary settling tanks, where higher-density solid particles and floating materials were removed. *Third*, the liquor passed to aeration tanks, the most important step in the process, where the oxygenation and mechanical mix created by the aerators, and other controlled conditions, allowed colonies of bacteria and protozoa to coagulate dissolved solids into flocks and to consume them. *Fourth*, these biological flocks—the activated sludge—would be further removed in the secondary settling tanks, reducing the effluent organic load by more than 90 percent of its biochemical oxygen demand (BOD). The treated effluent was discharged into the Capivara Pequeno river, and part of the activated sludge would return to the aeration tanks by way of a screw pump, providing extra nutrients to the microorganisms. This circular flow kept the process continuous. *Fifth*, the remainder of the dissolved solids combined with the sludge generated in the primary tanks in the sludge thickeners. The sludge at the bottom of these tanks was next pumped to the aerobic digestors, where the mineralization of the sludge took place. *Sixth*, the sludge was pumped for the final disposal into sludge ponds.

By 1982, Cetrel had doubled its treatment capacity from 31,100 to 62,200 m^3/day (55,600 kg DBO/ day), treating a volume of wastewater equivalent to the volume a city of 1,200,000 residents would generate. This expanded plant could remove 95 percent of BOD and 50 percent of ammoniacal nitrogen; the sludge ponds were also discontinued due to the generation of bad hydrogen sulfide (H_2S) odors at night. With the expansion of the plant, the primary settling tanks were converted into secondary settling tanks, because the Cetrel staff had found that the former were not needed, given the specific location and operational conditions of the plant. In addition, research studies developed in a pilot sludge plant operating in the wastewater facility, coupled with the technical advice of Charles Ganze of GCA, led Cetrel to adopt landfarming as the final solution for the disposal of biological sludge [3, 4].

While Cetrel had twenty-one industries connected to its industrial wastewater treatment system by 1979, after the doubling of capacity in December of 1982, it had forty industries connected: thirty-two petrochemical and chemical, two breweries, one paper mill, four manufacturing companies, and one copper mill [5]. This situation remained almost the same until Cetrel's second expansion in the early nineties.

Solid Hazardous Wastes Treatment
and Disposal

During the first few years of Cetrel's operation, a company called Limpec was in charge of doing an inventory and disposing of the solid hazardous wastes generated in the complex, despite not having prior experience with hazardous waste treatment, storage, and disposal. Previously, Limpec had been responsible only for domestic solid waste collection and treatment in Camaçari. To handle these petrochemical hazardous wastes, Limpec constructed and operated a hazardous waste landfill. However, as expected from its lack of experience, this company made some mistakes in disposing of hazardous wastes. At the beginning of 1983, Cetrel was given the responsibility of managing and disposing of the solid hazardous wastes. It enlarged the industrial landfill, built some oil farms, and had all the leachate collected and treated at the wastewater plant [6; 7, pp. 67-68].

The solid hazardous wastes were disposed of in hazardous waste disposal trenches and oil farms. Trenches were isolated with impermeable linings and a drainage system, and filled with solid or semisolid wastes that were compatible with each other. After they were filled to capacity, the trenches were permanently covered with an impermeable cover (pvc-made) to prevent the formation of leachates. The quality of the groundwater was checked through the collection of groundwater samples from monitoring wells located at various sites around the landfill. The oil farms were designed to treat wastes that could be degraded by the soil; they consisted of an impermeable layer of compacted clay, internal and external drainage systems, small dams on each side, and a reactive layer of soil, where the wastes were incorporated into the soil.

In 1984, CEPRAM enacted the first state hazardous waste regulation; in 1987, it revised and amended this regulation to make it more detailed and precise. A technical directive on hazardous waste incineration was added to the rule. At the federal level, the Associação Brasileira de Norma Técnicas (a Brazilian association similar to the American National Standards Institute—ANSI) issued a classification code for hazardous wastes in 1987, based on the French and American experiences.

According to Fontes Lima and Alves, after 1987, all of Cetrel's solid hazardous waste management practices were revised. New landfills were built with safer protections against leachate migration (e.g., the pvc membrane was replaced by a high-density polyethylene membrane, the size of the clay layer increased, twenty new monitoring wells were added). An important concurrent event was the federal government decision to establish a large, fine-chemicals industry in the complex by 1989, which would require the installation of an incinerator of liquid chlorinated hydrocarbons. In addition, an industry in the complex faced great difficulty in having 4,000 tons/y of vinyl chloride and polyvinyl chloride incinerated in the United States and Europe [8-10].

In short, all these new legal requirements and production needs contributed to inaugurating a new stage in solid hazardous waste management by the late eighties.

Cetrel—A Typical Public Bureaucracy? [11]

During Cetrel's first twelve years of operation, the state of Bahia had majority control and appointed two of Cetrel's three directors. It was therefore controlled by two different state secretariats: the Industry and Commerce (before 1979, it was under the Mines and Energy), and the Planning, Science, and Technology. The relationship established with Cetrel's customers—the businesses in the complex—was characterized by the Cetrel employers and managers interviewed as distant. Cetrel was not well-known by customers' employees and managers; neither did those realize that the quality of Cetrel's wastewater treatment process depended on the quality of the effluent discharged by their facilities (called "affluent" in the wastewater jargon).

For example, when plant operators of the latter visited Cetrel to learn about its operations, they used to complain and make jokes about the bad odor ("a catinga," "o fedor" da Cetrel), and hold their noses while walking in its premises. Cetrel operators would reply that the firm "stinks because you [the customers] send us 'stuff' that is difficult to treat in our wastewater plant. In other words, we stink because you stink" [12].

Before start-up and during the very first couple of years, Cetrel engineers in charge of operating the facility had to figure out how to treat the effluent, charge customers, and to deal with a host of other technical problems. One of the most important technical managers had already received a master's degree in sanitary engineering at Delft University in the Netherlands. Others visited foreign facilities to learn how to operate a centralized wastewater treatment system. The experience gained through visits to Dutch, American, and German plants was discussed and compared. The state bankrolled trial-and-error studies and experiments to adapt these experiences to local conditions, in an ongoing informal process of technology transfer and adaptation. As the company grew in size and scope, new treatment methods and techniques were gradually introduced.

Born out of state investments in a growth-oriented political and economic period, Cetrel's "founding fathers" had enough financial resources and political support to do their best to design and operate a state-of-the-art industrial wastewater treatment facility. There was continuity of plans and initiatives in successive authoritarian administrations, though state politicians belonged to separate political groups or factions and had their own personal interests within the same ruling party. Yet, despite the authoritarian "stability," Cetrel was a public company subject to the routine political interference common in state bureaucracies in Brazil.

Though financially controlled by the state, Cetrel never behaved as a regulatory enforcement agency. On the contrary, the management model rationale was based on the idea of a cooperative partnership with customers. This rationale appears quite clearly in Cetrel's slogan during this first phase: "the environment in good hands," which implied that citizens should trust Cetrel as an environmental steward. The slogan also suggests that managers believed that they represented civil society vis-a-vis the petrochemical industry, in spite of depending on the fees paid by the latter to finance Cetrel's operations. In other words, citizens could have rested assured that Cetrel would protect the environment on their behalf, since the environment was in good hands, that is, under the control of Cetrel managers.

While the state CEPRAM and CRA would write the regulations that guided the work of Cetrel, CRA was the state agency in charge of enforcing the law. Nevertheless, in practical terms, CRA would seldom enforce environmental standards. By the mid-eighties, CRA started its business-friendly orientation under the leadership of Durval Olivieri, a smart pro-business bureaucrat appointed to protect business interests.

As a quasi-state company, Cetrel had some legal enforcement powers to fine violators of effluent standards, but seldom did it use these powers to penalize them. On some rare occasions it would pressure "bad actor" companies to improve their effluents and pay for damages to the colony of bacteria, the heart of the wastewater treatment process [13].

Cetrel achieved stability and fared well until the mid-eighties, when it showed multiple signs of an internal crisis: First, the "sindicato"—Sindae—gained strength and went on strike for twenty-two days in October 1986. Second, the first cases of leucopenia started to appear, the beginning of a problem that persisted for several years, as described earlier. Third, the state of Bahia was under enormous financial pressures, with huge operational deficits. Fourth, the status quo in Bahia was challenged by the democratic wave that swept the country [14].

After the reform-minded governor, Valdir Pires, was elected, Sindae demanded that he appoint a labor-friendly technical director. Responding to this and other political pressures, the governor appointed Carlos Marighela, the son of a famous deceased Brazilian Communist leader [15; 16, p. 5]. However, despite the announced good intentions of the new state administration, during the mid- to late eighties, it became clear to the state administration that Cetrel needed a broader reform. Some old equipment needed to be replaced—its useful life was ending—the treatment capacity was overloaded, and the ongoing lack of investment caused obvious problems in the plant's operations. Sindae stayed on the offensive against management, systematically denouncing Cetrel's unfair treatment of the workers affected by leucopenia, and also the gradual firing of sick employees and union activists. In addition, the EIA/RIMA uncovered the environmental "dirty laundry" that demanded correction. Last, the incinerator required investments that the state could not afford [17].

Cetrel's operational performance and image was weak, and the public knew about it more than ever. Industrial customers decided that they would pay only the money necessary to implement the "Corrective Maintenance Plan" after Cetrel had replaced some top managers. From management's vantage point, this crisis was resolved only when two new managers came on board in 1988. In hindsight, it appears that a short transition phase to prepare the privatization of and improve Cetrel's image started with this new administration [18, 19]. Revealing evidence on this period was given by the headline of an editorial in a local newspaper that read: "A Cetrel em Questão" (Cetrel under Fire) [20, p. 5]. In this editorial, Ernesto Drehmmer, director-superintendent of Cetrel, wrote:

> Cetrel completed in February 10 years of effective operation. During all this period of daily work, in defense of the environment, it has never been so much "en vogue" as today, specially through criticisms, comments and opinions from people unaware of its project, operations, and mandates. We will try to reestablish the truth, within the current reality (emphasis in the original) [20, p. 5].

A plausible explanation for this administrative change is that businesses realized that they probably could not finance the expansion in the production capacity of plants in the complex unless they took over Cetrel's management. Pragmatic considerations may have combined with the increasingly influential neoliberal "creed" to create momentum for the privatization of Cetrel. Furthermore, it is also plausible that some business leaders were also converting or being forced to convert to a greener version of business behavior, after the EIA/RIMA exposed the accumulated environmental damage caused by the complex. It is important to mention here the two major positions about Cetrel's performance as a public company.

The first contention, held by several former and current managers, argued that Cetrel was an overstaffed (because of excessive political patronage), slow-moving bureaucracy—especially when reacting to crisis and problems—that was not prepared to have a meaningful dialogue with the customers. The latter would show their dissatisfaction by blaming the state government for the firm's internal problems. The second, held by those who disagreed with this negative balance, including Sindae officers, argued that Cetrel "crawled and walked before it could run, as any new business does." It viewed this negative assessment as a biased and skewed discourse that was tactfully used to justify the privatization of the company. This perspective claimed that this management discourse is a pro-privatization ideology that flourished in Cetrel by the late eighties, whose main contention was to blame every previous organizational problem on the out-of-date state control of Cetrel before privatization [21].

SECOND PHASE: COPENE TAKES OVER CETREL—
THE "COPENIZAÇÃO" OF CETREL" [22]

Several important events and trends combined in the late eighties to early nineties to produce this new phase in Cetrel. First and foremost, Cetrel changed ownership with privatization. From a company controlled by the state, it turned into a private company controlled by the polluters. Secondly, it became private after the state of Bahia had determined that the complex would not be licensed to expand unless it implemented new environmental protection programs. Third, the complex went through major productive restructuring, dramatically changing preexisting conditions. Fourth, national, international, and state trends toward market-oriented policies started to dominate the social, political, and economic landscape.

The joint effect of these factors on Cetrel's routine operations was such that it is not an exaggeration to theorize that new "rules of the game" emerged. Cetrel started to function in a totally new environment. It expanded its scope of action, reorganized its staff, modified its relationship with customers and the state, and switched to a corporate-dominated mode of operation. It became the Environmental Protection Company.

The Privatization of Cetrel

In October 1989 the House of Representatives of Bahia approved the bill that proposed the sale of Cetrel to the private sector, increasing its ownership in the company to 66 percent of the voting shares. Clearly, depending on the assessment of Cetrel's performance as a public company, one may favor or oppose the privatization of Cetrel.

To those who decry Cetrel's past, privatization was responsible for all the good changes that occurred afterward, implying that privatization caused a radical rupture with the past. For those who do not criticize the firm's past as harshly, privatization was, at best, a leverage in Cetrel's continuous process of organizational development; it had already achieved maturity by the time it became private. Some labor critics claimed that the new Cetrel operational scheme meant that "the fox [Cetrel] would take care of the henhouse [individual companies]," or that it was the same as "giving bananas for monkeys to take care of" [23].

According to Sindae, the state government lied about the true financial situation of Cetrel, because it did have enough funds to finance Cetrel's expansion. In reality, it was underselling Cetrel to the private sector [24]. Paulo Jackson Villas Boas, president of Sindae for six years (1986-1991), added a health and safety angle to the effects of privatization, in a 1992 interview with Cetrel's newspaper:

> We understand that the question of the privatization of Cetrel, combined with the contracting-out issue, is a way of undermining the protection of workers' health. We know that the complex has steadily promoted contracting-out, and

there are numerous cases of contractor employees affected by occupational illnesses or victims of some sort of workplace accident, who work without any safety. And, within Cetrel, these employees have been summarily fired by these contractors. And there is nobody complaining, nobody following them up, who can protect them against the very serious situation to which they are exposed [25, p. 2].

A quite different viewpoint was offered by the state secretary of Commerce and Tourism, Luiz Bacellar, who stated that "the state government cannot afford the new investments needed to expand and modernize Cetrel; these resources have been provided by the private sector" [26, p. 3; 27; 28].

A more in-depth perspective was given by Mascarenhas, who submitted that

[t]he state, sometimes, has the function of making up for the deficiencies in free enterprise. When the complex was established, the state investment in the environment was very important, because had the state not done it, the companies would have been burdened and lost their capacity to compete with the other existing [Capuava, São Paulo] petrochemical complex. This was one criticism of the opponents of the complex, that a noncompetitive industry would be established in Bahia. Against this background, the action of the state was very conscious. It invested upfront, made the system viable, and little by little, it withdrew. In fact, after the system matured, after the companies took over Cetrel, there were not any reasons for the state to continue leading the area. I support that the state continues to have a participation in the system, to the extent that the environment is a public interest issue. Nevertheless, the firms have conditions, duty and obligation to take care of the treatment of their own hazardous wastes [29, p. 2].

The debate around the causes and effects of the privatization of Cetrel still goes on in certain sectors of Bahian society and nationally. Nonetheless, the substantial transformation that Cetrel privatization suffered in the early nineties is undeniable and beyond controversy.

Cetrel: A Model in Environmental Protection [30]

Incineration

The fifth pollution control system started by Cetrel was the incineration of liquid chlorinated hydrocarbons (such as PCBs, pentachlorophenols, dichloro-benzene, nitrochlorobenzene, and others) installed in August 1991 to burn the wastes mainly produced by two companies in the complex: CPC and Nitroclor [31]. It was constructed as a result of state requirements that conditioned the installation of new units (Nitroclor, the fine-chemical "central" and Silinor) in the complex to the incineration of their wastes at high temperatures. Moreover, CPC had stored chlorinated hydorcarbons in large tanks since the start-up of its pvc plant in 1979 and had about 12,000 tons of them stored on-site by 1990.

According to Cetrel brochures, internal documents, and articles, the Swiss Sulzer technology incinerator has the nominal capacity to burn 10,000 tons of liquid waste per year, a 99.9999 percent destruction and removal efficiency, and a combustion efficiency of 99.99 percent [32-34]. It operates at 1200^0 C (2,192° F), an operational temperature that is claimed to strongly reduce the formation of dioxins [35, 36]. The incinerator was sited as near as possible to its customers to avoid transportation-related leaks and spills. Underground wells were positioned around the facility to monitor potential infiltration of the groundwater. Cetrel's laboratories routinely analyze the wastes and plant performance. Last, but not least, the incinerator is said to meet all Brazilian emission standards [37].

By the end of 1991, it had incinerated almost 2,200 tons of organo-chlorines and the test runs had confirmed its efficiency [38]. Nonetheless, a master's thesis study conducted by a Cetrel chemist found high emission levels of hydrochloric acid, chloride, and ammonia in areas affected by the operation of the incinerator [39].

Two additional pollution control systems began in 1992, the groundwater monitoring and the ocean disposal systems. Simultaneously, the construction work to expand and modernize the centralized industrial wastewater treatment plant ended in May 1992, while the construction of facilities for the temporary storage of hazardous wastes (silos, warehouses, and patios) concluded in June 1992 [40].

Groundwater Monitoring

The groundwater monitoring system is probably the most controversial environmental system operated by Cetrel, for several reasons. First, the complex is located on top of the main freshwater reservoir in Bahia, the São Sebastião aquifer. Rebouças wrote that about two hundred wells were drilled in the eighties, of which 50 percent were still in use by 1990 [41, 42]. Second, the state of Bahia did not have any clearly designated agency in charge of protecting the groundwater for many years. Thus, groundwater management has been haphazard. Third, the extent of groundwater contamination was unknown throughout the eighties.

These elements combined to generate a charged atmosphere in the nineties. Environmental groups and academics accused complex managers of purposefully polluting this strategic resource. Other commentators added that the siting of the complex over the aquifer would inevitably generate serious environmental problems.

According to Rebouças, the contamination of the groundwater with synthetic organic chemicals and toxic metals was first detected in the mid eighties. Later, the EIA/RIMA determined that there were many potential sources and causes for groundwater contamination: on-site waste-disposal systems, the wastewater treatment plant, storm water and industrial waste discharges, landfills, evaporation ponds and lagoons, transportation accidents, underground storage tanks, etc. [41]. In sum, there were several poorly controlled potential sources of contamination.

To resolve this problem, the EIA/RIMA recommended the design and application of a groundwater management plan divided into three phases: 1) physical resource definition, 2) groundwater monitoring, and 3) groundwater management.

CEPRAM Resolution 620 transformed this recommendation into law, and Cetrel was given the responsibility to monitor the groundwater in June 1992. With the help of an expert consultant, Cetrel set up the groundwater management plan together with its customers. The plan envisioned the operation of 340 monitoring wells, 114 production wells, nineteen pairs of multilevel monitoring wells, and twelve pump-and-treat wells; the elimination of the primary sources of contamination; an assessment of the secondary sources; the remediation of isolated areas; the shutdown of production wells in contaminated areas; and the operation of the hydraulic barrier.

According to Marinho et al., a major weakness of the groundwater management plan is the restricted public access to monitoring data and information [43]. This is, by the way, a general problem with much of the information generated by Cetrel.

Ocean Disposal System [44, 45, p. 18]

The ocean disposal system is composed of a standpipe, an almost seven-mile-long land outfall, an absorption tower, and a three-mile-long concrete-lined submarine outfall. The submarine part has 180 diffusers in the last .3 miles (500 m) that allegedly guarantee a dilution of 1:200 between the industrial effluent and the sea. Cetrel invested $35 million to build the ocean disposal system, under contract with the consortium Odebrecht-Concic.

To assess the impact of the industrial effluent on the marine ecosystem, Cetrel monitored it before (between April 1990 and December 1991) and after installation of the ocean disposal system (after August 1992). According to Cetrel, these oceanographic studies followed the guidelines provided by the American firms, Engineering Science and E.D. Grandle Associates. Eleven sampling stations were set up along the coast to monitor the evolution of the marine ecosystem, in particular to detect sea levels of nitrogen, phosphorus, carbon, and heavy metals.

Cetrel claimed that the start-up of this system enabled the polluted rivers in the area to recover, with the return of river life, oxygen levels, pH, Biochemical Oxygen Demand (BOD), and Chemical Oxygen Demand (COD), to levels that had existed before the construction of the complex [46]. Though touted by Cetrel staff as the best solution to reduce the pollution of the Capivara Pequeno and Jacuípe rivers, Cetrel's choice for the ocean disposal system was not free of controversies.

On the one hand, company staff argued that, among the different alternatives studied for the final discharge of the liquid effluents after the expansion of the complex, only two were economically viable and technically feasible: a) advanced (with the removal of BOD and nitrification) secondary treatment of the industrial effluent combined with tertiary treatment through photosynthetic lagoons (also called polishing lagoons); or b) secondary treatment combined with ocean disposal of the treated effluent. Cetrel's staff and consulting engineers considered the second alternative the best, since the lagoons would demand large amounts of land and not contribute much for increasing the removal of the organic pollutant load. They discarded CEPRAM Resolution 218/89—mandated tertiary treatment—on economic and technical grounds.

On the other hand, independent sanitary and environmental engineers preferred the EIA/RIMA- recommended tertiary treatment as the most environment friendly method. For example, First stated that the submarine outfall was a "high risk proposal" [47, p. 3]. A representative of the local environmental group Gamba, Renato Paes da Cunha, seemed to concur by adding that "the secondary treatment is insufficient to control environmental quality" [48, p. 3]. In addition, these opposing views believed that Cetrel was shifting pollution to a larger receiving body without doing enough to reduce pollution by heavy metals or persistent organic pollutants.

Cetrel answered this concern with the so-called "source control" or pretreatment program, which requires clients to discharge their effluents according to strict "Californian Ocean Plan" pollution-discharge standards. Thus, companies had to reduce and control the discharge of persistent organic chemicals listed by the EPA as priority pollutants under the Clean Water Act. Since many of these pollutants might not be treatable by Cetrel's activated sludge system, the only way to avoid polluting the sea would be to control for their discharge. Freire et al. wrote that the source pollution control program was conceived to reduce the pollutant load of the "Pólo" by 30 percent in five years, following the EPA Waste Minimization Assessment procedures [49, 50].

Wastewater Treatment Plant Expansion and Modernization

As mentioned before, the operational efficiency of Cetrel had reached a low point in the late eighties. One indicator of this low status is the 85 percent to 90 percent DBO removal and the less-than 65 percent COD removal in the wastewater treatment plant—values considered low for petrochemical wastewater [45, p. 17]. The expansion of the complex demanded a concurrent expansion and modernization of the wastewater treatment plant, which combined with the ocean disposal system to create a new, integrated, industrial effluent treatment system.

All the old operational units were totally renovated and modernized. For example, new submerged aerators were installed in the equalization basins, and cone-shaped systems (known as "Oxi Cap" covers) were installed in the aeration tanks to prevent the generation and dispersion of aerosols, odors, and splashes [45, p. 6]. The operation of the plant became automated. By 1997, operators could control most facility operations by looking at screens of portable computers, similar to the operators in control rooms of chemical plants. Lift stations can now be centrally monitored and operated. Equipment may be switched on and off very easily. In a word, Cetrel implemented state-of-the-art technology to run the wastewater facility.

The treatment capacity more than doubled to 148,000 m³/day, which is equivalent to the wastewater produced by a city of about three million inhabitants; the pollutant removal capability increased to 95 percent to 98 percent of the BOD and more than 80 percent of the COD. In fact, by 1992, Cetrel had two wastewater plants running in parallel, since most of the units were duplicated [51]. After the $40 million investment, Cetrel's industrial wastewater treatment capabilities changed from undercapacity to overcapacity, because the planned duplication of several plants in the complex did not occur.

Air Monitoring Network

According to Neves, when the complex started its operations in 1978, a meteorological station and a primary network to monitor sulfur dioxide and particulate matter concentrations in the air were installed in the area [52-55]. However, this equipment was not sufficient to meet the air-monitoring needs in the area affected by the complex. The EIA/RIMA pointed out that the expansion of the complex would require the use of an air-monitoring network to improve air quality monitoring and control. In addition, Neves noted that a survey carried out in 1991 by COFIC revealed that the population of neighboring communities—Dias D'Ávila, Camaçari, and Lamarão do Passé—had deep concerns regarding air quality, perceived as bad due to the emission of toxic gases that smelled bad and could intoxicate people [56].

CEPRAM Resolution 620/92 entrusted Cetrel to design and operate a multi-parameter, continuous air-monitoring network in the area affected by hazardous air pollutants. Firms pay for the operation of the network ($400,000/y) according to their emissions and the cost of monitoring for each pollutant emitted, i.e., fees are proportional to pollutant emission levels. So, Copene and a few other companies (such as Deten, Fafen, Acrinor, and Caraíba Metais) end up footing most of the bill [57, 58].

Before setting up the network, Cetrel hired a famous Brazilian air quality expert to help design it, using mathematical models and local climate parameters to calculate the atmospheric dispersion of pollutants [59]. An inventory of company emissions was elaborated. After this preliminary work, Cetrel decided in 1994 to establish a network of eight fixed air-monitoring stations, designed with French technology.

Four of these stations are complete stations that can continuously monitor the air concentrations of criteria pollutants—sulfur dioxide, nitrogen oxides (NO_x), carbon monoxide, ozone (two stations), and particulate matter—and volatile organic compounds (e.g., benzene, toluene, and xylene). They are located in strategic sites of neighboring urban communities. The remaining four are incomplete stations that can only monitor the air concentration of hydrocarbons, sulfur dioxide, and particulate matter. These are found in more remote and less-polluted areas [60]. A high-tech mobile unit installed in a multi-use van complemented the network, the Fourier Transform Infrared or FTIR [61].

Again, while there may be some technical controversy among local experts regarding the quality and correctness of the data collected, and the siting of the air stations, the most sensitive issue about the air- monitoring network might be the lack of free access to information [62]. Cetrel claimed that since it does not own the data, only CRA can provide public access to its reports. CRA, on the other hand, does not easily release the data to the public [63, 64].

After three full years of experience operating the network, Cetrel staff has been discussing with customers' managers how to reduce the emissions of hazardous pollutants found over the legal emission standards. In turn, Brazil's air quality emission standards follow EPA's National Emission Standards for Hazardous Air Pollutants (NESHAP).

According to Neves, the control of emissions of organic compounds, metals, and ozone should be the priority for the future. This may be a daunting task for the company because on the one hand, Brazil—as well as most developed countries—lacks standards for individual VOCs and metals, making it very difficult for Cetrel to propose a local standard based only on the experience of the Camaçari complex [65]. On the other, staff do not know why there are seasonal variations for some compounds, such as benzene, which has lower levels during the rainy season, while other chemicals have higher levels.

Beyond the pollution control systems already mentioned, Cetrel adopted several other programs that deserve mention. These programs will be described in the following sections, according to their relevance to the objectives of this research [66].

Occupational Health Program

According to the account of the current Cetrel health and safety team leader, Cetrel started to have a good health and safety program only after 1993. Some initiatives had been pursued before, but they were far and few between [67]. Monitoring campaigns to measure exposures to hydrocarbons in operational areas of Cetrel started in 1989, when Cetrel contracted with a Brazilian consulting firm to plan and execute an industrial hygiene program for the company [68].

Reports produced by the contractor indicate that the area and personal monitoring implemented in different sections of Cetrel, such as lift stations, equalization and aeration basins, landfarms, and hazardous waste landfills—in 1992 the incinerator was also included—followed the homogeneous exposure groups sampling methodology. Laboratory analysis of samples followed NIOSH guidelines [69]. Biological monitoring for benzene exposures was done by means of urinary phenol tests and blood exams.

Data collected in 1991showed low levels of exposure to benzene, toluene, xylene, 1-2 dichloroethane (dce), methylene chloride, 1,1,1 tricholoroethane, and chloroform. Therefore, the reports stated that Cetrel exposures did not violate Brazilian regulations, nor the U.S. Threshold Limit Values (TLVs) for these compounds. The contractor recommended that Cetrel set up an ongoing industrial hygiene program and monitor workers and workplaces every two months, during rainy and dry seasons. A list of potential chemicals to be routinely sampled was also prepared.

Cetrel employees democratically elected the "Comissão de Saúde" (health committee) in May 1992 to replace the CIPA as the labor-management committee in charge of representing their safety and health interests [70]. The actions of this health committee caused Cetrel to develop a comprehensive health and safety program that included:

- The organization of an information system for occupational accidents and injuries. Data on all occupational injuries and accidents from 1990 on were collected. A company health information system started to collect all information on employee visits to the medical service of Cetrel, composed of a part-time physician and a full-time licensed practical nurse.
- The continuation of the industrial hygiene and safety activities, such as area and personal monitoring of exposures to gases and vapors, monitoring of combustible vapors in lift stations, noise monitoring, and the company-wide installation of intrinsically safe tools and equipment.
- Training of employees in basic health and safety, use of personal protective equipment, and emergency response procedures [71].

While 1994 was marked by the gradual application of this program, in an atmosphere of struggles between the union and company regarding the role of the CIPA, 1995-1996 saw many accomplishments. Cetrel developed risk mapping of its facilities to comply with an NR-5 amendment, conducted a complex-wide emergency response drill, and implemented respiratory protection and personal protective equipment programs [72].

Health and safety staff wrote a manual describing all health and safety procedures for routine operations, to be followed by supervisors who authorize work orders. Some staff attended graduate courses and international conferences in occupational health and industrial hygiene to improve their technical skills and reduce the firm's dependence on external consultants [73].

Last, but not least, Cetrel began a workplace health promotion program titled, "QualiVida," to promote improved lifestyles of its employees through better nutrition, smoking cessation, reduced alcohol consumption, and increased physical activity. It is similar to workplace-wellness programs adopted in several corporations in the United States [74].

It appears that Cetrel has built a reasonably comprehensive health and safety program in the nineties, comparable only to the best companies in Brazil. Unfortunately, it has become a company-driven and dominated program with less participation from Sindae; yet it has accomplished many goals suggested by the union.

Organizational Changes

During the early years of Cetrel's reorganization process, the technical director of Cetrel defined:

> ... [t]he four links that composed the chain of technology and practices that would enable the company to achieve its main goal: excellence in environmental control in the area affected by the "Pólo Petroquímico de Camaçari ... Adopt the best internationally available treatment for liquid effluents of petrochemical industries; measure up to the most advanced technology for treating and disposing of solid hazardous wastes; monitor the environment and its natural resources; carry out solutions to the impact of the complex on nature, and protect the health of those who work in Cetrel to protect the environment [75, p. 3].

Underlying all these links, a fifth one was fundamental: Love of nature. The director-superintendent of Cetrel, José Antonio Andrade, added that Cetrel had two other targets: operational efficiency and cost reduction. But these were not as important as the quality of the service delivered. To the investments in the infrastructure (hardware), one must add administrative, philosophical, and behavioral changes (i.e., software changes).

According to these two managers, the application of $125 million in investments in the new environmental systems described before, and others not touched upon, contributed to elevate Cetrel's performance and technology to the same level of practices of petrochemical complexes that existed in developed countries [75].

Therefore, by the end of 1991, Cetrel's top managers laid out the framework for the organizational development of the company in the nineties. Under their leadership, Cetrel started many new programs and initiatives such as [76]:

- Creation of the newspaper *BEM-TE-VI*, which became the *Jornal da Cetrel* in 1993, and the weekly newsletter *Comunicação Direta* (Direct Communication). The newspaper published several interviews with prominent Brazilian environmentalists, intellectuals, politicians, administrators, and artists over the years [77].

- The Administrative Modernization Program, to improve the efficiency of company activities. Three high-level positions, two directors, and one mid-level manager were eliminated. The workforce was downsized from 319 to 220 "collaborators," and services were contracted out according to efficiency and cost reduction criteria [38].
- "Voluntários da Praia" (Volunteers of the Beach), a program sponsored by the employees' association (Grece) to clean up the beaches of Arembepe and neighboring communities.
- Implementation of a 500 ha (about 1.9 sq. miles) Ecological Park in Cetrel, under the guidance of the consultant Pedro Lima, a veterinarian and ornithologist, who since 1988 had started the "Program to Preserve the Flora and Fauna in Cetrel's premises."
- Optimization of operations, including human resource training and motivational meetings to "humanize" Cetrel's operations.
- The Corrective and Preventive Maintenance Program.
- Open dialogue with representatives of environmental groups (Gamba and Germen) and Sindae.
- Joint sponsorship with the International Association of Water Quality of the Third International Conference on Waste Management in the Chemical and Petrochemical Industries, held in October 1993 in Salvador.
- The "Fábrica Aberta" (Open Factory) Program, which opened Cetrel for community visits [78]. Because of this program, hundreds of visitors—high school teachers and students of neighboring communities, environmental experts, university professionals, etc.—had the opportunity to get to know Cetrel with "their own eyes."
- Comissão Técnica de Garantia Ambiental (CTGA)—Technical Committee for Environmental Assurance—a company committee legally responsible for self-auditing the environmental performance of Cetrel [79].

In November 1993, two new directors were appointed by the board of Cetrel: Carlos Eugenio Menezes and José Antonio Saraiva. Both had strong connections with Copene, and claimed that they would continue the work of the former administration [81]. The "Copenização" of Cetrel started during this administration, which also launched a host of new programs, including the Predictive Maintenance Program, the Operators and Supervisors Training and Certification Program, and the Total Quality Management (TQM) Program [82, 83].

The Cetrel operations manager stated that after these human resource development programs, routine operations improved a great deal. The BOD removal and other performance indicators improved substantially. Operators became more involved and integrated while running the plants. In a nutshell, this manager thinks that Cetrel up-skilled the core parts of its workforce [3].

By 1994, Cetrel had started the process of creating an all-encompassing environmental management system (SGA) coordinated by the CTGA. Menezes and Saraiva expressed the need for this new environmental management system in two different articles they wrote for the *Jornal da Cetrel* [84]. In the first, Menezes articulated the progress already made in the nineties and the future challenges lying ahead for Cetrel. In the second, Saraiva explained why Cetrel had decided "to adopt the ISO 14,000 certification as one of its main priorities." He argued that Cetrel had gone through a modernization and expansion of all its facilities that cost US$125 million. Besides, since 1992, the company had been very engaged in the Responsible Care program with the other companies in the complex. Therefore, Cetrel was ready to move forward and establish a pro-active environmental management style, which would be the next step in its continuous improvement process [84].

Voluntary Environmental Protection Marches In: The British Standard 7750 and the ISO 14001 Environmental Management Systems

Between January and September of 1995, Cetrel developed its environmental management system, which consumed a total of 14,000 hours of labor. Pereira and Kauss claimed that it was totally conceived and sized according to the BS 7750 criteria, considered a precursor of the International Standardization Organization (ISO) 14000 series [85-87].

Cetrel's strategy viewed the preparation needed for certification under BS-7750 requirements as a necessary step before ISO 14001 certification, i.e., with one organizational effort, two certifications would be achieved.

Following the requirements of BS-7750, Cetrel did a preparatory environmental review "to evaluate all the aspects of the organization, identifying its strong and weak points, the risks and opportunities as the bases for the establishment of the company's future Environmental Management System—EMS" [85, p. 225; 88]. Cetrel had to compile all the legal and regulatory requirements that it must comply with or that it follows voluntarily, including state, national, and international environmental regulations; identify and list all significant environmental effects, beneficial and adverse, that result from its activities, linking the effect with the environmental system that causes it; analyze its own environmental practices in detail; and assess the reactions received from previous environmental accidents, incidents, and situations of noncompliance with environmental regulations, policies, and procedures [89].

This new environmental management system reorganized Cetrel's operations and functions to meet the goals of the BS-7750 and also demanded a variety of initiatives:

a. Cetrel developed an environmental policy that set the context for the formulation of environmental objectives, which translated into multiple standard operating procedures. A fundamental principle of this voluntary initiative was to establish standards that would be more stringent than the Brazilian environmental legislation. Cetrel's BS-7750 environmental policy is composed of eight items [90]. The procedures created by the application of the EMS detail how these policy items should be executed on a day-to-day basis.

b. An environmental management system committee was formed to oversee the development of the system; to establish Cetrel's environmental policy, objectives, and targets; to participate in and provide support for the self-audit program and its follow-up; and to analyze and control use of the system. The EMS committee is composed of Cetrel's directors, managers, and the EMS coordinator, who coordinates several activities triggered by the system. An implementation group composed of fourteen staff members from several departments was also formed to coordinate the EMS.

c. Cetrel standardized its documentation, communication, operation, and monitoring functions. The EMS is described in the environmental management manual, which summarizes all the "general guidelines adopted by the Company to carry out environmental management systematically, identifying responsibilities, resources used, existing operational controls and relevant documentation" [85, p. 229]. The manual lists six environmental protection systems.

From the analysis of its environmental effects, Cetrel evaluated 132 effects, of which fifty-two were deemed significant after screening. Furthermore, it was found that Cetrel had to comply with six permits—for hazardous waste disposal, the temporary storage installations, the expansion of solid hazardous waste disposal system, the incineration unit, air and groundwater monitoring, and the liquid effluent system.

d. Cetrel established a specific internal system to verify compliance and noncompliance with BS-7750 requirements, through self-audits, measurements, documentation, and testing mechanisms that aim at continuous checking of its performance.

Taking advantage of the work done to get the BS-7750 certification, Cetrel adapted and converted previous documents and materials to get the ISO 14001 certification a few months later.

The ISO 14001 environmental policy is composed of seven items: continuous improvement/ pollution prevention, industrial waste and effluent reduction, environmental aspects/impact reduction, environmental liabilities elimination, communication with interested parties, support and improvement of the environmental legislation and regulations, and environmental objectives and targets.

Beyond minor cosmetic language modifications, the major change between the ISO 14001 and the BS-7750 policies is the explicit inclusion of pollution prevention in the company environmental policy. The same 132 aspects/impacts ("effects" in the BS-7750) were identified. Thirteen instead of eleven environmental objectives and targets were set, comprising an updated and more specific version than the list of objectives and targets of the BS-7750 standard [91]. Cetrel identified 521 procedures and operational instructions in the ISO 14001-tailored

EMS, compared with 425 in the BS-7750. The list of environmental protection systems has eight instead of seven systems, because the solid hazardous waste disposal was broken down into two systems [92]. Company programs listed in the ISO 14001 certification document included Source Control, Fauna Preservation in the Company Area, Environmental Education, and Reforestation of the Company Area, among others [85, p. 224; 93].

In conclusion, it is evident from company documents, my own observations, and interviews with Cetrel staff that once Cetrel got these certifications, all company activities fell under the purview of the new environmental management system. Operational efficiency of pollution control systems continued to improve, productivity increased, and new managerial practices and policies have been systematically introduced, such as the Total Productivity Management (TPM) [94].

The current director-superintendent of Cetrel argues that Cetrel's voluntary initiative credentials the firm as a business that follows internationally recognized environmental management standards. With the ISO certification, Cetrel achieved international excellence in environmental control. Therefore, Cetrel has given the complex a "green seal," a quality seal for environmental performance that makes the complex "environmentally correct." The ultimate result of the effort is that the exports of the complex will be better accepted in the demanding consumer markets of developed countries in Europe and North America [1, 95, 96].

In essence, this statement seems to suggest that the close integration of Cetrel with its customers reached a new level in the nineties—the Copenização of Cetrel, in which the management and treatment of hazardous wastes have become an integral part of the strategic planning of petrochemical businesses. Cetrel started this integration with the adoption of the Responsible Care Program by COFIC, which included codes of voluntary practices to be followed by chemical and petrochemical businesses. A common set of policies developed, unifying all companies in the complex.

As discussed earlier, this process suggests that corporate environmentalism may have come full-circle when private businesses increased their control of Cetrel. The business class not only set the local environmental pollution control agenda—and how it was to be done—but also controlled the execution of that agenda. Voluntary codes of conduct and environmental management systems became the dominant game in town. Moreover, and not less important, Bahian businesses integrated their local and national agenda with the international chemical business agenda. This is what the BS-7750 and ISO certification appears to have accomplished, once for all.

Beware ISO: The Standardization of Corporate Control [97, 98]

The first implication of the Cetrel's ISO 14001 EMS concerns the relationship between the ISO certification (and its precursor BS-7750), the importation of technologies and EMS systems to control environmental—and often occupational—hazards. The second implication involves the pros and cons of adopting voluntary environmental management systems to control environmental pollution. The third implication corresponds to the growing lack of democratic control over the impacts of hazardous technologies in Bahia [99].

Regarding the first point, it appears self-evident that since Cetrel was certified under ISO 14000 criteria, it has all the support needed to claim that it achieved internationally credible excellence in hazardous waste management and treatment. Therefore, it can also declare that its practices measure up to the best in the hazardous waste management business. In fact, the Cetrel public relations message stresses that it was the first company in its business activities in the world, and the second in Brazil, to get ISO 14001 certification [100].

If, as Bennett and Tickner claimed, the ISO 14001 standard is an international environmental management system that is the "international corporate agenda to substitute voluntary international standards for mandatory national standards embodied in regulations," then Castleman's double standard argument does not hold for Cetrel's case [87; 98, p. 37; 101]. In addition, when a common, corporate-driven, set of policies and standards may be applied worldwide, by definition they may negate the possibility of double standards of practices and policies in multinational companies with chemical plants operating in developed and developing countries.

This chapter described how Cetrel became certified as "compliant with" a voluntary environmental management system that may have the same shape and form all over the world. It also showed that Cetrel's environmental control systems adopted a wide range of modern end-of-pipe technologies, allegedly some of the best available in the market. Further, Cetrel's combination of best pollution control technologies and best environmental management practices fits the mainstream "green" discourse of oil and chemical industry leaders of developed countries, repeated loud and clear in Bahia [102, 103].

From the evidence presented above, one cannot but conclude that ISO 14000 suggests the concrete possibility of a common system, discourse, and standard for corporate environmental control practices and policies. This conclusion raises a second question: How good the ISO 14000 standards are if companies in developed and developing countries can "pass the test" and become ISO 14001-certified?

Bennett asserted that the ISO 14000 series does not "establish a standard for environmental protection, not does it measure environmental performance. Environmental performance is not audited, nor is there any cross-referencing between the auditing standards and the environmental performance standard. . . ." [98, p. 40]. In addition, ISO does not

> . . . establish absolute requirements for environmental performance beyond commitment, in the policy, to compliance with applicable legislation and

regulations and to continuing improvement. Thus, two organizations carrying out similar activities but having different environmental performance may both comply with its requirements [98, pp. 40-41].

Two hypothetical scenarios arise from the statement above: Two organizations in developed and developing countries may either comply or not comply with national regulations that have different levels of stringency—developed countries' regulations normally having stronger requirements. Even if both firms comply, the levels of requirements for the two companies may still differ a great deal. Thus, Castleman's double standards argument may hold even when these companies are ISO 14001-certified [104, 105].

However, this is not the most relevant aspect regarding Cetrel. Instead, the most important issue is the limitation of pollution controls in reducing or eliminating the environmental pollution generated by petrochemical production. While the ISO 14001 standard may not intend to validate all types of end-of-pipe controls as solutions to environmental pollution, it ends up doing so because it does not require performance standards above and beyond a company's status quo, nor is it grounded on a different environmental control paradigm [106].

Geiser provided substantive information in his writings to pinpoint the flaws of the mainstream "command and control," single media, and end-of-pipe pollution control policies. He proposed a paradigm shift toward pollution prevention, toxics use reduction, and cleaner production [107-112]. In summary, Geiser argued that

> . . . the move toward sustainable industry stems from the shortcomings of 25 years of pollution control regulations. Conventional environmental protection policy seeks to safeguard the public by setting conditions and limits on the release of contaminants. Except for some exposure prohibitions in occupational health and safety laws, governments have focused on wastes, emissions, and air and water quality while rarely intervening in the decisions of private firms about their selection of materials and technologies [110, p. 66; 113].

Citing Lee Thomas, a former EPA administrator, Geiser called this conventional approach "the strategy of the cork," that is, " . . . putting a cork in every pollution source you can find as quickly as possible," elsewhere called the "one-pipe-at-a-time" approach [109, p. 1; 114]. He also submitted that there is a need to go beyond assimilation and chemical-specific regulations, in the direction of integrating "industrial and environmental needs into a single vision of sustainable industrial development" [110, p. 67].

Therefore, even assuming that Cetrel may have the best available infrastructure and management in pollution control—which may enable it to perform beyond compliance with state environmental regulations—the ultimate issue is that petrochemical production in Bahia has released—and still releases—persistent chlorinated organic pollutants into the environment. Incineration of these chemicals still releases dioxins and furans into the air and contaminates the soil. Shifting the discharges of treated industrial wastewater to the sea may still seriously contaminate it over time with toxic chemicals, as the U.S. Great Lakes and the North Sea experience have shown. Groundwater treatment may never clean up past contamination.

The logical implication of the ISO certification is that Cetrel may have conveniently imported from the United States and Europe the best that can be done under the conventional paradigm, but the fundamental environmental impacts of the "Pólo" are far from being eliminated. Mitigation of these impacts certainly occurred, but their prevention looms large in the future. While the Cetrel staff is slowly trying to push its clients toward source control and pollution prevention practices, a commitment enshrined in Cetrel's environmental policy, much more remains to be done [115]. Commoner, after reviewing the impact of fifteen years of U.S. EPA regulations on environmental quality, said it better than anybody: "[T]he best way to stop toxic chemicals from entering the environment is not to produce them" [110, p. 67].

Last, but not least, there remains the issue of lack of societal, especially union and community, and state control over petrochemical production in Bahia. Adding to the arguments already made earlier for the whole complex, I posit that the ISO 14001 EMS gives Cetrel increased control over its own practices [116, 117]. Cetrel now knows a lot more about the occupational and environmental health impacts of its operations. However, while it has written standardized procedures to deal with societal complaints, the "Communication with Interested Parties" Program, it does not have to change operational procedures to handle these complaints, nor increase its transparency to inform the public about day-to-day releases, total emissions, and discharges.

The voluntary ISO EMS may have improved the firms' operations, yet it did not promote democratic relations with the public, its employees, and the state. The nature of this new ISO 14000 EMS game is undemocratic; decks are clearly stacked against popular control of corporate decisions. Neither the union, nor the state, nor neighboring communities around the complex, have had much say in the implementation of the EMS.

Bennett seemed to indicate that this lack of participation is inherent in the ISO standards when he wrote that ". . . there are very few examples of ISO conformity procedures being handled by joint committees of workers and managers [and governments, I would add]. The best that can be said is that some of the work on ISO conformity is done by employees who happen to be union members" [98, p. 38; 118].

ENDNOTES

1. This account of the changes in Cetrel is the version proposed by the current administration, as expressed in an interview with Carlos Eugenio Menezes,

director-superintendent of Cetrel, during the show "Face to Face," broadcast on July 15, 1997, Salvador, Bahia, by the local public television, TV Educativa. This account is also supported by former managers and current employees. However, disagreements do exist as to the causes and reasons for the changes. This debate will be addressed later in the chapter.

2. The description offered here is based on Cetrel's brochures of the mid-eighties. I chose to describe the old treatment process in order to highlight the changes that occurred when Cetrel expanded. During the same TV interview [1], the director of Cetrel affirmed that until the early nineties, the treated effluent was discharged into the Capivara Pequeno river in a ratio of 1/10 between the effluent and the river water, causing a sizable negative impact on the ecosystem.

3. Manoel Neiva, Cetrel's sanitary engineer in charge of wastewater operations, interview by author, tape recording, July 1997, Camaçari, Bahia.

4. These bad odors resulted from the nightly anaerobic digestion of sludge. The expansion also added a new aeration tank to the plant. According to this source, these modifications in Cetrel's wastewater operations were the first signs of the learning process that occurred in the first five years of operation of the plant; during these years Cetrel staff gained experience in operating the plant and added—or adapted—new technologies to the plant [3].

5. Cetrel brochure *Cinco Anos Tratando os Rejeitos Industriais do Pólo Petroquímico de Camaçari-Bahia*, (Five years treating the industrial wastes of the Pólo Petroquímico de Camaçari-Bahia), Camaçari, Bahia, 1984.

6. According to Francisco Fontes Lima and Francisco Alves Pereira, the treatment, storage, and final disposal of hazardous solid wastes were not adequately dealt with until 1984, because of the lack of technical knowledge and information in the early years of the complex [7]. They wrote that since Brazil and Bahia did not have specific regulations on hazardous solid waste management, the complex adopted the U.S. Resource Conservation and Recovery Act (RCRA) regulation; the hazardous solid wastes were classified as red wastes and the nonhazardous as green wastes [7, pp. 67-68].

7. Francisco Fontes Lima and Francisco Alves Pereira, "Avanços no Tratamento de Resíduos Industriais," (Advances in the treatment of industrial wastes), *Análise&Dados*, CEI, I, 4, pp. 67-68, March 1992.

8. According to several newspapers and company sources, by 1989 the complex generated 6,000 tons of organic solid waste, 10,000 tons of chlorinated hydrocarbons, and 50,000 tons of inorganic solid waste per year. See, for example, [9, p. 203; 10, p. 14].

9. José Artur Passos, Neuza Neves, and M.Q. Ferreira, "Handling and Processing of Hazardous Solid Wastes From Petrochemical Industries—Cetrel's Experience," *International Seminar on Hazardous Waste Management*, Salvador, Bahia, November 7-9, 1990, pp. 201-209.

10. *Jornal do Brasil*, August 13, 1989, p. 14.

11. The discussion that follows is a synthesis of interviews with former and current employees and managers of Cetrel, held in June and July of 1997 in Camaçari and Salvador, Bahia. Whenever feasible, I triangulated the factual information provided with written company documents, newspaper reports, and journal publications that address the issues touched upon in this section.

12. Interview by author with anonymous Cetrel employee, July 1997, Salvador, Bahia.
13. In these cases, the colony was affected by the discharge of a toxic chemical that was neither compatible with nor treatable by the activated sludge process. Bacteria would die, and the plant had to be temporarily shut down.
14. Therefore, political, economical, and health issues combined to shake the previous stability. The 1987-1988 Sindae's newsletter, *Gota D'Água*, reported that Cetrel employees were neither satisfied with the occupational health situation in the company nor with some decisions taken by management that were deemed arbitrary.
15. Yet, internal disputes within the left did not take long to appear. Sindae soon accused Marighela of political patronage, and he was later fired. The expression used by Sindae to denounce Marighela was that he was creating a "trenzinho da alegria" in Cetrel. "Trem da alegria" has no easy translation in English. It connotes that the director was illegally hiring several of his political supporters for positions in Cetrel. Marighela, on the other hand, accused right-wing groups and industry lobby pressures for his firing. He claimed that he was persecuted because of his left-wing politics, his pro-environment stances, and his opposition to the excessive costs of the soon-to-be installed incinerator. See [16, p. 5] for more details on Marighela's claims.
16. *Tribuna da Bahia*, Salvador, May 28, 1988.
17. Cetrel allegedly needed around $40 million dollars to finance the recuperation of equipment, the expansion of its facilities, and the installation of the incinerator. Since the state did not have the needed capital, the incinerator had been delayed, causing some companies to keep shipping chlorinated hydrocarbons for incineration in Mexico.
18. According to an interview with Fontes Lima, former director of Cetrel, one of the new administrators surveyed customers about their perception of Cetrel. Some companies answered that "Cetrel worked like a clock but it started to run late." The same source claimed that while businesses did not originally want to own Cetrel, they may have come to the conclusion that if Cetrel were not working correctly, they would not be able to get the money needed to finance the expansion of the complex [19].
19. Francisco Fontes Lima, interview by author, tape recording, July 1997, Salvador, Bahia.
20. *A Tarde,* June 26, 1989, p. 5.
21. Interview with current anonymous Cetrel employee, July 1997, Salvador, Bahia. This human development metaphor also suggests that from past good-faith mistakes, Cetrel employees and managers learned a great deal. As a result, the firm evolved and was ready to reach a new stage in its development. On the one hand, there is some truth to the claims of the privateers, as the crises in the mid- and late-eighties show. On the other, Sindae newsletters during the period called employees' attention to the purposeful campaign orchestrated by managers to demoralize the company. For example, the March 22, 1989 issue of *Gota D'Água* accused the new Cetrel managers of creating a climate of terror in the company. The story suggested that the actions of these directors could only be understood as either overt persecution against employees or a clear indication of a desire to privatize Cetrel.
22. I owe this characterization to a former director of Cetrel I interviewed, who implied that during the nineties the firm fell gradually under the managerial control of its main shareholder, Copene. In fact, by the mid-nineties, Cetrel had only two directors, instead of three. Both were former employees of Copene.

23. These are two popular sayings in Brazil, used by union leaders to connote that Cetrel would thereafter be controlled by the companies that generate the pollution, i.e., Cetrel would not be as free and independent to enforce treatment standards as it was as a state company. I owe the first quote to a Sindae leader; the second quote was attributed to Salvador Brito, a CUT health committee member, in *A Tarde*, August 15, 1989.

24. Sindae, "Carta aos funcionários" (Letter to Employees), undated and unpublished leaflet available at the union files kept at its headquarters in Salvador, Bahia.

25. Interview with Paulo Jackson, former president of Sindae, published in *BEM-TE-VI, Jornal da Cetrel* (Cetrel newspaper), year 1, no. 9, October 1992, pp. 1-4.

26. *Gazeta Mercantil*, August 23, 1989, p. 3.

27. In this same story [26], an important business leader told the reporter that "the Bahian business class was surprised with the decision of the government, because we were negotiating a new manner of rendering Cetrel more agile and dynamic, in order to enable it to properly handle the planned investment of $35 million dollars in two years" [26, p. 3]. It is obvious from this story that there were contradictions between business and government versions regarding the former's interest in buying Cetrel. Moreover, claims of corruption and bribery circulated in the union press at the time and are still present in progressives' accounts of the privatization process. In this regard, the situation in Bahia is not different from the privatization of many other state and federal companies. In fact, it is not different from the privatization of state-owned companies that occurred in many other countries in the world. For example, Martinez wrote that the IMF structural adjustment program includes privatization, which means, ". . . [to] sell state-owned enterprises, goods, and services to private investors. This includes banks, key industries, railroads, toll highways, electricity, schools, hospitals, and even fresh water. Although usually done in the name of greater efficiency, which is often needed, privatization has mainly had the effect of concentrating wealth even more in a few hands and making the public pay even more for its needs" [28].

28. Elizabeth Martinez and A. Garcia, "What Is 'Neo-Liberalism': A Definition for Activists," [102, p. 2].

29. Interview with José de Freitas Mascarenhas, current president of the Industrial Federation of the State of Bahia (FIEBA), former state Secretary of Mines and Energy (1971-1979), and also president of the Empresas Petroquímicas do Brasil (EPB), one of the enterprises of Odebrecht group; published in *BEM-TE-VI*, year 1, no. 10, November 1992, pp. 1-4.

30. This is the connotation of the Portuguese title of a 1997 Cetrel publication that summarizes all the environmental systems and programs it managed and operated. I decided to adopt it here because I think it represents very well the current culture of the organization. Even a quick look at Cetrel's brochures and documents makes clear that the company has developed a systemic approach to its hazardous waste and environmental management practices. This may have happened as a result of a) the predominance of the technical views of its engineers in shaping the company's culture, and b) the adoption of the international environmental management systems (EMS) jargon disseminated by the ISO. No matter what the reasons for the adoption of this approach were, I find it useful to view the components as particular systems (though they are actually subsystems) of a larger environmental management system.

31. The incinerator was supposed to have started up by 1988. Despite the initial planning for joint state and private sector financing, the $25 million incinerator was totally financed by the four companies that use it, in proportion to the volume of wastes produced by each.

32. For example, P. Cain and Manoel Neiva, "The Incineration of Hazardous Liquid Wastes Generated by the Petrochemical Complex at Camaçari-Brazil," [33, pp. 39-46].

33. *International Seminar on Hazardous Waste Management*, Salvador, Bahia, Nov. 7-9, 1990.

34. Jayme Sarmento, "Considerações Sobre a Implantação da Unidade de Incineração da Cetrel," Cetrel's unpublished internal document, May 1987.

35. This argument was made by Sarmento, who was then the coordinator of the incineration unit. A paper written in English by a Sulzer representative at the International Hazardous Waste Seminar held in Bahia in 1990 stated that ". . . most of the polychlorinated dibenzodioxins and dibenzofuranes, especially the well-known 2, 3, 7, 8-TCDD are products which are synthesized within the unburnt soot particles on their way through the furnace and boiler. 300° C to 700° C is the temperature range in the core of the particle for the synthesis. . . . Every kilogram of soot (solid unburnt matter) contains on average 50 μg of PCDD and PCDF, of which 1 μg of 2,3,7,8-TCDD" [36, pp. 173-174].

36. Giovanni Ghelffi, "Disposal of Chlorinated Hydrocarbons through Incineration. Discussion of Four Major Incineration and Gas Treatment Problems: 1. Decomposition Rate and Inhibition Effect, 2. Free Chlorine Formation, 3. Nitric Oxide Formation and 4. Dioxin and Furan Formation," [33, pp. 167-174].

37. Sarmento wrote that Cetrel staff visited several incinerators in industrial areas in Germany, France, and the U.K. in 1986. In an interesting line of argument, he also described the incinerator as a chemical plant in a complex where there are many other chemical plants, whose furnace is a chemical reactor in an area where there are many other chemical reactors. Therefore, he claimed that the risk created by the incinerator is similar to the risk associated with any other chemical and petrochemical plant [35].

38. *BEM-TE-VI*, year 1, no. 2, January 1992.

39. Elisabeth Couto, "Medidas De Ácidos Fortes E Seus Sais Em Uma Área Do Complexo Petroquímico De Camaçari—Incinerador De Resíduos Líquidos Da Cetrel" [Measurements of Strong Acids in an Area of the Camaçari Petrochemical Complex—The Incinerator of Liquid Hazardous Wastes of Cetrel], master's thesis, Federal University of Bahia, 1996.

40. Since the addition of these facilities complemented the existing industrial landfills, I will only mention them here without further details. They were built to temporarily store hazardous wastes before their incineration.

41. A. C. Rebouças, "Groundwater Protection in a Petrochemical Complex Region, Camaçari, Bahia, Brazil," [33, pp. 147-155].

42. According to an interview with Paes de Andrade (tape recording, July 1997, Salvador, Bahia), a former director-superintendent of Copene, the groundwater in the area of the complex was never supposed to have been used, because Copene had access to enough surface water to supply all companies. However, severe droughts in the region in the eighties forced Copene to dig deep wells to prevent future water supply crises. Simultaneously, state agencies lost control of permitting of well perforation, and

allowed wells to be dug within company premises. As a result, contamination of the soil and the groundwater became widespread. Andrade believed this was a serious mistake.

43. Márcia Marinho, Yvonette Medeiros, Iara Oliveira, Franciso Negrão, and Dária Nascimento, "Diagnóstico Preliminar do Gerenciamento dos Recursos Hídricos do Pólo Petroquímico de Camaçari (COPEC)-BA," unpublished draft manuscript (available from the author), Salvador, Bahia, 1997.

44. The information provided below is based on [45, p. 18].

45. *Disposição Final dos Efluentes Líquidos da Cetrel: A Escolha de Um Corpo Receptor Ideal* (Final Disposal of Cetrel's Liquid Effluents: The Choice of an Ideal Receiving Body), Cetrel, Camaçari, Bahia, undated publication.

46. BOD and COD are laboratory methods used in the wastewater treatment industry to detect biological and chemical pollution levels, respectively.

47. *A Tarde*, August 16, 1989, p. 3.

48. *Gazeta Mercantil*, August 23, 1989, p. 3. This debate is another example where representatives of civil society voiced disagreement with decisions taken by company staff. While Cetrel staff claim that their decision was the best technical decision possible, they had to consider the arguments put forward by opposing experts.

49. Paulo Freire, Domingos Neto, and D. Carvalho, "Source Pollution Control Program at the Camaçari Petrochemical Complex: Overall and Individual Improvements," *Proceedings of the Third International Conference On Waste Management in the Chemical and Petrochemical Industries*, Salvador: Bahia, 1993, pp. 61-72.

50. In this article, the authors reviewed the improvements in Cetrel pollution control systems made in the early nineties [49]. They focused almost exclusively on wastes [49]. Therefore, pollution prevention means mostly reduction in wastes, i.e., pollutant loads, not control at the source. It appears that these Cetrel staff incorrectly considered control at the source to mean only the reduction of the effluents released into the wastewater treatment system, as well as waste minimization.

51. Interview with Cetrel operations team leader, July 1997. Before expansion, the old facility had two aeration tanks and six settling tanks. The new facility also has two aeration tanks and six settling tanks.

52. Neuza Neves, "Air Monitoring at Camaçari Petrochemical Complex," *Water Science & Technology*, 33, 3, pp. 9-16, 1996.

53. The account that follows is based on this article [52], as well as on a personal interview with the author, who is Cetrel's team leader for managing the air monitoring system [54]. Tavares submitted that this station was not only poorly operated but also that there was poor quality control and assurance of the data [55].

54. Neuza Neves, interview by author, tape recording, July 1997, Camaçari, Bahia.

55. Tania Tavares, personal communication with author; also interview, tape recording, July 1997, Salvador, Bahia.

56. Eduardo Machado, professor of anthropology and sociology at the Federal University of Bahia, also conducted several interviews with inhabitants of Camaçari in 1996-97 that corroborate these survey findings. Personal communication with the author, 1997-98.

57. For example, in 1996 Copene generated 42.95 percent of the particulate matter, 36.37 percent of the SO_2, 2 percent of the CO, 58.48 percent of the No_x, and 33.14 percent of the organics, in *Cetrel: Relatório de Monitoramento do Ar, Relatório Anual*, 1996, p. 15.

58. According to Neves, some companies have complained about this method of figuring costs out, under the argument that those companies that have a better inventory of emissions end up paying more than their fair share. Allegedly, companies with poor inventory of emissions pay less in spite of emitting more hazardous pollutants [54].

59. Tania Tavares, a well-known local expert on air quality issues, suggested that since the experience of Cetrel consultants was mostly based on urban air pollution in São Paulo, they emphasized the monitoring of conventional (SO_2, NO_x, ozone, and particulate matter) air pollutants. Moreover, Brazilian air regulations followed U.S. EPA regulations of the 1970s, which also concentrated on urban air pollution [55].

60. The complete stations can also monitor meteorological conditions, such as wind speed and direction, luminosity, humidity, etc. Cetrel staff in charge of managing the network visited Canada (Sarnia) and the U.S. (Bayport and Houston area) prior to buying equipment and operating the network. These visits aimed at learning about the technologies and methodologies adopted by some petrochemical complexes to monitor air pollution. The travel report produced by the staff, in which they summarized the feedback and recommendations given by Canadian and American professionals they interviewed, makes it clear that there was a conscious effort to see and learn how the equipment performed under field conditions.

61. This high-tech mobile unit was bought for $500,000 from an American company called Environmental Technologies Group (ETG). Neves wrote that when it was bought, it was the first mobile unit operating in South America [52]. It is based on infrared spectroscopy, which allows for the simultaneous monitoring of 200 different compounds at a distance of up to about .4 miles form the emitting source. However, this unit did not perform in real life as well as expected. At first it was used, incorrectly, as a mobile unit. In 1996, the FTIR became another fixed station located within the complex. Neves told me that Cetrel had stopped using it due to operational problems and difficulty in getting proper maintenance for the equipment [54]. In addition, ETG folded. It is my impression that Cetrel staff feel somewhat embarrassed and disappointed by the purchase of such high-cost equipment, with lower than expected results.

62. Tavares claimed that at the time Cetrel did not have skilled professionals to make technically correct decisions regarding what to monitor and where to locate the stations. For example, she claimed that particulate matter (and to a lesser extent NO_x) are not important parameters to monitor in petrochemical complexes. Instead, hydrocarbons should have been the priority parameter. She summarized her criticism by judging the air-monitoring network partially "out of focus" [55].

63. Management of information is probably the "Achilles heel" of the environmental management systems of the complex. CRA seems to be a captured agency, with few skilled staff and a director who is closely associated with the companies in the complex. The notion of regulatory agencies being "captured" or "co-opted" by the interests they were supposed to regulate is discussed in [64, p. 25].

64. Ronald Brickman, Sheila Jasanoff, and Thomas Ilgen, *Controlling Chemicals: The Politics of Regulation in Europe and the United States*, Cornell University Press, Ithaca, New York, 1985.

65. Tavares believes that this is related to the lack of toxicological data for individual organic chemicals [55].

66. It goes without saying that I will not cover in this research all the programs implemented by Cetrel in the last seven years. Therefore, I must choose, among many programs, the ones that have closer relationship to the arguments of this book. The trade-off of this choice is not to address other important company programs.

67. Interviews with Cetrel's health and safety team leader, July 1997, Camaçari, Bahia. Although this statement may be considered self-serving, I tend to believe that the benzene and other crises of the mid- to late eighties in Cetrel lends credence to it. My interview with Sindae representatives, as well as Sindae newsletter stories, also confirm this assessment of Cetrel's health and safety program in the eighties.

68. This firm is located in S. Paulo and called Ecologica. It hired internationally known Brazilian experts (such as Dr. Rene Mendes) to guide and evaluate the field work in Cetrel.

69. Several reports provide data on workers' exposures in Cetrel. I intend here to describe briefly the types of activities developed in the industrial hygiene program, without evaluating the quality and appropriateness of the program. Area samples were collected through samplers set 1.5 m above the floor, a height close to workers' breathing zone. Personal samples were collected through activated charcoal sampling tubes and sent later to S. Paulo for toxicological analysis. Three monitoring campaigns were performed in March, June, and December of 1991.

70. This more-democratic committee was short-lived. By 1995, the management-controlled CIPA came back to the scene, reflecting the weakening of Sindae's presence in Cetrel during 1994. An example of this process is Cetrel's initiative to try to block the entrance of officers and the occupational physician of the "sindicato" into company premises. Cetrel had previously invited the "sindicato" to attend lectures to be delivered during the 1994 "Health Week." The union newsletter that denounces the incident has the following headline: "Cetrel, cresce a falta de respeito" (Cetrel: Lack of Respect Is Growing), in *Gota D'Água*, December 6, 1984, p. 2.

71. The emergency procedures followed the Accident Preparedness for Emergencies at the Local Level (APELL) methodology designed by the United Nations Industrial Development Organization in the eighties. Cetrel had large emergency incidents in 1982, 1992, 1995, and 1997, caused by the illegal discharge in Cetrel's industrial wastewater of flammable solvents and toxic chemicals above the permitted levels. Consequently, explosion and fires occurred in lift stations, employees had to be evacuated, and/or the colony of bacteria was temporarily damaged. In the 1992, 1995, and 1997 episodes, Cetrel was able to identify the violator and recuperate the money spent with fixing the problems. CRA also assessed fines to the companies that dumped the chemicals into the wastewater treatment system. Those three incidents had ample coverage in the local media and company press. Examples of this coverage may be seen in *A Tarde*, July 7, 1992, p. 3, and October 10, 1997, front page. The latter reads: "Vazamento força a evacuação da Cetrel" (Spill forces the evacuation of Cetrel). The story describes how Cetrel had to evacuate its employees for a whole day, as a result of the discharge of benzene or pyrolisis oil in Cetrel's pipeline network. Four victims stayed under observation in a local hospital after feeling dizziness, headaches, a burning sensation in the eyes, nausea, and throat irritation. Right below the headline, the front page has a large picture of contract workers wearing half-mask respirators while draining the spill in a lift station.

72. During this period Sindae lost power as Cetrel consolidated its internal restructuring. Consequently, management increased its control over Cetrel's health and safety program. Personal interview with Sindae's representatives, July 1997, Salvador, Bahia.

73. By 1995-1996, health and safety staff had started to use the FTIR to monitor exposures to a larger variety of organic compounds. Cetrel also bought new state-of-the-art equipment (Summa canisters) in 1996 to perform personal monitoring. The laboratory gas chromatography tests required to analyze the personal samples have since been done in Cetrel's laboratory. Nevertheless, Cetrel continues to rely on consultants to advise staff on how to implement the program and to perform specific tasks that are not available in-house.

74. Cetrel used a Centers for Disease Control and Prevention (CDC) questionnaire called Risk-Quest, which allows for the determination of lifestyle risk factors of each individual surveyed. Therefore, Cetrel has an individual risk profile for all employees. In 1996 it launched programs to educate and reduce these risks.

75. *BEM-TE-VI,* year 1, no. 1, December 1991, p. 3.

76. According to several issues of *BEM-TE-VI.*

77. For example, it interviewed Gilberto Gil, a very famous Brazilian singer; Marília Pera, a famous actress; Edgar Teles and José Mascarenhas, two of the founding fathers of Cetrel; the late Betinho, a famous social activist; Jair Meneghelli, former president of CUT, and others.

78. According to Fontes Lima, this program reflected a more open stance toward environmental management. It was adopted by Cetrel after one staff member saw its implementation in a conference held in New Orleans, which was part of Cetrel's initiative to keep ongoing contacts with foreign technical expertise. The "Open Factory" program is also part of Cetrel's commitment to the Responsible Care codes of practice [19].

79. The CTGA is based on an old Brazilian concept called "alvará," which is a license or permit for the legal operation of businesses. The CTGA fits within the shift from state-driven enforcement to voluntary compliance by companies. The rationale for the CTGA is that, since committee members are legally registered, reports produced have legal value. They are official company environmental reports. Therefore, committee members may be personally liable for violations of environmental laws and regulations. In addition, if the state finds false information on the reports, they may be held liable for producing it [80, pp. 33-34]. Fontes Lima argued that the "alvará" is a demonstration of "public faith" on professional expertise [19]. He added that the CTGA aims at holding professionals and managers responsible for environmental conditions in companies. If something goes wrong in a given company, one knows whom to hold responsible for the problem. In his opinion, the CTGA is a self-audit committee that registers a company environmental program in the CRA, following guidelines provided by the Responsible Care program [19].

80. Ronaldo Martins, "Comissão Técnica de Garantia Ambiental," *Bahia Análise&Dados,* CEI, 3, 1, pp. 33-34, June 1993.

81. *Jornal da Cetrel,* year II, no. 16, 1992, p. 3.

82. According to the team leader of operations, before the training program each of the five operator shifts had its own procedures, with lack of uniformity between and among them. Opportunities for mistakes were too high. After to taking the courses,

operators had to pass a written test with a minimum grade of 70/100. After all standard operating procedures (SOPs) had been written, operators were given one week to study them before taking a series of written and performance tests. The operators had to be 100 percent proficient in the critical or emergency procedures and 70 percent proficient in the routine procedures. Eighty percent of the operators were approved in their first test. If a given operator did not pass the first time, he would have two or three more chances [3].

83. The TQM started through the implementation of the Japanese 5 S program, a management and policy model whose main ideas are summarized by five words starting with the letter S. Thus, the acronym 5S. They mean: Seiri=Organization; Seiton=Order; Seizo=Cleanliness; Seiketsu=Hygiene; and Shitsuke=Discipline. This model altered several internal procedures of Cetrel, affecting procurement, maintenance, and other areas. In *Comunicação Direta*, no. 76, August 26, 1994.

84. The first article was published in *Jornal da Cetrel*, year III, no. 19, 1994, p. 2; the second, in *Jornal da Cetrel*, year III, no. 20, 1994, p. 2.

85. Francisco Alves Pereira and Amir Kauss, "Cetrel's Environmental Management System (BS-7750): An Advanced and Innovative Project," *Water Science & Technology*, 33, 3, pp. 223-237, 1996.

86. Cetrel managers were aware that the ISO 14,000 series would be based on the BS-7750, so they knew that the effort to get BS-7750 certification would also enable them to get the ISO 14,001. Moreover, the same organization, the Bureau Veritas Quality International, certified Cetrel in both standards. The International Standardization Organization (ISO) is an independent federation of 100 national standards bodies, established in 1946. The standards developed by ISO comprise mainly product and process specifications. The national standards bodies are composed mainly of private interests, with, in some cases, government participation. The structure of the organization is based on technical committees, which may establish subcommittees and working groups, as needed. The national bodies may form Technical Advisory Groups to develop a unified national position on a proposed standard [87].

87. Joel Tickner, "Will ISO 14000 Deter Cleaner Production?" *New Solutions: A Journal of Occupational and Environmental Health Policy*, vol. 8(3), pp. 285-308, 1998.

88. Pereira noted that the preparatory review was like a "snapshot"of Cetrel before the implementation of the EMS.

89. The EMS is composed of 425 procedures and operational instructions (244 of the former; 181 of the latter), of which fifteen are EMS procedures [85, p. 225]. It is beyond the scope of this research to assess Cetrel's performance and compliance with BS-7750, a task that would require an analysis of these procedures. Here, I concentrate on what I consider to be the most important environmental policy issues.

90. Continuous improvement of environmental management, adoption of new environmental technologies, reduction of industrial effluents and wastes, reduction of environmental effects, elimination of environmental liabilities, communication with interested parties, compliance and improvement of environmental legislation, and compliance with and dissemination of objectives and environmental targets. Appendix 4 shows the environmental policy of Cetrel in full.

91. For example, one objective of the BS-7750 list reads, "Optimise Operations of the Incineration Unit." In the ISO 14001 list, a similar objective reads, "To exceed the

legal standards for air pollutants emissions at the Liquid Incineration Unit." By comparing the two lists, it appears that the ISO list focuses more on specific tasks and targets than the more generally stated BS-7750 list.

92. The temporary storage of solid waste-class I, and the processing and final disposal of solid waste-class II. This classification of class I and II follows the Brazilian Association of Technical Norms (ABNT) criteria. The ABNT is the Brazilian representative on the ISO technical committees. The process of preparation for the certifications also created a new slogan in Cetrel: "Escreva como voce faz, e faça como voce escreveu" (Write how you do [your job], and do [your job] as you wrote).

93. Source control here means controlling the effluent discharges of a list of priority pollutants by client companies, a connotation that differs from the clients controlling their discharges at the source.

94. Though I am not addressing here all the changes that took place after 1996, it is worthwhile commenting on the TPM management concepts. The TPM is a management model that aims at maximizing the effectiveness of Cetrel's operational system by involving all Cetrel employees in the goal of zero losses, that is, no operational problems in any equipment, using a train-the-trainer program and small group activities. The eight points that constitute this model include: specific improvement of equipment, autonomous maintenance, planned maintenance, education and training, preventive maintenance, quality maintenance, safety and environment, and TPM in offices. The slogan of the model says, "to keep the highest level of production all the time; to keep the highest level of productivity all the time, and to keep the rhythm of changes, improvements and transformations." In *Comunicação Direta*, no. 195, p. 1, April 18, 1997.

95. Concerns with business image and product acceptability in environmentally aware societies are the fundamental economic reasons why business leaders in Bahia perceive the ISO certification as a strategically important issue. Based on Darwich survey data on company-reported exports for 1996, the main markets for the "Pólo" are, in descending order: the U.S., Argentina, Germany, South Africa, Uruguay, France, China, and Japan [96, p. 109]. Considering that exports play a smaller role on business decisions than the internal market, one cannot underestimate the role of managerial fashions and the current strength of the ideology of "green modernity" in shaping Cetrel's decisions. This ideology claims that "to be modern is also to be green" and is promoted nationally by neoliberals as Brazil's only alternative to leap forward and join the circle of developed countries, the G-7.

96. Luciana Darwich, "Gerenciamento Ambiental no Pólo Petroquímico de Camaçari," master's thesis, Núcleo de Pós-Graduação em Administração, Federal University of Bahia, May 1996.

97. I owe part of this subtitle to the article, "Beware ISO" [98].

98. David Bennett, "Beware ISO," *New Solutions*, 7, 3, pp. 37-45, Spring 1997.

99. Though these three implications may be somewhat interrelated, I address them separately to emphasize my three main criticisms against Cetrel's ISO 14001 certification.

100. *Cliente Cetrel* (Cetrel client), year 1, no. 2, Jul/Aug/Sept 96. This is Cetrel's quarterly newsletter for the clients of Cetrel. Many national prizes and awards have been given to Cetrel as a result of these accomplishments. There is no question that it has since become a model environmental management company in Brazil, receiving dozens of visitors annually who want to learn about its environmental systems.

101. Though it is easier to limit the validity of this argument to Cetrel in the nineties, it is my contention that from the very beginning of its operations Cetrel had aspirations to be as good as the best in the business. Chapter 6 will go over this argument in more detail. I recognize that my argument is also a stretch of Castleman's argument [104] because Cetrel is not a subsidiary of a multinational company. I am alluding here to the fact that Cetrel could be compared with a similar company in petrochemical complexes of developed countries, such as the U.S., Germany, or Canada.

102. Joshua Karliner, *The Corporate Planet: Ecology and Politics in the Age of Globalization*, Sierra Club, San Francisco, chapter 2, "The Greening of Global Reach; Corporate Environmentalism Comes of Age," pp. 30-57.

103. Tickner also stated that ". . . ISO 14000 has been promoted as the most systematic and comprehensive means to achieve global corporate sustainable development and environmental protection. It has been sold to industry world-wide by its potential to bring easier regulatory oversight and more market share (Mass Environ, 1996). ISO 14000 books, newsletters, conferences, and consulting services have become commonplace" [87, p. 21].

104. Barry Castleman, "The Double Standards in Industrial Hazards," in Jane Ives, ed., *The Export of Hazards,* Routledge & Kegan Paul, Boston, pp. 61-89, 1985.

105. Tickner argued that "Since the ISO definition of a firm is fundamentally site specific, there is no guarantee that a transnational company will maintain the same standards world-wide. While the ISO 14000 series is claimed to be a global environmental management standard, companies need only comply with 'applicable' local laws and regulations. Thus, a multinational company may be significantly less 'friendly' towards the environment in a country with lesser environmental standards, such as India, than in the U.S. If a country does not have a specific law (e.g., on waste disposal), there is no requirement that the issue be addressed in the EMS" [87, pp. 13-14].

106. Tickner offered a solid criticism of the ISO 14001 in the article mentioned above [87]. He criticized the ISO 14001 on the following grounds: ISO 14001 does not stimulate pollution prevention or cleaner production; it ". . .does not place actual requirements on companies (or requires firms to set goals) to reduce their emissions, wastes, or chemical use . . ."; it harmonizes procedures, products, and systems across businesses and countries, but does not provide minimal requirements for environmental protection as regulatory standards do; it proposes a limited perspective toward continuous improvement, but focuses only on continuous improvement of the EMS; it ". . . leaves wide discretion to the firm (and thus the auditor in plan certification) in determining what is important to identify, measure, or improve upon;" it only requires audits "to determine whether or not the environmental management system conforms to the standard and has been properly implemented and maintained;" it lacks public participation, and "does not provide any additional information on environmental impacts of a firm to the public, and may even restrict access to information" [87, pp. 13-14].

107. See, for example, [108, 109, 110, 111]. A more recent article is [112]. In these papers, Geiser described the origins and evolution of these concepts, and provided definitions for them.

  Pollution Prevention is defined in the U.S. Pollution Prevention Act (42 USCA 13101) as source reduction. Source reduction means any practice which: reduces the amount of any hazardous substance, pollutant, or contaminant entering any waste stream or otherwise released into the environment (including fugitive emissions) prior to recycling treatment or disposal; and reduces the hazards to public health and the environment associated with the release of such substances, pollutants, or contaminants. The term includes equipment or technology modifications, process or procedure modifications, reformulation or redesign or products, substitution of raw materials, and improvements in housekeeping, maintenance, training, or inventory control. The term source reduction does not include any practice that alters the physical, chemical, or biological characteristics or the volume of a hazardous substance, pollutant, or contaminant through a process or activity which itself is not integral to and necessary for the production of a product or the providing of a service.

Toxics Use Reduction is defined in the Massachusetts Toxics Use Reduction Act (TURA) as:

> In-plant changes in production processes or raw materials that reduce, avoid or eliminate the use of toxic or hazardous substances or generation of hazardous byproducts per unit of product, so as to reduce risks to the health of workers, consumers, or the environment, without shifting the risks between workers, consumers, or parts of the environment. In Commonwealth of Massachusetts, House Bill no. 6161, pp. 7-8, June 1989.

Cleaner Production is defined by the United States Environmental Program (UNEP) as "the continuous application of an integrated preventive environmental strategy to processes and products to reduce risks to humans and the environment" [112].

108. Ken Geiser, "The Unfinished Business of Pollution Prevention," *Georgia Law Review*, vol. 29, pp. 473-491, 1995.
109. Ken Geiser, "Toxics Use Reduction and Pollution Prevention," *New Solutions,* 1,1, pp. 1-8, Spring 1990.
110. Ken Geiser, "The Greening of Industry: Making The Transition to a Sustainable Economy," *Technology Review*, pp. 66-72, August/September, 1991.
111. Ken Geiser, "Protecting Reproductive Health and the Environment: Toxics Use Reduction," *Environmental Health Perspectives Supplements,*, vol. 101, suppl. 2, pp. 221-225, 1993.
112. Ken Geiser, "Establishing a General Duty of Precaution in Environmental Protection Policies in the United States: A Proposal," in *Protecting Public Health and the Environment,* Carolyn Raffensperger and Joel Tickner (eds.), Island Press, Washington, D.C., pp. xxi-xxvi, 1999.
113. As argued in chapter 3, Geiser noted that "conventional regulations, such as those developed under the Clean Air Act and Clean Water Act, are based on the assumption that the environment has an unlimited capacity to assimilate small amounts of contaminants with negligible risk. By establishing emission standards, this approach proposes that the environment dilutes or transforms chemicals so thoroughly that they become mere traces and do little damage" [110, p. 66].
114. For the second characterization, see Roy Manik, "Toxics Use Reduction in Massachusetts: The Whole Facility Approach."
115. Based on my interviews with several Cetrel staff and managers, I cannot deny that some of them understand the need to push client firms to adopt greener practices. Yet,

they also understand that customer companies own and pay for the services provided by Cetrel, i.e., there is only so much they could do as a waste management service contractor owned by inherently polluting companies. Moreover, they recognize that only a few companies are moving toward pollution prevention without resistance. Personal interviews with Cetrel staff, July 1997.

116. Jennifer Nash and John Ehrenfeld argued that ". . . these codes [ISO 14000, Responsible Care, and other codes] are created and maintained by industry, and individual firms are responsible for ensuring that they comply." They also argued that ". . . codes potentially strengthen corporate legitimacy." When comparing regulation with private codes they wrote that private codes "provide public access to information only in select cases," while regulation "provides public access to information on compliance" [117, p. 19].

117. Jennifer Nash and John Ehrenfeld, "Code Green: Business Adopts Voluntary Environmental Standards," *Environment*, 38, 1, pp. 16-45, January/February 1996.

118. Sindae reacted to the ISO 14001 certification with a leaflet titled, "A Cetrel Merece ISO?" (Does Cetrel Deserve ISO?), 1997 (available from author), in which it accuses the company of keeping the "sindicato" in the dark, contracting out bargaining unit jobs, violating the contract, as well as establishing authoritarian relationships with the union and its employees. It was my observation that Cetrel employees participate in company activities and support the goals of the company, yet they complain about overwork, low salaries, and management arbitrariness.

CHAPTER 6

Environmental Management Policies in the Gulf Coast Authority: A Case Study of Pollution Control Policies in the Center

This chapter is a case study of the historical evolution of environmental management policies and practices in the Gulf Coast Waste Disposal Authority (GCWDA or GCA), the hazardous waste management and treatment authority of the Houston-Galveston region of Texas. It is a focused case study of the implementation of the end-of-pipe pollution control "model" in Texas [1-3]. It addresses these events by dividing them into three chronological phases: the early (1970s), the middle (1980s), and the late (1990s) years. The most important aspects in each phase are examined through the lenses of the legal, economic, regulatory, institutional, or political determinants for GCA's waste management policies.

THE EARLY YEARS: "POLLUTION CONTROL AGENCY SAILING INTO TROUBLED WATERS" [4]

GCA was created to control the environmental pollution of the Galveston Bay region. It was a state intervention to mitigate the market's failure to safeguard the natural environment against the domestic and industrial pollution generated by a booming petrochemical production area. This state intervention preceded the *environmental policy system* that emerged in the early seventies. According to Gotllieb,

> In just four years, between 1970 and 1974, an extraordinary range of legislative initiatives, regulatory activities, and court action came to the fore. These established a broad and expansive *environmental policy system* centered around efforts to control the environmental by-products of the urban and industrial order. Through this system, a vast pollution control, or environmental protection, industry was created, including engineering companies,

law firms, waste management operations, and consulting firms specializing in environmental review, standard setting, or other new environmental procedures (emphasis added)[6, p. 125].

GCA must be considered a local component of the contemporary, late sixties to early seventies, mainstream trend to manage and control water and air pollution. In GCA's case, this pollution derived from chemical and petrochemical production in the post-Second World War period. Under this characterization, GCA exemplifies, in the Gulf Coast region, the environmental management and policy systems developed for the whole nation. Thus, it is no coincidence that GCA had to face the economic, legal, organizational, and political challenges presented by these new systems.

Economic Troubles:
The Bond and Taxes Controversies

In chapter 2, it was established that GCA was given the statutory power to levy a property tax up to 10 cents per $100 of assessed valuation after elections in three counties, and to issue municipal bonds to finance its operations. These provided two primary sources of funds to set the agency in motion. In 1970, voters defeated a referendum to permit GCA to exercise its taxing powers—54 percent against it, 46 percent for it. As a result, GCA started to issue revenue bonds as early as July 1971, by issuing $3.6 million worth of revenue bonds for the city of Houston to assist it in upgrading some of Houston's waste treatment plants. In December 1971, GCA issued $10.5 million in bonds.

The issuance of municipal bonds to finance waste treatment plants—and other pollution control equipment—had the objective of giving an incentive to industry and the state to build and operate these facilities, because a) industry paid lower interest rates on municipal bonds than on industrial bonds, and b) the facility paid no sales tax on the equipment that was delievered to the plants. Industry paid the debt service on the bonds issued, the operating cost of the facility, and 7.5 percent of the average annual debt service as a management fee. GCA collected these fees for the service provided and had a steady source of income to support its operations. For municipalities and other public bodies, the authority had the "buck-passing" [7, 8] role, serving as a financing agency by "providing a method for securing funds to combat pollution" [9].

The financial role and status of GCA generated an ongoing controversy throughout the early and mid-seventies. Some state politicians did not agree with GCA's financial role and tried to block state appropriations for the agency under the argument that it was "but an army of industry" [10]. In 1973, J. Kent Hackleman, a GCA board member who represented Harris County, asked, on behalf of the Taxpayers' Rights Association, for a formal written Texas Attorney General's opinion regarding the constitutionality of the act that had created GCA.

He stated that "the unlimited issuance of tax-free municipal bonds with little or no control and no vote of the people is clearly not in the best interest of the taxpayers" [11, p. 8/A; 12; 13]. By 1973, the Texas legislature had passed a bill that allowed local governments to finance industrial air pollution control facilities. The law allowed industry to finance air pollution control improvements through long-term tax-exempt bonds issued by local governments and guaranteed by industry. Before such bonds were issued, they had to be approved by the attorney general of Texas after the Texas Air Control Board certified the air control facilities to be essential for controlling air pollution. Critics of the bill argued along the same lines that Hackleman did, raising concerns regarding the misuse of public funds, tax benefits to industry, potential damage to city budgets, and the lack of public benefit by this subsidy to industry [14, 15].

Another thorny issue faced by the agency concerned the tax exemption of properties signed over to GCA by industrial customers. In 1974, the Texas Attorney General, John Hill, ruled that the properties signed over to GCWDA by Champion Paper in Harris County were not exempt from local property taxes. GCA had received the properties in 1973 when it contracted with five local industries to control their wastes [16, 17]. Those who argued that GCA had to pay property taxes, such as Galveston County Tax Assessor-Collector C. R. Johnson, defended their position by saying that GCA's practice of building or operating pollution control equipment was "a new gimmick to avoid paying property taxes" [17, sec. 1, p. 12]. He claimed that GCA was a business "and their benefits go to businesses" [17, sec. 1, p. 12], and "directly assessed the waste treatment facilities built by the authority for treating the industrial waste of the Union Carbide Corporation plant in Texas City" [18, p. 1].

GCA's general manager, Jack Davis, countered that "the basic tenet of our government is that one unit of government cannot tax another unit, because the power to tax is also the power to destroy" [19, p. 1]. Davis also stated that "properties owned by the authority should have the same exemption as provided other units of government" [19, p. 1; 20].

By 1975, after assessing that the attorney general's ruling was wrong, GCWDA sued in Galveston County asking for a state judge to declare it exempt from taxes under state statutes. Judge Donald Markle, of the District Court of Galveston County, ruled on June 1976 that property owned in the name of the authority, operated and controlled by the authority, "was entirely exempt from ad valorem property taxes" [21, p. 2]. In addition, "the value of property owned by the [a]uthority but controlled and used by industry was taxable to industry" [21, p. 2]. Therefore, the court clarified that only property under control of industry would be taxable. By 1975, the authority had built, acquired, or financed almost $200 million in pollution control equipment. By 1979, it had already "passed the $500 million mark in financing of pollution control facilities," mostly used by industries in the Houston area to clean up air and water emissions [22]. After going through these legal hurdles, the authority became an almost self-sufficient agency, able to bankroll or facilitate pollution control investments in the area through the bond market.

Regulatory Aspects:
A Pollution Control Model Is Born

Though GCA was created a few years before the passage of the 1972 Water Pollution Control Act Amendments (known as the Clean Water Act or CWA), it anticipated the implementation of some policy concepts put forward by the Act. Two of those concepts were the joint treatment of industrial and municipal wastewater, and the regionalization of wastewater treatment systems. GCA's 1970-1975 Five Year report stated that "it is the first agency of its kind in Texas, and possibly in the United States, that was established as a regional agency to approach pollution control problems in a complete estuarine system, i.e., the Galveston Bay" [23, p. 5].

The state of Texas was also given credit for being three years ahead in "[creating] areawide waste treatment management agencies . . . in areas that have significant water quality problems" [23, p. 5]. Thus, from the regulatory perspective, GCA embodied the implementation of Clean Water Act requirements in the Galveston Bay area. Given the novelty of the system proposed by this act, and the inexperience of the recently created Environmental Protection Agency—it began operations in 1970—it is no surprise that GCA sailed on troubled "regulatory waters" during the seventies.

For one, some local city and county officials, to whom GCA was "just another agency in the bureaucratic boondoggle of state local and water pollution groups" [5] resisted GCA's interference in their internal affairs [24]. In addition, GCA had to comply with different state and federal regulations enacted by the state of Texas Water Quality Board (TWQB) and the federal EPA. For example, one newspaper report described the "grumbling" of board members about federal EPA "actions and requirements even as they took another step to comply with federal regulations so as to remain *in control of* water pollution in the state" (emphasis added) [25].

This ongoing conflict became highly visible when the EPA's regional administrator, Arthur Busch, decided to issue permits to individual industries in the ship channel and to GCA. TWQB Director Hugh Yantis Jr. protested this decision because it "goes against state policy and would make more difficult our program and that of the GCWDA toward integrated industrial regional waste disposal systems" [25].

After public hearings to discuss the protests of TWQB and GCA were held, Busch issued a joint permit that included both an individual company—Champion Paper—and GCA in the permit. The struggle between EPA and GCA continued until 1974, when the EPA finally issued GCA a permit to operate the Washburn

Tunnel plant under its own name. Actually, GCA also had to get a second state permit to operate its plants.

The essence of the argument was that GCA and the TWQB believed that the permits should all be issued in the name of GCWDA, since it treated the combined effluents of several industries. These organizations claimed that by giving permits to individual industries, the EPA would undermine the joint and combined wastewater treatment model.

Jack Davis, GCA general manager during the period, manifested the opinion that

> ... We had a recent administrator—EPA administrator in Dallas—who didn't like joint treatment of industrial wastes. We started out putting our first one [plant] together, and he [Mr. Busch] said, "It won't work." He said, "It's just like all the women on the block throwing their laundry together, and it won't work." ... If you had one big washing machine and the ladies were trying to wash it, and you did colored loads on Tuesdays and whites on Thursdays, it would work, and it would be cheaper. It's really that simple. You just have to control what goes in. It is workable—and it does work! [26, 27].

On the other hand, Arthur Busch, a former Rice University professor, was a well-known, outspoken critic of regional systems, including the GCWDA, before he joined the EPA in 1972. He argued that "all dischargers under the law must have a permit and this includes GCWDA," because he was concerned that "the GCWDA-industry contracts for treatment could prevent proper enforcement and interfere with the legal rights of citizens to file pollution suits" [28, p. 4A].

Arthur Busch's view of GCWDA's "contracting away its enforcement responsibilities" [28, p. 4A] is similar to the view of union leaders of Bahia described earlier. His criticism reflected the potentially conflicting role of a public body that simultaneously had legal enforcement powers and delivered services under contract with private industrial customers.

These two roles raised ambiguous situations for a public or semi-public agency, forcing it to, sooner or later, make an option between enforcing waste discharge permits—the law—or treating and managing the wastes generated by the customers—its cash cow. This conflict was resolved early by GCA's board decision to downplay the enforcement and regulatory activities, because of "lack of capital and lack of citizen support for another enforcement agency, as perceived from the citizen's vote" [29, p. 1]. In addition, as once stated by Davis, "the [a]uthority should not try to be both an operator and a regulator" [30]. GCA then became an implementing agency.

Those contradictions notwithstanding, GCA's modus operandi was fundamentally affected by compliance with the National Pollutants Discharge Elimination System (NPDES) set forth in the Clean Water Act. The water pollution regulatory system established in this Act became the centerpiece of GCA's operational model, because it determined the pollutant loads allowed to be discharged into the environment. To comply with these legal limits, GCA designed—or purchased—treatment technologies, management systems, and monitoring strategies.

It charged customers based on hydraulic, organic chemicals, nitrogen, and total suspended solids loadings, materializing the "polluter pays" aspects of the model. Pretreatibility studies were performed to assess the compatibility of industrial discharges with GCA's wastewater treatment capabilities, mostly defined by the activated sludge treatment system's ability to destroy or absorb the pollutants received in the wastewater treatment plants.

Relating the quality of its final effluent to the quality of industries' discharges to its plants—the effluents of GCA's customers become GCA's influent—GCA oversaw pretreatment standards that were almost completely under its sole purview. As an exception to GCA's mediator or facilitator role, it could fine companies that violated the specifications of the pretreatment permit, i.e., GCA's regulatory functions were limited to pretreatment issues. Over the years, both the state and the federal government would track compliance by reviewing GCA compliance with their NPDES permits [31].

Improving the water quality of GCA's effluent became the driving force behind all practices and procedures—GCA's wastewater management model—adopted in its early years, because the quality of the effluent would indicate how much pollution control had been achieved. Furthermore, this model fit nicely within the assimilative capacity paradigm, because it proposed only to reduce pollutant loads to levels deemed safe to the natural environment, without incorporating any concerns with pollution prevention or questioning how safe is safe.

In a word, the reduction of pollutant levels in the final effluent of GCA's wastewater plants was a measure of regulatory compliance, operational efficiency, and technological expertise; this reduction also was a measure of the extent that Galveston Bay and the Houston Ship Channel were recovering from the previously accumulated chemical and organic pollution. GCA's management model achieved significant success in the seventies in implementing this pollution control model, whose logic can only be traced to the regulatory framework created in the 1970s. By the late seventies, GCA treated more than 90 percent of the waste load from Texas City industries and about a third of the waste load from the Houston Ship Channel [32].

Municipal Operations

The municipal operations of GCA were also guided by the requirements of the Clean Water Act, which required "the establishment of integrated, area-wide or regional waste collection, treatment and disposal system while eliminating the proliferation of individual plants because of their economical and operational disadvantages" [23, p. 16].

Accordingly, the authority designed areawide plans that revolved around the concept of service areas that would have one central plant, whose limits would be defined by estimates of population growth and geographical conditions. Applying this concept to the Galveston Bay area, GCA built, operated, and helped finance several municipal wastewater plants during the seventies. Nevertheless, it had to overcome political and economic problems to implement the regionalization of city and county wastewater facilities. The most important setback happened in the Cypress Creek watershed [33].

Institutional Growth

While GCA had started as a very small organization composed of a few employees in the early seventies, by the late seventies it had dozens of employees, experienced leadership and board members, and well-developed programs and objectives. By 1980, GCA operated one landfill in Texas City, a class I permitted landfill that received sludge and other industrial solid and liquid wastes; four centralized industrial wastewater treatment facilities: the Bayport facility, the Washburn Tunnel facility, the 40-Acre facility and the American facility; seven centralized municipal wastewater treatment plants; ten sewage treatment facilities, and it managed five municipal water districts. In addition, it had already operated several other municipal facilities and the Tenneco industrial wastewater plant throughout the seventies [34-37].

GCA development in the 1970s focused mostly on its industrial and municipal wastewater management and treatment missions, clearly enunciated in state and federal statutes. Yet, Public Law 92-500 also required that GCA start to engage in solid waste disposal issues. In the early seventies, it surveyed municipal and industrial solid waste needs and inventoried landfill capacity in the area, evaluated disposal alternatives, recommended cost-effective solutions for transferring and final disposal of municipal solid waste, located solid waste transfer stations, etc. These activities were guided by the idea that the best orientation for the actions of the authority in the solid waste area would be to assist local governments through intergovernmental partnerships.

This was the solid waste policy that drove GCA to operate the Galveston landfill, contracted with four Texas City industries in 1974—Union Carbide, Monsanto, Texas City Refining, and Marathon Oil Company—that provided the funds to plan, construct, and operate the facility. These companies purchased 90 percent of the landfill capacity, while 10 percent was reserved by the "[a]uthority for public use such as the clean up of abandoned waste sites. In addition, a perpetual care fund was established "to ensure care of the site for the protection of future generations" [34, p. 7]. According to Davis, "it [the landfill] was selected as a model project by the U.S. EPA for a film on landfill operation" [30].

To address the problem of more than 12 million tons/y of hazardous waste generated in the Gulf Coast area, and the new requirements of the 1976 Resource Conservation and Recovery Act (RCRA), the authority proposed a Waste Management Center. This center was a source of lasting and widespread conflicts with local politicians and community groups.

THE MIDDLE-YEARS: "THERE IS JUST NOT A PLACE NAMED 'SOMEWHERE ELSE,' TEXAS" [38, 39]

Background

After the enactment of the 1976 RCRA and its regulation by the late seventies, many materials that were not considered hazardous before the passage of the act were defined as toxic or hazardous. According to GCA publications, in 1978, GCA management assessed the impact of this new classification on the Houston area and came to the conclusion that a new hazardous waste disposal facility to serve industries in the area was needed. The staff conducted a market survey and determined the types and quantity of wastes that would require proper disposal. By doing an investigation of processes, physical equipment, corporate policies, financial capability, and other parameters, GCA staff devised "an environmentally acceptable disposal arrangement utilizing those physical facilities which were considered appropriate for the type of waste produced in the Houston-Galveston metropolitan area" [40].

This arrangement was composed of three main parties: GCWDA, an incinerator contractor, and a chemical fixation contractor. GCWDA would own the land and hold permits, provide laboratory facilities to assure an internal quality control program, and assume responsibility for long-term site management. The incinerator contractor would build and operate the incinerator, including pretreatment and resource recovery equipment for organic waste materials. The chemical fixation contractor would construct and operate the chemical fixation process, and provide pretreatment and resource recovery devices for inorganic waste materials. Moreover, the latter would also control ash and scrubber sludges derived from incineration [40].

By 1980 GCA publicly announced plans to build a modern toxic waste disposal facility to destroy toxic waste. The facility was supposed "to accept hazardous waste and route it through high technology processes that convert it to a harmless, inert product" [34, p. 7]. The components of the center included two rotary kiln incinerators, one liquid combustion device, extensive pretreatment and product recovery facilities, waste materials storage, chemical fixation process equipment, a fixation product deposition area, a laboratory, administration, maintenance and related facilities, and utility control facilities.

The center was supposed to be a public-private partnership that "would bring out the best of both sectors," and treat 520,000 tons of hazardous wastes/year [41].

Davis once compared the center to a shopping center "whose owner [GCA] provides streets to the building and leases space to the people who are operating a dress shop, barber shop, or whatever" [41-44].

GCA chose two companies to participate in the center: Stablex, a British company that owned the Stablex process—by which liquid, solid wastes, and sludges turned into "safe synthetic rock"[45]—and the IT Corporation, a U.S. corporation "with a history of success with the rotary kiln incinerator" [41].

In order to select the best site for the center, GCA carried out an extensive review process based on criteria that included proximity to population, distance to major transportation routes, general subsurface soil characteristics, existing air quality, site elevation, and proximity to industrial generators. About twenty potential sites were considered, of which one was chosen, near the Ellington Air Force Base, in South Harris County. A "fatal flaw"evaluation of this site was done to determine the site's environmental acceptability. State and federal agencies were consulted to make sure that the evaluation took into account their regulatory requirements. After this detailed planning process, GCA finally concluded that the site met all requirements.

GCA then started its public information program to display and explain the project to different constituencies before formally filing the permit application and official public notice. GCA staff met with environmental groups, such as the Sierra Club and the Audubon Society, elected officials—such as mayors, state representatives and senators—City of Houston Public Works Department officials, area civic groups, homeowners, and businesses near the site, to get feedback on the project.

By Davis's account, all these stakeholders agreed that the high technology center was good, the location was acceptable, and that there was a clear need for a waste destruction facility in the area [40, 41, 46]. By the time GCA filed the regulatory permit application, in June 1980, community opposition to the siting of the center in Pasadena had started to emerge. This movement profoundly affected GCA's "neutral technical certainties" and had a big impact on GCA's ability to deal with hazardous wastes during the eighties. For the first time in its ten-year history, the authority had to respond to the public's perception concerning hazardous waste issues. The "Not in My Backyard" (NIMBY) movement appeared on the local scene with all its fears, outrage, and political militancy.

The Local NIMBY Coalition

The members of the heterogeneous ad hoc coalition that opposed the siting of the center in Pasadena included citizen groups, headed by the Citizens Against Polluting Our Neighborhoods (CAPONE), the cities of Houston, La Porte, Seabrook, and Pasadena, Harris County, the Clear Creek City Water Authority, the Clear Lake City Civic League, and a couple of local hazardous waste management businesses [47]. A quick look at the actors in this multifaceted coalition, and the reasons why they opposed GCWDA, reveals several fundamental hazardous waste policy questions that arose in the early eighties.

CAPONE was the catalyst of this coalition. This 250-member grassroots organization was formed specifically . . . "to oppose the siting of the 200-acre chemical waste disposal facility on Highway 3" [48]. The group claimed that the facility "may be an answer to disposing of hazardous wastes, . . . but should be located in an industrial area and not near homes and schools" [48]. It mobilized the local community to actively oppose the siting of the facility in Pasadena. Davis observed that "they [CAPONE members] acknowledged the harsh implications of the name, but stated that they felt it would take forceful measures to impact the proposed facility" [40, 49].

Based on a series of interviews with CAPONE members, Mackay, Jr. wrote that "a feeling of frustration is what motivated the formation of this anti-establishment body" [50, p. 82]. He claimed that CAPONE members represented a wide variety of interests and that some of them even worked for industries that generated wastes. Moreover, these average citizens felt outraged when they realized that a public, or quasi-public agency had become so autocratic and paternalistic. CAPONE members, "with some dark hints of the tactics of the sixties," also helped defeat longtime state senator, "Babe" Schwarz, a staunch supporter of GCWDA [50, p. 82].

Gottlieb offered an excellent analysis of the role of citizen-action or community empowerment groups like CAPONE [6, chap. 5]. He argued that the Love Canal dramatic events became "a staging ground for the development of a new movement that was primarily about community empowerment" [6, p. 176]. This movement was characterized as the "NIMBYites," and was attacked by the waste industry's trade press as carriers of the "NIMBY Syndrome" [6, p. 190].

Yet, the most powerful member of the coalition was the City of Houston. A City of Houston lawyer advised GCA's counsel that the city would not oppose the project if it was relocated to an industrial area. If GCA persisted with its application, the city "would utilize all avenues of opposition, including appeals to any issued permit" [40]. Contemporary press reports suggest that the City of Houston had concerns regarding contamination of drinking water of Southeast Houston residents, and the proximity of major residential and commercial areas [51].

The City of Pasadena and Pasadena residents claimed that the center could increase trucking of toxic wastes in their communities, with the potential for spills of hazardous materials, cause adverse effects on residential property values, and attract additional industries to the area. The Malone Company, on the other hand, charged in the first public hearing to review GCA's permit application that GCA's project—the state "would present unfair competition with private industry" [52, p. 13A; 53, p. 1; 54]. Mackay, Jr. quoted Paul Malone, president and chairman of the board, as saying, "This is the first time in my long career that I have been threatened with extinction through actual business competition by a creation of the state legislature. On top of that, it was started with tax money, a part of which was generated by the Malone Company. Socialism—that's all it is!" [50, p. 158].

After almost a year of court battles and political pressure, and about $500,000 in investments, GCA withdrew its applications for permits from the Texas Department of Water Resources and the Texas Air Control Board on March 1981. The two contractors would instead seek the permits themselves [55]. Still, GCA did not give up the idea of the center, and announced an alternative site in the Bayport Industrial District, located in Southeast Harris County.

Again, nearby community residents opposed the siting of the facility "in their backyards," even though one local community, Taylor Lake Village, appointed a committee to evaluate the project over several months. During this evaluation process, Stablex withdrew from the project, because it disagreed with GCA on long-term contracting needed for the issuance of bonds.

The final blow to this second siting option was the EPA's announcement in February of 1981 that it would allow increased landfilling of liquid hazardous wastes. This decision created uncertainty in business plans for new hazardous waste facilities and led the incinerator contractor for the Bayport site to lose interest in participating in the project.

Responding to these successive failures, GCA backed off from its proposal and decided to assess "our hazardous waste program in light of regulatory developments and public perceptions of siting and disposal" [40]. In 1982, GCA asked the Keystone Center in Colorado "to design and direct a workshop process, to include regional opinion leaders from all the various disciplines and interests involved in hazardous waste management, and to develop a public review/facility siting process for our area" [56; 57, p. 1]. All throughout the eighties, GCA faced community opposition to the construction or expansion of solid and hazardous wastes treatment projects [58].

Political Aspects:
The Greg Cantrell Series on GCA

By the early 1980s, a *Galveston Daily News* reporter, Greg Cantrell, wrote a series of eleven highly critical articles on the Gulf Coast Authority. These articles synthesized the political debate around GCA in the seventies, named and gave voice to its harsh critics, and offered rich material concerning GCA's political troubles. The GCA general manager and board members tried to respond to every single accusation with letters to the editor of the newspaper, suggesting that GCA did not take them lightly. This section reproduces the essence of the debate between the reporter and GCA.

In the introductory article, titled, "Gulf Coast Authority: A creature of the state," Cantrell wrote that right after its creation there were two supportive views regarding GCA: Some saw it as "the best last hope for a deteriorating Galveston Bay," while others saw it as a "saviour of Houston's heavily polluted" ship channel. Citing a study on pollution problems in the area, Cantrell noted that critics would say that "in a state where government is widely reputed to favor big business . . . it was easy for a skeptical public to reach skeptical conclusions about an agency that helped industry and filed no enforcement actions" [59, pp. 1A-2A].

In addition, he echoed criticisms that claimed that GCA: began with too many powers; was a "little monster, since it was both a regulator and one of those being regulated," and "a clear case of corporate welfare"; was not a state agency "but a company and a business"; had evolved "into a governmental entity in direct competition with private waste disposal firms"; and was given "most favored nation treatment by the state" [59, pp. 1A-2A].

These arguments were amplified and detailed in the following ten articles, which also accused GCA of being too cozy with the Texas Department of Water Resources, a major industrial polluter in the area, and a violator of U.S. environmental regulations.

In summary, the Cantrell series attacked GCA from left and right perspectives, creating a mix of unfounded factual evidence and solid political views. Yet, the series demonstrated that the critics and supporters of GCA had strong economic, political, and ideological reasons not to accept the new agency [60].

Those who owned small hazardous waste businesses in the area feared unfair economic competition from "big brother." Those who had libertarian views wanted GCA to disappear from the scene. Those who were critical of the collusion between state and business interests challenged GCA on the grounds that Texas needed strong enforcement of environmental regulations, not a dubious "implementing agency."

Both on the right and the left, there was the view that GCA represented "corporate" welfare. Municipal and county governments and politicians at times opposed the authority due to turf or jurisdictional battles regarding control of solid waste or wastewater management.

Defenders of the agency, on the other hand, tended to coalesce under the argument that GCA was the only rational way for a regional environmental crisis to be solved, i.e., a regional problem demanded a regional solution. Besides, given the existence of several other regulatory agencies in the area, there was a need for a neutral "facilitator," who should solve, not regulate, the environmental problems in the area [61]. In other words, they defended limited state intervention to promote pollution control in the area. While they favored state intervention, they were not interested in colliding with the interests of the rich and strong Texas petrochemical industry. Industry representatives appear to have agreed with GCA and supported its existence and growth over the decade, as the next section shows.

Regulatory Aspects: The POTW and Pretreatment Standards Controversies

The POTW Status of GCA's Industrial Facilities

In 1981, an old dispute with the EPA came to a conclusion, after a consent decree was issued by the courts in Texas. The dispute had revolved around the legal status of GCA's industrial treatment facilities: Were these facilities Public Operated Treatment Works (POTW) or not? If they were, should they be allowed to have industrial permits or not?

The consent agreement between EPA and GCA (U.S. District Court Southern District of Texas) specified that all wastewater treatment plants operated by GCA were public owned treatment works, "as that term is used in every portion of the Clean Water Act except the provisions relating to the receipt of federal construction grant monies" [62, 63].

According to GCA's attorneys, "[T]his is what we have been trying to have the Environmental Protection Agency recognize for many years" [62]. The consent decree also required that the industrial wastewater treatment facilities be "permitted by the Texas Water Commission and Region VI of EPA as though they were industrial direct dischargers" [64]. GCA agreed that the effluent limits for each of GCA's industrial facilities would be a sum of the best practicable technology (BPT), best conventional technology (BCT), or best available technology (BAT), as appropriate for the industrial contributors.

Clean Water Act Pretreatment Regulations

Section 307 (b) (1) of the Clean Water Act states that the EPA administrator must develop

Pretreatment standards for the introduction of pollutants into treatment works ... which are publicly owned for the pollutants which are determined not to be susceptible to treatment by such treatment works or which would interfere with the operation of such treatment works.

With respect to toxic pollutants, the Act allows municipal agencies to grant removal credits to indirect industrial dischargers of toxic substances, as part of their local pretreatment programs. These credits are supposed to reflect the pollutant removal achieved by municipal plants and prevent the construction of costly and duplicative treatment plants by categorical industries [65]. In a word, it was a mechanism to avoid redundancies of treatment facilities.

In 1987, the EPA adopted the pretreatment standards to industrial users of POTWs, the Organic Chemicals, Plastics, and Synthetic Fibers Category Effluent Limitations Guidelines, Pretreatment Standards, and New Source Performance Standards (40 CFR 414). These pretreatment standards required that "each industrial chemical plant that produces wastes under these rules must pretreat their [sic] wastewater to the same standards as if it were being discharged directly to a receiving stream, if they [sic] are to discharge to a publicly owned treatment works" [67].

The purpose of this regulation was to protect the typical POTW against interference or pass-through problems [68]. Nevertheless, if applied to GCA's customers, the regulation would render GCA's industrial POTWs "virtually useless," because it would require these customers "to treat their wastewaters to a level that is equivalent to the industrial direct discharger best available technology standards before the wastes are discharged to the POTW" [64].

GCA argued emphatically that EPA's revisions to the pretreatment standards would be "duplicative, unduly expensive and would jeopardize the existence of three of GCA's four industrial POTWs, without materially improving the quality of the respective wastewater discharges" [69]. Davis qualified this issue as the "most critical issue the [a]uthority has ever faced." He went on to say that the rule would make obsolete a total of $126 million in capital equipment [67].

To counter the threat posed by this EPA rule, GCA, together with its customers and other similarly affected agencies and industries: a) lobbied the U.S. Congress to amend the CWA to exempt or exclude them from the pretreatment requirements of section 307 of the CWA, b) filed a lawsuit in the Fifth Circuit of Appeals in New Orleans, and c) petitioned the EPA for a stay and relief from the pretreatment regulation [70, 71]. In fact, GCA was told by EPA officials that it would be difficult for EPA to find a solution to GCA's case because it "was unique to any other situation in the nation" [72, 73].

GCA lost its ability to use the removal credits until one of these initiatives provided some resolution to the conundrum. As a result of this legal obstacle and other business conditions, AMOCO decided to purchase the American facility in late 1989. Therefore, GCA lost one of its facilities before the legal battle came to conclusion in the nineties.

Institutional Consolidation

In contrast to the GCA of the seventies, the GCA of the eighties is an institution that strived for improvements in its operational performance, consolidation of its institutional mission, and of its research and development capabilities. During the first three years of the decade, it had to "weather the storm of an economic downturn in the Houston economy," a crisis that affected GCA's activities, because of its dependence on service fees to finance its operations [74]. In other words, the health of the industrial economy in the Houston-Galveston area has a direct impact on GCA's ability to grow.

This economic crisis, coupled with success stories, led GCA to concentrate efforts on "efficient operation and development of programs within our defined statutory authority that will sustain our basic operations" [74, 75]. One such success was recognized by the Water Pollution Control Federation report titled, "Decade of Progress," which praised GCA's effort to control the water pollution in the Houston Ship Channel during the seventies. It stated that ". . . while environmentalists pronounced the channel dead in 1970, state and federal agencies began to work on the remains. The lower channel has now been restored to the point where it provides a habitat for fish and other aquatic life—and the fish are thriving" [76, p. 1; 77].

During the eighties, the municipal operations experienced significant growth, with the construction or expansion of regional facilities. A landmark event occurred when GCA contracted, in 1987, with the City of Houston to dispose of thirty-five to forty-four dry tons/day of sludge from the Sims Bayou Wastewater Treatment Plant [78, p. 3; 79]. By 1988, GCA operated nineteen domestic wastewater treatment plants, six of which were regional and served multiple city and water district customers [80].

On the industrial treatment front, GCA achieved better operational results by replacing older equipment with state-of-the-art technologies, introducing innovations in sludge handling and joint treatment of industrial and municipal wastewater, and gradually improving the compliance record of its facilities. Performance studies and evaluations conducted by consulting groups and university professors ranked GCA's facilities among similar plants in the area and pointed out areas for improvement [78, p. 5; 81].

On the solid waste front, GCA encouraged resource recovery, also called waste-to-energy, projects in Galveston County and other areas, due to the lack of landfill capacity to accommodate area needs. It also promoted seminars and conferences with state and federal agencies in order to find coordinated and common solutions to the solid waste problems in the region [82].

During the eighties GCA also developed some health and safety activities. It trained employees to respond to emergency response to hazardous waste spills and to work safely in hazardous waste operations, had all industrial facilities monitored for chemical exposures, and provided annual check-ups for its employees. The Washburn facility won an award in March 1989 for working a year without a lost time injury [83].

In sum, the middle years were years of community opposition and legal struggles. The former set the political boundaries for GCA's expansion. The latter could dramatically reduce GCA's infrastructure. Thus, GCA ended the decade with an improved operational performance and a much better understanding of its legal and political limits.

THE LATE YEARS: GCA SAILS INTO CALM WATERS

While the seventies were once called "troubled waters," the nineties can only be called "calm waters" by comparison. The most controversial issues in the history of the authority had, without a doubt, happened in the preceding two decades, when it was hit from right and left before it could consolidate its political, economic, and legal boundaries. The political and court battles of the eighties also taught GCA the minefields to avoid and the probable smoother paths for its institutional development. Nevertheless, GCA still had to resolve and settle issues that developed in the late eighties, such as the CWA amendment referred to in the previous section. These are the topics discussed in the following section.

Regulatory Aspects

The battle to amend the CWA came to closure only in October 1992, when Public Law 102-389 passed. This law has special provisions for industries discharging to wastewater treatment facilities operated by GCWDA. These industries were finally exempted from meeting categorical pretreatment standards established under section 307 (b) of the Clean Water Act.

GCA and its allies were able to overcome the regulatory hurdle by changing the language of a major environmental statute, the CWA, suggesting that GCA and its industrial allies used their political muscle quite effectively. Compared to this obstacle, all other regulatory aspects faced by GCA were minor. They involved GCA's industrial customers' compliance with new EPA regulations such as the 1990 Clean Air Act Amendments or CWA categorical pretreatment standards. [84].

Despite the fact that most GCA's customers in the Bayport Complex—and probably elsewhere—are part of the Responsible Care Program, GCA's literature does not even mention any of the voluntary protection programs en vogue in the nineties [85]. Judging by the information collected for this book, it appears that GCA does not see these programs as important strategic developments. While this lack of emphasis on voluntary protection may be explained by GCA's very early commitment to cooperation with industry, it still suggests a remarkable indifference to the prevailing petrochemical businesses discourse regarding regulatory issues in the nineties.

Institutional Aspects: "New Environmental Vistas Opened" [37, 86]

For the most part GCA continued in the nineties along the "waste management road" paved in the 1980s by EPA regulations. Yet, it introduced new environmental initiatives to its agenda by 1994, when it adopted several special environmental education programs and projects.

GCA developed a unique grocery produce compost program in partnership with a supermarket chain, a program to mulch discarded Christmas trees involving six area churches and a large building materials retailer, and introduced the limited use of biosolids as a soil amendment for nonfood crops, such as day lilies. In addition, many authority employees participated in a "massive river banks cleanup program" in the spring of 1994 [87-89].

In 1996, GCA adopted the Laboratory Management Information System (LIMS), that allows all GCA's facilities to be on line and transfer laboratory data as soon as it is validated by the system. GCA's lab has put the facility "among the top industrial laboratory to be found anywhere" [88, p. 14].

On the municipal operations front, in 1994, GCA replaced the old gaseous chlorination system used to disinfect domestic wastewater in the Alief Wastewater Treatment Plant with a new sulfur dioxide disinfection/dechlorination system. It also introduced in 1994 a new ultraviolet disinfection system in the Blackhawk facility, composed of a series of lights operating in the UV spectrum to disinfect the wastewater as it passes between the rack of bulbs.

On the industrial operations front, the most important milestone was the start-up in 1997 of the Odessa South Regional Facility in the City of Odessa. For the first time in its history, GCA, in partnership with the City of Odessa and Huntsman Corporation, is operating a joint municipal/industrial wastewater treatment plant located 500 miles away from its original tricounty boundaries. This wastewater plant has allegedly "provided an attractive to lure for industrial businesses," and additional jobs in the area [89, p. 5].

On the solid waste front, the highlight of the nineties was the construction of Y cells at the Campbell Bayou Facility, the landfill operated by GCA in Texas City. This cell is "an elaborate structure . . . that includes three feet of compacted clay, an impermeable liner, and leachate collection system to ensure that what goes in the cell stays there or is collected for treatment" [89, p. 10]. It provides for the disposal of nonhazardous industrial solid waste materials primarily from two companies: Union Carbide Chemicals and Plastics, and Sterling Chemicals.

During the nineties, GCA also wrote standard operating procedures for hazardous jobs in a new health and safety manual, which includes confined space entry, lockout-tagout, hazard communication, hot work, emergency response operations, and more. As of 1997, GCWDA operated three industrial wastewater treatment facilities, seven municipal wastewater plants, an industrial solid waste landfill, two solid waste transfer stations, a central laboratory, and other service facilities. The GCA of the nineties can thus be considered an example of a well-established institution, whose mission and operations are no longer challenged in any significant way.

THE EVOLUTION OF THE BAYPORT FACILITY

GCA started operating the Bayport plant on November 1974, when the plant treated the effluent of about ten companies. By 1976, the plant had expanded with the addition of a third clarifier, modifications to the two existing clarifiers, and an aeration basin. This first expansion aimed at improving flow monitoring and sludge recycling, coupled with the addition of two new customers, the Quaker Oats Company and Rexene Polymers. The August 1976 GCWDA newsletter claimed that the quality of the effluent was good enough to support aquatic life such as gambusia fish, as well as birds, such as mallards [90]. In October 1976, GCA purchased the Bayport facility from the Friendswood Development

Company, after three-and-a-half years of negotiations, at a cost of $7,180,000. It employed 20 people, had 6.5 million gallons-per-day capacity, and treated the wastewaters from 20 petrochemical industries [91].

In March 1977, Bayport staff stopped supplying industrial water to the Bayport Industrial Complex for Friendswood. The Coastal Industrial Water Authority (CIWA) installed a new surface water system to replace the previous water supply system, which was based on ground wells, ground and elevated storage tanks, and a booster pump station. This replacement was supposed to help alleviate the problem of land subsidence in the Bayport Area [92]. In 1979, a second expansion of the Bayport facility took place, almost doubling its capacity. As a result of this expansion, the Bayport facility manager expected a "better effluent quality with the ability to meet new permit standards and increased loadings" [93, p. 1]. GCA requested a new permit to allow "greater flow from Bayport to the [c]hannel due to new industries coming onstream by January 1982" [93, pp. 1-2; 94; 95].

In 1982, GCA spent $1.5 million in tax-exempt bonds to finance the purchase of twenty-two subsurface jet aerators to increase the water temperature in the Bayport facility treatment ponds, because low temperatures were slowing the breakdown of organic matter and creating overloading of the treatment process [96, 97]. Moreover, the bonds would also finance sludge dewatering and plant aeration additions in the following two or three years. In 1985, a new belt-press installation replaced the old filter press, providing additional capacity to treat an increased amount of wastewater. Once again, Bayport expanded to match the needs of increased petrochemical production in Bayport.

By 1991, Bayport was treating the effluent of about forty industries in the Bayport Industrial District, along with municipal sewage from Shore Acres and the Bayshore Municipal Utility District. Responding to increased demands for treatment capacity and a need for general improvements, a series of projects were planned in the early nineties [98, 99].

The last expansion occurred in 1995-1996, a project that involved a massive Bayport facility improvement program. It cost about $30 million and involved substantial changes to the facility, aimed at refurbishing the plant to increase the Bayport facility's capacity to treat additional wastewater from Hoechst Celanese, which decided to discontinue the use of deep well injection as a treatment method [100]. Furthermore, GCA and Bayport industrial customers anticipated that new EPA volatile organic compounds (VOCs) air emission regulations would require tighter control of these emissions.

According to the GCWDA 1997 annual report [89], the changes included:

a) the replacement of the open concrete collection channel that collected the organic streams of the Bayport Industrial Complex by an above-ground pipeline that allows for vapor recovery, easier detection of leaks, and less costly repairs;

b) process improvements such as an additional aeration unit, a second step aeration utilizing a jet aeration system similar to the one existing in the first step of the treatment process, an additional sixth clarifier, a new air control emissions system that takes any potential air emissions from the lift station into the biological treatment system, and an upgraded lift station;

c) a synthetically lined emergency spill basin.

With these improvements, the Bayport facility saved energy, increased its flow and treatment capacity, reduced the total quantity of sludge that requires dewatering, and improved its operational efficiency. In general, the improvements and expansions of the Bayport facility were conditioned by the business cycles of the local petrochemical industry and its effects on the Bayport complex. As the local economy expanded, so did the Bayport plant. Therefore, this brief summary of the evolution of the Bayport plant mirrors the evolution of the Bayport complex throughout the last thirty years.

Last, a very important component in the evolution of the Bayport facility was the building of a cooperative relationship with its industrial customers. For one, facility staff had to analyze every company waste characteristic to make sure that it didn't create a problem for the treatment system. This examination involved detailed knowledge of petrochemical production processes and required strong trust between facility managers, because of industry's concerns with trade secrets. [101]. Bayport staff—and GCWDA as a whole—dealt with customers individually or collectively, depending on the situation. For example, if Bayport staff needed to talk about operating costs, or needed to upgrade the plant, they talked to companies as a group.

In the Bayport complex, there are no written contracts between GCA and its customers. The relationship is based on a "gentlemen's agreement" between the parties, coupled with an application for discharge into Bayport treatment system. This business-related connection between the polluters and the authority evolved over the years into an essential part of GCA's organizational culture.

The Bayport Complex

Starting with only ten industries in the late sixties, the Bayport complex had twenty in 1976, more than thirty by 1980, forty in 1991, and more than fifty by 1997 [102]. Most of the growth in the 1980s and 1990s was determined by the expansion of the fine- and specialty-chemistry sector of the petrochemical industry, which is considered the high-tech segment of the industry [103].

ARCO Chemical owns a chemical facility that produces propylene oxide, tertiary butyl alcohol—a compound used to produce oxygenate fuels such as methyl tertiary butyl ether (MTBE) or ethyl tertiary butyl ether (ETBE)—and various derivatives including propylene glycol. ARCO, one of the largest integrated enterprises in the petroleum industry, claimed in 1996 that it was the world's largest producer of MTBE and propylene glycol, the second largest producer of polyol, and the third largest producer of styrene [104].

Rohm and Haas owns a plant that produces biocides, chemicals used to "keep products and processes free from bacteria, fungi, and algae," and monomers such as acrylic acid and its derivatives, and methyl methacrylate and its derivatives. Rohm and Haas claimed to be the largest producer of acrylic monomers in the world by 1994 [105].

Hoechst Celanese owns a plant that used to be a Celanese plant. The facility uses ethylene to produce ethylene glycol and ethylates, which in turn are used to produce polyester fibers and antifreeze; uses propylene to obtain acrylic acid, and natural gas to produce methanol and acetic acid. The latter is combined with ethylene to produce vinyl acetate [106].

Akzo Nobel, a Swedish corporation, owns a plant that produces hydro-processing and fluid cracking catalysts, used by refineries to crack vacuum gasoil and resid into products such as LPG, gasoline, and/or diesel fuel. Akzo Nobel also owns facilities in Asia, Latin America, and Europe.

The companies in the complex formed a loose, low-profile association called Association of Bayport Companies (ABC), which has represented their collective interests on a "as-needed" basis. In addition to the lobbying efforts described earlier in this chapter, most of the activities carried out by the ABC have concentrated either on industry-sponsored programs such as the Responsible Care Program, or regulatory-driven obligations. For example, Bayport complex industries participate in three separate community advisory panels (CAPs)—the Laporte, the Bay Area, and the Seashore CAPs [107, 108].

Since many of the plants in the complex are subsidiaries of large global chemical corporations that follow the codes of conduct proposed by the Chemical Manufacturers Association Responsible Care program, they have developed voluntary environmental programs to address community concerns. Some of these programs follow European guidelines, such as the Environmental Management and Audit System (EMAS), which are stricter than the ISO 14,001 standards [109]. Moreover, these corporate programs try to address community reactions to company information produced to comply with the 1987 SARA Title III Toxics Release Inventory (TRI) regulations, which require companies to inform state and federal EPA about their emissions and discharges to air, land, and water [110, 111].

The Factory Regime in the Bayport Complex [112]

Labor union power and presence in the Bayport complex has been quite limited, according to several former Oil, Chemical, and Atomic Workers regional and local leaders interviewed for this research [113].

As the U.S. oil and petrochemical industry restructured in the early eighties, firms in the complex tended to switch to a hegemonic-despotic regime. Therefore, the growth of the complex from the mid- to late-eighties spread the hegemonic-despotic factory regime to the majority of the companies. During the early to mid-eighties Bayport companies implemented Total Quality Management programs, contracted out maintenance jobs, downsized the workforce, and increased automation of processes [114, 115]. In addition, corporations reduced their plant and management staff through the use of early retirement buyouts, or attrition. An interesting account of this period is offered by *Chemical Business*:

> . . . The chemical industry is very cyclical, particularly the petrochemical end of the business, with a notably rough ride in the 1980's. The slump in the early part of the decade was countered by the boom in the latter part of the 1980's, right now [1990] the industry is heading back down again. . . . The financial climate of the 1980's added to the pressure for profitability, with *a major reorganization of the industry as the theme*. The threat of takeovers forced many companies to prepare defenses by cutting back . . . (emphases added) [116, p. 41].

Thus, it would be plausible to assume that the size of the permanent workforce in Bayport also decreased while the contract workforce increased. By the same token, overwork increased, fewer senior workers remained, and costs were trimmed.

In the nineties, the shrinking, mostly white salaried workforce, still got good wages—twenty to twenty five dollars an hour—and benefits, while the mostly Hispanic (Mexican) contract employees got lower salaries—between ten to fourteen dollars an hour—and limited or no benefits. In addition, the contractor employees still worked under worse health and safety conditions than permanent employees [117].

Former OCAW leaders claimed that it had been very challenging to organize either segment of the workforce. In the case of contractor employees, organizing was thwarted because they were highly mobile, might not speak English, were relatively well-paid for their education levels and skills, and feared management's retaliation. In the case of the "permanent" workforce, it was difficult because wages in the industry were far superior to other sectors, leading average workers not to perceive their need for a union to represent their collective interests [118].

Yet, former OCAW sources maintained that organized labor has indirectly impacted environmental or occupational health and safety policies in Bayport through the contracts negotiated with oil corporations. These contracts allegedly established policies and procedures patterns that became the benchmark for most companies in the Gulf Coast area. Along this line of reasoning, firms would implement better policies and pay better wages to prevent unionization of their facilities. Another potential labor effect may derive from the political pressure the union exercises to have new standards enacted and better enforcement of existing laws.

After the former OCAW lost thousands of members—with the corresponding loss of "power in the numbers"—during the eighties, it became less and less able to accomplish this pressure. In short, labor has not been able to effectively counter the local petrochemical industry, which restructured the petrochemical workplace according to its short-term and strategic business needs.

Toxic Release Inventory Data on Bayport Facilities

EPA TRI data collected between 1988 to 1995 shows that Bayport industries produce a host of highly toxic chemicals that may cause severe acute and chronic diseases. These chemicals include ethylene glycol, ethylene oxide, methanol, propylene, vinyl acetate, acetaldehyde, ammonia, and others. In 1995, the zip code (77507) in which the Bayport complex is located—Pasadena, Texas—ranked in the top 20 percent of all zip codes in Texas ". . . in terms of cancer hazards, air releases of recognized carcinogens, air releases of recognized developmental toxicants, and air releases of recognized reproductive toxicants" [119, 120]. The top cancer and noncancer risk was ethylene oxide [119, 120]. Also, in 1995, this zip code was responsible for, among other emissions, 368,118 pounds of recognized carcinogens, 517,686 pounds of suspected carcinogens, 1,583,302 pounds of suspected cardiovascular or blood toxicants, 1,369,646 pounds of kidney toxicants, and 2,412,773 suspected neurotoxicants [121].

Between 1988 and 1995, TRI data shows that in this zip code there was a reduction in stack air releases, fugitive air emissions, and land and water releases, while there were increases in underground injection, total environmental releases, and total off-site transfers. The total environmental releases increased from 15,929,949 pounds in 1988 to 16,185,249 pounds in 1995, after reaching a sharp reduction in 1991 [122].

Although these data on toxic emissions in the area of the Bayport complex were submitted by companies without further verification by EPA, they still constitute a strong tool with which communities and environmental activists can demand further reduction in chemical emissions and wastes. In addition, grassroots environmental groups in the United States were able to organize a right-to-know network (RTKnet) to provide technical assistance in interpreting the data and organizing activities around pollution prevention issues.

CONCLUSION

This chapter intends to demonstrate that throughout its history GCA allegedly emphasized "cooperation with industry, economy of scale through regionalization, and environmental safeguards" [123, p. 2]. From the beginning, GCA managers and board insisted on a pragmatic approach to EPA's pollution abatement requirements, which led them to steer the authority toward the implementation of pollution control facilities in the area.

Accordingly, GCA has always tried to develop a partnership with the local petrochemical industry to facilitate its compliance with the massive federal, state, and local environmental policy system. Further, the chapter shows how GCA wastewater plants grew according to the national and international business cycles of an oil-based market economy, especially in the case of the Bayport wastewater treatment facility.

An initially innovative regional waste management agency turned, over the years, into a mainstream pollution control advocate, a pollution control consultant to businesses, and a financial backer of pollution control investments in the Gulf Coast area. In a word, GCA became a state agency whose logic was probusiness, that is, a public body that operated like a business, as once stated by a GCA general manager. This contradictory role of the agency generated many controversies.

While in its first decade GCA was challenged from the regulatory, financial, and legal standpoints, in the eighties the authority had to wage the most significant political battles against local communities and small businesses. These confrontations with the public around the siting of hazardous waste facilities prevented the authority from coordinating "rational" market solutions to the hazardous waste crisis and raised all sorts of disputes and debates concerning the role of the state—GCA—in this sector of the economy.

During the eighties, the authority was also gradually defeated in its intent of facilitating the implementation of areawide hazardous waste management policies. When challenged by neighborhood working- and middle-class groups and interests, which constituted the basis of the local grassroots environmental movement, GCA fought back for nearly a decade. Finally, it changed its plans, retreated, and found alternative courses to accommodate industry's needs. The alliance of communities, small businesses, local governments, and politicians in the region mounted a strong resistance that ended up "winning the day." GCA finally found the limits for its expansion within the area by the end of the decade.

After this tense period GCA "retreated" to its core wastewater and municipal solid waste operations and expanded to other areas of Texas—Odessa—in the nineties. In addition, it increased its outreach to communities through public education and communication programs to gain more public legitimacy and support.

While it is clear that GCA actions significantly reduced the water and air pollution in the Galveston Bay area, seldom did GCA propose pollution prevention policies as an alternative to prevent Galveston Bay pollution, even after the concept became well-known in the early nineties. One major reason for the sustained dominance of pollution control policies may be the fact that the petrochemical industry would not be viable under a different paradigm—one that proposed the elimination or reduction of toxic production.

Following this line of reasoning, the authority would have been forced to abide by "controlling pollution one pipeline at a time," or "several pipelines at a time" in a more rational joint treatment system. Perhaps this policy course may be solely explained by GCA's almost complete dependence on waste management contracts with industrial customers.

One should look, however, beyond strict economic reasons to understand the nearly total absence of or reference to waste prevention alternatives in GCA's discourse. The picture that seems to emerge from the analysis of the history of environmental policies adopted by GCA is the overwhelming and ongoing hegemony of the oil and petrochemical industry in the Gulf Coast region. As the evolution of the Bayport complex suggests, this well-established business hegemony grew even stronger after the industrial restructuring of the early eighties. Petrochemical businesses imposed a more authoritarian version of the hegemonic factory regime. An already weak labor actor became even weaker.

Given this probusiness power balance, GCA, first and foremost, was willing to implement only policies that matched the economic, political, and ideological interests of this industrial sector. It has never opposed the status quo that favored the fundamental interests of the local petrochemical industry. On the contrary, it joined industry to fight EPA's refusal to grant GCA power to control industrial effluents. In short, GCA has always acted as a "quasi-public spokesperson" for industry.

While the pollution control paradigm has offered the general guidelines for the creation of the national environmental policy system, GCA applied it locally in close association with industry. Thus, it is not far from the truth to argue that GCA was captured by the petrochemical industry's political, economic, and ideological viewpoints. Paradoxically, GCA does not develop in the nineties a public relations message that emphasizes voluntary compliance, despite the fact that some of its customers do advocate for and practice these policies in their facilities.

Whether GCA's policies could ever have been different is a question that I leave open to further debate. Nevertheless, the evidence discussed in this chapter suggests that probably not, since in the "Lone Star," the "Oil Republic of Texas," the state has had a long tradition of playing according to this industry's music.

ENDNOTES

1. The term *model* is used here to characterize a set of GCA's policies and practices that together may be interpreted as an economic, organizational, and technological paradigm for hazardous waste management and treatment, especially for liquid hazardous wastes. The components of the model will be detailed throughout the chapter. Texas is an example in the United States, which in turn is an example of a country in the center.

2. To avoid the limitation of an unilateral focus in the Brazilian case, this chapter is an effort to take a look at the "center" side of the "center-periphery" dynamic discussed in chapter 1, even though lack of resources prevented the same in-depth look. Moreover, I agree with the criticism often made by observers in developing countries, who argue that intellectuals from developed countries tend to be ethnocentric and not

look at both sides of this center-periphery relationship. For an example of this criticism, see [3].

3. David Barkin, "Building Trinational Solidarity in an Era of Free Trade," *New Solutions*, 3, 4, pp. 3-10, Summer 1993.

4. This is the title of a newspaper story that describes the origins and initial tasks of GCA [5]. I used this title for the section because it communicates well the problems faced by GCA in its early years.

5. Susan Caudill, *Houston Post*, Sunday, February, 8, 1970.

6. Robert Gottlieb, *Forcing the Spring: The Transformation of the American Environmental Movement,* Island Press, Washington, D.C., 1993.

7. Pasadena Mayor Clyde Doyal, in [8].

8. Susan Caudill, *Houston Post*, February, 8, 1970.

9. Patsy Jackson report, *Galveston (Texas)Daily News,* July 20, 1972.

10. State Rep. Rex Braun (from Houston), cited in [9].

11. J. Kent Hackleman, quoted in Ernest Bailey article, *Houston Post*, October 29, 1973, p. 8/A.

12. Hackleman, an outspoken opponent of giving financial breaks to industry, was not reappointed to GCA's board. According to a Houston Post story, he "has incurred disfavor by opposing the GCWDA's procedure of selling municipal type bonds—at a reduced rate—in behalf of various industries so the industries can install pollution control equipment at less cost" [13, p. 4A]. In the same report, Hackleman affirmed that "the board is sympathetic to industry," and that "whatever industry wants, industry gets" [13, p. 4A]. Summarizing his point of view, he said, "To me, cleaning up is part of the cost of doing business. I know that sounds old and hackneyed to many people, but that's the way I feel about it" [13, p. 4A].

13. *Houston Post*, September, 6, 1975, p. 4A.

14. This is the summary of the arguments provided in *Gulf Coast Comments* (GCA newsletter), December 1973, vol. 1, p. 1. See also [15], in which it is reported that Rep. "Nick" Nichols, Democrat-Houston, introduced a bill to strip authority from the GCWDA and other units of government to issue controversial pollution control bonds. Nichols also accused GCWDA of acting as a "front for the industrial polluters" [15].

15. "GCWDA target of Nichols bill," *Houston Post*, May 7, 1975.

16. These industries were: Champion, Petro-Tex Chemical Corporation, Atlantic Richfield Co. (ARCO), Air Products and Chemicals Corp., and Crown Central Petroleum Co. Joe Resweber, attorney for Harris County, asked Hill for an opinion regarding the tax exemption issue in September 1993. One of the motives for this tax controversy is revealed by Pasadena school superintendent Forest Watson's statement that the "GCA takeover of the Washburn Tunnel waste treatment plant in Pasadena removes $6 million in property from the schools' district rolls" [17, sec. 1, p. 12].

17. Rad Sallee, *Houston Chronicle*, April 30, 1974, sec. 1, p. 12.

18. *Gulf Coast Comments*, vol. 4, p. 1, July 1976.

19. Davis, *Gulf Coast Comments,* vol. 4, p. 2, August 1976.

20. Davis wrote a longer piece defending the tax exemption in the agency newsletter, where he submitted that ". . . since football stadia, gymnasia, auditoriums, and many other developments owned by governmental bodies are not taxed, industrial waste

treatment plants owned and operated by the [a]uthority are not, and should not be subject to taxation by other units local government" [p. 1]. Moreover, industry contracting with the authority did not receive any tax benefit; it was true that industry got lower interest rates, but it should be given the same rights that are utilized by another industry using a municipal system. In the latter case, industries utilize municipal wastewater facilities and are not assessed ad valorem taxes on those facilities, even though they serve industry. In *Gulf Coast Comments*, Vol. 4, p. 4, 1976.

21. *Gulf Coast Comments*, vol. 4, p. 2, August 1976.
22. This quote is from GCWDA Tenth Anniversary—1970-1980 report. Roy Hatch, the first chairman of GCA's board, declared in 1970 in a meeting to the Clear Lake Chamber of Commerce that he estimated it would probably take ten years "to get the job done at a cleanup cost of $500 million." In *Spaceland Star* (League City, Texas), News Citizen edition, May 1, 1970.
23. "Gulf Coast Waste Disposal Authority Five Year Status Report," 1970-1975, p. 5.
24. The same story [5] also reports that Senator Criss Cole, the founding father of GCA, said that the original bill included eight counties, reduced to three in the final bill due to "political considerations" [5].
25. *Houston Post*, June 13, 1973.
26. Alan Borner to Charles Goode, personnel director of GCA, March 20, 1981, available in the historical files of GCA, Pasadena, Texas. The letter had attached to it an edited version of Davis's presentation to the Northeast Conference on Hazardous Waste. This conflict between EPA and GCA is the first in a series of conflicts between both agencies. Charles Ganze, GCA operations manager, agreed with the view that GCA has had a long history of trying to be independent from the EPA regulatory environment [27].
27. Charles Ganze, interview by author, tape recording, May 1997, Pasadena, Texas.
28. *Houston Post*, p. 4A, June 20, 1973.
29. *Comments* (GCA's newsletter), vol. 9, p. 1, January 1991.
30. Jack Davis, "Hazardous Waste: Challenge for Today and the Future," paper presented at the Cape Town Conference of the International Association on Water Pollution Research, Cape Town, S.A., 1982.
31. Ganze actually told me that "We [GCA] assist industry to comply with regulations" [27]. Ganze is a biologist who has worked for GCA for the last 26 years. Over the years he received awards, such as the Willem Rudolfs Medal of the Water Pollution Control Federation in 1974, for outstanding contribution to industrial waste control, and got several promotions. He now holds one of top managerial positions in the authority, that of industrial operations manager.
32. *Comments*, vol. 9, p. 2, January 1981.
33. In July of 1973, the authority was asked by the Texas Water Quality Board (TWQB) to assume responsibility for centralized sewage treatment for the Cypress Creek watershed, after the San Jacinto River Authority (SJRA) resigned. GCA took over existing contracts between the SJRA and districts in the watershed. GCA spent significant amounts of money and effort to implement regionalization there, and started to operate fourteen municipal plants. Despite GCA's willingness to bankroll the program, it met staunch political opposition from water districts and could not continue. In 1976, the authority requested that it be relieved of the responsibility. The

TWQB released GCA from its order. This account is based on an unpublished and undated GCA internal document.

34. "GCWDA 1980 Annual Report."

35. The Tenneco plant treated the industrial wastewater of Tenneco Chemical, Inc.

36. For a summary of the chronology of GCA milestones in the 1970s, see [37]. In my two visits to GCA in 1996 and 1997, I reviewed GCA's historical files, including press reports, and interviewed several staff. In contrast to Cetrel, I did not find nor hear of any significant health and safety problems in GCA during the seventies. Though this lack of evidence does not rule out the occasional incidence of workplace accidents and exposures to toxic chemicals in the routine operations of GCA's facilities, it suggests that no major work environment crisis occurred in the early years of the authority. Yet, a GCA staff told me that GCA did not have a formal health and safety program until the eighties. In fact, GCA is not covered by OSHA regulations, because Texas does not enforce federal OSHA regulations in public workplaces.

37. "Gulf Coast Waste Disposal Authority 1994 Annual Report, Twenty-Fifth Anniversary, 1969-1994."

38. This quote is attributed to Joe Teller by Davis. Teller was at the time GCA's deputy general manager for hazardous waste [30].

39. The account that follows is based on several internal documents, articles, and position papers written by GCA management, local and national newspaper reports, and leaflets issued by groups that opposed the siting of the Waste Treatment Center.

40. Jack Davis and D. Harkey, "An Innovation With Opposition: Hazardous Waste Management in the Houston Area," paper presented at the American Society of Civil Engineers Fall Convention, October 1992.

41. Quote from Jack Davis, paper presented at the Northeast Conference on Hazardous Waste, 1981, available in the archives of GCA in Pasadena, Texas.

42. A local environmental reporter called the center a "one-stop dumping"[43, p. 10A] or a "one stop shopping center" [44, p. D].

43. Harold Scarlett, *Houston Post*, p. 10A, August 19, 1979.

44. Harold Scarlett, *Houston Post*, p. D, April 27, 1980.

45. Harold Scarlett described this way the end result of the treatment process in an article [44, p. D]. A group of GCWDA board members and executives, along with local officials and Texas politicians visited Stablex facilities in Thurrock, twenty miles east of London, to see how the process worked. Scarlett quoted Hackleman, described as a former maverick member of GCA's board, as saying that ". . .it was fascinating to watch them bring in loads of just horrible stuff, neutralize it and then use it to reclaim land" [44, p. D]. They also visited the first plant that used the same process, located in Brownhills, near Birmingham, in operation since 1974.

46. Davis also narrated this public information process elsewhere the following way: "We contacted every person who ever lived, had a business, or otherwise were involved in that area and told them what we were doing. We hand carried the package. We didn't send it late either. We knocked on every door. . . . We had four public meetings with area residents and business people and things were just going on smoothly. Most of them understood it. Everybody said 'Well you know it looks like a good process, but why don't you go somewhere else?'" [41]

47. The environmental groups Sierra Club, Galveston Bay Conservation and Preservation Association (GCBPA), and the Toxic Substances Task Force also participated in the

coalition. The hazardous waste businesses that opposed the center were Malone Co., a Texas City based family-owned waste disposal company, and Liberty Waste Disposal Company of Chambers County. There was a broad press coverage of this coalition. For examples, see articles of Joe Chapman, *Pasadena Citizen*, p. 3, November 20, 1980; Greg Cantrell's reports, *Galveston Daily News*, July 25, 1980, and December 20, 1980; *Houston Chronicle*, p. 2, September 11, 1980; and Ralph Bivins' report, *Daily Citizen*, pp. 1-2, August 30, 1980.

48. Letter of Sandra Clarke to a local newspaper. In 1981, Carlos Byars reported that Ralph Morrissey, a CAPONE spokesperson, said, "the group had been passing out leaflets calling the proposed facility a "Harris County Love Canal," even though it knows such a description is not valid." Quote from Byars, *Houston Chronicle*, January 7, 1981.

49. During the period when GCA was attempting to obtain a permit for the Waste Management Center, Joe Teller is reported to have said to Davis, "Jack, I've checked out the entire map of Texas, and there just is not a place named somewhere else" [30].

50. Bentley Mackay, Jr., "Texas Triangle Denizens Hope to Hobble Raging Bureaucratic Bull," *Solid Wastes Management*, p. 82, April 1981.

51. For example, the *Houston Chronicle* reported on Sept. 11, 1980 that the city was negotiating to purchase the land east of the Ellington base for construction of a major drinking water facility [Sec. 1, p. 2].

52. Monica Reeves, *Houston Post*, p. 13A, September 17, 1980.

53. Greg Cantrell, *Galveston Daily News*, p. 1, September 17, 1980, reported the positions of the opposing parties during the official public hearing held on September 16, 1980, at San Jacinto College in Houston.

54. Two of the hot issues covered by the local press—yet not necessarily the most relevant—during the period after the public hearings were the controversy regarding the technical director of Malone Co., Clifford Washington, and the effectiveness of the Stablex process. GCA filed a court petition against Washington, an outspoken critic of the center, on the grounds that he had faked his academic credentials (master's degree in chemistry and doctoral degree in public health at the University of California-Los Angeles) and falsely posed as a hazardous waste expert. The Stablex process was questioned based on evidence provided by a Michigan attorney and New Hampshire studies that the end result of the fixation process was not as impervious to water as claimed by the firm. Additional information from England also showed that the process had flaws and was under severe criticism there. For examples of this coverage, see Harold Scarlett, "Criticism Crisis," *Houston Post*, August 31, 1980, p. D; Carlos Byars, "Agency Questions Background of Foe," *Houston Chronicle*, August 28, 1980, sec. 1, p. 10; and Harry Turnbull, "Stablex: Is It Really Safe? *Daily Citizen*, January 18, 1981, pp. 1-2.

55. Davis explained that "public pressure showed that GCWDA was not getting their message across." In addition, "there are several obvious effects of this change that need emphasis. As a public agency, we are concerned about the public's understanding of what we are doing and how these activities affect them. . . . Initially, we believe that the permit process will be facilitated by allowing the Operators to develop and explain their own technology throughout the permit proceedings." In Joe Chapman, *Pasadena Citizen*, pp. 1, 3, March 13, 1981.

56. The Keystone Center is a nonprofit educational organization founded in 1975. The Keystone Program on Science and Public Policy "seeks to advance public understanding and improve governmental and private sector decision making in some critical areas where science and broad public purposes intersect." The principal tool to achieve this goal is the "policy dialogue," in which individuals approach one another on a person-to-person basis, "to bring out areas of potential consensus" [57, p. 1].

57. "Siting Waste Management Facilities in the Galveston Bay Area: A New Approach, "Report of the Keystone Workshops on Siting Nonradioactive Hazardous Waste Management Facilities," p. 1, 1983 (available at GCA, Texas).

58. Communities opposed the Bellaire transfer station, the siting of an incinerator in Texas City, etc. For examples, see Carlos Byars, *Houston Chronicle*, "Citizens Oppose Bellaire Waste Transfer Station," April 18, 1980, and Davis's comments about a group called RASH (Residents Against Siting Here) that opposed the siting of a hazardous waste incinerator in Texas City. In Davis's letter to Honorable Chet Brooks, May 1988, p. 5, available in GCWDA's files. Moreover, communities also claimed that GCA's wastewater plants violated EPA permits, and complained about the bad odors emanating from the facilities. For examples, see "Waste Station Foes Claim Authority Violated Its Permit at Bayport Site," *Houston Chronicle*, October 24, 1980, sec. 1, p. 13.

59. Greg Cantrell, *Galveston Daily News*, December 6, 1980, pp. 1A-2 A.

60. For example, Cantrell accused GCA of misconduct in acknowledging existence of toxic pesticides in a Bayport landfill. GCA refuted his evidence with documents that showed his information was inaccurate. See Davis's Commentary to the report, "The Phosvel Incident," unpublished memo available in GCA's files. The account that follows is based on this series, on GCA's positions on the issues debated, as well as on several newspaper stories mentioned in this chapter.

61. For example, in 1980, Davis said, "Our effort is in solutions, not regulations." In *Comments*, vol. 8, p. 2, February-March 1980.

62. Quote from a memorandum to GCA dated June 24, 1981, in which the law firms Baker & Botts and Vinson & Elkins described and explained the contents of the consent decree. See [63].

63. United States v. Crown Central Petroleum Corp., Atlantic Richfield Corp., Gulf Coast Waste Disposal Authority, and the state of Texas. U. S. District Court, Southern District of Texas, Houston Division, Consent Agreement Civil Action No. H-80-484, September 11, 1981.

64. Dick Brown's, GCA's general manager, letter to EPA's assistant administrator for policy, planning, and evaluation, March 18, 1992.

65. EPA classified U.S. industries into categories according to their sic codes before issuing National Categorical Pretreatment Standards. In 1986, the Third Circuit of Appeals held that the removal credits of CWA, section 307 (b) were not valid until EPA promulgated comprehensive sludge management regulations according to section 405 (d) of the CWA. These regulations should "insure that a treatment process was not simply transferring toxic materials from the water phase to the solid phase and would end up as an environmental problem where sludge disposal occurred." Cited in [66, p. 17]. The CWA amendments of 1986 granted a stay of this portion of the 3rd Circuit's decision concerning sludge management until August 31, 1987,

when EPA had to promulgate those regulations. In the meantime, no third-party plaintiff could take actions against EPA or POTWs that had previously received removal credits.

66. Charles Ganze and Dick Brown, "Increasing Regulations Result in Decreasing Operational Efficiency," paper presented at the Third International Conference on Waste Management in the Chemical and Petrochemical Industries, Salvador, Bahia, October 1993.

67. Jack Davis's memorandum to GCA board of directors asking the board to approve that GCA initiate a lawsuit against EPA's pretreatment standards, December 9, 1987.

68. Interference is defined as "a discharge which alone or in conjunction with a discharge or discharges from other sources, both: a) inhibits or disrupts the POTW, its treatment processes or operations, or its sludge processes, use or disposal, and b) therefore, is a cause of violation of any requirement of the POTW NPDES permit." Pass through is "a discharge which exits the POTW into waters of the U.S. in quantities or concentrations which, alone or in conjunction with a discharge or discharges from other sources, is a cause of violation of any requirement of the POTW's NPDES permit." Definitions provided in GCA's implementing revisions to the approved pretreatment program for the Washburn Tunnel, 40-Acre, American, and Bayport facilities, April 20, 1989.

69. John White, environmental counsel to GCA, memorandum to GCA board of directors, December 4, 1987.

70. The lawsuit, filed by the Synthetic Organic Chemical Manufactures Association (SOCMA), the Chemical Manufacturers Association (CMA), and some fifty companies, aimed at the CWA. Representative Joe Chapman proposed a bill to the House. The American Bayport Coalition, a group of companies in the Bayport complex, petitioned EPA. See [71, pp. 4-5].

71. John Black, "EPA'S 'Waste' Plans Could Cripple Bayport," *Bayshore Sun*, pp. 4-5, May 1988.

72. Quote from Larry Jenson, EPA official [71, p. 5].

73. The environmental counsel to GCA, John White, seemed to confirm Black's report in an undated memo to Jack Davis, where he wrote that ". . . EPA representatives in attendance [to a meeting sponsored by the Association of Metropolitan Sewer Authorities held in Chicago on March 25, 1987] stated that a legislative amendment would be the best course of action to resolve the "removal credits" dilemma.

74. Jack Davis, GCWDA 1984 Annual Report.

75. Davis also said in 1980 that ". . . we will continue to promote well-established effective methods of pollution abatement through operating our own facilities as well as through financing support from tax-exempt [a]uthority bonds. But we will also continue to investigate innovative procedures for waste treatment and to provide technical assistance to help those outside the [a]uthority find better answers to our common problems." *Comments,* July-August 1980, vol. 8, p. 1.

76. *Comments,* May 1983, vol. 11, p. 1.

77. Another important success was GCA's issuance of more than $500 million in bonds between 1970 and 1981 to finance pollution control facilities for cities and industry. *Comments,* January 1981, vol. 9, p. 2, 1981.

78. GCWDA 1982 Annual Report.

79. Davis wrote that "a study of regional sludge disposal methods continues to be a prime effort. Cleaning the air and water leaves a residue of solids that must be also handled in an environmentally safe and acceptable manner. We intend to give a major effort to that goal in the coming year" [78, p. 3].

80. GCWDA Highlights and Activities, April 1988.

81. This report also mentioned that ". . . an analysis of the permit violations in 1982 indicated that, for the most part, they [permit violations] were due to accidental spills, or inordinate loadings (process changes, turnarounds, etc.) by our industrial customers rather than to poor operation or inoperative facilities" [78, p. 5].

82. A permit application for a hazardous waste incinerator in Texas City was filed in 1986, but GCA withdrew the application in 1989 because "area industries have reduced the amount of toxic waste they produce." According to Joe Teller, then GCA's special projects manager, "the commercial people have stepped up and meet the need, and it has never been our Board's intention to compete with private enterprise." Galveston County Commissioners Court, Annual Report for 1989. In a report titled, "No Haste on Waste," reporter Chuck Stevick wrote that ". . . the GCWDA proposal made Wednesday is generally the same one it made during several months it courted the city in late 1987 and early 1988. It calls for the construction of a facility in the south part of town that will burn garbage and generate electricity." In *Texas City Sun*, p. 1, July 6, 1989.

83. According to the GCA newsletter, Radian corporation's industrial hygiene evaluation did not find any significant employee exposure to chemical hazards. In *Comments*, vol. 12, p. 2, May 1984. The training was required by EPA's RCRA and OSHA's Hazardous Waste and Emergency Response Operations (HAZWOPER) standard.

84. Compliance with these new regulations proved to be expensive in some cases, as the improvements of the Bayport facility in the mid-nineties demonstrated. The next section will detail this point further.

85. Later in this chapter I will provide more evidence regarding this point.

86. Although there were several other institutional developments in the nineties, this section will refer only to the milestones described in GCA annual reports.

87. GCWDA celebrated its 25th anniversary in 1994. Not surprisingly, it sponsored and/or launched a series of new activities during that year. According to the 1996 and 1997 Annual Reports, GCA employees participated in the River, Lakes, Bays, and Bayous "Trash Bash," to foster volunteer environmental cleanups of these bodies of water; GCA sponsored the distribution of teaching materials to area schools, with municipalities and the state of Texas, to foster environmental education in high schools, parks, and community events; and the authority sponsored a permanent backyard composting demonstration, as part of a state-operated environmental education center located at Sheldon Lake State Park, northeast of Houston.

88. GCWDA 1996 Annual Report.

89. GCWDA 1997 Annual Report.

90. It had pictures that showed fish and birds surviving in the plant's effluent [21, p. 3].

91. These companies were: The Armak Co., Bayport Molding Inc., Big Three Industries, Calgon Corporation, Celanese Chemical Co., Choate Chemical Co., Dart Industries, Dixie Chemical Co., FMC Corporation, Goodyear Tire & Rubber, Grover Tank & Manufacturing Co., Haldor Topsoe, Inc., Hercules, Inc., Liquid Air, Inc., Liquid Carbonic Corporation, Lubrizol Corporation, Oxirane Chemical Co., Southwestern

Bell Co., Velsicol Chemical Corporation and Quaker Oats Company. As can be inferred from this list, the complex was a mix of plants owned by large corporations such as Goodyear and Lubrizol, and smaller companies such as Dixie or Calgon. In *Gulf Coast Comments*, October 1976, vol. 4, p. 2.

92. *Gulf Coast Comments*, April 1977, vol. 5, p. 2.

93. *Gulf Cost Comments*, September 1979, vol. 7, pp. 1-2.

94. These improvements were also a reaction to community complaints about offensive odors in the area adjacent to the plant. Davis acknowledged the problem when he declared that ". . . we very frankly have had a bad odor problem at the Bayport Facility for the past several months." In addition, he stated that ". . . we sincerely regret any discomfort our problem may have caused the surrounding communities" [95].

95. "GCDWA Board Tackles Solving Odor Problems," *Bayshore Sun*, April 26, 1979, p. 11A.

96. *Comments*, September 1982, vol. 10.

97. The GCA 1983 Annual Report explained that "this change from surface to subsurface aerators is expected to retain an extra four to six degrees temperature which would otherwise be lost to the surrounding air. Bacteria or 'bugs' work better at warmer temperatures."

98. *Comments*, March 1991, p. 1.

99. The improvements, such as climate-controlled buildings along the collection channels, new lift stations to handle a higher volume of wastewater, and above-ground tanks and new piping, aimed at providing the "necessary capacity to meet the needs of the Bayport industrial area for the next twenty years." In *Comments*, November 1992, p. 1.

100. Jim Kowalick, Bayport facility manager, described this program as "the most ambitious improvement program ever undertaken by the [a]uthority." In *Comments*, February 1995, p. 1.

101. Before being allowed to build a plant in the Bayport complex, firms had to agree to have its wastewater treated by the Bayport facility. Moreover, Bayport staff had to do a feasibility and pretreatability study to check that the plant's effluent could be treated in the facility.

102. By 1988, the Bayport Industrial complex had forty-three plants employing around 5,700 people representing a collective investment of about $2.3 billion. These figures were mentioned by Marcel Olbrecht, then president of the Bayport Industrial Association, in an interview with the *Bayshore Sun* [71, p. 4]. Appendix 5 lists all the companies that were part of the complex in 1997.

103. Customers were chosen according to the volume of wastewater treated by the Bayport wastewater treatment facility, i.e., they are some of the largest industrial customers of GCA in Bayport.

104. In http://www.arco.com./Corporate/reports/SAM96/dwchem.htm. ARCO has facilities in Asia, Europe, and Latin America.

105. Biocides are used in paints, personal care products, coatings, dishwashing detergents, wood preservatives, etc. In http://www.rohmhaas.com/businesses.dir/biocides.html and /Monomers.html. Rohm and Haas also has facilities in Asia, Europe, and Latin America.

106. In http://www.hoechst.com/esha/CGI/view.pl?WNR=63. Hoechst Celanese owns a marine terminal in the Bayport complex as well. This German-based corporation has subsidiaries in Europe, Asia, and Latin America.

107. Here I am not going to detail the activities of these committees, because they are beyond the scope of this research. The CAPs emerged as a result of EPA Superfund Amendments and Reauthorization Act (SARA) of 1986, Title III, the Emergency Planning and Community Right to Know Act. In general, they deal with local community awareness and emergency response issues. Bayport staff may also participate in the monthly meetings of the CAPs, especially when they discuss questions that relate to wastewater treatment, such as bad odors or emergency spills, and in the Local Emergency Planning Committees (LEPC) [108].

108. Jim Kowalick, Bayport plant manager, interview by author, tape recording, May 1997, Pasadena, Texas.

109. Jim Kowalick told me that GCA Bayport customers indicated to him that they did not believe the authority should seek ISO 14,001 certification. In addition, the customers suggested that it would be a good idea for GCA to follow the ISO guidelines without formally applying for certification. It appears that Bayport customers did not want to pay for the certification process either, "because it would be a waste a money" [108].

110. For examples of corporate environmental or safety and health policies, see http://www.arco.com/Corporate.ehs/ehs.htm, and http://www.celanese.com/84-envir.htm (environmental policy) or http://www.celanese.com/81-emplo.htm (health and safety policy). According to an EPA factsheet on the Toxics Release Inventory, section 313 of the Emergency Planning and Community Right to Know Act (EPCRA) requires manufacturers to report releases of more than 600 designated toxic chemicals to the environment. The reports are submitted to the U.S. EPA and state governments. EPA compiles this data in an online, publicly accessible, national, computerized Toxics Release Inventory (TRI). Facilities are required to report on off-site transfers—transfers of wastes for treatment or disposal at a separate facility—and on pollution prevention activities and chemical recycling. Reports must be submitted on or before July 1 each year and must cover activities that occurred at the facility during the previous year [111].

111. EPA factsheet "What Is Toxics Release Inventory," available at http://www.epa.gov.

112. The lack of resources, the paucity of previous work on the political economy of the complex, and the restricted access to company data limited the depth of the discussion about the factory regime in the Bayport complex. Nevertheless, I believe it is important to at least characterize its general contours, based on tape-recorded interviews with former OCAW leaders and Bob Otto, plant manager of Nova Molecular Technologies, Inc., held on May 1998 in Pasadena, Texas.

113. One of these former OCAW leaders referred to the managerial class in the Bayport complex as a "good old boy" network, or "the ultimate good boy network." Interview by author, May 1998, Pasadena, Texas. In addition, he told me that the Bayport complex has been able to keep "a low profile" in the area. These leaders did not know much about the plants in the complex either, with the exception of the two former OCAW organized facilities, Calgon and Petrolite. The latter was only recently organized, while the former was organized over a decade ago. I could not find any written accounts of major confrontations between workers and managers in the

complex, confirming the testimony of former OCAW leaders, one of whom had worked in the Calgon plant for many years.

114. The former OCAW international staff representative in the area, Jim Lefton, was highly critical of these work management innovations. He claimed that despite the introduction of a series of new management programs, "nothing ever changes," wasting firms' money and resources. Further, employees participated in numerous meetings to "pick the workers' minds on how to downsize and streamline operations." As a result, these programs helped eliminate work and jobs. In his own words, these programs ". . . [i]nstead of rewarding people for making the operations more productive would throw people out on the streets" [115].

115. Jim Lefton, personal interview, May 1998, Pasadena, Texas.

116. S. Randel, *Chemical Business,* October 1990, p. 41.

117. Another former OCAW member, Bill Early, a member of a maintenance crew at Amoco Corporation's refinery at Whiting, Indiana, stated in the same Business Chemical report, that his plant ". . . is run as hard as possible for as long as possible, with management hoping for the best. When the units are shut for turnarounds, the crews repair only what is necessary, eliminating non-immediate repairs to shorten down time. . . . As a maintenance worker, I see the schedule lying around, and I see things crossed off—things management feels they can live without repairing this time" [116, p. 41]. This account from another former OCAW member confirmed the opinions expressed in my interviews with former OCAW leaders. In addition, it coincided with the opinion of a Cetrel maintenance worker I interviewed in Brazil in July 1997, who commented on the effects of contracting out in Camaçari.

118. Jim Lefton, the former OCAW International Union representative for District 4, which includes Texas, Louisiana, and Oklahoma, told me a folk story that reveals the political awareness of an average local petrochemical worker, who tends to be a conservative, well-paid, and white male Texan. Two guys were driving a car on highway 225. One of them was not from the area. As they passed by the Citgo refinery, the out of towner complained about the bad odors coming from the refinery. He said: "Man, it stinks." The local guy, a petrochemical worker, replied: "Yes, it smells like money to me" [115].

119. These data were produced by the Environmental Defense Fund Polluter Locator database, which is based on the EPA TRI database [120]. See "1995 Rankings: Major Chemical Releases or Waste Generation in Zip Code 77507."

120. The electronic address for the Environmental Defense Fund Polluter Locator database is http://www.scorecard.org.

121. The list goes on to include suspected respiratory toxicants, endocrine toxicants, gastrointestinal and liver toxicants, skin or sense organ toxicants, reproductive toxicants, and recognized reproductive toxicants. See "1995 TRI Pollution Releases Sorted by Health Effect" [120].

122. The Bayport facility also falls under the TRI reporting requirements because it stores more than the threshold amounts of chlorine [108].

123. *Comments,* February-March, 1980, vol. 8, p. 2.

CHAPTER 7

Dependent Convergence: Comparing Cetrel and GCA Histories

HISTORICAL-STRUCTURAL FOUNDATIONS

It is worth reviewing some important historical-structural features of Cetrel and GCWDA discussed in previous chapters. Both companies are small to medium-size firms, whose growths—as best shown in the GCA's case by the evolution of the Bayport complex—have been closely associated with the business cycles of the petrochemical industry in Bahia and Texas. Their growth resulted from market conditions favorable to the oil and petrochemical sectors of the national economies, since most of their production is consumed in the internal markets. Nevertheless, the two companies have been, at least marginally, affected by the international business cycles of the petrochemical industry, since most investments in the petrochemical industry are driven by long-term capitalist planning.

Cetrel is an almost twenty-year-old firm born from managed capitalism, i.e., through state planning that aimed at mitigating and controlling, instead of preventing, the negative environmental impacts of petrochemical production [1, 2]. State of Bahia managers in charge of environmental affairs believed that managing and treating industrial wastewaters constituted state-of-the-art technology in controlling water pollution. They claimed at the time that Cetrel had adopted the best hardware and software available in developed countries. The hardware—plant equipment—was made nationally, and the software—by which the plant was operated—was based on foreign models.

The GCA is an almost thirty-year-old firm born from state intervention to control free-market failures that had generated a regional environmental crisis. Interestingly enough, even in the United States case, one can see the "visible hand" of corporate planning in the formerly Exxon-owned Bayport plant. The GCA is part of a much larger petrochemical region that includes several hubs of petrochemical production that are neither integrated nor centrally planned. Thus, it has managed the wastes of at least three smaller petrochemical complexes, located in Texas City, Bayport, and the ship channel, composed of subsidiaries of large multinationals and mid-sized plants.

Cetrel, on the other hand, has managed the wastes of a larger concentration of nationally owned plants in a single complex. In addition, it has treated a large volume of toxic wastes produced by a petrochemical refinery—Copene—that supplies downstream companies with basic chemicals, while the GCA does not. This central structural difference probably accounts for the development of major work-environment and environmental crises in Camaçari—the benzene and the environmental pollution crises described in previous chapters—but not in the comparable Bayport complex.

Perhaps reflecting the political economy of these petrochemical production areas in both countries, the business associations representing petrochemical interests have been more closely integrated and active in Bahia than in Texas. The history of the Camaçari complex suggests that petrochemical business leaders in Bahia organized a cadre of business intellectuals that played a major role in formulating a hegemonic ideology and a set of policies to deal with political opposition from subordinate classes. They helped create the "Petrochemical Republic of Bahia," where the interests of the local petrochemical industry are portrayed as the general interests of the people of Bahia. Labor fiercely resisted this hegemony, and actively fought against it throughout the eighties, but, in the end, was defeated.

In contrast, the Texas situation shows a loose network of business leaders that got together only when legal crises, such as the pretreatment guidelines, developed. This apparent business weakness, however, may be explained by the oil and petrochemical industry's long-established and consolidated hegemony in Texas, i.e., business organizations appeared on the scene only when significant threats arose. In the "Oil and Petrochemical Republic of Texas," the interests of these industries have been portrayed, and accepted, as the general interests of the people of Texas for decades now. Communities mounted a strong resistance against the treatment in their backyard of the wastes generated by this industry, but never challenged this industry's control of production decisions.

Table 1 synthesizes the analysis of actors involved in shaping the policies implemented in both companies.

Social Actors [5]

This section discusses the roles played by the most important actors identified in documents, interviews, field trips, and participant observations in both organizations. The actor analysis summarized here assumes that environmental and occupational health policies result from social processes that involve conflict and negotiation among social strata [6].

Table 1. Cross-National Comparisons
An Actor Analysis Comparison between Cetrel and GCA [3, 4]

Social actors	Cetrel	Gulf Coast Authority
Management	Public/private majority control by the state in the '70s and '80s; private in the '90s	Quasi-public agency. "Government that operates like a business."
Labor	Strong opposition after benzene crisis.	Not present
Community/ environmental groups	Opposition by late '80s. Not active before and after.	Strong opposition in the '80s. Not very active before and after.
Industry	Strongly supportive, especially after privatization.	Always strongly supportive.
State bureaucracy/ politicians	Supportive at the state and federal levels.	Federal EPA opposed single permit and POTW status. Local and state politicians divided on several occasions. Texas bureaucracy supportive.
Small businesses	Not relevant.	Strongly opposed hazardous waste treatment center.
Courts	Not relevant.	Settled regulatory and jurisdictional conflicts between the EPA and GCA.
Academia	Important role in the EIS process.	Mostly supportive. Somewhat split during the NIMBY movement.

Management

The GCA has always been a quasi-public authority, almost completely financed by the fees charged to its municipal and industrial customers. A board is appointed by elected officials to oversee routine operations, providing an indirect public accountability mechanism. Cetrel's financing was similar to that of the GCA during the period when it had majority state control. By the early nineties, industrial customers had gained almost complete control over it. After privatization, Cetrel continued to be a nonprofit waste management and treatment service firm, but has been administered by managers who closely represent the local petrochemical producers. In a word, while the GCA has always been *a government agency that operates like a business,* Cetrel has changed from the GCA model into *a nonprofit business that operates like a for-profit business.*

Labor

In the case of Cetrel, Sindae—and to a lesser extent Sindiquímica—was the major actor to protest and mobilize against the environmental and occupational crises associated with petrochemical production in Camaçari. This active opposition emerged in the mid-eighties, after the redemocratization of Brazil and the recognition of the leucopenia epidemic. Sindae's political pressure on Cetrel managers and state agencies led to the elimination and reduction of occupational exposures to toxic chemicals during the late eighties. By the early nineties, however, the "sindicato" had lost power, and it became less and less able to influence Cetrel's work-environment policies.

In GCA's case, labor did not have a visible influence on its policies, since the authority has always been a nonunion workplace. In addition, union density in the Gulf Coast area has been small and has not affected GCA's practices to a significant extent, if at all.

Community/Environmental Groups

Local grassroots coalitions played a major role in determining how far the GCA could go in its attempts to coordinate hazardous waste policies in the area during the eighties. In Cetrel's case, however, this type of coalition had only had an ephemeral impact by the late eighties. In both cases, these coalitions forced the GCA and Cetrel to set up stricter control technologies.

Communities resisted some of the policies of these companies in several ways. They spread rumors and information about the consequences of the policies; voiced their dissatisfaction with bad odors, chemical spills, and explosions; and actively organized neighborhood rallies against exposures to hazardous chemicals.

Industry

Industry has always been the backbone of both companies, expressed differently at different moments of each company's history. The petrochemical industry provided economic support, political support, human resources, and the ideological constructs that underlay their growth and legitimization. If there is one social actor that has never shown overt opposition to the existence and growth of the two companies, it is GCA's and Cetrel's petrochemical customers.

Not coincidentally, the industry has also been one of the most powerful social actors in both societies, at local and national levels. Therefore, the waste management policies adopted by these companies are fundamentally, though not exclusively, the policies that industry liked or that it did not veto when it disliked them. In Cetrel's case, the relationship between industry's needs and Cetrel's policies became clear and transparent in the nineties, when the former was privatized. That was the period when corporate environmentalism flourished in the Camaçari complex.

In addition to the points made above concerning the local petrochemical industry's hegemony, the GCA's close relationship with industry has also been a conscious choice of its board since the early seventies, when GCA's taxing powers were voted down by the electorate.

Governments and Politicians

Born as a creature of federal and state Brazilian governments, Cetrel has had steady support from politicians, and federal and state officials for most of its history, except for some progressive state legislators in the mid- to late-eighties, who tried to reform its practices. GCA, on the other hand, had ongoing support from Texas bureaucrats, but solid opposition from local politicians, local managers, and some federal EPA officials. Ranging from mere turf battles with city mayors to principled disagreements with EPA, GCA had to sail into troubled waters throughout the seventies and eighties before the Gulf Coast political and regulatory waters became smooth.

Federal representatives were key in supporting GCA's amendment to the Clean Water Act, which included a special provision granting relief for the authority regarding the EPA OCSPF pretreatment guidelines (chapter 6). This was a very important and decisive political victory for GCA and the local petrochemical industry.

Small Businesses and the Courts

Since these two actors are relevant only to the GCA, I grouped them together. Following the American political tradition of checks and balances between the executive, the legislative, and the judicial branches of government, the courts played an important role in settling conflicts among EPA, politicians, and GCA. These conflicts involved interpretations of environmental and tax laws that had profound implications for GCA's survival. The Public Operated Treatment Works (POTW) consent decree settled the issue of ownership of plants. The decision concerning the tax-exempt nature of the bonds issued by GCA settled the financing of pollution control facilities and equipment. Therefore, the courts were very important in helping GCA leave troubled legal waters in the seventies and eighties.

Small businesses in the hazardous waste field challenged GCA on one of the most sacred grounds of the American system of beliefs, the free enterprise system. Accusations of socialist planning, unfair competition by the state, and the like permeated the discussion around the Hazardous Waste Center proposed by GCA. These small-business interests provided leverage to the local grassroots environmental movement. Together, they mustered enough power to defeat the authority's hazardous waste planning goals, and clearly set political and economic boundaries for the future actions of the GCA.

Academia

Academia has apparently played a more important role in Cetrel than in the GCA. While the Federal University of Bahia (UFBA) has supplied Cetrel with qualified people to plan and operate the environmental control systems, it has also trained or hired some of its most important critics. The latter have given technical advice to the labor and environmental movements in Bahia and helped these movements stage counter-hegemonic strategies and actions. These progressive experts—physicians, sociologists, engineers, etc.—contributed a great deal to the debate over the causes of and the solutions for the environmental crises of the mid- and late-eighties.

In contrast to Cetrel, the history of the GCA seems to suggest that local colleges and universities have not played such a critical role in the Gulf Coast region and have for the most part supported the authority. For example, some GCA board members were professors at the University of Texas Medical Branch (UTMB) and Rice University; other former GCA managers joined the faculty of the University of Houston at Clear Lake.

Table 2 sums up the policy outcomes, which took the form of regulatory and technological outcomes.

Waste Management Policy Outcomes

Environmental Policy Paradigm

Both firms adopted the pollution control paradigm as a policy guideline to their operations. In the early years, they had to struggle with a certain degree of ambiguity concerning the contradiction between enforcement and implementation of environmental regulations. Nevertheless, sooner rather than later, GCA and Cetrel undertook the role of implementing organizations; they operated pollution control equipment, provided technical solutions to municipalities (GCA) and petrochemical businesses (Cetrel and GCA), and applied the requirements of their respective environmental policy systems to their regions.

The GCA also had a considerable financial role in the Gulf Coast area by providing tax-exempt money to support private businesses' investment in pollution control technologies and devices.

Pollution prevention policies became, on paper, part of Cetrel's practices in the mid-nineties, while the GCA does not refer to those policies in its publications. Yet, some large GCA Bayport customers have carried out waste minimization procedures in their facilities, as corporate environmental reports suggest.

Table 2. A Policy Outcome Comparison between GCA and Cetrel

Waste management policy system outcomes	Cetrel	Gulf Coast Authority
Policy paradigm	Pollution control of all environmental media. "Polluter pays" principle.	Pollution control of all environmental media. "Polluter pays" principle.
Regulatory	Federal and state regulations (EIS, CRA discharge permits) CRA Resolutions. EPA standards.	Clean Water Act, RCRA, and Clean Air Act, and state, county, and local regulations. Permit-driven system.
Self-regulation	Responsible Care, BS-7750, ISO 14001	Responsible Care
Technology	Dependent on foreign technology. Imported BAT, BPT from developed countries (U.S., Japan, Germany, and Switzerland).	Easy access to U.S. technology. Mostly U.S. BAT, BPT.
Environmental systems operated throughout history	Industrial wastewater treatment plant. Solid hazardous waste disposal. Two incinerators. Ocean-disposal system groundwater and air monitoring.	Regional municipal and industrial wastewater treatment facilities. Solid waste disposal and treatment. Equipment services (a mobile dewatering unit, a solid dredging unit).

Regulatory Outcomes

There is no question that GCA has had to comply with a larger body of detailed federal, state, and local environmental regulations than Cetrel. Moreover, the former had to deal with a wider variety of regulated customers, municipal and industrial, than the latter.

These regulations cover water and air pollution (the Clean Water and Clean Air acts); solid and hazardous wastes collection, storage, treatment, and disposal (the Resource Conservation and Recovery Act [RCRA] and the Solid Waste Disposal Act [SARA]); and the clean up of contaminated sites (the Superfund Amendments and Reauthorization Act).

This U.S. environmental policy system was based on a pollution control strategy that set ". . . 'acceptable levels' of emissions and then tried to regulate industry's installation of pollution control equipment that achieved this 'acceptable level' " (emphases in the original) [7, p. 6].

Moreover, not only have the GCA's industrial customers been regulated by the same statutes, but they have also had to comply with other occupational and environmental laws. For example, in the late eighties, SARA Titles I, II, and III established "a nationwide public right to know about local chemical usage and releases," that eased community awareness and preparedness for chemical accidents [8, p. 168; 9; 10].

Not surprisingly, Cetrel has had to comply with less detailed and broad environmental and occupational regulations than the GCA. It also has dealt with fewer government bodies, especially at the county and city levels, for it has always been in charge of treating the wastes of only one petrochemical complex, without any other municipal or regional responsibilities. The state of Bahia CRA has been the main regulator of Cetrel's discharges and activities, typically included in several CRA Resolutions. The federal and state regulations requiring environmental impact studies before permitting expansion of the "Pólo," and the operation of the new facilities, make up the basis of the regulatory framework with which Cetrel has had to comply.

At times, due to the lack of specific national and state environmental regulations in several areas, such as incineration and groundwater cleanup, Cetrel was allowed to operate without clear regulatory guidance. In these special instances, it tried to follow the EPA and other European environmental standards, which it used as guidelines or references until such a time as state or federal regulations were enacted. As the body of environmental regulations grew in the nineties, these instances disappeared. Yet, over the years, Cetrel has been ahead of state regulations on many occasions.

Self-Regulation Outcomes

In the arena of voluntary compliance and initiatives, one finds a remarkable difference between Cetrel's big effort to play by the rules of the international environmental management systems—based on voluntary certification of environmental management policies—and GCA's near-indifference to them. While both companies have operated under some quite similar "solutions instead of regulations" principle for decades, it is almost paradoxical that Cetrel has been much more aggressive in the pursuit of ISO and BS-7750 certification than its U.S. counterpart.

Cetrel had its environmental management systems certified by the BS-7750 and the ISO standards in the mid-nineties, after a concerted organizational effort to follow the perceived direction signaled by the global chemical and petrochemical market. In contrast, the GCA has not yet moved in that direction. By the early nineties, the vast majority of GCA customers had joined the CMA Responsible Care program, introducing the world of voluntary environmental protection into GCA's agenda [11]. Still, the corporate activities triggered by this new voluntary environmental policy have not affected GCA's policies and public relations messages significantly.

Technology Outcomes

Chapter 6 has already established the centrality of the water discharge permits as the main component of GCA's pollution control "model" [12]. The EPA's requirements for best-available technologies (BAT), best-practical technologies (BPT), or best-feasible technologies—depending on the environmental statute considered—set the direction for the technological development of the U.S. waste management industry. These waste control technologies were for the most part designed to meet the polluters' need to comply with the acceptable levels set in the permits. Ashford, Geiser, Karliner, and several other U.S. observers noted that these technologies do not interfere much with what is produced or how it is produced, focusing instead on the wastes and by-products generated in a given process [2; 13-17; 18, pp. 33-34].

In the Bayport plant case, it seems that industrial customers of the GCA had to finance the purchase of newer technologies whenever EPA requirements became stricter or when community concerns about odors and toxic emissions required action [19].

As referred to above, most of the expansion in Cetrel's pollution control activities was based on requirements triggered by the Brazilian environmental impact assessment law. While the technical cooperation with GCA and foreign professionals started very early in Cetrel's life, it was mostly during the nineties that Cetrel deliberately imported regulatory standards and their rationale to operate new environmental control systems [20].

For example, it adopted the EPA and European standards associated with manufacturers' guidelines to operate the two incinerators. In fact, Cetrel imported pollution control packages that included foreign technology developed to comply with foreign standards. Foreign manufacturers usually provided initial training to Cetrel staff, and maintenance for the equipment.

The case of the Fourier Transform Infra-Red (FTIR) is an interesting counter-point to this trend. Cetrel imported an expensive air quality monitoring technology whose effectiveness had not yet been accepted in the American market. It imported this high-tech hardware especially to monitor air levels of volatile organic compounds (VOCs), even though the EPA had not yet developed standards for air emissions of these pollutants. As a result, Cetrel had no guidelines to gauge the application of the equipment to the reality of the Camaçari complex. Adding insult to injury, the Brazilians did not have enough scientific and technical expertise to elaborate national VOC standards or to maintain the equipment properly. When the U.S. manufacturer folded, a big operational problem arose.

Though guided by the best of intentions, this example illustrates Cetrel's, i.e., Brazil's, technical and scientific limitations in finding solutions to the environmental and occupational health problems derived from petrochemical production. While the importation of untested high-tech foreign technology may be an exceptional case, it also demonstrates the dependent role of Brazil in the global economy [21-25]. Cetrel decided to look elsewhere for technology that would allow it to monitor for these emissions, because Brazilian companies—or Brazilian subsidiaries of multinationals—did not produce similar hardware, nor the software to operate it. In addition, the importation of foreign-developed solutions has been a hallmark of Cetrel's "best-in-the-business" practices and its message of the nineties [26].

Environmental Control Systems

Cetrel evolved in twenty years into a horizontally integrated waste management company that oversees the collection, storage, treatment, and disposal of hazardous wastes generated in the Camaçari complex and monitors the air and groundwater in the area affected by it. GCA, on the other hand, did not achieve such a broad scope. The latter consolidated its operations around regional industrial and municipal wastewater, and solid waste management and treatment operations. Cetrel's total investment in environmental control infrastructure amounted to more than $250 million over twenty years, while GCA's amounted to $147 million in assets and $1.6 billion worth of bonds to finance pollution control equipment and waste treatment projects.

LESSONS LEARNED

There are many reasons to believe that the political, cultural, economic, ethnic, and other important contexts in which GCA and Cetrel have operated are substantially different. These different contexts illustrate the expected large difference between a rich state in the richest country of the world—Texas and the United States, respectively—and an emerging state in an emerging country— Bahia and Brazil. Nevertheless, a historical-structural comparison shows several common features between GCA and Cetrel.

Roughly speaking, the general political and economic environments in which GCA and Cetrel operated are similar. The U.S. environment could be condensed under the title, "The Oil and Petrochemical Republic of Texas." The Brazilian environment could be summarized as, "The Petrochemical Republic of Bahia." The former reflects the hegemony of this industry in a liberal-democratic market economy. The latter reflects a similar hegemony in an initially authoritarian period, followed by a liberal democracy after the fall of the Brazilian dictatorship in 1985. In both cases, the petrochemical bourgeoisie has been the most powerful social actor.

While the older GCA was born to abate decades of water pollution accumulated in the Galveston Bay watershed and the Houston Ship Channel, Cetrel was born to mitigate or reduce the future pollution of rivers and watersheds in Camaçari, using the GCA as a model.

Managing and treating wastes generated by the same industry, GCA and Cetrel have developed several commonalities. *First*, they have followed the same environmental or waste management policy paradigm, the pollution control model. *Second*, they have shared the application of this paradigm to their areas, which translated into similar end-of-pipe technologies, regulations, and modes of operation. *Third*, they have shared almost identical supporters. Industry, the state, and the media have most of the time been behind both of them. In addition, for over a decade they were both quasipublic firms. The GCA has had a regional focus, while Cetrel has had a local focus.

Several points of divergence also exist. GCA has financed the installation of hundreds of millions of dollars in pollution control equipment in the Gulf Coast area, while Cetrel never did. GCA is responsible for the management and treatment of municipal wastewater and solid waste, while Cetrel is not. Cetrel is ISO 14,001 certified, while GCA is not. On the other hand, GCA customers have to inform the public about their environmental emissions and discharges, while Cetrel customers do not. Cetrel became a private firm, while the GCA remained quasi-public. Access to information is, consequently, easier in the latter.

In GCA's case, political opposition from local communities, politicians, and small businesses—without significant labor union presence—coupled with several long-lasting legal obstacles and battles, prevented it from becoming an all-encompassing hazardous waste management authority in the Gulf Coast region.

In contrast to GCA, state and federal Brazilian environmental laws combined with environmental and political-economic crises in the late eighties to facilitate Cetrel's expansion to areas other than wastewater and solid waste management. In spite of strong labor union opposition—Sindae and Sindiquímica—to the environmental and occupational health crises in the "Pólo," Cetrel was given more power to carry out the environmental controls required by the state. Therefore, the social struggles led by two different sets of social actors caused these organizations to take quite different shapes and scopes by the late nineties.

Cetrel managers now brag about it being a modern, internationally recognized waste management firm that matches if not outranks its U.S. counterpart. They claim that Cetrel should benchmark itself against European waste management companies, since GCA did not keep up with its recent progress. Besides, they equate the high degree of pollution control with the greening of petrochemical production in Camaçari.

Even if one discounts a bit of exaggeration in these views, the Brazilian company and the American company are playing on the same level field. These companies are as similar in the nineties as ever, though this book did not compare their operational performances. In both cases, end-of-pipe pollution controls have decreased the amount of environmental pollution in their areas.

The two companies have probably achieved—or are close to achieving—the point when marginal pollution control improvements remain feasible, but are not cost-effective. While Cetrel operates a wider range of environmental control technologies than GCA, at the environmental policy level they are quite close.

Therefore, one cannot argue for the existence of double standards in their practices, as recognized by GCA and Cetrel managers [27]. The authority may have had to comply with stricter regulations than its Brazilian counterpart. Its operations did not cause an occupational health crisis. Yet, I would argue that overall they followed similar models and had arrived at parallel levels of development by the early nineties.

Finally, the cross-national comparison between both companies suggests that it is possible for certain industries in newly industrializing countries to adopt environmental management policies and procedures that converge with the ones carried out in developed countries. While this example of a capital-intensive petrochemical industry does not disprove the much-talked-about, export-of-hazards argument formulated by Castleman [22-24], it certainly weakens its generalizability. The cross-national comparison undertaken here also indicates that the same pattern of convergence may have occurred in other petrochemical industries in developing countries, where the state bankrolled the creation and development of the industry.

Moreover, this comparison offers a methodological contribution to the double standards and export-of-hazards debate. To verify the existence of double standards between and among countries with different levels of development, or even within similar levels of development, concrete analyses of concrete cases have to be done before general conclusions can be drawn—particularly when deeply ingrained cultural stereotypes about the meaning of developed and developing countries are involved.

Environmental or occupational standards and regulations are social creations of social actors in different historical periods of these societies. They are not automatic consequences of industrial economic development. Thus, there is no natural law that prevents social actors in developing countries from achieving the same level of environmental and occupational protections achieved in developed countries. By the same token, populations in the former countries may potentially obtain the same level—convergent levels—of environmental and occupational protection that developed countries have, or even higher.

The fact that the same level of protection is not as common as divergent levels should not be solely explained by the relative discrepancy in economic growth or development, measured by indicators such as Gross National Product (GNP). Often, these differences result from the particular history and outcomes of the social struggles between those who pollute the work and general environment in their search for profits and those who oppose them. Policies and legal outcomes of this ongoing struggle determine the levels of protection achieved in each society.

The job of the investigator is to identify the actors, analyze their history, and try to explain why and how the standards differ or are similar.

CONCLUSION

Initial empirical evidence collected in Bahia and Texas established that Cetrel and GCA have developed a long-term interaction and technical cooperation process. Based on this evidence, this book described and analyzed the process of importation of petrochemical technologies and technological controls by the petrochemical industry of Bahia. To interpret the policy developments that led to the importation of these controls, it reviewed the history of the occupational and environmental policies in Cetrel, emphasizing the struggles that led Brazilian social actors to adopt these policies. In addition, it examined the same aspects of the history of GCA to provide a comparative reference to the Brazilian case.

A combination of four theoretical arguments grounded the understanding of this historical process: the dependency perspectives, the double standards, the theory of class formation, and the political economy of occupational disease. Guided by this interdisciplinary theoretical framework, this research led me to the following set of conclusions, which together constitute what I call dependent convergence between Cetrel and GCA.

The Double Standards Argument

The double standards and export-of-hazards arguments proposed by Castleman et al. are useful for regulatory and technological comparisons between plants owned by multinational companies in developed and developing countries. For example, in the aftermath of the Bhopal disaster, such comparisons showed wide discrepancies in environmental safeguards between the Union Carbide plants in Bhopal, India, and Institute West Virginia. His argument springs from an economic development paradigm—the structural approach to dependency perspectives—that sees countries divided into divergent economic development stages, closely related to their levels of industrialization and economic development.

According to this perspective, countries are either developed or under-developed, industrialized or industrializing, with some countries in inter-mediate stages, called newly industrializing countries or semiperipheral. Developed countries—the "center"—unilaterally determine what happens in economically dependent developing countries, or "the periphery." From the per-spective of many public health scholars in developed countries, such as Castleman [22, 23], Navarro [24], LaDou [25], Thébaud-Mony [28], the "center" exports hazardous technologies to peripheral or semiperipheral countries, which import them due to their subordinate role in the international capitalist economy.

Following this line of reasoning, progressive—and some mainstream—intellectuals in the United States and Europe focused most of their attention on the export side of the underlying export-import relationship that is always present in such economic transactions. These intellectuals have studied and correctly criticized the export of hazardous technologies, products, wastes, and factories to developing countries, which accept them as a "trade-off" for their much-needed and desired industrialization. They found many situations where the controls applied to these technologies in peripheral countries were divergent from similar controls adopted in the "center."

Many progressive scholars and activists have also pointed out that this thirty-year-long trend may reach a climax with the much-heralded globalization of the economy in the nineties. According to them, the downward harmonization of environmental, occupational, and consumer protection standards promoted by several recent regional trade agreements, such as NAFTA, has become a common side effect of the global free trade agenda. To counter this trend, they have proposed strong labor and environmental side agreements that would protect labor and the environment in the "center" against the "Third Worldization" of these countries.

Yet, the history of the work environment and environmental policies carried out in the Camaçari petrochemical complex and Cetrel pointed in a direction different from the one suggested by the export-of-hazards argument. Multinational companies did not open a subsidiary in the "Pólo," through which they exported hazards to Bahia. It was the Brazilian government that decided to develop the petrochemical industry in Bahia.

In the interesting Brazilian case, the local branch of the native petrochemical industry grew as a state-planned association between foreign, Brazilian private, and Brazilian state capital, each controlling a third of the investment. The Brazilian government created, in Peter Evans' words, an "oligopolistic community" [29, p. S210] to manage the new industry, with the objective of reducing Brazilian dependence on petrochemical imports. The military dictatorship claimed that Brazil had no other viable recourse but to import production technologies and pollution control models from developed countries. A necessary price to pay for this strategic economic development would be to allow some multinationals and foreign capital to profit from joint ventures with Brazilian state and private capital.

A few petrochemical multinationals licensed their proprietary technology to become partners in a long, tripartite economic and political alliance, which later became a bipartite alliance after the privatization of state assets in the early nineties. In short, the Camaçari Petrochemical Complex was an economic development project associated with a "state-led," yet still dependent, development strategy.

Therefore, an understanding of these development policies required this book to focus on the import side of the import-export relationship, highlighting the perspectives of the importers of these hazardous technologies and controls. In addition, that history also suggested the need for a closer look at both sides of this relationship—Bahia and Texas—because a) a close and long-term interaction between GCA and Cetrel have developed over the years, and b) the export-import relationship is a dyad, in which one side does not exist without the other.

From this alternative vantage point, Brazilian social actors have been the main actors that decided on the environmental and occupational policies carried out in the Camaçari petrochemical complex. The process of importation of hazards is thus fundamentally determined by national or internal actors, dynamically interacting with foreign actors.

While Brazil is still viewed as dependent, it is also seen as a sovereign country that has had enough power to decide its own economic development, work-environment, and environmental policies. The work-environment and environmental policies, regulations, technologies, and paradigms adopted in Bahia should be understood as historical-structural outcomes of the social struggle between and among social actors. The dialectical interactions between human agency and political-economic structures play the essential role in explaining the policy outcomes of this struggle.

Interaction Between National and
Foreign Actors in Peripheral Countries

In the early seventies Cetrel and GCA started their informal technical cooperation. Planners and technical staff from Bahia took the initiative to come to the United States to learn from GCA's experience with petrochemical and industrial wastewater treatment. They became particularly interested in knowing how the Bayport plant operated and managed the industrial wastewater of the Bayport Industrial Complex or Park.

No commercial interests were involved in either side of the relationship. GCA was a quasi-public authority and had no self-interest in selling equipment to Cetrel. Cetrel was a not-for-profit public company and had no interest in buying equipment from GCA. When the Camaçari complex started to operate in the late seventies, the U.S. petrochemical industry had already had a ten-year history with centralized wastewater treatment.

Cetrel learned a great deal from GCA's pollution control experience and applied it to run the industrial wastewater treatment plant. Cetrel also imported, coupled with GCA's experience, the U.S. environmental pollution control paradigm, which was a social compromise to abate pollution without interfering in management's right to decide what is produced and how. Brazilian professionals adopted in Cetrel a Brazilian, i.e., authoritarian, version of the "solution to pollution is dilution" model they saw in Texas and elsewhere, aiming at mitigating the negative effects of the known hazards of petrochemical production.

Their actions, however, were not sufficient to avoid or prevent the adverse health and environmental consequences of those hazards [30]. On the contrary, they were only at the beginning of a long learning curve. It was too little, but not too late.

Over the years, Cetrel has interacted with GCA and a host of other waste management companies. Conferences, seminars, and mutual visits, provided excellent opportunities for international technology transfer and informal information exchange. In about ten years, Cetrel managers and staff learned how to operate the wastewater treatment plant efficiently. Nevertheless, the "dependent pollution" created by the technologically dependent development pattern resulted in overt environmental and health crises that drove local subordinate classes—labor and middle classes—to challenge the status quo of production decisions. The petrochemical elite's solution to these crises required the importation of more sophisticated pollution control technologies (the hardware) and regulations (the software). Again, managers in Bahia imported corporate solutions to environmental pollution problems, as Karliner classified incineration, hazardous waste landfills, and other waste management technologies implemented by Cetrel [18]. These solutions contributed to reestablishing the temporarily weakened hegemony of the local petrochemical bourgeoisie.

This example seems to suggest that actors in peripheral countries may import controls from the "center" to resolve social crises originated by the health and environmental consequences of hazardous technologies.

Social Struggles and Occupational and Environmental Crises in the Camaçari Complex

As the local high-tech and capital-intensive petrochemical industry matured by the mid-eighties, it generated acute and chronic chemical, physical, ergonomic, and biological hazards that are common to petrochemical production the world over. Not surprisingly, this industry polluted the environment and exposed petrochemical workers and local communities to high levels of toxic chemicals.

Wooding provided a good theoretical framework to explain the environmental and occupational health developments in Bahia when he wrote that

> . . . the problems arising from the nature of the productive process itself (environmental contamination, community and workplace health and safety, toxic waste disposal, etc.) have been—and are—a major challenge to governments in both the U.S. and Europe. Ultimately they lead to the creation of new demands and new social and political forces to articulate them [31, p. 44].

Subordinate classes, led by Sindiquímica, Sindae, and later CUT, mobilized against wage losses—the strike of 1985—and the work-environment crises. First, a smaller benzene crisis occurred in Cetrel. Later, a much larger benzene crisis affected the whole complex. The democratization of Brazilian society and a countrywide political-economic crisis, combined with these local environmental and occupational health crises, in the mid- to late-eighties, to challenge the authoritarian version of the hegemonic factory regime of the complex.

Social actors on the left and right have searched for models to resolve or manage these crises. The Left's campaign against the environmental and occupational health crises forced businesses to accept the importance of the problem and to increase control of the toxic emissions derived from petrochemical production.

Sindiquímica, environmental groups, and their allies in the state apparatus adapted Italian and other European countries' ideas and experiences on how to organize workers to fight chemical pollution and capitalist exploitation. They applied in Bahia a "Brazilianized" version of the "Italian workers' " model and the Italian network of occupational health clinics [32]. Yet, they did not propose a *preventive alternative* to pollution control. Pollution prevention was not on their radar screen at the time.

Employers, who had already imported and "Brazilianized" the United States—and to a lesser extent European—pollution control paradigm and technologies, followed suit. To set up the new state requirements for pollution control systems and practices, the ruling petrochemical elite imported new end-of-pipe "corks," in part due to the lack of Brazilian technologies to address these problems. They did not propose any pollution prevention alternative, either.

Thus, on both sides of the political spectrum, the human agency of Brazilian social actors combined their creativity and independent action with their cultural, political, and ideological dependence on foreign models and technologies. As a result, an apparent convergence with the standards of protection common in developed countries emerged [33, 34].

Yet, the installation of new pollution control equipment was not an *automatic and natural* consequence of petrochemical industrialization, as convergence theorists would argue. Instead, this convergence in standards of protection occurred as a result of the strong local social struggle to control the technological hazards created by dependent petrochemical industrialization. In fact, it took the emergence of an epidemic, over almost a decade, for the technological hazards to be perceived as serious occupational and environmental health problems [35].

The expression "dependent convergence" could probably articulate this reality better than either one word alone. Brazil converged around developed countries' standards because of social struggle, cultural and technological dependency, and international solidarity [36].

The Texas Pollution Control Model and the U.S. "Environmental Policy System"

The U.S. environmental crisis of the late sixties also affected the Galveston Bay region of Texas, especially the Galveston Bay and the Houston Ship Channel. The Gulf Coast Waste Disposal Authority should be understood as a state intervention to mitigate the pollution in these two bodies of water against the domestic and industrial—especially oil and petrochemical— pollution generated in the Houston metropolitan area. GCA is, therefore, a quasi-public regional authority that epitomizes, in the Gulf Coast region, the mainstream trend of the early seventies to manage and control the water pollution of watersheds.

It is an important part also of the national institutional apparatus developed across the United States to carry out the environmental policy and management system engendered by the newly enacted environmental laws and regulations. In short, GCA is a creature of the state, born to deal with an existing environmental crisis. From the beginning, GCA developed a cooperative partnership with the local petrochemical industry to enable the latter to comply with the growing federal, state, and local environmental policy system.

This system was grounded on the pollution control paradigm and the "polluter-pays" principle. During the seventies, GCA installed its basic environmental control infrastructure, composed of many municipal, and four industrial, wastewater plants. In addition, it had to face financial, regulatory, and legal hurdles that involved the federal EPA, and counties and municipalities in the area. GCA won most of these initial battles.

During the second decade, GCA had to carry on a sustained political confrontation with communities, small businesses, politicians, and local officials concerning the siting of hazardous waste facilities in the Houston-Galveston area. This time around, GCA was not able to defeat the challenge of the "Not in My Backyard" (NIMBY) coalition. After years of unsuccessful attempts to site a high-tech hazardous waste treatment center in the area, it backed off and consolidated its operations around municipal solid waste and domestic wastewater treatment, as well as centralized industrial wastewater treatment. In the nineties, GCA increased its outreach to communities through public education and communication programs, aiming at improving its public image.

The Bayport complex evolved parallel to the booms and busts of the regional oil and petrochemical market. Composed of subsidiaries of large petrochemical corporations and structurally different from the Camaçari complex, it does not have the same history of labor union struggles against environmental and occupational health crises. On the contrary, firms in this complex were remarkably able to keep a low profile and prevent unions from organizing workers, except for three plants. This task was made easier by the traditional hegemony of the oil and petrochemical industries in the area.

During the eighties, the Bayport complex also went through productive restructuring, as happened with most oil and petrochemical corporations in the area. Workplace health and safety and environmental control policies followed the requirements of OSHA and EPA until the late eighties, when most companies adopted the voluntary Responsible Care Codes of Conduct. Nevertheless, GCA did not get certified by the ISO 14001 standards.

In summary, the analysis of the history of environmental policies adopted by GCA and the Bayport complex indicates the overwhelming and ongoing hegemony of the oil and petrochemical industry in the Gulf Coast region. Hence, as referred to before, pollution control policies—which do not challenge manage-ment's basic authority—prevail, rather than pollution prevention.

"The Petrochemical Republic of Bahia" and "The Oil and Petrochemical Republic of Texas"

By the early nineties, the "dependent convergence" referred to above con-solidated. Sindiquímica went "down the hill" and lost power, and with it, the ability to influence business decisions. At the national level, Brazil entered the neoliberal decade. The "Pólo" expanded and went through a broad productive restructuring, importing ideas and concepts that had been the Zeitgeist in the United States during the productive restructuring of the eighties.

Starting in the late eighties, competitiveness, productivity, and quality dis-courses spread throughout businesses in the complex like an epidemic. Con-tracting out, Total Quality Management, and Responsible Care policies became the new management doctrines.

Concentration of capital changed the "Pólo" gradually into an "Oligopólo." At Cetrel, "the solution to pollution is pollution control" model gained momentum after its privatization in the early nineties. In a word, corporate environmentalism "came to town" and stayed throughout the nineties. The new Post-Fordist and neoliberal hegemonic project of the petrochemical industry won the day, causing Bahia to look similar to Texas in many aspects.

In both places, the petrochemical industry shaped workplaces and local societies to consent to its hegemony. In Texas, whites and Hispanics have danced to its music for decades. In Bahia whites, mulattos, and Afro-Brazilians have been doing the same for over a decade now. During the nineties, Cetrel seemed to believe that Brazilian music is even better than American. Also, Brazilians would say that "Cetrel quer ser mais realista que o rei." ("Cetrel wants to be more royal than the King"). Yet, the king may already be naked.

Economic Globalization and Dependent Convergence

Brazilian intellectuals adopted and adapted "The Oil and Petrochemical Republic of Texas," assimilationist ecological paradigm, to build "The Petro-chemical Republic of Bahia." By the late eighties, the petrochemical industry was already global. The environmental pollution control industry was booming. When the Bahian petrochemical industry increased its subordinate, or dependent, integration in the global market in the early nineties, it had no difficulty in finding choices for solutions to its environmental and occupational health problems. Sooner rather than later, it applied the market-based policy "package" of the big players in the industry to local realities. It restructured, downsized, and adopted some prescriptions of the Responsible Care program. By the mid- to late-nineties, a new period in environmental management policies flourished in Camaçari, summarized in chapter 3 by the slogan, "the solution to pollution is voluntary pollution control."

Cetrel's BS-7750 and ISO 14001 certifications prompted the local petrochemical industry to claim that it plays by the rules of the world's best in the waste management business. Cetrel claims to have given the "Pólo" a "green seal" that is widely recognized in the global market of environmental pollution control. These claims actually mean that within a twenty-year period, similar production-related problems led to similar, now voluntarily installed, end-of-pipe controls [37].

Thus, by the late nineties, the fundamental problems of the Brazilian industry had become the same as those of the petrochemical industry in developed countries. Globalization of the economy may have brought developed and developing countries to a level playing field as far as petrochemical waste management policies and technologies are concerned.

In both situations, the limitations and successes of more and better waste management technologies are clear, although developed countries have easier access to state-of-the-art knowledge and have more resources to apply them. In both cases, investments in pollution control strategies are close to providing only marginal efficiencies. In both cases, a new paradigm to eliminate wastes is urgently needed.

Contradicting this potential trend for the petrochemical and other rich industries, the globalization of the world economy may strengthen Castleman's export-of-hazards argument [22, 23], because multinationals have now more power to "open" the economies of developing countries to their exports. This is what the free-trade agenda is mostly about, as Barkin and Lemus suggested [38]. Yet, the importing countries are still part of the process; they need to be taken into account in more detail in order for the assertion fully to explain the social conflicts that may emerge in the future.

ENDNOTES

1. This approach should be considered similar to the environmental strategy that Ashford called secondary prevention. He used this term when analyzing different strategies to address accidental releases of chemicals. In that context, secondary prevention strategies ". . . impose engineering and administrative controls on an existing production technology," while primary accident-prevention strategies ". . . utilize input substitution and process redesign to modify a production technology" [2, p. 51].
2. Nicholas Ashford, "Policies for the Promotion of Inherent Safety," *New Solutions*, 7, 4, pp. 46-52, Summer 1997.
3. GCWDA 1994 Annual Report.
4. GCWDA 1997 Annual Report.
5. While this list is not exhaustive, it covers the most important actors that played prominent roles in the history of Cetrel and GCA. Another influential player throughout their history has been the media (which includes the press). Media coverage

of the two firms has been for the most part supportive. Yet, when political and legal crises developed, the public was able to get enough information about their substance. In Cetrel's case, critical media coverage occurred only after the censorship of the press was de facto abolished in the early 1980s. The benzene crises in Cetrel and the Camaçari complex, especially the latter, were widely covered by local and national media outlets. In addition, the labor press reached a vast number of workers and residents in the Salvador metropolitan region. In GCA's case, local newspapers, such as the *Galveston Daily News*, echoed the existing wide spectrum of criticisms against GCA during the early eighties. Other newspapers, such as the *Houston Post* and the *Houston Chronicle*, also covered the main incidents in GCA's life. Therefore, to a large extent, the media publicized the social struggle and the actions of social actors to solve the crises that have occurred in both companies. This is not to say, however, that the media supported civil society in all these struggles.

6. For more details on social actors, see Appendix 1.
7. Gary Cohen, "Why Organized Labor Needs a Coherent Strategy on Chlorinated Chemicals," *New Solutions*, 7, 4, pp. 6-9, Summer 1997.
8. Sanford Lewis, "Federal Statutes," in [9, pp. 209-234].
9. *Fighting Toxics: A Manual for Protecting Your Family, Community, and Workplace*, Gary Cohen and John O'Connor, eds., Island Press, Washington, D.C., 1990.
10. Other recent examples include the 1992 OSHA Process Safety Management and the 1997 EPA Risk Management plans.
11. A review of many corporate environmental reports provides overwhelming evidence that most of GCA's industrial customers follow the Responsible Care program.
12. Progressive environmentalists ironically call the permits the "license to pollute."
13. These authors are some of the best-known commentators who discuss the relationship between pollution control technology and regulations in the United States. For more discussion on this issue, see [2; 14; 15; 16; 17; 18, pp. 33-34].
14. Ken Geiser, "The Unfinished Business of Pollution Prevention," *Georgia Law Review*, vol. 29, pp. 473-491, 1995.
15. Ken Geiser, "Toxics Use Reduction and Pollution Prevention," *New Solutions,* 1,1, pp. 1-8, Spring 1990.
16. Ken Geiser, "The Greening of Industry: Making The Transition to a Sustainable Economy," *Technology Review*, pp. 66-72, August/September, 1991.
17. Ken Geiser, "Protecting Reproductive Health and the Environment: Toxics Use Reduction," *Environmental Health Perspectives Supplements,*, vol. 101, suppl. 2, pp. 221-225, 1993.
18. Joshua Karliner, *The Corporate Planet: Ecology and Politics in the Age of Globalization*, Sierra Club, San Francisco, 1997.
19. As referred to in chapter 6.
20. Chapter 2 described Cetrel's interaction with GCA staff and Japanese and European professionals in the seventies and eighties. Chapter 5 provided evidence of Cetrel's sponsoring of international conferences and seminars to discuss "state-of-the-art" waste management policies and technologies.
21. The typical case is the importation of obsolete or hazardous technologies from developed countries, as Castleman [22, 23], Castleman and Navarro [24], LaDou [25], and others publicized. From the perspective of the developed countries, one would have to call it the export of obsolete or hazardous technologies. In turn, I'd argue that

the exportation of hazardous technologies may trigger the future exportation of technology controls.

22. Barry Castleman, "The Double Standards in Industrial Hazards," in Jane Ives, ed., *The Export of Hazards,* Routledge & Kegan Paul, Boston, pp. 61-89, 1985.

23. Barry Castleman, "The Migration of Industrial Hazards," *International Journal of Occupational and Environmental Health,* 1(2), pp. 85-96, April-June 1995.

24. Barry Castleman and Vicente Navarro, "International Mobility of Hazardous Products, Industries and Wastes," *International Journal of Health Services,* 17(4), pp. 617-633, 1987.

25. Joseph LaDou, The Export of Environmental Responsibility, *Archives of Environmental Health,* 49(1), pp. 6-9, 1994.

26. This public relations message is coherent with contemporary Brazilian culture. It is not unusual for large segments of the Brazilian elite to claim that the country's "manifest destiny" is to imitate or copy the experience of more advanced countries in order to quickly become part of the developed world. In the case of the importation of pollution controls, Brasil had to import solutions to the problems created by imported technological hazards.

27. Personal interviews with Cetrel and GCA managers conducted during visits to both companies in 1997.

28. Fernanda Giannasi and Annie Thébaud-Mony, "Occupational Exposures to Asbestos in Brazil," *International Journal of Occupational and Environmental Health,* 3, 2, pp. 150-157, April-June 1997.

29. Peter Evans, Reinventing the Bourgeoisie: State Entrepreneurship and Class Formation in Dependent Capitalist Development, *American Journal of Sociology,* Supplement, (88): S210-247, 1982.

30. Initially, petrochemical hazards were managed and controlled in Bahia through a pollution control paradigm, and sometimes technologies, imported from at least three developed countries, the United States, Germany, and Japan, as discussed in previous chapters.

31. John Wooding, "Dire States: Workplace Health and Safety Regulation in the Reagan/ Thatcher Era," Ph.D. dissertation, Brandeis University, 1990. In spite of referring to scenarios in developed countries, his insight also applies to Bahia.

32. The neologism, "Brazilianized," connotes that Brazilian actors learned the models and technologies, and gave them a Brazilian face, i.e., these actors transformed the original imported ideas and equipment into something else. Again, the human agency of Brazilians adapted or modified these technologies to fit them into local social, political, economic, and cultural conditions. For example, Brazilian engineers learned that the activated sludge treatment system works differently in warmer climates than in temperate climates. This finding caused them to change the design of the wastewater plant in the early eighties.

33. The use of the word, "dependence," here without qualification is probably a bit misleading. Progressive and conservative groups in Brazil have a long history of trying to imitate or adapt foreign experiences to Brazil. This trend results in part from a long history of cultural, political, and scientific dependence on the metropolis, whichever this may be—Portugal, France, England, or the United States. A Brazilian literary critic calls the end result of this trend "as idéias fora de lugar" ("the ideas out of place"), to allude to the fact that Brazilian intellectuals tend to acritically imitate foreign ideas that

do not necessarily correspond to Brazilian realities. On the other hand, Brazilian elites and middle class, as in any other country, also have a long history of participating in international networks—scientific, political, or commercial—that enable them to know "the best" that other countries have done to solve their problems. Thus, the importation of ideas and technologies is actually a dialectical synthesis of both aspects, dependence and international networking. For more details on Brazilian dependence on foreign ideas, see [34].

34. Roberto Schwarz, *Ao Vencedor as Batatas*, Livraria Duas Cidades, São Paulo, Brazil, 1992, p. 169.

35. Theoreticians of the convergence theory proposed in the late sixties to early seventies that industrialization was ". . . the common denominator for all developed societies" [31, p. 44]. Further, ". . . In establishing the process of industrialization as a common factor for all *advanced* societies it [the theory] emphasizes that the problems they face (and their solutions) will tend to converge" (emphasis in the original) [31, p. 44].

36. In the cases discussed in this book, convergence probably happened because Brazilians of all political colors imported models and paradigms that were proven social answers—in developed countries—to the pollution problems derived from petro-chemical pollution. Whereas, on the one hand, convergence was a result of corporate dependence on foreign technologies, on the other, it resulted from international solidarity among progressive forces, which transferred successful models for worker and community struggles against environmental and workplace pollution. At the end of the day, the environmental and occupational health policies and controls that prevailed in Bahia were Brazilian versions of international corporate solutions to petrochemical pollution, clearly reflected in the contemporary aggressive public relations messages of Cetrel.

37. Brazil, as many other newly industrializing countries, did not have the financial resources and expertise to design and produce its own solutions to environmental pollution. In the seventies, it imported the technology that created environmental and occupational hazards. Later, it imported the technology to control those hazards.

38. David Barkin and Blanca Lemus, "The Impact of Integration on Mexico's Workers: Why GATT, NAFTA, WTO, and OECD Are Important," *New Solutions, A Journal of Environmental and Occupational Health Policy*, 8, 2, pp. 243-252, 1998.

APPENDIX 1

Research Design

This study used in-depth historical case studies to discuss Cetrel's importation of petrochemical hazards, policies, and technologies, from the perspectives of social actors in Brazil. It is composed of three instrumental case studies, purposefully chosen to illustrate the specific issue of importation of hazardous technologies and control policies by social actors in the Camaçari Petrochemical Complex and Cetrel [1, p. 250; 2].

Menendez wrote that this perspective tries to capture the viewpoint of these actors by focusing on them as subjects or units of description and analysis, and recognizing them as agents of change. The underlying implication of this view of reality is that potentially a variety of actors function in different locations of the social structure. These actors may have similar practices and representations, but they may also have distinct and conflictive knowledge and perceptions regarding health, exposures, and the work environment. Thus,

> . . . [t]o recover the viewpoint of the actor as an academic and/or political methodology in modern societies means to recognize that social structures refer to conditions of inequality and difference generated at the ethnic, religious, political, and economical levels, and express themselves not only through the different actors but also through their social relations [3, p. 240].

Brown and Fee expressed a similar notion when they wrote that

> Actors perceive their realities through historically and culturally specific prisms; notions of scientific objectivity are but aspects of a particular paradigm. Historians are relatively casual about methodology, resistant to claims of a timeless truth, and highly sensitive to context-dependent meanings [4].

Menendez noted that a relational actor analysis of social actors or classes assumes that those are dynamic builders of their reality, which is not totally determined by their positions within the social relations of production [3]. The social relations of production define only the social boundaries for an analysis of positions that discounts the description of concrete actors in their class transactions. Conversely, the actor analysis developed in this study assumes that social actors should be understood by means of a relational approach. The structure is what is produced by the actors in their social interactions. In this approach, researchers should listen to all meaningful key actors that intervene in a given process and describe in relational terms the characteristics and conditions of their knowledge.

Moreover, Menendez argued that the viewpoints or perspectives of these actors should be guided by a methodological principle that underscores the existence of possible meaningful differences within cultures, social classes, ethnic groups, community, and genders. No single unit can, explicitly or implicitly, be expressed by a single viewpoint [5].

The research design chosen in this study centers around two historical case studies of Cetrel and the Gulf Coast Waste Disposal Authority. The Cetrel case study is an in-depth, focused analysis of the evolution of Cetrel's environmental, and to a lesser extent occupational, policies. The GCA case study provides a historical reference for comparisons with Cetrel.

Before addressing these two case studies, this study situates them in their national and regional legal, physical, political-economic, and social contexts. The case studies are followed by a cross-case comparative analysis that identifies thematic commonalities and discrepancies between the two cases.

This research fits within the tradition of qualitative research. Creswell defined qualitative research as

> ... [a]n inquiry process of understanding based on distinct methodological traditions of inquiry that explore a social or human problem. The researcher builds a complex, holistic picture, analyzes words, reports detailed views of informants, and conducts the study in a natural setting [1, p. 15].

According to Yin, case studies should be chosen when 1) a researcher has little control over phenomena under study; 2) the significance of independent, dependent, superfluous, or contextual variables is unclear; and 3) considerable heterogeneity across situations is expected but comparison across them is desired [6]. All these conditions applied to the contexts of Cetrel and the Gulf Coast Waste Disposal Authority.

Stake also noted that the intellectual products of case study research include direct observation and interpretation of statements, activities, events, categorical aggregation, the derivation of patterns within and among situations, and generalizations [7]. The time and place boundaries of the Cetrel and GCA case studies were determined by the history of these two institutions. Cetrel was created in 1975 and is located in Camaçari, state of Bahia, Brazil, while GCA was created in 1969 and is located in Pasadena, Texas, United States.

The two case studies are narrated through a chronology of phases associated with major events, in the Cetrel case, or with time periods, in the GCA case. Both case studies conclude with a within-case analysis that provide a summary discussion of the major aspects of each case. This study covers work and general environment aspects in different chapters, according to the importance of each in the history of Cetrel and GCA. While serious work environment crises occurred in Bahia, environmental issues were the most important in Texas. Yet, by focusing on either of the two aspects, the other is also indirectly covered, because emissions of petrochemical plants tend to have a simultaneous impact on the general and work environments [8].

Due to time, access to information, and financial constraints, this research also had to deal with the limitations of concentrating on Cetrel and GCA. These two waste management companies treat the wastes of dozens of petrochemical companies that are not addressed by this study. This could lead to false assumptions about the extent to which Cetrel and GCA histories represent their history.

No assumption is thus made regarding the specific history of each company in the petrochemical complexes where Cetrel and GCA operate. Nevertheless, given the high level of integration between the latter and their customers, it is reasonable to assume that there may be a parallel between the environmental and occupational policies carried out. In Cetrel's case this was truer in the nineties than before. In GCA's case, this integration was more indirect and subtle, but still very present throughout its history [9].

DATA COLLECTION METHODS

Table 1 lists the types of information obtained from key informants or sources for each social actor.

For each social actor, key informants were selected through a combination of nonprobabilistic, purposeful sampling methods, in particular the snowball-sampling technique and the theory-based sampling technique [10]. Key informants are "individuals who provide useful insights into the group [actors] and can steer the researcher to information and contacts" [1, p. 60; 11; 12]. Key informants were identified through newspaper clips, company documents, scientific articles, videos, and informal contacts with unions, university professionals, and staff of the Cetrel and GCA.

All key informants were interviewed in person, most via semistructured interviews that lasted for approximately one to two hours. Yet, field conditions also required that some important interviews be conducted in an unstructured format. The purpose of semistructured interviews is to allow the researcher to guide the interview in a certain direction, through the use of interview guides that contain a list of topics or questions that need to be covered during the interview. Specific interview guides were prepared for the two major sources of information of this research, i.e., Cetrel and GCA.

The interviews in Bahia were administered over a period of two months between June and August 1997. Interviews in Texas were initially administered in May 1997 and continued in March 1998 [13]. Confidentiality of responses and identities was discussed prior to the beginning of the interviews. Interviews were taped when authorized by interviewees, transcribed, and reviewed for coding of

Table 1. Types of Information by Source

Information type/ information source	Interviews	Observation	Documents	Audiovisual materials
Sindiquímica				
Occ. Physician	Yes		Yes	Yes
Former H&S Officer	Yes		Yes	
Sindae				
Occ. Physician	Yes		Yes	
H&S Officer	Yes		Yes	
Cetrel				
Management	Yes	Yes	Yes	Yes
Employees	Yes	Yes	Yes	
Former Director	Yes			
COFIC				
Former Superint.	Yes			
Public Relations Staff			Yes	
FUNDACENTRO				
Ind. Hygienist	Yes		Yes	
Occ. Physician	Yes			
Fed. Univ. of Bahia				
Faculty (several)	Yes		Yes	
GCWDA				
Operations Manager	Yes			
Bayport Manager	Yes	Yes	Yes	
Technical Staff	Yes		Yes	Yes
Bayport Complex				
Plant Manager Nova	Yes			
OCAW				
Health&Safety Activist	Yes			
Local Union Officer	Yes			
Internat. Represent.	Yes			

major themes. To preserve confidentiality, some informants were given a fictitious name or identified by a generic category such as a worker, staff, manager, or union officer. When there was no clear need to preserve confidentiality, informants were identified by their real name [14]. Photographic and audiovisual materials were used to document and analyze technologies and work methods used to manage and treat hazardous wastes in both companies.

This research also reviewed the Brazilian scientific literature on the Camaçari Petrochemical Complex; doctoral and master dissertations on occupational health in Brazil and the U.S.; public health, occupational, environmental health, and trade journals; union and daily newspapers, company publications and documents; and a variety of Internet Web sites. In short, as Table 1 shows, this research applied techniques that are common in case- study research: observation, interviews, and document review [15].

To strengthen the credibility and validity of the data collected, triangulation of data and sources was conducted whenever possible [16]. In addition, before developing the analytical framework to interpret the history of the "Pólo"and Cetrel, the author 1) searched to validate the data collected in the field by submitting it to criticism from competent university professionals in Bahia, and 2) had a number of individual and collective discussions with sources who were very familiar with the history of the complex.

RESEARCH LIMITATIONS

Case-study research is not sampling research. It serves primarily to provide an in-depth understanding of a particular topic. Therefore, the findings of any one case study may not be generalizable to other situations. The cases studied in this book may or may not be representative of other petrochemical industries in developing countries. Only by conducting other case studies in these countries can one assess how representative the Cetrel and GCA cases are. Yet, this research intends to provide in-depth case descriptions and analyses that could be useful for further international research and support the comparability of its findings.

Two main threats may reduce the external validity—or transferability—of these research findings and conclusions: contextual and information biases. The first bias derives from the difficulty in apprehending complex historical, political, economic, cultural, and ideological contexts of two very diverse countries and societies. This challenge is further complicated by the length of time covered by this book, which ranged from the late 1960s to the late 1990s.

The second bias derives from the logistical complexity of checking for the reliability of information sources located in two different countries, who speak two different languages, and who perceive their own reality with particularly biased lenses [17].

Data collected for this study may not have been sufficient to account for gender, national, and cultural biases. In addition, this study did not always have enough data to account for internal conflicts or disagreements within each social actor, i.e., labor, industry, etc.

While the research methods used may have helped to prevent and control for these threats, a possibility still remains that cultural and information biases were not accounted for properly. On the one hand, the author's U.S.- Brazil binational experience may have strengthened his ability to interpret these bicultural and binational biases. On the other, his own national and personal biases may have made this task overwhelming in some instances. This book provided Brazilian and English versions of words, titles, and expressions as often as possible to enable readers to understand the cultural meanings attached to them. Yet, some expressions are so culturally bound to the Brazilian and Bahian view of the world that they may not make sense at all to other cultures.

ENDNOTES

1. Robert Creswell, *Qualitative Inquiry and Research Design: Choosing among Five Traditions*, Sage, Thousand Oaks, Calif., 1989.
2. In addition, the choice for the cases studied in this study was motivated by 1) empirical evidence that suggested interesting counterarguments to Castleman's double-standards propositions, and 2) Brazil and the U.S. have been an intrinsic part of the life and professional experiences of the author. These experiences enabled the author to have a deep understanding of the particular occupational and environmental health realities in both countries. This research in fact follows the combined traditions of focused case studies and cross-national comparative studies, by undertaking two in-depth Brazilian case studies and one U.S. case study.
3. Translated from Eduardo Menendez, "El Punto de Vista del Actor: Homogeneidad, Diferencia e Historicidad" (The point of view of the actor: Homogeneity, Difference and Historicity), *Relaciones*, no. 69, pp. 239-269, Invierno 1997.
4. Elizabeth Fee and Theodore Brown, "Why History?" *American Journal of Public Health*, 87, 11, pp. 1763-1764, 1997.
5. While this concern was always present in the procedures selected to collect data for this research, the author was not able to apply it in all instances, due to time and resource constraints. For more details on actor analysis, see [3].
6. R K Yin, *Case Study Research: Design and Methods*, revised ed., Sage, Thousand Oaks, Calif., 1989. Yin also wrote that a case study "is an empirical inquiry that investigates a contemporary phenomenon within its real life context, when boundaries between phenomenon and context are not clearly evident, and in which multiple sources of evidence are used" [p. 4].
7. RE Stake, *The Art of Case Study Research*, Sage, Thousand Oaks, Calif., 1995.
8. This is not to say that there are no exceptions to this trend. Sometimes, only workers are affected by fugitive emissions in a facility. By the same token, emergency leaks or explosions may affect neighboring communities without harming workers.
9. For example, the author assumed, based on evidence collected in some companies of the Camaçari complex by Antonio S. Guimarães, that large similarities exist between Cetrel's factory regime and the prevailing factory regime in the "Pólo" (see chapters 1 and 4). In GCA's case, there was no solid evidence to back the same assumption.
10. The snowball- or chain-sampling technique is a technique in which the researcher locates one or two key individuals and asks them to name other likely informants. Creswell defined it as a strategy where the researcher "identifies cases of interest from people who know people who know what cases are information rich" [1, p. 119]. While he used this definition as a criterion for the selection of cases, it also applies to the selection of informants after the selection of a case is made [1].

11. Key informants may also be defined as ". . .individuals who possess special knowledge and who are willing to share their knowledge with the researcher" [12, p. 39].

12. Patricia Hudelson, *Qualitative Research for Health Programmes,* World Health Organization, Geneva, Division of Mental Health, 1994.

13. Before conducting the field work, the author spent two weeks in Bahia to assess the viability of conducting field work in the complex and the availability of secondary sources of information.

14. The vast majority of interviewees did not mind being taped and did not require confidentiality.

15. The author visited Cetrel several times for one month, where he could observe a host of aspects that are indirectly reported in this research. Access to company employees and documents was not difficult, since Cetrel managers allowed the author to conduct this investigation. Nevertheless, given the conflictive nature of the history of labor-management relations in Bahia, the author could not always disclose the exact goals of this research to all parties involved in the conflicts.

16. Creswell noted that ". . . Stake places emphasis on sources of data and suggests that the researcher triangulate differently based on 'data situations' in the case"(emphasis in the original) [1, p. 251]. The author triangulated the sources of information collected for this study whenever feasible, by comparing newspaper sources with interviews and company documents. Fortunately, it was possible to have three or more sources of information for many events, such as the benzene crises. In a few cases, however, the author had only one source of information to rely on, such as information on the Bayport complex. Whenever sources of information contradicted each other, the author either tried to report both or used multiple sources of data to support or contradict one of them.

17. For example, most of these sources were male, a characteristic of the petrochemical labor force in Texas and Bahia. Since gender is an important factor in risk perception, this gender bias may have affected the analysis of the benzene crisis provided in chapter 4.

APPENDIX 2

The Petrochemical Industry

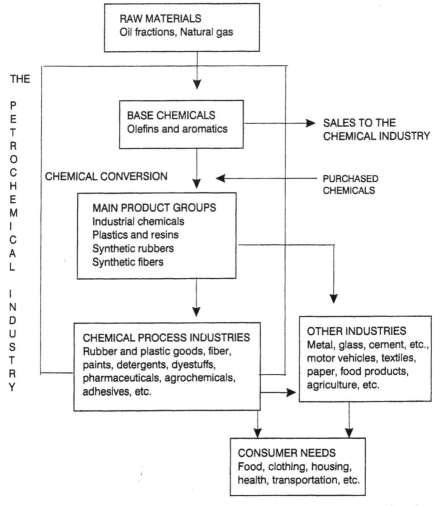

Source: Keith Chapman, *The International Petrochemical Industry: Evolution and Location,* Basil Blackwell, Cambridge, Massachusetts, p. 26, 1991.

APPENDIX 3

Timeline of the History of the "Pólo Petroquímico de Camaçari"

1978	1982	1986	1990	1994	1998
Start-up of Complex		Benzene Crisis at Cetrel + EIS/RIMA ('87-'88)	Benzene Crisis at Nitrocarbono ('90)	Globalization →→ BS-7750, ISO ('95-96)	↑↑
☞☞ Authoritarian-Hegemonic Factory Regime	☞ Strike ('85)				
			Responsible Care Early 90s	↑↑↑↑↑↑	↑↑
		Restructuring Late 80s	☞ Hegemonic Despotic Factory Regime ↑↑↑↑↑↑	↑↑↑↑↑↑↑	↑↑
		Expansion Late 80s	of Complex Early 90s		
			Privatization of Cetrel ('91)		

APPENDIX 4

CETREL S.A. Environmental Policy

1. Continuous Improvement/Pollution Prevention

To maintain a continuous improvement of environmental performance, emphasizing the utilization of new environmental technologies, optimization of the waste- and effluent-treatment processes—especially by adopting pollution-prevention practices—and environment-monitoring activities in order to guarantee better results in environmental protection.

2. Industrial Waste and Effluent Reduction

To support and encourage actions to control and reduce effluent generation, industrial waste, and air emissions, with the application of source-control programs.

3. Environmental Aspects/Impacts Reduction

To assure excellent standards of operation, allowing a significant reduction in adverse effects/impacts resulting from Cetrel's environmental protection activities and practices.

4. Environmental Liabilities Elimination

To prevent and to pursue the elimination of any form of environmentally adverse effects resulting from Cetrel's activities or generated by industrial waste- and effluent-systems users, by working in cooperation with the industries involved and environmental-control agencies.

5. Communication with Interested Parties

To maintain a permanent dialogue with all parties involved—employees, suppliers, neighboring communities, clients, shareholders, environmental control agencies, and the public in general—through environmental-education programs and social communication.

6. Support and Improvement of Environmental Legislation and Regulations

To assure the management of industrial wastes and effluents, as well as environmental monitoring systems in accordance with the environmental legislation, regulations, standards, practices, and procedures in force governing the development and improvement of the environmental-protection programs.

7. Environmental Objectives and Targets

Cetrel's environmental objectives and targets were established on the basis of significant environmental aspects/impacts, in compliance with the standards and regulations in force, to support the demands of the interested parties and the economic aspects resulting from the company's activities. The objectives and targets are annually updated and published in the company's official bulletins and available for consultation at the Environment Management System Coordination and at Cetrel's communication sector.

Source: Cetrel S.A.—Environmental Protection Company, p. 8.

APPENDIX 5

Bayport Facility Industrial Users in 1997

AIR Liquide America Corp. Bayport
Air Liquide America Corp. La Porte
Air Products, Inc.
Akzo Nobel Chemicals, Inc.
ARCO Chemical Co.
Bayou Cogeneration Plant
Baytank (Houston), Inc.
Bealine Service Company, Inc.
CBSL Transportation Services, Inc.
Calgon Corp.
Carpenter Co.
Catalyst Resources
Chemical Research &Licensing, Inc.
Chusei (U.S.A.), Inc.
City of La Porte
City of Shore Acres
Clear Lake Cogeneration Co.
Dahlen Transport Co.
Dianal America, Inc.
Dixie Chemcial Co., Inc.
E.I. Dupont de Nemours Co., Inc.
Eval Company of America
FMC Corp.
Fina Oil and Chemical Co.
The Goodyear Tire & Rubber Co.
Graver Tank & Manufacturing Co., Inc.

Haldor Topsoe, Inc.
Hoechst Celanese Corp.
Hoechst Celanese Chemical Group, Inc.
Hoyer USA, Inc.
Huntsman Chemical Corp.
Kaneka Texas Corp.
Liquid Carbonic Specialty Gas Corp.
Lonza, Inc.
Lubrizol Corp.
Lyondell Polymers Corp.
Montell U.S.A., Inc.
Montgomery Tank Lines, Inc.
Nisseki Chemical Texas, Inc.
Noltex L.L.C. Soarnal
Nova Molecular Technologies, Inc.
Oxychem Petrochemicals
PPG Industries, Inc. (two plants)
Petrolite Corp.
PatroUnited Terminals, Inc.
Revak Enterprises, Inc.
Rohm & Haas Co.
Southern Ionics, Inc.
Tri-Gas Industrial Gases
Velsicol Chemical Corp.
Zeneca Ag Products
Zeon Chemicals, Inc.

Index

Academia and cross-national
comparisons, 220
Accidents/injuries, rewards based on low
reporting of, 117
See also Health and safety issues
Administrative Modernization Program,
Cetrel's, 160
AFL-CIO, 117
Air monitoring network, 156–157
Akzo Nobel, 200
Alief Wastewater Treatment Plant, 197
Alma Ata Primary Care Conference, 129
Almeida, Rômulo, 49
AMOCO, 38, 194
Antarctica, 108
ARCO, 38, 39, 198–199
Argentina, 35
Asbestos, 10
Associação Brasileira de Norma Técnicas,
147
Associação Proquímicos, 115
Association of Bayport Companies
(ABC), 39, 200
Association of Petrochemical Industry
Workers (ASPETRO), 48
Association of Workers Occupationally
Contaminated by Organo-
chlorines (ACPO), 1–2
Audubon Society, 189
Australia, 35
Auto industry, Brazilian, 128
Automation of operations, 82, 84

Bacellar, Luiz, 152
Bahia state, 46–47
See also individual subject headings

Banco Econômico group, 43
BASF, 3
Bayport Industrial Park, 36–39, 197–202,
223, 232, 242, 253
See also Gulf Coast Waste Disposal
Authority
BEM-TE-VI, 159
Benzene crises in COPEC
causality of the problem, employers/
labor organizations argue over,
126
Cetrel
antecedents, 108–109
disease, the production of, 108–111
health-hazard evaluation, 111–115
Chemical Workers Union, 115–119
collective bargaining around health/
safety, historical development of,
128–130
definition of the problem, employers/
labor organizations argue over,
125–127
evolution of work environment/
environmental policies in
COPEC, 72–73
Fundação José Silveira study,
123–124
integration of production and
processing, 107–108
laws and agreements, 127–130,
132–136
Nitrocarbono, 119–123
Operação Caça Benzeno, 122–123
Ordinance 3, 132–133
overview, 107–108
regulations, development of new,
130–132

[Benzene crisis in COPEC]
size of the problem, employers/labor organizations argue over, 125–126
solution to the problem, employers/ labor organizations argue over, 126–127
summary/conclusions, chapter, 136–138
Tripartite Working Commission, comprehensive standards developed by, 133–136
Benzene working groups (GTBs), 134–135
Best available technology (BAT), 193, 223
Best conventional technology (BCT), 193
Best practicable technology (BPT), 193, 223
Biochemical oxygen demand load (BOD), 39
Board of Administration of Petrobrás, 49
Boas, Paulo, 151–152
Bonds and Gulf Coast Waste Disposal Authority, 182–184
"Brazilian Wastewater Technicians Study Industrial Facility Questions," 52
British standard 7750, 161–163
Buffer zone around COPEC, 50
Bureaucracy and perception of industrial disease, 23
Busch, Arthur, 184, 185
Businesses and the courts, cross-national comparisons and small, 219–220

Camaçari Petrochemical Complex (COPEC)
background, 42–44
Cetrel, the creation of, 51–53
creation of, history of the, 48–50
political economy of, 44–48
public relations and media messages, 53
social structure of the state, 47
social struggles and occupational/ environmental crises in, 230–231

[Camaçari Petrochemical Complex (COPEC)]
timeline, historical, 249
See also Benzene crises in COPEC; Evolution of work environment/ environmental policies in COPEC
Campbell Bayou Facility, 197
Cantrell, Greg, 191–192
Capacities, class, 19
Capital, centralization/concentration of, 82
Capitalism
modernization theories vs. world-system view, 12–15
production politics in advanced, 20–21
Capivara Pequeno River, 154
Caprolactam, 119
Carbocloro S/A, 1
Carbon monoxide, 157
Carbon tetrachloride, 1
Cardoso, Fernando H., 64
Career advancement, 69–70
Carlos Magalhães, Antonio, 50
Caustic soda, 1
Ceman (Central de Manutencão), 44
Center for Sanitary Surveillance of the S. Paulo Health Department, 130–131
Centralization/concentration of capital, 82
Centralized industrial wastewater treatment model, 52
Central Única dos Trabalhadores (CUT), 70, 84, 117–118, 121, 133–134
Certification processes and benzene crises in COPEC, 134
CESAT and disease diagnosis, 118, 120
Cetrel (Brazilian waste management company), 2, 44
centralized industrial wastewater treatment model, 52
contract fees, 52
cooperative partnership with customers, 149
Corrective Maintenance Plan, 150, 160
creation of, 51–53
dilution as solution to pollution, 73–76

[Cetrel (Brazilian waste management
company)]
first phase: public company
bureaucracy, typical public, 148–150
solid hazardous wastes treatment/
disposal, 147–148
wastewater treatment, industrial, 146
inorganic effluent system, 52
labor-management relationship, 109
liquid organic effluent system, 51
overview, 145
policy, S.A. environmental, 251–252
research design, 242
second phase: privatization
air monitoring network, 156–157
effects and causes of privatization,
debate over, 151–152
environmental protection, a model
in, 152–157
expansion/modernization,
wastewater treatment plant,
155–156
groundwater monitoring, 153–154
health program, occupational,
157–159
incineration, 152–153
ocean disposal system, 154–155
organizational changes, 159–161
voluntary environmental protection:
British standard 7750/ISO
14001, 161–166
solid hazardous waste treatment and
disposal system, 52–53
See also Cetrel under Benzene crises
in COPEC; Cross-national
comparisons; Occupational/
environmental health/safety
policies of Cetrel/GCA,
evolution of
Champion Paper, 183
Chemical Business, 201
Chemical Manufacturers Association,
127, 200
Chemical Workers Union (Sindiquímica)
benzene crises in COPEC, 115–119,
122
factory regime in COPEC, 68–70

[Chemical Workers Union
(Sindiquímica)]
historical background, 115
merging with Stiep/Sindipetro, 87
organizing under adverse conditions,
67–68
research design, 242
strike of 1985, general, 70–72
wages, 83–84
Chile, 11
China dust, 1
Chloracne, 1
Chlorinated hydrocarbons, liquid, 147,
152–153
Chlorine, 1
Chloroform, 158
Ciquine, 108, 120
Citizens Against Polluting Our
Neighborhoods (CAPONE),
189–190
Class conflict and perception of industrial
disease, 23
Class formation, the theory of, 18–21
Clear Creek City Water Authority, 189
Clear Lake Civic League, 189
Clinical approaches to controlling
industrial disease, 24
Clorogil S/A, 1
Coastal Industrial Water Authority
(CIWA), 198
COFIC (Committee for the Industrial
Foment of Camacari), 43–44,
78–80, 89, 156, 242
Collective bargaining around
health/safety, historical
development of, 128–130
Collor, Fernando, 63–64, 83, 131
Comments, 52
Committee for the Industrial Foment of
Camaçari (COFIC), 43–44,
78–80, 89, 156, 242
Communist party (PCB) in Brazil, 48, 70
Community advisory panels (CAPs), 200
Community/environmental groups and
cross-national comparisons, 218
Companhia Siderúrgica Paulista
(COSIPA), 122, 125, 130, 135

Compensation for occupational diseases, 24–25
Competitiveness, 81
Consent, authoritarian/labor-capital relations and workers', 81
Contracting out productive/support services, 81–82, 84, 86, 88, 201
Control systems, cross-national comparisons and environmental, 224
Coordination of Science and Technology, 75
COPEC. *See* Camaçari Petrochemical Complex
Copene (Companhia Petroquímica do Nordeste), 44, 70–71, 81, 107, 119–120
Core countries and international division of labor, 13–14
Corruption, 63–64, 131
COSIPA (Companhia Siderúrgica Paulista), 122, 125, 130, 135
Costs of health/safety regulations and the export/migration of hazards, 9
County Council to Protect the Environment of Cubatão, 1
CPC, 152
Croce, Mr., 40
Cross-national comparisons
 actor analysis
  academia, 220
  businesses and the courts, small, 219–220
  community/environmental groups, 218
  governments and politicians, 219
  industry, 218–219
  labor, 218
  management, 216–217
 double standards argument, 227–229
 economic globalization and dependent convergence, 233–234
 hegemony of petrochemical industry, 233
 historical-structural foundations, 215–216
 lessons learned, 224–227

[Cross-national comparisons]
 peripheral countries, interaction between foreign/national actors in, 229–230
 policy outcomes, waste management control systems, environmental, 224
  environmental policy paradigm, 220
  overview, 221
  regulatory outcomes, 221–222
  self-regulation outcomes, 222–223
  technology outcomes, 223–224
 summary/conclusions, chapter, 227
CUT (Central Única dos Trabalhadores), 70, 84, 117–118, 121, 133–134

Davis, Jack, 183, 185
de Andrade, Paes, 126
"Decade of Progress," 194–195
Democratization of Brazilian society, 63, 230
Dependency
 chronic technological, 36
 cross-national comparisons, 233–234
 historical-structural/relational/unorthodox approach to, 15–18
 inclusive theory of export-import of hazardous technologies, 3
 structuralist/globalist/orthodox approach to, 12–15
 See also individual subject headings
Despotic regimes, hegemonic, 20–21
Developed to developing countries, export/migration of hazards from, 2–3, 7–12
 See also individual subject headings
Dibenzodioxins, 1
Dichloroethane, 158
Dilution as solution to pollution, 73–76
Direct Communication, 159
Diseases. *See* Health and safety issues
Disinfection/dechlorination systems, 197
Double standards argument, 9–11, 226, 227–229
Dow Chemical, 43
Downsizing, 84, 86

Downstream linkages for the petrochemical industry, 34–35
Drehmmer, Ernesto, 150
DRT (regional office of the Labor Ministry), 114, 119, 120–121, 135
Dual societies and modernization theories, 13
Dupont, 38

Ecological Park in Cetrel, 160
Econometric analysis of international investment location decisions, 10
Economies of scale and petrochemical industry, 34
EIA/RIMA solution, 76–80, 145, 149, 153–156
Ellington Air Force Base, 189
Embasa, 113, 115
Emergency response training, 110
Emschergenossenschaft, 40
End-of-pipe controls, 165
Engineering ethic and perception of industrial disease, 23
Environmental issues
    Cetrel as a model in environmental protection, 152–157
    cross-national comparisons, 220
    Europe, 200
    1970s, environmental policy system emerging in, 181–182
    See also Evolution of work environment/environmental policies in COPEC; Occupational/environmental health/safety policies of Cetrel/GCA, evolution of
Environmental Management Division (GMA) of COFIC, 78–80, 89
Environmental Management System (EMS), Cetrel's, 161
Environmental Protection Agency (EPA), 9, 41, 74, 155, 184–185
Environmental Resources Center (CRA), 76, 78, 88, 149, 222

Environment Program of the Center for Research and Development (CEPED), 75
Ernesto Geisel, Gen., 44–45
Estireno, 120
Ethical orientations and perception of industrial disease, 23
Ethylene oxide, 202
Ethyl tertiary butyl ether (ETBE), 199
European Union, 86–87, 200
Evolution of work environment/environmental policies in COPEC
    first phase
        health policies, national/state environmental, 73–76
        health policies, occupational, 72–73
        industry: ten years of unconditional state support, 64–67
        labor: ten years of militancy, 67–72
        lost decade to neoliberal decade (1978-1985), 62–64
        national political-economic aspects, 62–64
        overview, 61–62
    second phase: global/restructured/neoliberal complex
        health policies, national and state environmental, 88–90
        health policies, occupational, 87–88
        industry, 80–83
        labor, 83–87
    summary/conclusions, chapter, 90–91
    transition period: EIA/RIMA solution, 76–80
Executive Group of the Chemical Industry (Geiquim), 49
Export/migration of hazards from developed to developing countries, 2–3, 7–12
    See also individual subject headings
Exxon, 37, 38, 41

Factory regimes, 20, 68–70, 84, 200–201, 230
Federal Water Pollution Administration, 39

Feedstocks for petrochemical industry, 34
Fisiba, 108
Força Sindical, 134
Fordism, 20, 81
Foreign capital/direct investment, 35, 45–46
Fourier Transform-Infra-Red (FTIR), 223
Fragmentation and dismantling of factory work organization, 81–82, 86
France, 1, 49, 156
French Oil Institute, 45
Friendswood Development Company, 198
Fundação José Silveira (FJS) study, 123–124
Fundacentro health hazard evaluation, 111–115, 120, 242
Fungicides, 1

Galveston Bay, 39, 40, 186, 187, 224
  See also Gulf Coast Waste Disposal Authority
Galveston Daily News, 191–192
GCA. See Gulf Coast Waste Disposal Authority
Geiquim (Executive Group of the Chemical Industry), 49
General Confederation Of Italian Workers (CGIL), 121
Germany, 3, 40, 52
Globalization
  cross-national comparisons, 233–234
  dependency, globalist approach to, 12–15
  labor, decline of, 85–86
Goodyear, 38
Government
  Camaçari Petrochemical Complex, 44–48
  cross-national comparisons, 219
  disease, occupational, 21–25
  evolution of work environment/ environmental policies in COPEC, 62–64, 66–67
  Gulf Coast Waste Disposal Authority, 40, 181–182, 231–232

Gramacho, Moema, 115–116, 118–119
Great Lakes, 166
Greenbelt around COPEC, 50
Groundwater monitoring, 153–154
Grupo Ambientalista da Bahia (GAMBA), 78
Guerra, Celso, 125
Gulf Coast Waste Disposal Authority (GCA/GCWDA), 2, 3
  Bayport facility, evolution of the, 36–39, 197–202, 232
  consulting and public hearings, 40–41
  contract signings, 41
  COPEC planners visit, 52
  early years
    economic troubles: bonds and taxes, 182–184
    growth, institutional, 187–188
    municipal operations, 186–187
    regulatory aspects: birth of pollution control model, 184–187
  state intervention to mitigate market's failure to safeguard environment, 40, 181–182, 231–232
  hegemony of petrochemical industry, 230, 232–233
  joint waste treatment facility, 41–42
  late years, 195–197
  middle years
    background, 188–189
    consolidation, institutional, 194–195
    NIMBY (not in my back yard) movement, 189–191
    political aspects: Greg Cantrell, 191–192
    regulatory aspects: POTW status and pretreatment standards, 193–194
  overview, 181
  research design, 242
  summary/conclusions, chapter, 202–204
  See also Cross-national comparisons; Occupational/environmental health/safety policies of Cetrel/GCA, evolution of

Hackleman, J. Kent, 182–183
Hazards from developed to developing
      countries, export/migration of,
      2–3, 7–12
   See also individual subject headings
Health and safety issues
   Association of Workers Occupationally
      Contaminated by Organo-
      chlorines, 1–2
   CESAT and disease diagnosis, 118, 120
   Cetrel, 157–159
   collective bargaining around health/
      safety, historical development of,
      128–130
   contracting out productive/support
      services, 88
   dilution as solution to pollution, 73–76
   diseases, occupational
      compensation for, 24–25
      control measures, 24
      production of disease, 22
      recognition of disease, 22–23
   evolution of work environment/
      environmental policies in
      COPEC, 72–76, 87–90
   factory regime, challenging the, 230
   Gulf Coast Waste Disposal Authority,
      195
   pentachlorophenolate, 1
   rewards based on low accident reports,
      117
   See also Benzene crises in COPEC;
      Occupational/environmental
      health/safety policies of
      Cetrel/GCA, evolution of
Hegemony of petrochemical industry,
      20–21, 23, 224, 230, 232–233
Hexachlorobenzene (HCB), 1
Hill, John, 183
Historical development of the
      petrochemical industry, 33–34
Historical-structural approach to
      dependency, 15–18
Hoechst Celanese, 200
Houston Ship Channel, 186, 195, 224
   See also Gulf Coast Waste Disposal
      Authority

Hunstman, 38
Huntsman Corporation, 197
Hydrogen sulfide, 112

Identity, class, 20
Importation of hazards, role of national
      actors in the, 2–3, 7–12
   See also individual subject headings
Import substitution policies, 35, 81
Incineration, 147, 149, 152–153,
      165–166
Inclusive theory of export-import
      hazardous technologies, 3
Industrial Development Council of the
      Ministry of Industry and
      Commerce (CDI-MIC), 49
Industrial hygiene approach to controlling
      industrial disease, 24
Informal workers, 82
Injuries/accidents, rewards based on low
      reporting of, 117
   See also Health and safety issues
Inorganic effluent system and COPEC,
      52
INSS, 135
Instrumentalist view, 14
Integration of tasks rather than
      specialization, 82
InterAmerican Development Bank (IDB),
      49
Interchangeability of tasks/workers
      through team-based work, 82
Internal Committee for the Prevention of
      Accidents (CIPA), 109, 113, 130,
      134, 158
Internal Week to Prevent Occupational
      Accidents (SIPAT), 117
International Association of Water
      Quality of the Third International
      Conference on Waste
      Management in the Chemical
      and Petrochemical Industries
      (1993), 160
International Labor Office (ILO), 131
International Monetary Fund (IMF),
      62, 63

International Standardization
   Organization (ISO), 88,
   161–166, 225
Inter-Union Committee for Workers
   Health (CISAT), 128
Inter-Union Department for the Study of
   Health and the Work Environ-
   ment (DIESAT), 129
ISO. *See* International Standardization
   Organization
IT Corporation, 189

Jacuípe River, 154
Japan, 43, 45–46, 81
Japanese Consultant Institute, 50
Joanes River, 42
Johnson, C. R., 183
Jornal da Cetrel, 159, 161
Just-in-time (JIT) processes, 81

Kawasaki, Masaji, 50
Keystone Center, 191

Laboratory Management Information
   System (LIMS), 196–197
Labor issues
   Bayport Industrial Park, 201–202
   career advancement, 69–70
   Cetrel and labor-management relations,
      109
   consent, authoritarian/labor-capital
      relations and workers', 81
   contracting out productive/support
      services, 81–82, 84, 86,
      88, 201
   core/periphery countries and
      international division of labor,
      13–14
   cross-national comparisons, 218
   evolution of work environment/
      environmental policies in
      COPEC, 67–72, 83–87
   globalization and decline of labor,
      85–86

[Labor issues]
   lost decade to neoliberal decade
      (1978-1985), 63
   National Mobilization Day Against
      Benzene Contamination, 133
   shiftwork, 70
   strikes
      auto workers (1978), 128
      common way to solve health/safety
         problems, 129
      1985, general strike of, 70–72
   Tripartite Working Commission,
      comprehensive standards
      developed by, 133–136
   workers' compensation, 115, 131
   See also Chemical Workers Union;
      Unions
Landulpho Alves (RLAM) refinery, 44
Latin America, economic development
   and industrialization of, 10–11, 16
Layoffs, 83
Lázaro de Freitas, Antonio, 119
Legislation
   Brazil
      Brazilian Environment Act (1981),
         74–75
      Law 3.237, 127
      Law 6.514, 127
      Law 3163, 75
      Law 3858, 75
      National Environmental Policy
         (1988), 74
   United States
      Clean Air Act, 196, 221
      Clean Water Act, 155, 184–186,
         193–194, 196, 221
      Public Law 92-500, 187
      Reauthorization Act, 221
      Resource Conservation and
         Recycling Act (RCRA) of 1976,
         108, 188
      Solid Waste Disposal Act (SWDA)
         of 1987, 200, 221
      Superfund Amendments (SARA), 221
Leukopenia, 107, 112–113, 115, 121, 125,
   130
   See also Benzene crises in COPEC

Liberation movements, national, 14
Licensing, technology, 35
Lighting, Cetrel and improper, 112
Limpec, 147
Liquid chlorinated hydrocarbons, 147, 152–153
Liquid organic effluent system, 51
Liver disorders, 1
Location of petrochemical industry in proximity to oil/natural gas fields, 33–34
Lula da Silva, Luis I., 63, 86
Lyondell Citgo, 38

Magalhães, Antonio C., 50
Malone, Paul, 190–191
Malone Company, 190, 191
Management and cross-national comparisons, 216–217
Maquiladora factories, 11
Marathon Oil, 187
Mariani group, 43
Marighela, Carlos, 149
Market-based/management-oriented instruments used for environmental management, 89
Markle, Donald, 183
Marlboro men path of migration/export of hazardous industries, 11–12
Marxist analysis of class consciousness, 19
Maximum allowable concentrations, 74
Media
  benzene crises in COPEC, 116–118
  Camaçari Petrochemical Complex, 53
  Gulf Coast Waste Disposal Authority, 191–192
Médici, Gen., 49
Menezes, Carlos, 160–161
Metal Workers Union, 122, 130
Methylene chloride, 158
Methyl tertiary butyl ether (MTBE), 199
Mexico, 11
Migration/export of hazards from developed to developing countries, 2–3, 7–12
  See also individual subject headings

Ministry of Health, 130
Ministry of Labor, 114, 119, 120–121, 127, 130–132, 135
Ministry of Social Welfare, 125, 131
Mitsubishi, 43
Modernization theories vs. world-system view, capitalism and, 12–15
Moema Gramacho, 115–116, 118–119
Monopoly, technological, 35
Monsanto, 41, 187
Movimento Democrático Brasileiro (MDB), 62
Multinational companies exporting banned products/technologies, 7–8

National Association of Manufacturers, 9
National Bank for Economic Development (BNDE), 45
National Confederation of Industry (CNI), 132
National Council of the Environment (CONAMA), 75
National Development Plan (PND), 44–45
National Emission Standards for Hazardous Air Pollutants (NESHAP), 157
National Health Conference (1986), 129
National Institute for Workers Health (INST), 121
National Institute of Social Welfare, 131
National Institute of Social Welfare (INPS), 115
National Mobilization Day Against Benzene Contamination, 133
National Oil Council (CNP), 49
National Petrochemical Plan, 65, 66
National Pollutants Discharge Elimination System (NPDES), 185–186
National Workers' Health Conference (1986), 129
Neoliberal agenda, 63, 64
  See also second phase under Evolution of work environment/ environmental policies in COPEC

NIMBY (not in my back yard) movement, 189–191, 232
Nissho-Iwai, 43
Nitrocarbono, 119–123
Nitroclor, 120, 152
Nitrogen oxides, 157
Noise levels at Cetrel, 112
Norquisa, 69
North American Free Trade Agreement (NAFTA), 228
North Sea, 166

Occupational/environmental health/safety policies of Cetrel/GCA, evolution of
class formation, the theory of, 18–21
dependency, historical-structural/relational/unorthodox approach to, 15–18
dependency, structuralist/globalist/orthodox approach to, 12–15
hazards, export/migration of, 9–12
overview, 8
political economy of occupational disease, 21–25
summary/conclusions, chapter, 25
See also Evolution of work environment/environmental policies in COPEC
Occupational Safety and Health Administration (OSHA), 9
Ocean disposal system, 154–155
Odebrecht group, 43, 82
Odessa South Regional Facility, 197
Odors, Cetrel and foul, 109, 110, 112
Oil, Chemical, and Atomic Workers International Union (OCAW), 39, 242
Open Factory Program, Cetrel's, 160
Operação Caça Benzeno and benzene crises in COPEC, 122–123
Operators and Supervisors Training and Certification Program, Cetrel's, 160
Ordinance 3, 132–133
Ordinance 14, 135

Organization for Economic Cooperation and Development (OECD), 11
Orthodox approach to dependency, 12–15
Oxychem, 38

Package deals path of migration/export of hazardous industries, 11
Paes de Andrade, 126
Paraguaçu River, 42
Particulate matter, 157
Partido do Movimento Democrático Brasileiro (PMDB), 62
Patent monopoly, 35
Paths of migration of hazardous industries from North to the South, 11–12
Pentachlorophenolate, 1
Pentatetraper plants, 1
Perc, 1
Peripheral countries and production/control technologies/labor issues, 13–14, 35, 229–230
Permanent Benzene Commission (CNP), 134
Permanent workers, 82
Petrobrás, 44, 46, 49
Petrochemical industry
fundamentals of the, 33–36, 247
hegemony of, 20–21, 23–24, 224, 230, 232–233
See also individual subject headings
Petroquisa, 46
Phenol, 1, 132
Pimentel, Marcelo, 132
Pires, Valdir, 76, 149
Plan to Prevent Environmental Risks (PPRA), 135
Polychorinated byphenils (PCBs), 1
Political economy of COPEC, 44–48
Political economy of occupational disease, 21–25
Pollution havens path of migration/export of hazardous industries, 11
Polyvinyl chloride, 147
POTW. See Public operated treatment works

Predictive Maintenance Program,
    Cetrel's, 160
Pretreatment programs/standards, 155,
    193–194
Privatization programs, 63, 69
    See also first phase under Cetrel
Production politics in advanced
    capitalism, 20–21
Productive restructuring and decline of
    labor, 85–86
Productivity, 81
Progil Société Anonyme, 1
Program to Prevent Benzene Exposures
    (PPEB), 131
Program to Prevent Occupational
    Benzene Exposures (PPOEB),
    134
Promotions, 70
Propylene glycol, 199
Propylene oxide, 199
Proquímicos, 67
Protective equipment, personal, 110
Public contamination from disposal of
    untreated chlorinated hazardous
    wastes, 2
Public health ethic and perception of
    industrial disease, 23
Public operated treatment works (POTW),
    193–194, 219

Qualitative research, 240
Quality as the main business principle,
    introduction of, 81

Reagan, Ronald, 62
Refinery Workers Union (SINDIPETRO),
    48, 87, 122
Registry of benzene
    producers/consumers/transporter,
    134
Regulations
    benzene crises in COPEC, 130–136
    cross-national comparisons,
        221–223
    export/migration of hazards, 9

[Regulations]
    Gulf Coast Waste Disposal Authority,
        184–187, 193–194
    Ordinance 3, 132–133
    Ordinance 14, 135
Relational approach to dependency,
    15–18
Research and development (R&D), 35
Research design
    actor analysis, 239–240
    data collection methods, 241–243
    limitations, research, 243–244
    overview, 239–241
    qualitative research, 240
Respiratory protection, improper, 112
Responsible Care Program, 89, 127, 196,
    200, 233
Rhodia, 1
Rhône-Poulenc, 1, 43
Rice University, 220
Rigotto, Raquel, 131
Rohm & Haas, 38, 200
Ruhr Valley Authorities, 40
Ruhrverband, 40
Runaway shops, 9

Safety issues. See Health and safety issues
Saraiva, José, 160–161
Sarney, José, 63
Schwarz, Babe, 190
Scientific ethic and perception of
    industrial disease, 23
Shiftwork, 70
Sierra Club, 189
Sims Bayou Wastewater Treatment Plant,
    195
Sindae, 114, 116, 122, 149, 242
Sindicato Proquímicos, 115
SINDIPETRO (Refinery Workers Union),
    48, 87, 122
Sindiquímica. See Chemical Workers
    Union
Skilled workers, 82
Skin eruptions, 1
Sobrinho, Armando, 119
Social structure of the state and COPEC, 47

Socio-medical model, 128
Soda, caustic, 1
Solid hazardous wastes treatment/
    disposal, 52–53, 147–148
Source control program, 155
Southern Pacific Railroad, 38
Specialization, integration of tasks rather
    than, 82
Special Secretariat of the Environment
    (SEMA), 74
Special Services for Safety Engineering
    and Occupational Medicine
    (SESMT), 127, 130
Stablex, 189
State Council of the Environment
    (CEPRAM), 75–76, 78, 88, 147,
    149, 154, 156
State Environmental Resources Manage-
    ment System (SEARA), 75–76
Statistical process control, 81
Steel industry, 9
Sterling Chemicals, 197
Stiep, 87
Strikes. *See under* Labor issues
Structural adjustment programs (SAPs),
    62–63
Structuralist approach to dependency,
    12–15
Sulfur dioxide, 157
Sulzer technology, Swiss, 153
Sumitomo, 43
Swiss Sulzer technology, 153

Taxes and Gulf Coast Waste Disposal
    Authority, 182–184
Taylor Lake Village, 191
Team-based work, interchangeability of
    tasks/workers through, 82
Technical Committee for Environmental
    Assurance (CTGA), 160
"Technical Subsidies to the Safety and
    Health Division of the Ministry
    of Labor," 132
Technological monopoly, 35
Technology outcomes and cross-national
    comparisons, 223–224

Temporary workers, 82
Tertiary butyl alcohol, 199
Tetrachlorobenzene, 1
Tetrachloroethylene, 1
Texas, Gulf Coast region of, 38–39
    See also Gulf Coast Waste Disposal
    Authority
Texas Air Control, 191
Texas City Refining, 187
Texas Department of Water Resources,
    191
Texas Natural Resources Conservation
    Commission (TNRCC), 40
Texas Water Quality Board (TWQB), 39,
    184–185
Thatcher, Margaret, 62
Thomas, Lee, 165
Threshold limit values (TLVs), 127, 158
Time Weighted Technological Reference
    Values (VRT-MPT), 134
Toluene, 112, 158
Total productivity management (TPM),
    81
Total quality management (TQM), 81,
    160, 201
Toxic Release Inventory (TRI), 200,
    202
Trade agreements, regional, 228
Training
    benzene crises in COPEC, 134–135
    emergency response, 110
Transnational companies exporting
    banned products/technologies,
    7–8
Tricholoroethane, 158
Tripartite Working Commission and
    benzene crises in COPEC,
    133–136

Ultraviolet disinfection systems, 197
Union Carbide, 41, 187, 197
Unions
    Bayport Industrial Park, 39, 201
    benzene crises in COPEC, 114–115,
    122–123
    Cetrel, 149

[Unions]
   collective bargaining around health/
      safety, historical development of,
      128–130
   Companhia Siderúrgica Paulista, 130
   European Union, 86–87
   political-ideological issues, confusion
      around, 87
   See also Chemical Workers Union
United Nations Conference on Human
      Environment (1972), 74
University of Houston, 220
University of Texas Medical Branch
      (UTMB), 220
Unorthodox approach to dependency,
      15–18
Untreated chlorinated hazardous wastes,
      illegal disposal of, 2

Villas Boas, Paulo, 151–152
Vinyl chloride, 9, 147
Volatile organic compounds (VOCs), 157,
      223
Voluntary protection programs, 161–166,
      196, 222–223
Volunteers of the Beach, Cetrel's, 160

Wages
Bayport Industrial Park, 201
Cetrel, 109
diseases, compensation for
      occupational, 24–25
evolution of work environment/
      environmental policies in
      COPEC, 70, 83–84
factory regime, challenging the,
      230
workers' compensation, 115, 131
Washburn Tunnel Facility, 41, 184–185,
      195
Wastewater treatment, industrial, 146,
      155–156
Water Pollution Control Federation,
      194–195
White blood cell counts, 112, 125
Workers' compensation, 115, 131
Workers' Health Program (PROSAT),
      118
World Bank, 63
World-system approach to dependency,
      12–15

Xylene, 158